DISTRIBUTED COMPUTING

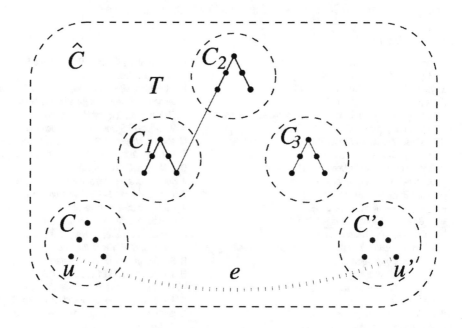

SIAM Monographs on Discrete Mathematics and Applications

The series includes advanced monographs reporting on the most recent theoretical, computational, or applied developments in the field; introductory volumes aimed at mathematicians and other mathematically motivated readers interested in understanding certain areas of pure or applied combinatorics; and graduate textbooks. The volumes are devoted to various areas of discrete mathematics and its applications.

Mathematicians, computer scientists, operations researchers, computationally oriented natural and social scientists, engineers, medical researchers, and other practitioners will find the volumes of interest.

Series Volumes

Peleg, D., *Distributed Computing: A Locality-Sensitive Approach*
Wegener, I., *Branching Programs and Binary Decision Diagrams: Theory and Applications*
Brandstädt, A., Le, V. B., and Spinrad, J. P., *Graph Classes: A Survey*
McKee, T. A. and McMorris, F. R., *Topics in Intersection Graph Theory*
Grilli di Cortona, P., Manzi, C., Pennisi, A., Ricca, F., and Simeone, B., *Evaluation and Optimization of Electoral Systems*

DISTRIBUTED COMPUTING

A Locality-Sensitive Approach

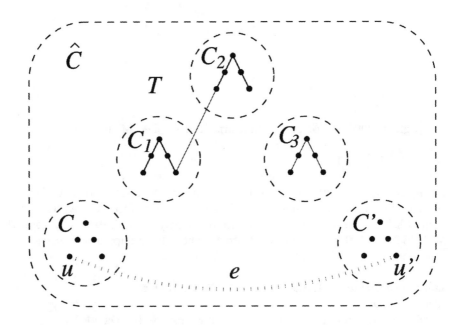

DAVID PELEG

The Weizmann Institute of Science
Rehovot, Israel

siam

Society for Industrial and Applied Mathematics
Philadelphia

Copyright © 2000 by Society for Industrial and Applied Mathematics.

10 9 8 7 6 5 4 3 2 1

Library of Congress Cataloging-in-Publication Data
Peleg, D. (David)
   Distributed computing : a locality-sensitive approach / David Peleg.
      p. cm. – (SIAM monographs on discrete mathematics and applications)
   Includes bibliographical references and index.
   ISBN 0-89871-464-8
      1. Electronic data processing – Distributed processing. I. Title. II. Series.

QA76.9.D5 P43 2000
004'.36—dc21

                          00-033836

siam is a registered trademark.

To Rina, Asaf, Itai, Noa, and Daniel

Contents

Preface

Distributed computing concerns environments in which many processors, located at different sites, must operate in a noninterfering and cooperative manner. Each of the processors enjoys a certain degree of autonomy: it executes its own protocol on its own private hardware and often has its own independent task to complete. Nevertheless, the processors must still share certain common resources and information, and a certain degree of coordination is necessary in order to ensure the successful completion of their individual tasks.

In the last two decades, we have experienced an unprecedented growth in the area of distributed systems and networks, and distributed computing now encompasses many of the activities occurring in today's computer and telecommunications world. Virtually any large computerized system currently in use is distributed to some extent. The applications of distributed computing range from computer and telecommunication networks to distributed database systems and from large financial and economic systems to industrial control mechanisms. In all of those applications, the need to ensure the smooth, coordinated and noninterfering operation of many remote processors is one of the most challenging tasks faced by the application's designers and operators.

One of the main themes of recent research in distributed network algorithms concerns better understanding of and coping with the issue of *locality*. Most traditional network algorithms do not take locality into consideration and do not exploit locality in any nontrivial way. Due to the increasing complexity and cost as networks become larger, it becomes significantly harder to use many of those traditional protocols for performing various network control and management tasks. On the other hand, such global knowledge is not always essential, and many seemingly global control tasks can be efficiently achieved while allowing processors to know more about their immediate neighborhood and less about the rest of the world. Moreover, whenever considering a local subtask that only involves vertices located in a small region in the network, one would like the execution of the subtask to involve only sites in or around that region, at a cost proportional to its locality level.

In order to be able to achieve this type of dependency on locality in distributed network algorithms, it is necessary to develop a robust and general methodology for addressing locality in distributed algorithms. The purpose of this book is to provide an overview of such a methodology, termed *locality-sensitive distributed computing*, whose basic idea is to utilize locality in order to both simplify control structures and algorithms and reduce their costs. This book presents a systematic development of a theory of locality-sensitive distributed network algorithms and describes some of the recent developments in this area.

On the way to achieving this goal, Part I of this book also provides an introductory exposition of some basic issues in distributed network algorithms. The intention is mainly to introduce the material most relevant to the various aspects of locality which are developed in later parts of this book. This intention reflects itself in the selection of topics and problems discussed. The coverage focuses on a number of key problems and topics—such as broadcast, tree construction, maximal independent sets and coloring, synchronizers, routing, local queries and resource finding—chosen as examples serving to illustrate the ways in which locality enters the picture and its effects on the design and analysis of various algorithmic solutions for those problems.

Subsequent parts of the book are organized as follows. The development of the locality-sensitive methodology involves the definition of several types of *locality-preserving (LP) network representations* and the development of novel clustering and decomposition techniques for their construction. The main types of LP representations are reviewed in Part II of this book, which focuses on clustered and skeletal representations. The presentation concentrates on the relevant graph-theoretic notions and their fundamental properties.

Part III combines the two topics discussed in the previous two parts and develops the locality-sensitive approach to distributed network algorithms. In particular, it first deals with construction algorithms for distributedly setting up the necessary LP-representations, and then demonstrates the applicability of the approach via illustrating a number of example applications.

This book grew out of lecture notes developed for a course given at the Weizmann Institute in 1992, 1996, 1997 and 1999 on distributed network algorithms and the locality-sensitive approach.

I would like to thank all of those who read parts of this book at various stages and made helpful comments, including (in alphabetic order) Meir Cohen, Amos Guller, Oded Goldreich, Yehuda Hassin, Yoel Jacobsen, Eyal Shai, Maria Shneerson, Sergei Soloviev, Wasserkrug Segev and Lihi Zelnik-Manor.

Many more have participated in the research efforts leading to the development of the theory described in this book. Of those, I have personally benefited from collaborating with a number of people, including (in alphabetic order again) Noga Alon, Baruch Awerbuch, Judit Bar-Ilan, Amotz Bar-Noy, Bonnie Berger, Jean-Claude Bermond, Lenore Cowen, Tamar Eilam, Juan Garay, Cyril Gavoille, Oded Goldreich, Dick Karp, Guy Kortsarz, Shay Kutten, Nati Linial, Yishay Mansour, Stephan Perennes, Alex Schäffer, Jeff Ullman, Eli Upfal and Avishai Wool.

Finally, I wish to thank my wife, Rina, and my children, Asaf, Itai, Noa and Daniel, for their patience and continuous support during the long period it has taken me to complete this book.

Chapter 1

Introduction

1.1 What is distributed computing?

In order to define a distributed system, one safe approach is to consider first what a *centralized* system is. We usually think of such a system as composed of a single controlling unit. Thus in a centralized system, at most one autonomous activity is carried on at any single moment. In contrast, the main characteristic of a distributed system is that there may be many autonomous processors active in the system at any moment. These processors may need to communicate with each other in order to coordinate their actions and achieve a reasonable level of cooperation, but they are nonetheless capable of operating by themselves.

Another significant characteristic of a distributed system is that it is rather nonuniform. For instance, the processors participating in it may be (and often are) physically distributed in different geographic locations. They are often rather different in size and power, architecture, organizational membership and so on.

Consequently, there exists a wide spectrum of types of distributed systems, ranging from parallel computing systems to wide-area communication networks. One of the main parameters of this spectrum is the *coupling level* of different processors in a distributed system, which may vary significantly from one application to another. In a tightly coupled system (e.g., a parallel machine), the processors typically work in tight synchrony, share memory to a large extent and have very fast and reliable communication mechanisms between them. In contrast, in a loosely coupled distributed system (e.g., a wide-area communication network), the processors are more independent, communication is less frequent and less synchronous and cooperation is more limited.

The *type* and *purpose* of cooperation in a distributed system may also vary greatly. Certain systems (again best exemplified by parallel machines) are designed with the idea of exploiting the possibility of processor cooperation in order to enable us to handle large, complex problems. Thus in such a system, a typical goal would be to harness the processors together for the purpose of solving a problem in collaboration.

However, more often than not, a distributed system is based on much more "individual" goals. Such a system has to serve individual users, who are mostly interested in their own private activities. These activities may sometimes involve communication with some other specific users or servers in the system. For instance, a user may wish to access a data bank located at a different site. However, the cooperation required by the user in this case is limited to guaranteeing that the transaction it is interested in will be performed successfully (from its own point of view) i.e., that it will be performed correctly and eventually terminate (preferably fast) and possibly also that it will not harm or disturb the (concurrent or subsequent) activities of other users in the system (or just as importantly, that it will not be significantly disturbed by the activities of the other users). In such a setting, the most desirable situation in a distributed system is to be able to supply the user with a *centralized view* of the system, i.e., to make the distributed nature of the system transparent to the user, and let it act as though it is the only user of the system, and the system is composed of a single entity, located in one place.

In other words, the main distinction between the above two extreme approaches is that the former attempts to use cooperation between processors in a "constructive" sense in order to achieve a difficult goal together, whereas the latter attempts to exploit cooperation in a "preventive" sense, trying only to ensure that different individual processes do not disturb each other. In reality, actual systems usually provide a mixture (to a varying degree) of both extreme types of cooperation.

This view of distributed systems dictates also the types of algorithms we are interested in when discussing distributed systems. Rather than algorithms for specific data-processing tasks or scientific computations, we will typically be interested in various *system* protocols, providing services and control functions to the users of the system. Typical examples of such problems include

- various communication services, such as routing, broadcast or end-to-end communication,

- maintenance of control structures, such as the construction of spanning trees of various types (BFS, SPT, MST), topology update or leader election,

- resource control activities, such as load balancing, tracking mobile resources, managing global directories such as name servers and managing various queues in the system.

1.2   A basic framework for distributed systems

There are numerous models for distributed systems, differing from one another on a large number of important factors and parameters. One major distinction is between the *message passing* and *shared memory* models. Message passing models treat communication explicitly. Namely, whenever a processor wishes to communicate with another, it must send it a message, using some available communication media. In contrast, in a shared memory system, processors do not speak to each other directly. Instead, the model assumes the existence of some common memory, storing variables that are shared by all processors. These shared variables can be written to or read from by all processors, with the exact mechanism for doing so depending on the particular variant of the model. Clearly, these variables can also be used for communication between processors, among other things.

Within the scope of this text, we shall restrict ourselves to systems based on the message passing model and exclude from discussion the shared memory model. The reason for this choice is that while the shared memory model is a commonly studied one, it is more suitable for discussing very tightly coupled concurrent or parallel systems, in the sense described above. In such systems, where the different processors tightly share their activities, it may be desirable to abstract away communication issues and develop methodologies based on as much similarity to the sequential model as possible. Indeed, in parallel computing, this trend has led to adopting the so-called Parallel Random Access Machine (PRAM) model as one of the most common machine models, at least as far as theoretical study of algorithms is concerned. The issue of locality, however, arises mainly in physically distributed systems based on actual (wide-area or local-area) communication networks. Hence for discussing locality issues, it is necessary to keep the communication aspect explicit in the model, rather than hide it.

Even when limiting ourselves to message passing communication networks, there are still a large number of alternative communication modes available. In this book, we concentrate on *point-to-point* communication systems, which allow direct information exchange between specific pairs of sites. In contrast, a number of other models (which will not be addressed here at all) can be grouped together under the title of "broadcast" networks. These include Ethernet and radio-based networks, and the main characteristic separating them from the point-to-point communication model is that they allow a single message to be delivered simultaneously to a *number* of recipients, rather than just one at a time.

Technically, the type of communication network we shall be dealing with is described by a connected undirected graph whose vertices represent the sites of the network (see Figure 1.1). Each site may consist of an autonomous processor, equipped with some local (main and secondary) storage facilities and possibly some specific equipment. Each site also serves a collection of users hooked to it via some local I/O devices.

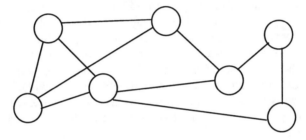

Figure 1.1: The communication network underlying a point-to-point message passing distributed system.

The edges represent bidirectional communication channels connecting the different sites. (Historically, some systems used to have unidirectional communication links, but most current systems provide channels allowing bidirectional communication as their standard, hence it may not be worthy to dwell on this distinction.) A vertex may communicate directly only with its neighbors, and messages to nonneighboring vertices u and v must be sent along some path connecting them in the graph.

A more refined model of the way communication is carried is as follows. Each vertex has a number of *ports*, i.e., external connection points. Every communication channel connects two ports at adjacent vertices. A processor sends a message to its neighbor by loading it onto the appropriate port. When this message arrives at the destination processor, it is stored in a local buffer. We will mostly abstract away these details, but we will need to address them when discussing issues to which they are directly relevant, such as routing policies.

This description of the local architecture of a processor highlights the fact that from the processor's point of view, the other end of its adjacent channels is an external entity and is not directly accessible in any way. In particular, it allows us to consider a model in which a processor does not know the identity of its neighbors and even one in which processors are essentially "anonymous components," which can be easily replaced or interchanged. Nevertheless, whenever convenient, we ignore the port assignments in the definition of the communication network and refer essentially to the underlying graph, i.e., we interchange the set of channels with the corresponding collection of vertex pairs.

1.3   Issues unique to distributed computing

Let us say a few words on the issues and concerns that most distinguish the distributed setting from the sequential one.

1.3.1   Communication

One central issue in the distributed setting is the need for communicating information between different entities participating in the system's activities. This aspect is virtually nonexistent in centralized computing (except at the very low level of hardware considerations). This leads to the need for characterizing, developing and analyzing methods for information exchange.

A crucial point implicit in the above statement is that communication does not come "for free" and has certain costs associated with it. Moreover, there may be limits to the speed at which we can transmit information and the amounts of information that can be transmitted. Hence communication should be treated as a *computational resource* and efforts should be made to use it wisely. In fact, in certain situations, this cost dominates other, more traditional costs (e.g., processing time and storage capacity) involved in the computational process at hand. Many theoretical papers on distributed algorithms reflected this situation by including in their model the assumption that local processing at the sites of the system comes for free and the only costs of a task are those associated with the communication involved. While this assumption is useful for highlighting the issue of communication and focusing on efficient ways to use it, care should be exercised in employing it, since it is easy to abuse it and end up with algorithms that are useless due to unrealistically high local processing requirements.

1.3.2   Incomplete knowledge

In the centralized setting, the processor carrying out the computation has full knowledge of every relevant piece of information about what happens before and during the computation. In particular, the input is known in its entirety to the processor at the outset of the computation. Every data item obtained during the computation is known and available, and so on.

In the distributed setting, a processor constantly needs to cope with the fact that it has only a partial picture of the system and the ongoing activities. A central aspect of this phenomenon concerns the fact that crucial elements of the *computation* may be hidden away. For instance, a vertex may not know the entire *input* to the problem at hand, which may be physically distributed among the sites, but only the part stored in it locally. The vertex may not be certain about which other vertices participate in, or are aware of, the computation that it originates. It certainly does not know for sure in which stage of the computation each of the participants is currently at, and so on. This may lead to obvious difficulties in coordinating the joint activities of the processors on a common task.

Another major manifestation of this "partial information" phenomenon which the processors must cope with is that processors do not necessarily know much about the surrounding *environment*. In particular, a variety of alternative models are discussed in the literature concerning the extent of topological knowledge available at the various sites. At the one extreme lies the model known as *anonymous networks*. This model assumes that the vertices of the network are indistinguishable and have no identifying labels and that initially a vertex knows nothing on the topology of the network. A somewhat more realistic model assumes that vertices are equipped with unique identifiers and that each vertex knows the identity of its neighbors, and perhaps also an estimate for the number of vertices in the system, or its diameter. More permissive models allow a vertex to know the topology of its entire neighborhood (or region) according to some partition of the network into subnetworks. Finally, the most powerful model assumes that complete topological knowledge of the network is maintained at every vertex.

1.3.3 Coping with failures

In a centralized environment, protection from failure is evidently just as important as in a distributed system. However, it is somewhat less subtle and more "straightforward": a bug in the software or hardware may cause the program to terminate abnormally or even crash the system. A hardware failure may even crash the entire computer. But in all of these cases, there's nothing to do but find the source of failure, fix it and go on to retry.

In the distributed setting, things are more complicated. On the one hand, more things might go wrong and lead the computation astray. The spectrum of failure types that might occur includes transient failures and more permanent ones and ranges from software or hardware failures at some of the machines, causing a machine to temporarily malfunction or even go down, to severe communication problems involving the disconnection of a link, or more transient communication errors causing, say, the loss or corruption of a message.

On the other hand, in a multiprocessor setting, the failure of one component may not necessarily cause *other* processors to go down. This allows us to aim at the more ambitious goal of ensuring that the system continues to function properly and does not collapse even in the presence of some (processor or link) failures. In fact, this promising potential for overcoming or at least tolerating failures has been one of the central motivations which promoted research and development in the area of distributed computing. Consequently, much of the activity in the area is dedicated to the development of *fault-tolerant* algorithms. Such algorithms are expected to go on executing properly and producing correct results (namely, the same results they were supposed to produce had no failures occurred at all), despite occasional failures at some of the machines or the communication links.

Clearly, there are cases where this goal cannot be achieved. For example, if most processors malfunction, then it is difficult to successfully complete any computation based on reaching some consensus between the processors. Also, in case the computation critically depends on some inputs, the destruction of that data could irreparably disable the computation. Moreover, even in case the algorithm is capable of completing its task successfully, it is clear that its performance might be hindered by the presence of failures.

1.3.4 Timing and synchrony

Understanding the concept of time and developing systematic methodologies for dealing with it is one of the most active areas of research in the field of distributed computing. One cardinal notion in this context concerns the level of synchrony provided by the system. In order to illustrate this notion, it is common to concentrate on two extreme models: the fully synchronous model and the totally asynchronous one.

Let us define these two extreme models in more detail.

The synchronous model: In the fully synchronous network, it is assumed that all link delays are bounded. More precisely, each processor keeps a local clock, whose pulses must satisfy the following property: A message sent from a processor v to its neighbor u at pulse p of v must arrive at u before pulse $p+1$ of u. Thus in effect, one can think about the entire system as driven by one global clock. The machine cycle of each processor can be described as composed of the following three steps:

1. Send messages to (some of) the neighbors.

2. Receive messages from (some of) the neighbors.

3. Perform some local computation.

Local computation is assumed to take negligible time compared to message transmission. Hence virtually the entire cycle is spent by each processor on waiting to receive the messages sent to it by its neighbors at the start of the cycle.

The asynchronous model: In an asynchronous model, in contrast, algorithms are event driven, i.e., processors cannot access a global clock in order to decide on their action. Messages sent from a processor to its neighbor arrive within some finite but unpredictable time. This has the implication that clocks are rather useless, at least as far as communication is concerned; in particular, one cannot rely on the time elapsed in waiting in order to deduce that a message was not sent from a neighbor by a certain time or that the message was lost; it can always be the case that the message is still on its way. It is also impossible to rely on the ordering of message arrivals from different neighbors to infer the ordering of various computational events, as the order of arrivals may reverse due to different message transmission speeds.

Clearly, both of these models are extreme to the point of being somewhat unrealistic. Indeed, more realistic models have been proposed in various papers in the literature. Such models attempt to capture systems exhibiting a certain limited degree of synchrony, e.g., based on an envelope providing upper and lower bounds on message transmission times.

However, these two extreme models have proved very useful for studying the behavior of a variety of problems and issues, as they help to define and limit their potential behavior in intermediate models. In particular, a lower bound or an impossibility result proven for a certain problem in the fully synchronous model will be extremely useful as it applies to every other intermediate model as well. Analogously, an algorithm developed for a certain problem in the fully asynchronous model implies that an algorithm of the same complexities (or better) exists for every other model.

Moreover, even if the system at hand does adhere to an intermediate "limited synchrony" model, it may be better to avoid relying on such an assumption while possible and to design the algorithm assuming total asynchrony, as the alternative requires careful definition of the partial synchrony assumptions, potentially complicates the algorithmic design and exposes the algorithm to yet one more possible type of failure (i.e., the danger that the system will temporarily violate its synchronization guarantee).

Asynchrony and nondeterminism: A striking phenomenon of the asynchronous model, which strongly affects the behavior of asynchronous distributed computations, is that it is inherently *nondeterministic*. This holds true even when the protocols used are strictly deterministic and use no randomization whatsoever. The reason for this is that the model contains an inherently nondeterministic component, namely, the ordering of message deliveries, which in the fully asynchronous model is completely arbitrary.

The cause for this assumption is that the executions of any particular protocol are strongly affected by the timing and speed of actions taken by the underlying communication network, which in turn are affected by other events concurrently occurring in the system. Thus the order in which messages arrive may differ from one execution to another and may subsequently affect the way the computation continues.

As a result, it may happen that running precisely the same algorithm twice, on precisely the same inputs, would yield completely different executions, terminating with different outputs. We refer to such executions as different *scenarios* of the execution. This pathological behavior has grave consequences on issues of correctness and complexity in distributed algorithm design.

As an example, consider the following simple system, described in Figure 1.2. The protocols specified for processors v_1 and v_2 require them to send their input bit x to v_3, and v_3's protocol requires it to wait until getting a message, print the incoming message and halt. Even though all three protocols are deterministic, in an asynchronous system the output printed by processor v_3 may be either 0 or 1, regardless of which of the two processors v_1 and v_2 has sent its message first. This is because the output clearly depends on the speeds in which the two network channels deliver the two messages, and those speeds are not controlled by the protocols of the processors and, moreover, might change from one execution to the next.

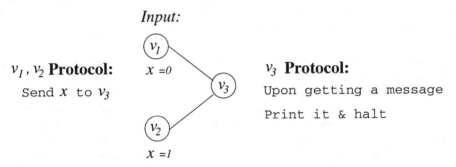

Figure 1.2: An algorithm with a potentially nondeterministic execution in the asynchronous model.

1.3.5 Algorithmic and programming difficulties

The special nature of distributed computing implies in particular that a new style is needed for describing distributed algorithms. This is particularly true for asynchronous systems.

A *protocol* is a local program executed by a vertex in the network. A distributed algorithm consists of n protocols, each dedicated to one of the vertices. The protocol governs the way the processor modifies the local data and exchanges messages with neighboring processors. In a *synchronous* system, the protocol of each processor should specify, in every step, the local computations performed and the messages sent by the processor.

In contrast, in a distributed *asynchronous* setting, the algorithm must be described as *event driven*. By this we mean that the code of each local protocol is composed of a list of commands of the type:

"On event X, do Y."

The event X is typically the arrival of a message containing a certain information, and the Y component of the command is composed of a sequence of steps to be taken in response to the event X. The process executed in a vertex spends its time idly waiting for an event X (among the ones specified in its list of instructions) to happen, whence it performs the corresponding Y and resumes its waiting state.

It is worth pointing out that algorithm design and programming in the distributed setting involves several complications not encountered in the centralized setting. This is due to all the points raised earlier, including especially asynchrony, and the implied nondeterministic nature of a distributed program. As all possible executions must be correct, the design of a correct distributed algorithm involves what may be thought of as coping with a hidden *adversary*, which has control over the network's actions at any given execution. Discussing and analyzing the properties of distributed algorithms, and proving their correctness, also turn out to be considerably more challenging and problematic in the distributed setting than in the sequential one, and methods for formally reasoning about the behavior of distributed systems are among today's most active research areas in the field.

1.4   Locality-sensitive distributed algorithms

Let us now introduce and briefly discuss the main topic of this book, namely, *locality-sensitive distributed algorithms*. This discussion is primarily geared towards readers with some prior familiarity with the area of distributed network algorithms, and the uninitiated reader may find this section difficult to follow; it would be best in this case to skip Section 1.4 completely for now and get back to it after reviewing (at least partially) Parts I and II of this book.

Traditional protocols for performing various global network control and management functions, such as routing, broadcast and topology update, are based on requiring all sites to maintain full information (of various forms) about what happens in the network. As distributed networks grow larger, it becomes increasingly harder to use many of those traditional protocols, as their information requirements become problematic over large networks. The difficulty lies not only in the increased need for memory, but also in that the task of maintaining and updating this global information becomes increasingly more complex and resource consuming.

At the same time, it should be realized that global knowledge is not always essential. Many common network control tasks can be achieved in a local manner with no substantial performance degradation by utilizing "locality of reference," namely, relying on the fact that performing these tasks requires processors to know more about their immediate neighborhood and less about the rest of the world. Furthermore, certain tasks are local in nature and only involve vertices located in a small region in the network. In such a case, one would like the execution of the task to involve only sites in or around that region. Further, it is desirable that the cost of the task be proportional to its locality level. Even in a global operation, it is in many cases possible to distinguish suboperations of local nature, whose costs can be considerably reduced by utilizing this locality of reference.

In order to be able to achieve this type of dependency on locality, it is necessary to develop a robust and flexible methodology for addressing locality in distributed algorithms, based on a coherent and general theory. Such a theory should include several components. Specifically, we list the following three ingredients:

(a) a general framework, complexity measures and algorithmic methodology,

(b) suitable graph-theoretic structures and efficient construction methods, and

(c) adaptation to a wide variety of applications.

1.4.1   Locality-preserving network representations

The approach presented here is based on the natural and fundamental concept of *locality-preserving network representations* (or *LP-representations*, for short), i.e., representations whose structure faithfully captures the topology of the network itself.

A variety of different types of LP-representations have proved extremely useful in a number of areas, including robotics and computational geometry, distributed computing, communication networks, graph algorithms and combinatorial optimization. The basic premise behind employing such representations is that using them (as a substitute for using the entire network) allows us to maintain a smaller amount of information (namely, remember fewer edges, know less about the structure of the graph and so on), thus reducing the computational and storage *costs* involved. The price to be paid is that using sparse, approximate representations incurs a certain loss of *accuracy*. (The precise meaning of "accuracy" and "costs" differs from one application to another and depends on the specific measures of interest.) Naturally, these two parameters are correlated, hence the extent of this accuracy degradation depends on the degree to which the employed representation preserves the topology of the network.

Our focus is on general techniques for imposing a locality-preserving organization on an *arbitrary* given network and on ways of using such an organization for deriving more efficient distributed algorithms.

Different types of LP-representations come equipped with different cost, efficiency and quality measures. As it turns out, the choice of network representation is in fact a central consideration affecting the complexity of the derived solution for many well-known network problems, e.g., synchronization, deadlock prevention, resource management, routing, mobile users communication and others. For that reason, it is important to develop a precise understanding of the different types of LP-representations available to us, their potential and their limitations, in a uniform manner. The ultimate goal in this area is designing network structures and representations which may be thought of as "distributed network" analogues of efficient data structures used in the area of sequential computing.

LP-representations can be classified into two main types, *clustered representations* and *skeletal representations*.

Clustered representations: The first type of LP-representations is based on grouping the vertices of the graph into small connected subsets (clusters) based on certain desirability considerations. There are two inherent criteria of interest for cluster design. The first parameter is the "depth" or "radius" of the cluster (defined formally later on), intuitively measuring its locality level. The second criterion is the level of "interaction" or "overlap" between clusters, which can be formally measured as the maximum number (over all vertices) of clusters containing a particular vertex. As explained above, these parameters directly relate to the efficiency of any application based on the clustered representation at hand, and hence typically one would like to keep both measures as low as possible. The clustering is often designed hierarchically, i.e., using several different levels of clusters (ranging from many small clusters on the lower levels, to few large ones on the higher levels), in a way suitable for the application in mind.

Skeletal representations: The second type of LP-representations consists of representations based on sparse spanning subgraphs of the network itself. The most common example for a sparse spanning subgraph is a spanning tree. Using a spanning tree as our representation achieves the ultimate sparsity (assuming connectivity must be guaranteed), but locality is not well preserved; two neighboring vertices in the original network might be very far apart in the spanning tree. One central type of skeletal representations that aims to remedy this deficiency of spanning trees is based on the notion of *graph spanners*, which appear to be the underlying graph structure in various constructions in distributed systems and communication networks. Intuitively, spanners can be thought of as a generalization of the concept of a spanning tree, allowing the spanning subgraph to have cycles, but aiming towards maintaining the locality properties of the network. These locality properties revolve around the notion of *stretch*, namely, the (worst) factor by which distances increase in the network as a result of using the spanner edges alone and ignoring nonspanner edges. Other kinds of skeletal representations are based on particular types of spanning trees with special locality properties, e.g., low *average* stretch, or simultaneously low root-to-all distances and low total weight, or on collections of spanning trees with similar properties.

1.4.2   Utilizing LP-representations for locality-sensitive computing

Let us now briefly review the main ideas of the locality-sensitive approach. Informally speaking, a "global" algorithm is one that makes no attempt to restrict its activities to the specific regions of the network directly related to its task. Such an algorithm might require all the vertices of the network to collect, maintain and distribute information related to its tasks, regardless of their direct involvement.

In contrast, the locality-sensitive approach attempts to restrict activities to the relevant regions. One natural approach is based on using a clustered representation. Intuitively, the idea is to cover the network by (possibly overlapping) logically connected clusters and to develop a solution method based on this clustered organization. Essentially, neighborhood and proximity information other than that captured by the cluster structure is disregarded. Hence a distributed protocol based on such a clustered organization will require a vertex to participate only in those activities that occur in the clusters it belongs to. Consequently, the cost of a task tends to depend on its locality properties *in the clustered representation*: a task involving a single cluster is relatively cheap, whereas a task requiring cooperation between sites from different clusters would be more expensive.

Clearly, in order for this approach to be useful, the clustered representation must conform to the topological structure of the network. For instance, if the application involves communication between neighbors, then any two neighboring vertices must appear together in some cluster. Hence the need for LP-representation.

The crucial observation that drove research efforts on the problem of designing efficient clustered representations is that the graph-theoretic criteria of cluster radius and overlap discussed above are tightly related to the significant complexity measures of distributed network algorithms. In virtually all applications considered in the literature so far, smaller cluster radii in a given cluster collection directly translate into lower time complexities, due to the fact that computations are performed inside clusters. At the same time, low overlap guarantees low memory requirements, since each vertex is actively involved in (and thus stores information for) only the clusters it belongs to. Finally, and perhaps most importantly, the message complexity of cluster-based protocols turns out to be strongly dependent on both parameters (typically on their product).

Finally, let us discuss the ways in which the other type of LP-representations, namely, skeletal representations, can be utilized in the distributed context. More specifically, let us consider the spanner representation. A spanner can be used in any given application without changing the algorithm in any way, simply by ignoring the communication channels that do not belong to the spanner and thinking of the network as if it consists of the spanner edges alone. Consequently, in most applications, the relevant "quality" parameter measuring the performance degradation of the solution would be the stretch factor of the spanner, and the number of edges in the spanner would serve as the "cost" parameter. In other words, the expected effects of using a spanner are that the solution might be less accurate (to the extent that the network topology is relevant) and less costly (since fewer edges are used). Hence in order to guarantee a reasonable quality–cost trade-off for such an application, one is mainly interested in finding sparse spanners with small stretch factor.

Bibliographical notes

A number of excellent textbooks are available on the basics of distributed computing, including [Ray86, Tel94, Lyn95, Bar96a, AW98]. The textbooks listed above have some partial overlap with the topics covered in Part I of this text. Good sources on some related areas include [BHG86, BG92, M89]. An early report on distributed network algorithms is [Sha86].

Part I

Basics of distributed network algorithms

Chapter 2

The distributed network model

This chapter provides the definitions for the basic model components and computational notions (such as algorithms and executions) in a distributed message passing system. It should be clear from the earlier discussion that these notions may sometimes change in accordance with the specific characteristics of the model at hand. However, the general structure of a system and a computation going on in it can be described in a rather uniform way, with some variation regarding the specific details, such as the communication mode.

2.1 The model

2.1.1 The system components

The communication model consists of a point-to-point communication network, described by a simple connected undirected graph $G = (V, E)$, where the vertices $V = \{v_1, v_2, \ldots, v_n\}$ represent network processors and the edges represent bidirectional communication channels operating between them.

Occasionally we may consider as our network model a *multigraph*, namely, a graph allowing some vertex pairs to be connected by more than one edge. Nevertheless, most of our normal course of discussion will be restricted to plain graphs. In some cases we shall assume that the graph is weighted, i.e., associate a weight function ω with the set of edges E. Such edge weights may have a variety of interpretations, according to the application at hand. One possible application may be to associate with each edge $e = (u, w)$ a weight $\omega(e)$ representing the *capacity* of the communication channel connecting u and w. This kind of interpretation provides an alternative mechanism for introducing a multigraph model, as it enables us to represent a collection of m multiple edges connecting two vertices u and w by a single edge $e = (u, w)$ with an appropriate weight $\omega(e) = m$. Other common interpretations for edge weights may relate to the actual length of the edges (i.e., the distance between their endpoints) or to their current traffic load.

Initially, unique identifiers are assigned to the processors of the graph G. For concreteness, we may assume that these identifiers are taken from an ordered set of integers $S = \{s_1, s_2, \ldots\}$, where $s_i < s_{i+1}$ for every $i \geq 1$. Thus an ID-assignment is a one-to-one mapping $ID : V \to S$. (Whenever no confusion arises, we might ignore the distinction between the vertex itself and its identifier, i.e., we may refer to the vertex v as either v or $ID(v)$ interchangeably. However, some issues discussed later on depend expressly on the properties of the chosen ID-assignment. Clearly, when discussing those issues we will have to strictly obey the distinction between these two separate notions.) These identifiers should be thought of as fixed and assigned to the processors on the hardware level. Later on, we will discuss situations in which it may be beneficial to assign other types of labels to vertices in our network on a higher software level, e.g., for routing purposes.

Communication is carried out as follows. Each vertex v has $deg_G(v)$ *ports*, i.e., external connection points, numbered 1 through $deg_G(v)$. The set of edges adjacent to the vertex v contains precisely $deg_G(v)$ edges, with exactly one edge connected to each port of v. Every edge (u, v) in E corresponds to a pair $((u, i), (v, j))$, where $1 \leq i \leq deg_G(u)$ and $1 \leq j \leq deg_G(v)$, representing a channel connecting port i of u to port j of v (see Figure 2.1). The vertex u sends a message to its neighbor v by loading it onto the appropriate port, i. This message is then received by v through its port j. More specifically, each vertex has one input buffer per adjacent link, and each arriving message is placed in the input buffer and is read from the buffer by the processor. It is assumed that at most one message (in either direction) can occupy a communication channel at any given time. Hence the channel becomes available for the next transmission from u to v only after the previous message is removed by the receiving processor from the input buffer.

For simplicity we adopt the common assumption that the allowable message size is $O(\log n)$ bits, so a message can carry a fixed number of vertex identifiers (including, in particular, those of its sender and destination).

2.1.2 Some graph terminology

Our discussion of distributed network algorithms and their complexity makes frequent use of some basic graph-theoretic terminology. Let us next introduce some of the notions and graph parameters which occur intensively later on.

Distances

For two vertices u, w in an unweighted graph G, let $dist_G(u, w)$ denote the length of a shortest path in G between those vertices, where the length of a path is defined as the number of edges in it. (We sometimes omit the subscript G where no confusion arises.)

When dealing with a weighted graph $G = (V, E, \omega)$, the edge weights may be thought of as representing the lengths of the edges. In that case, we let $dist_G(u, w)$ denote the *weighted* length of a shortest path in G between u and w, where the weighted length of a path $(e_1, \dots, e_s)$ is $\sum_{1 \leq i \leq s} \omega(e_i)$.

This definition is generalized to sets of vertices U, W in G in the natural way, by letting $dist(U, W)$ denote the minimal distance $dist(u, w)$ between any two vertices $u \in U$ and $w \in W$,

$$dist_G(U, W) = \min\{dist_G(u, w) \mid u \in U, w \in W\}.$$

(We sometimes substitute w for a singleton $W = \{w\}$.)

In certain cases, we need to talk about the *unweighted* distance between two vertices u and w in a weighted graph G. This distance, denoted $dist^{un}(u, w, G)$, is defined by

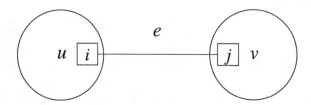

Figure 2.1: The edge $e = (u, v)$ and the ports it connects.

measuring the distance between u and w looking at G as an unweighted graph, i.e., it is the minimum number of hops necessary to get from u to w.

Diameter, radius and depth

Definition 2.1.1 [Diameter]: *Let $Diam(G)$ denote the (weighted or unweighted) diameter of the network G, i.e., the maximal distance between any two vertices in it:*

$$Diam(G) \;=\; \max_{u,v \in V} \{dist_G(u,v)\}.$$

Throughout, we denote $\Lambda = \lceil \log Diam(G) \rceil$.

In a weighted graph G, let $Diam^{un}(G)$ denote the unweighted diameter of G, i.e., the maximum unweighted distance between any two vertices of G.

Definition 2.1.2 [Radius and center]: *For a vertex $v \in V$, let $Rad(v,G)$ denote the distance from v to the vertex farthest away from it in the graph G:*

$$Rad(v,G) \;=\; \max_{w \in V} \{dist_G(v,w)\}.$$

Let $Rad(G)$ denote the radius of the network, i.e.,

$$Rad(G) \;=\; \min_{v \in V} \{Rad(v,G)\}.$$

A center of G is any vertex v realizing the radius of G (i.e., such that $Rad(v,G) = Rad(G)$). In order to simplify some of the following definitions, we avoid problems arising from 0-diameter or 0-radius graphs, by defining $Rad(G) = Diam(G) = 1$ for the single-vertex graph $G = (\{v\}, \emptyset)$.

Observe that for every graph G,

$$Rad(G) \;\leq\; Diam(G) \;\leq\; 2Rad(G). \tag{2.1}$$

When discussing spanning trees, we sometimes use the *depth* parameter as the analog of radius (or diameter) in general graphs.

Definition 2.1.3 [Depth]: *The depth of a vertex v in rooted tree T is its distance from the root, r_0, of the tree:*

$$Depth_T(v) = dist_T(v, r_0).$$

The depth of the rooted tree T is the maximum depth of any vertex in it or, alternatively, its radius with respect to its root r_0:

$$Depth(T) = Rad(r_0, T).$$

Neighborhoods

The concept of vertex neighborhoods plays a central role in our later treatment of clustered graph representations. The *neighborhood* of a vertex $v \in V$, denoted $\Gamma(v)$, is the set of its neighbors in the graph, namely, those vertices connected to it by an edge. We extend this definition to include v itself in $\Gamma(v)$, and we also look at the generalized concept of *ρ-neighborhood*, defined as follows.

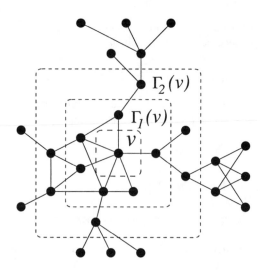

Figure 2.2: The neighborhoods $\Gamma_0(v)$, $\Gamma_1(v)$ and $\Gamma_2(v)$ of a vertex v in an unweighted graph.

Definition 2.1.4 [ρ-neighborhood]: *The ρ-neighborhood of a vertex $v \in V$ is the collection of vertices at distance ρ or less from it in G:*

$$\Gamma_\rho(v, G) \;=\; \{w \mid dist_G(w, v) \le \rho\}.$$

(When G is clear from the context, we write simply $\Gamma_\rho(v)$.) Note that in particular, $\Gamma_0(v) = \{v\}$.

Since we are dealing with *unweighted* graphs, the traditional notion of the neighborhood $\Gamma(v)$ coincides with our definition for $\rho = 1$, namely, $\Gamma_1(v)$. Moreover, our generalized definition corresponds to the natural extension of $\Gamma(v)$ (see Figure 2.2).

Tree levels

When dealing with a rooted tree with root r_0, it is convenient to stratify its vertices in various ways. We will be using three types of stratification schemes. The most common one is a simple top-down *layering* of the vertices. Layers are numbered $0, 1, 2, \ldots$ from the root downwards. Hence we have the following definition.

Definition 2.1.5 [Tree layers]: *Layer t of a rooted tree T with root r_0 consists of all vertices at (unweighted) distance t from the root. The* layer number *of the vertex v is denoted by $L(v)$.*

Our two other stratification schemes are defined bottom-up. For a vertex $v \in V$, let $\mathtt{Child}(v)$ denote the set of v's children in T.

Definition 2.1.6 [Tree max-levels]: *The* max-level *of a vertex v in a rooted tree T is the depth of the subtree T_v rooted at v, denoted by $\hat{L}(v) = Depth(T_v)$. More explicitly, $\hat{L}(v)$ is defined as follows:*

$$\hat{L}(v) \;=\; \begin{cases} 0 & \text{if } v \text{ is a leaf,} \\ 1 + \max_{u \in \mathtt{Child}(v)}\{\hat{L}(u)\} & \text{otherwise.} \end{cases}$$

Definition 2.1.7 [Tree min-levels]: *The* min-level $\check{L}(v)$ *of a vertex v in a rooted tree T is defined as follows:*

$$\check{L}(v) = \begin{cases} 0 & \text{if } v \text{ is a leaf;} \\ 1 + \min_{u \in \text{Child}(v)}(\check{L}(u)) & \text{otherwise.} \end{cases}$$

Observe that these definitions of "levels" in a tree may yield rather different level numbers (see Exercise 1).

2.1.3   The computational model

Let us now present a formal description of the computational model. The computation is governed by an *algorithm* Π, composed of n *protocols* $\Pi_1, \ldots, \Pi_n$, with each Π_i residing at the processor v_i. Consequently, each protocol Π_i can be modeled for the purpose of this algorithm as a state machine with state set Q_i, containing a predefined initial state $q_{0,i}$ such that at any given moment, processor v_i is at some state q_i of Q_i.

Similarly, at any given time each communication link $e_i = (u, v)$ is at some state $\bar{q}_i$ from the state set $\bar{Q}_i$. The state $\bar{q}_i$ is composed of two components, denoted $\bar{q}_{u \to v}$ and $\bar{q}_{v \to u}$, one for each direction of the link. Letting $\mathcal{M}$ denote the collection of possible messages that processors may send each other throughout any execution of the algorithm, each of the two components $\bar{q}_{u \to v}$ is an element of $\mathcal{M} \cup \{\lambda\}$, with $\bar{q}_{u \to v} = MSG \in \mathcal{M}$ signifying that the message MSG is now in transit from u to v and $\bar{q}_{u \to v} = \lambda$ representing the fact that the channel is currently empty in that direction.

At the beginning of the computation, all processors v_i are in their initial state $q_{0,i}$ and all communication links e_i are empty (i.e., their initial state is $\bar{q}_{i,0} = \langle \lambda, \lambda \rangle$).

The execution of a distributed algorithm consists of *events* occurring at various places in the network and affecting the involved processors. Each event is either a *computation event*, representing a computation step of a single processor, or a *communication event*, representing the sending or delivery of a message. Each communication event has the form SEND(i, j, MSG) or DELIVER(i, j, MSG) for some $MSG \in \mathcal{M}$. Thus the repertoire of possible events includes the following:

1. Event COMPUTE(i): the processor v_i executes an internal operation, based on its local state, and possibly changes its local state.

2. Event SEND(i, j, MSG): the processor v_i sends out a message $MSG \in \mathcal{M}$ on some communication link e_l (destined at a neighbor v_j).

3. Event DELIVER(i, j, MSG): the message $MSG \in \mathcal{M}$ (originated at some processor v_i) is placed by the communication link e_l into the input buffer at its destination v_j.

The computation in a distributed system can be described by a sequence of configurations, capturing the current state of the processors and communication links. Each event changes the state of some processor, and possibly also that of some edge, and thereby changes the configuration of the system.

Formally, a *configuration* is a tuple $C = (q_1, \ldots, q_n, \bar{q}_1, \ldots, \bar{q}_m)$ where q_i is the local state of processor v_i and $\bar{q}_j$ is the local state of edge e_j. The *initial configuration* is the vector $(q_{0,1}, \ldots, q_{0,n}, \bar{q}_{0,1}, \ldots, \bar{q}_{0,m})$.

We model a computation of the algorithm as a (possibly infinite) sequence of configurations alternating with *events*. The execution of algorithm Π on a graph of topology G

with initial input I at the processors is denoted $\eta^{\Pi}(G, I)$. Formally, an *execution* η of an algorithm is a sequence of the form

$$\eta = (C_0, \phi_1, C_1, \phi_2, C_2, \ldots),$$

where each C_k is a configuration C_0 is the initial configuration and each ϕ_k is an event. Furthermore, the application of ϕ_k to C_{k-1} results in C_k, in the natural way. That is, if ϕ_k is a local computation event of processor v_i (namely, a COMPUTE(i) event), then the only change in C_k with respect to C_{k-1} is in the state of v_i, and specifically, the state of v_i in C_k is the result of applying v_i's transition function to the state of v_i in C_{k-1}. Likewise, if ϕ_k is a SEND(i, j, MSG) event, then the only changes in configuration involve the states of the involved parties, v_i and the edge e_l connecting it to v_j (in particular, the state change of v_i reflects the fact that the message has been sent, and in e_l's state, the $\bar{q}_{v_i \to v_j}$ component of the state $\bar{q}_l$ changes from "λ" to "MSG"). And finally, if ϕ_k is a DELIVER(i, j, MSG) event, then the only changes in configuration involve the states of v_j and the edge e_l connecting it to v_i, which are updated to reflect the fact that the edge is empty again and that v_j's input buffer on edge e_l now contains an additional message MSG. We adopt the convention that a finite execution ends with a configuration.

Some additional requirements must be imposed on executions. In the asynchronous model, an execution is *legal* if each processor has an infinite number of computation events and if whenever the state of some communication link changes to some $MSG \in \mathcal{M}$, it changes back to λ within finite time (or in other words, each SEND event can be mapped in a 1-1 fashion to a subsequent DELIVER event, so that every message sent is delivered at some later point in the execution). It is often convenient to assume also that processor v_i has a computation event immediately after each delivery event of the form DELIVER(j, i, MSG).

In the synchronous model, processors are required to execute in lock-step. An execution is *legal* if, in addition to the legality constraints specified for the asynchronous case, the computation events occur in *rounds*. Each processor is allowed exactly one computation event in each round, and all computation events of round r appear after all computation events of round $r - 1$. Furthermore, all messages sent in round r are required to be delivered before the computation events of round $r + 1$.

2.1.4   Predefined structures

The network model as presented so far portrays a preliminary setting of a *clean network*, in which nothing is available to the users except the basic mechanisms provided by the network. However, in actual actively operating systems, there often exist a host of knowledge and information structures designed to aid and simplify computational processes on the system.

For instance, as discussed earlier, different models for partial topological knowledge may be implemented, giving the sites some additional knowledge on their surroundings. But even without allowing processors to know much about the topology explicitly, it is possible to supply them with implicit topological knowledge by setting up various structures in the network.

As a typical example, it is possible to set up a spanning tree in the network, namely, a cycle-free set of edges connecting all the vertices. Assuming the spanning tree is known to all the vertices, it can be used for performing various communication tasks, as elaborated on in later chapters.

At this point it may be useful to dwell a little on what we mean when saying that a given spanning tree T is "known" to all processors. In the sequential setting, knowing a tree T means having direct access to some precise description of T, e.g., a data structure representing it. In contrast, in the distributed context, "knowing the tree" by vertex v does not necessarily mean that v needs to know the *entire* tree structure, but only that it knows which of its neighbors in the graph are its neighbors in the tree and which are not. As a concrete implementation, each processor v connected to $d = deg_G(v)$ edges $e_1, \ldots, e_d$ may store d Boolean variables $X_1, \ldots, X_d$ as in Figure 2.3(a), with

$$X_i = \begin{cases} 1 & \text{if } e_i \text{ is a tree edge,} \\ 0 & \text{otherwise.} \end{cases}$$

In case the tree is rooted at some vertex r_0, a more appropriate representation may require each vertex to know which of its neighbors in the graph is its *parent* in the tree T, which are its children and which of its edges in the graph are not tree edges at all. Hence each vertex v should have a variable $parent(v)$ specifying (the edge leading to) its parent and a set variable $child(v)$ listing (the edges leading to) its children (see Figure 2.3(b)).

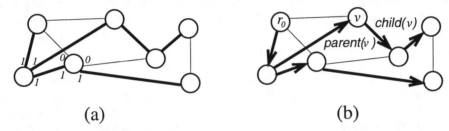

(a)   (b)

Figure 2.3: Possible representations for a spanning tree in the network: (a) for an unrooted tree,   (b) for a rooted tree.

Other types of useful structures, which are discussed at length in later parts of this book, may be based on an arbitrary marked subnetwork of the graph or on various kinds of hierarchical decompositions of the graph.

Yet a more implicit representation of topological knowledge may be hidden in assuming that a *routing* service is available in the network. Such a service responds to requests for sending messages from one vertex to another by delivering the message from its sender to its requested destination as efficiently as possible. While the processors using such a service are unaware of the underlying mechanism, and do not gain any topological knowledge directly, they nevertheless benefit from an implicit structure designed to ensure routing along short paths.

2.2 Complexity measures

The question of evaluating the performance of our algorithms raises some interesting issues special to the distributed setting. Again, let us contrast the situation with what happens in the sequential case. There, our common complexity measures are the *time* and *space* required by the algorithm. In the distributed setting, the corresponding measures are more subtle to define, and additional measures become relevant as well.

2.2.1 Time complexity

The time complexity of a sequential algorithm is measured by the number of steps it takes from start to finish. Thus although the execution of the algorithm may be halted and resumed several times by the operating system, its complexity measure is robust against these changes.

In a multiprocessor setting, the possibility exists that the program segments involved in our algorithm at the various processors are swapped into and out of execution at different times, resulting in a situation where a process at one site awaits messages from another vertex in which the corresponding process is currently halted. Again, there seems to be no other alternative but to assume, for the purpose of analysis, that the algorithm is run by the system in "stand-alone" mode, with no other activities concurrently taking place. However, delays incurred at one processor as the result of having to wait for information computed at another cannot be ignored away. In other words, it is not enough to count the number of steps taken by each processor, as forced gaps in its operation must be taken into account as well.

Formally, time complexity is defined as follows.

Definition 2.2.1 [Synchronous time complexity]: *The* time complexity *of a synchronous distributed algorithm Π on the network G, denoted* $\mathsf{Time}(\Pi, G)$, *is the number of pulses generated during the execution of Π on G in the worst case (namely, over every legal input for Π stored initially at the processors of G), from the time the first processor began the execution until the last processor has terminated.*

(Again, we sometimes omit the parameter G when it is clear from the context.)

For an asynchronous algorithm, this definition is meaningless, since even the simple algorithm in which a processor v sends a single message to a neighbor u has unbounded time complexity, recalling our assumption that the time this message may require to arrive at its destination is unbounded. Therefore we adopt the following definition.

Definition 2.2.2 [Asynchronous time complexity]: $\mathsf{Time}(\Pi, G)$ *is the number of time units from the start of the execution of Π on G to its completion in the worst case (namely, over every legal input for Π on G and in every execution scenario), assuming that each message incurs a delay of at most one time unit.*

Recalling that asynchronous computations are inherently nondeterministic, we note that here, the term "worst case" refers to all possible inputs as well as to all possible scenarios over each input.

Let us stress that this assumption may be used only for performance evaluation and does not imply that there is a bound on delay in asynchronous networks. Note that this assumption does not restrict the set of possible scenarios of the algorithm in any meaningful way. This is because any scenario involving message transmissions longer than one time unit can be transformed into one involving only transmission times between 0 and 1 without changing any of the ordering properties of the execution, by scaling all the transmission times by the appropriate factor, namely, the longest actual transmission time of a message during the execution.

2.2.2   Space complexity

Next, let us consider space complexity. Although we mainly consider the total memory requirements of an algorithm, in some cases we would also consider the maximum *local* memory requirements at any particular vertex.

Definition 2.2.3 [Space complexity]: *The* total space complexity *of an algorithm Π on the network G, denoted* $\mathsf{Mem}(\Pi, G)$, *is the total number of memory bits used by the algorithm in the network in the worst case (namely, over every legal input for Π on G and in every execution scenario). The* maximum space complexity *of an algorithm Π on the network G,* *denoted* Max_Mem(Π, G), *is the maximum number of memory bits used by the algorithm at any processor in the network in the worst case (namely, over every legal input for* Π *on* G *and in every execution scenario).*

Assuming a certain level of total memory requirements Mem(Π, G), the more sensitive measure Max_Mem(Π, G) may enable us to identify algorithms achieving a more balanced distribution of their memory requirements.

2.2.3   Message complexity

In sharp contrast with centralized computing, there is a third complexity measure which plays a critical role in the distributed model, namely, the cost of communication. Its main role is to fill an acute void left by the measure of time complexity. In centralized computing, the time complexity of an algorithm is used to simultaneously evaluate two inherently different parameters, which are

1. *the completion deadline*, namely, the time by which the client(s) may expect to get the outcome of their computation, and

2. *the cost*, namely, the expected number of operations required for the computation.

In the distributed setting, these two parameters are no longer linked to each other, since computations can be sped up by sharing the work among many processors. Therefore, while estimation of the completion deadline is still achieved by the notion of time complexity, the cost of the computation is now evaluated using *message complexity* as the main measure. As explained earlier, communication is often viewed as the major cost in a distributed algorithm.

Example 1:   *Four algorithms.*

In order to illustrate this distinction, let us consider the following four algorithms, executed on the complete graph on vertices $\{0, \ldots, n-1\}$ with an edge connecting every two vertices. In algorithm Π_A, a single message MSG is sent from vertex 0 to vertex 1. In algorithm Π_B, a different message MSG_i is sent (in parallel) from every vertex i to vertex $(i+1) \bmod n$. In algorithm Π_C, a single message MSG originated at vertex 0 is repeatedly passed on in a chain from each vertex i to its successor vertex $(i+1) \bmod n$. Finally, in algorithm Π_D, vertex 0 sends (simultaneously) a separate message MSG_i to every other vertex i.

As far as completion deadline performance is concerned, algorithms Π_A, Π_B and Π_D are very efficient, requiring one time unit to complete, while algorithm Π_C is slow and requires $n-1$ time units. On the other hand, our message complexity measure (to be defined essentially as the number of messages sent by the algorithm) will classify these algorithms differently, viewing algorithm Π_A as efficient (since it involves a single message transmission) and algorithms Π_B, Π_C and Π_D as inefficient, having complexity $\Theta(n)$.   □

Let us point out that in the "stand-alone" scenario discussed earlier, it may be that the measures of time and space are sufficient for evaluating the quality of our algorithms and the "cost" of a computation is not a very significant factor. After all, in this mode all that a client cares about is the waiting time. Consequently, one may raise the question of why we should bother to estimate the message complexity of our algorithm, rather than focusing on time alone.

One answer to that has to do with the fact that in many systems, communication has an associated cost besides its implications on time. It may be that the users of the algorithm have to pay the network administration for using the network, according to the amounts of information they transmit.

However, even when time is our primary consideration, message complexity is significant. To understand that, it is important to remember that in reality, the algorithms will often be executed in an active, multiuser network with many other activities happening at the same time. Here is where the issue of message complexity comes into the picture. It may indeed be true that the ultimate measure of efficiency is time, hence message complexity is meaningful only insofar as it captures this issue. However, when evaluating an algorithm in stand-alone mode, it is hard to estimate its impact on the entire network performance. This performance is determined to a very large extent by the performance of the communication subsystem, whose efficiency (in terms of propagation and queuing delays for messages) is influenced to a very large degree by the load on the message queues in the various sites. Consequently, by bounding the total amount of communication used by a particular algorithm in stand-alone mode, we obtain a handle on the amount of extra work that this algorithm will impose on the network when used in practice.

Our message complexity measure is defined as follows. The *basic message* length is assumed to be $O(\log n)$ bits. In some cases, when the discussion focuses on communication and ignores time, it may be convenient to assume that longer messages are allowed, but their cost is evaluated by viewing them as composed of a sequence of basic messages and charging proportionally to their length (i.e., a message of length $L > \log n$ is viewed as $\lceil \frac{L}{\log n} \rceil$ basic messages).

Definition 2.2.4 [Message complexity]: *The* message cost *of transmitting a basic message over an edge is 1. The* message complexity *of a distributed algorithm Π on a network G, denoted* Message(Π, G)*, is the total number of basic messages transmitted during the execution of Π on G in the worst case (i.e., over every legal input for Π on G and in every execution scenario).*

2.2.4   Weighted cost measures for communication tasks

The efficiency of communication in a computer network critically depends on the delays existing on the various links at any given moment. These delays, caused by high traffic loads of currently transmitted and queued messages, are usually modeled in communication network theory by representing the network as a *weighted* graph $G = (V, E, \omega)$, where a positive weight $\omega(e)$ is associated with each edge of the graph. For an edge $e = (u, v)$, the weight $\omega(e)$ represents the expected time it will take a message currently enqueued by u to be transmitted on the channel e until it is delivered at v.

Nevertheless, in the distributed algorithms literature it is commonly accepted that in analyzing the performance of network control and management algorithms, it is reasonable to make the simplifying assumption of unit weight (or simply unweighted) edges. Subsequently, one may adopt the definitions given above for the Message and Time complexity measures, which are based on postulating that sending a basic $O(\log n)$-bit message over an edge requires one time unit and costs one communication unit.

The justification for this assumption is twofold. First, network control and management algorithms typically use relatively short messages compared to the traffic generated by the end users of the system. Moreover, control messages usually receive higher priority and therefore do not suffer the queuing delays facing user traffic. Hence for studying the performance of various basic network control mechanisms and management protocols, this simplistic unweighted modeling is sufficient to capture the behavior of the system. Indeed, in most of the following chapters we will concentrate on this type of unweighted cost analysis.

This line of thinking is no longer valid once we shift our attention to the design of communication protocols for providing facilities such as the routing and broadcast of user-originated messages. Consider, for instance, a routing algorithm whose primary goal is to select and set up routes for transmitting traffic between various end users. It may still be true that the cost of the algorithm's internal messages at the route-design stage is immaterial for the two reasons mentioned above. However, it is crucial that the *output* produced by the routing algorithm, namely, the routes themselves, be optimal or near-optimal with respect to the actual delays, since the traffic that will actually be shipped along those routes will be mostly user traffic, which as discussed earlier may both be very large and have low priority.

It follows that for evaluating the quality of the "message delivery" solutions produced by a communication protocol, delays must be taken into account, and hence weighted graphs should be used to model the network.

Consequently, let us next define a *delay-related* cost measure for communication, to be used in our analysis of end-user routing and broadcast services.

Definition 2.2.5 [Communication cost]: *The* communication cost *of transmitting a basic message over an edge e is the weight $\omega(e)$ of that edge. The* communication cost *of the communication operation Π on the network G, denoted* $\mathrm{Comm}(\Pi, G)$, *is the total cost of the messages sent during the execution of Π in the worst case (i.e., over every legal input for Π on G and in every execution scenario).*

2.2.5   Global and specific complexity bounds

We close this section with a brief discussion of our terminology concerning *bounds* on complexity. We will use the standard $Big - Oh$ and $Omega$ notation, albeit with slightly more involved semantics than usual. Instead of giving a formal definition, let us illustrate these notions via a number of examples.

The bounds we state usually refer to the worst case. In particular, upper bounds are *global* in nature, i.e., an upper bound applies to any network in the particular class of networks under discussion and holds under every input and execution. Hence when we say that "algorithm Π has time complexity $O(n \log n)$ on the class of planar graphs," we mean the following:

> There exists a constant $c > 0$ such that for every n-vertex planar graph G, $\mathrm{Time}(\Pi, G) \leq cn \log n$, or more specifically, for every legal input for Π (stored initially at the processors of G), in every execution scenario of Π on G, the algorithm will terminate within time at most $cn \log n$.

In contrast, for lower bounds in the worst case, when we say that "the algorithm Π has time complexity $\Omega(n)$ on arbitrary graphs," we mean the following:

> There exists a constant $c > 0$ such that for every $n \geq 1$, there *exists* an n-vertex graph G such that $\mathrm{Time}(\Pi, G) \geq cn$, or more specifically, there *exist* a legal input for Π and an execution scenario of Π on G in which the algorithm terminates after time of at least cn.

This is what we may call a *specific* or *existential* lower bound. On the other hand, we may sometimes be interested in a stronger statement, providing a *global* lower bound for every graph in the given class. For instance, the statement "the algorithm Π has time complexity $\Omega(n)$ on *every* graph" means the following:

> There exists a constant $c > 0$ such that for *every* n-vertex graph G, $\text{Time}(\Pi, G) \geq cn$, or more specifically, there exist a legal input for Π and an execution scenario of Π on G in which the algorithm terminates after time of at least cn.

In other words, while in both cases the bound holds for some specific input and scenario, the difference is that an existential lower bound only implies the existence of some specific network in the class under discussion for which the bound holds, whereas a global lower bound must hold for every network in the class.

A similar distinction applies for lower bounds on the complexity of problems, rather than algorithms. In particular, when we say "problem X has time complexity $O(n \log n)$ on the class of planar graphs," we mean that "there exists an algorithm Π for X with time complexity $O(n \log n)$ on the class of planar graphs." In contrast, when we say that "a (global or existential) lower bound of $\Omega(n)$ applies for the problem X," we mean that "a (global or existential) lower bound of $\Omega(n)$ applies for every algorithm Π for X."

Let us conclude with a brief discussion of a common metaphor for analyzing lower bounds based on representing the situation as a *game* against an *adversary*. In the distributed network context, the participants playing the game (namely, the algorithm designer and the adversary) have the following powers:

- The *algorithm designer* controls the *protocols* of the processors. This includes, in particular, deciding which messages are to be sent by each processor, to whom and when (or following what events).

- The *adversary* controls the *external system*. This includes, in particular, selecting the inputs to the problem, relying on full knowledge regarding the structure of the protocol and determining the behavior of the communication channels. The latter means that the adversary decides the order in which queued messages are to be scheduled for transmission (unless explicitly specified by the protocol of the sending processor). Moreover, in an asynchronous network, the adversary also controls the transmission speeds (and hence the delays) for each message sent by the protocol.

2.3   Three representative models

The above discussion should make it clear to the reader that there is a huge variety of different models one can employ in studying the behavior of distributed systems. Indeed, the number of different models considered in the literature is only slightly lower than the number of papers published in this field. However, it is still possible to identify a number of prototypical models that were defined and used (albeit with many minor "internal" variations) for various purposes. For instance, there were typical model classes used for studying issues related to fault tolerance, others dedicated to the study of dynamic changes in networks, yet others dedicated to the study of the nature of time and the effects of asynchrony in the distributed setting and so on.

In the present text, we shall deliberately restrict our spectrum of models (and analogously, the range of issues and problems discussed) by fixing certain characteristics of the model as follows.

1. We shall completely ignore the (extremely important) issue of fault handling. Thus our algorithms will be based on the assumption that the network at hand is fault free and that processors are fully reliable. Moreover, we will focus on algorithms geared at static topologies, and we will not consider dynamic changes (i.e., additions or removals of vertices and communication links).

2. We assume that the vertices of the network are equipped with unique identifiers, i.e., we shall not consider the anonymous model (although we may, on occasion, remark on the possible effects of assuming anonymity). Moreover, we will usually assume that the identifier $ID(v)$ of each vertex v is of $O(\log n)$ bits.

3. We assume that local computation is free. Again, we shall usually try to minimize the abuse of this assumption and derive algorithms employing reasonably low local computation per step. We shall also try to point out explicitly whenever individual processors are required to perform a "global" (e.g., $O(n)$ sequential time) computation.

These restrictions clearly limit the immediate applicability of the results discussed. Nevertheless, we feel that this choice is well justified from a didactic point of view, as the concepts and techniques studied are better introduced and easier to digest in the more restricted setting outlined above.

On the other hand, a number of important parameters of the model will be left deliberately "nonuniform," in the sense that their specification (and hence the resulting model) will vary from one algorithm to another. This includes, for instance, the topological knowledge possessed by the processors: some of the algorithms presented will be based on the assumption that processors know a good deal about their environment (e.g., their neighborhood to some distance, or the total number of processors in the network, or the entire topology, or some bound on the network's diameter or maximum degree), while other algorithms will make use of minimal assumptions (e.g., the identity of the neighbors) or none at all.

Another property left to vary between chapters is the existence of various *weights* on the edges and vertices of the network. While most of the time we will assume an unweighted network, in certain applications we will consider weighted networks with various interpretations for the weights.

Finally, under the above guidelines, we will focus in what follows on three major model classes that were traditionally used in the literature in the aim of understanding the role of three fundamental *obstacles* arising in the distributed setting, namely, *locality, congestion* and *asynchrony,* and their adverse effects on the *time and message complexities* of distributed network algorithms. We shall consequently refer to these three model classes as the $\mathcal{LOCAL}$ model, the $\mathcal{CONGEST}$ model and the $\mathcal{ASYNC}$ model.

The $\mathcal{LOCAL}$ model is aimed at focusing on the effects of the localized nature of executions of distributed network protocols on the time requirements of the problems at hand. It therefore abstracts away difficulties arising from other factors, such as congestion and asynchrony, in order to expose the precise limitations stemming solely from this phenomenon. Consequently, this model allows messages of unlimited size (thus doing away with congestion problems) and unlimited local computation (thus enabling the solution of every problem in time proportional to the network's diameter by allowing the vertices to exchange among themselves all the information known to them). This model also assumes that communication is synchronous and that all the vertices wake up simultaneously and start the computation at the same round.

The $\mathcal{CONGEST}$ model is aimed at focusing on the effects of the *volume* of communication, specifically the congestion created at various bottlenecks in the network, on the time and message complexities of the protocol. This model thus enforces the $O(\log n)$ bit limitation on the maximal message size. This model has both a synchronous and an asynchronous version, and the results are sometimes insensitive to this distinction. We will not usually make the assumption of simultaneous wakeup in this model (although again, most results are insensitive to this parameter).

Finally, the $\mathcal{ASYNC}$ model is geared towards understanding the effects of asynchrony. It will therefore assume asynchronous communication without simultaneous wakeup. This model has versions allowing both limited and unlimited size messages, and many typical results are insensitive to this distinction.

Bibliographical notes

A number of common standard models for distributed systems appear in the literature. Our basic framework of a point-to-point communication network follows numerous references in the literature (cf. [LL90, Lyn95]). Among the first papers that paved the way to the systematic study of distributed network algorithms in this model are [Dij74, Gal76, GMS77, LeL77, Gal82, GHS83].

Exercises

1. Give an example for a (small) tree with a vertex whose level, max-level and min-level are *three different* numbers.

2. (a) State and prove an inequality relating $L(v)$, $\hat{L}(v)$ and $Depth(T)$ for a vertex v in a rooted tree T.

   (b) Characterize the vertices v for which equality holds.

3. Let PRUNE(T) be a procedure eliminating an arbitrary leaf from the tree T, and consider a tree T' obtained from T by a number of repeated applications of Procedure PRUNE(T). For a vertex $v \in T'$, let $L_T(v)$ and $L_{T'}(v)$ denote, respectively, v's layer number in T and T' and similarly for $\hat{L}$ and $\check{L}$. Disprove, prove or strengthen each of the following claims:

   (a) $L_{T'}(v) \leq L_T(v)$.

   (b) $\hat{L}_{T'}(v) \leq \hat{L}_T(v)$.

   (c) $\check{L}_{T'}(v) \leq \check{L}_T(v)$.

4. Consider an n-vertex network $G = (V, E)$, $V = \{v_1, \ldots, v_n\}$. The *individual messages (IM)* task requires vertex v_1 to deliver a (distinct) $\log n$-bit message to every other vertex in the network along some prespecified shortest route. Prove or disprove each of the following claims regarding the message complexity of the problem.

   (a) **[Upper bound]:** Message(IM) $= O(nD)$ (or there exists a constant $c > 0$ such that for every network G as above, Message(IM, G) $\leq cnD$).

   (b) **[Lower bound]:** Message(IM) $= \Omega(nD)$ (or there exists a constant $c > 0$ such that for every $n \geq 1$, there exists an n-vertex network G as above for which Message(IM, G) $\geq cnD$).

   (c) **[Global lower bound]:** There exists a constant $c > 0$ such that for every network G as above, Message(IM, G) $\geq cnD$.

5. Consider the IM task of the previous question in the synchronous $\mathcal{CONGEST}$ model. Prove or disprove each of the following claims regarding the time complexity of the problem.

   (a) **[Upper bound]:** Time(IM) $= O(D)$ (or there exists a constant $c > 0$ such that for every network G as above, Time(IM, G) $\leq cD$).

   (b) **[Upper bound]:** Time(IM) $= O(n)$ (or there exists a constant $c > 0$ such that for every network G as above, Time(IM, G) $\leq cn$).

(c) [**Lower bound**]: $\text{Time}(IM) = \Omega(D)$ (or there exists a constant $c > 0$ such that for every $n \geq 1$, there exists an n-vertex network G as above for which $\text{Time}(IM, G) \geq cD$).

(d) [**Global lower bound**]: There exists a constant $c > 0$ such that for every network G as above, $\text{Time}(IM, G) \geq cD$.

6. Repeat the previous question in the $\mathcal{LOCAL}$ and the $\mathcal{ASYNC}$ models.

Chapter 3

Broadcast and convergecast

3.1 The broadcast operation

The broadcast operation is one of the most fundamental primitives of distributed network algorithms. It has been given many algorithms in several frameworks, and its properties and applications have been extensively studied.

In this chapter, we will use the broadcast operation as an illustration to the basic notions defined in the previous chapter. We will therefore discuss the problem in both the synchronous and the asynchronous models. We will mainly examine the time and message complexities of various solutions.

Formally, the problem of *broadcast from a single source* can be stated as follows.

Definition 3.1.1 [Broadcast]: *The broadcast operation is initiated by a single processor* r_0*, called the* source*. The source has a message, initially kept on a special input buffer. This message needs to be disseminated from the source to all vertices in the network.*

We observe the following simple global lower bounds for the complexity of the broadcast operation.

Lemma 3.1.2 *For any broadcast algorithm B and any n-vertex network G,* $\mathsf{Message}(B, G)$ $\geq n - 1$ *and* $\mathsf{Time}(B, G) \geq Rad(r_0, G) = \Omega(Diam(G))$*, in either the synchronous or the asynchronous model.*

Proof: The bound on the number of messages follows from the need to deliver at least one message at each destination vertex in the graph. The time bound stems from the need to reach the farthest destination, which is at distance $Rad(r_0, G)$ away. (Recall Inequality (2.1) on the relationship with the network diameter.) $\square$

Let us remark that a stronger lower bound of $\Omega(|E|)$ holds for the clean network model (in which vertices know nothing on the topology), as we will see in Chapter 23 (Theorem 23.2.2).

3.2 Tree broadcast

A common strategy for broadcast is to use a spanning tree T of the network rooted at the source of the broadcast, r_0. Given such a tree T, the message is transmitted from the root to all its children, and each internal vertex of the tree getting the message from its parent forwards it to all its children. We refer to this algorithm as the *tree broadcast* algorithm and denote it by $\text{TCAST}(r_0, T)$.

The tree broadcast algorithm relies on the preexistence of a spanning tree T, which is known to all processors (in the distributed sense, as discussed in Section 2.1.4). In case such a tree is not available, it has to be constructed first. Note, however, that the problem of constructing a spanning tree from a single initiator is equivalent in terms of message complexity to the problem of broadcasting a single message. This follows from the observation that any broadcast algorithm can also be used to build a tree in the network. Specifically, given a broadcast algorithm B, apply it on the graph G and define a spanning tree T_B by defining the broadcast source as the root r_0 of the tree and fixing the parent of a vertex $v \neq r_0$ in the tree T_B to be the neighbor from which v has received the first message. T_B is guaranteed to be a spanning tree, since the broadcast algorithm ensures that the broadcast message reaches all the vertices. Hence the message complexity of spanning tree construction is at most that of broadcast, and the message complexity of broadcast is bounded by that of spanning tree construction (plus $O(n)$).

The complexities of the tree broadcast algorithm are easy to analyze. In an asynchronous network, the message might progress at different speeds on the different branches down the tree (see Figure 3.1). However, after t time units, the message must have reached (at least) all the vertices at layer t of the tree (namely, at distance t from the root r_0, as defined in Section 2.1.2). Hence we have the following lemma.

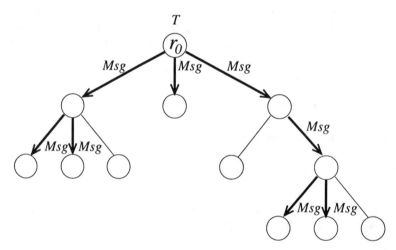

Figure 3.1: An intermediate stage in the execution of the tree broadcast Algorithm TCAST.

Lemma 3.2.1 *For every n-vertex graph G with a spanning tree T rooted at r_0,* $\text{Message}(\text{TCAST}(r_0, T)) = n - 1$ *and* $\text{Time}(\text{TCAST}(r_0, T)) = Depth(T)$.

Clearly, certain trees T might have depth much larger than the network's diameter. It follows from this analysis that the tree most appropriate for the purpose of performing an efficient broadcast is a *breadth-first search tree*, defined next.

Definition 3.2.2 [Breadth-first spanning tree]: *The* breadth-first spanning tree, *or* BFS tree, *of G with respect to a given root r_0 is a spanning tree T_B with the property that for every other vertex v, the path leading from the root to v in the tree is of the minimum (unweighted) length possible.*

(The name "BFS tree" stems from the fact that it is exactly the tree tracing the edges examined by a breadth-first search of the graph originating at the source.) For such a tree, we get the optimal complexities for broadcast, matching the lower bounds of Lemma 3.1.2.

Lemma 3.2.3 *For every n-vertex graph G with a spanning BFS tree T w.r.t. r_0,* $\mathsf{Message}(\textsc{Tcast}(r_0, T)) = n - 1$ *and* $\mathsf{Time}(\textsc{Tcast}(r_0, T)) \leq Diam(G)$.

3.3   The flooding algorithm

One of the most basic and well-known algorithms for broadcast in a point-to-point communication network is the *flooding* algorithm, henceforth named $\textsc{Flood}$. This algorithm, which is the natural one to apply in the absence of any preconstructed structures in the network, achieves its task by simply forwarding the message over *all* links. Algorithm $\textsc{Flood}$ is described formally in Figure 3.2.

For the source r_0 **do:**
Send the message on all outgoing links.

For vertex $v \neq r_0$ **do:**
Upon receiving the message for the first time (over an edge e):

  1. Store the message on the output buffer;

  2. Forward it on every other edge.

Upon receiving the message again (over other edges):
    Discard it and do nothing.

Figure 3.2: Algorithm $\textsc{Flood}$.

It is easy to verify that this description yields a correct broadcast algorithm. A formal proof of that fact is implicit in the time analysis given in the proof of the following lemma.

Lemma 3.3.1 $\mathsf{Message}(\textsc{Flood}) = \Theta(|E|)$ *and* $\mathsf{Time}(\textsc{Flood}) = \Theta(Rad(r_0, G)) = \Theta(Diam(G))$ *in both the synchronous and asynchronous models.*

Proof: Each edge delivers the message at least once and at most twice (once in each direction), hence the message complexity. As for the time complexity, it is straightforward to verify (by induction on t) that after t time units, the message has already reached every vertex at a distance of t or less from the source, i.e., the entire t-neighborhood $\Gamma_t(r_0)$. (Note that in the asynchronous model, the message may actually have reached many additional vertices beyond $\Gamma_t(r_0)$.) $\square$

In view of the discussion in Section 3.2, we observe that Algorithm $\textsc{Flood}$ implicitly constructs a directed tree $T = T_{\textsc{Flood}}$, rooted at the source r_0 and spanning all the vertices of the network, with the parent of each nonroot vertex v in T being the vertex from which v has received the message for the first time.

An important distinction between the structure of the tree $T_{\textsc{Flood}}$ in the synchronous and asynchronous models is revealed by the following lemma.

Lemma 3.3.2 *Let T be the spanning tree constructed by Algorithm $\textsc{Flood}$ as described above. Then in the synchronous model, T is a BFS tree with respect to the source r_0, hence* *its depth is Rad(r_0, G). In contrast, in the asynchronous model, T may be of larger depth (up to $n - 1$).*

Proof: For the synchronous model we observe (by induction on t, as in the previous lemma) that the message reaches the vertices at distance t from r_0 after *precisely* t time units, hence their depth in the tree T is precisely t. In the asynchronous model, the message may travel faster on some paths and slower on others, and consequently T is not guaranteed to preserve distances. (See Figure 3.3).   □

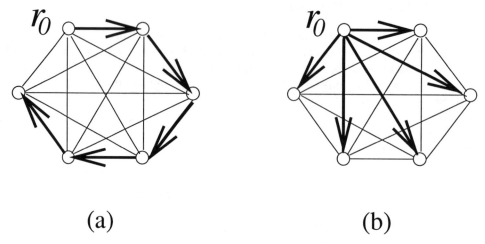

(a)   (b)

Figure 3.3: (a) A possible execution of Algorithm FLOOD in an asynchronous network. The arrows indicate, for every vertex $v \neq r_0$, the direction from which v received the message for the first time, hence the edges of the implied spanning tree T_{FLOOD}. (b) The execution in a synchronous network, and the resulting tree.

3.4   Convergecasts

One element that is missing from the basic broadcast algorithms described above is a mechanism that will enable the source to detect the fact that the broadcast operation has completed. This component of the problem is usually known as "termination detection."

  A simple method of achieving termination detection for the broadcast algorithm (sometimes called "broadcast with echo") is based on collecting back acknowledgements in a leveled fashion on a spanning tree. The process of collecting information upwards on a tree is called *convergecast* and is the subject of this section.

3.4.1   Acknowledgement echos

Acknowledgements of receiving the broadcast message can be efficiently gathered on a spanning tree T of the network by the following convergecast process. Upon getting the message, a vertex v has to do the following. If v is a leaf in the tree T, then it immediately responds by sending up an *Ack* message to its parent. If v is an intermediate (nonleaf) vertex in T, then it must first collect *Ack* messages from all its children and only then may it send an *Ack* message to its parent. We refer to this algorithmic technique, illustrated in Figure 3.4, as Procedure CONVERGE(*Ack*).

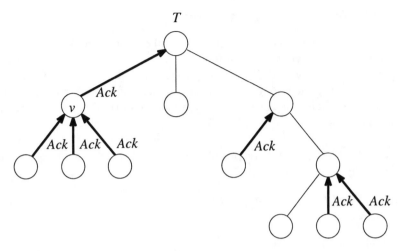

Figure 3.4: The convergecast process resulting from applying Procedure CONVERGE(Ack) over the spanning tree T.

Notice that the meaning of an Ack message sent up from a vertex v in the tree is not only an acknowledgement of receiving the message, but also a "joint acknowledgment," representing all the vertices in T_v, the subtree of T rooted at v and signifying that each vertex in T_v has received the message. In particular, the source receives Ack from all its children only after all vertices in the graph have received the message.

Lemma 3.4.1 *On a tree T, the message and time complexities of the convergecast process carried by Procedure* CONVERGE *are* Message(CONVERGE(Ack)) $= n - 1$ *and* Time(CONVERGE(Ack)) $\leq Depth(T)$.

Using the convergecast process, it is possible to augment the broadcast algorithms described earlier and get a broadcast algorithm with acknowledgements, namely, one in which the source can detect the termination of the broadcast.

In particular, for the tree broadcast algorithm TCAST, this additional "echo" stage can be performed over the same tree used for the broadcast. Hence both the time and message complexities of the algorithm increase only by a constant factor.

As for the flooding algorithm, recall that this process constructs a spanning tree T of the network. This tree can be used for the convergecast. Hence in this algorithm, a vertex v sends Ack to its parent only after the subtree of T rooted at v has been constructed *and* all its vertices have received the message. By Lemma 3.3.2, in the synchronous model this tree is a BFS tree and therefore the complexities again at most double. Unfortunately, in the asynchronous model, it is not possible to guarantee that the "echo" phase ends with the same time complexity as the broadcast itself, by the same lemma.

Lemma 3.4.2 *Applied to a network $G = (V, E)$ with diameter D, the complexities of the "broadcast with echo" algorithm* FLOOD&ECHO *are as follows.*

1. Message(FLOOD&ECHO) $= O(|E|)$.

2. Time(FLOOD&ECHO) $= O(D)$ *in the synchronous model and* $O(n)$ *in the asynchronous model.*

3. *In both models, the message MSG reaches all vertices by time D.*   □

3.4.2 Global function computation

The setting in which the convergecast process is useful can be generalized further, to include the computation of various types of global functions. Suppose that each vertex v in the graph holds an input X_v, and we would like to compute some global function $f(X_{v_1}, \ldots, X_{v_n})$ of these inputs. Suppose further that f falls into the class of operations defined next. Such functions (possibly without the third property in the definition) are sometimes referred to as *semigroup functions*.

Definition 3.4.3 [Semigroup functions]: *A function f is a* semigroup function *if it enjoys the following three properties.*

1. *f is well-defined for any subset of the inputs (i.e., $f(\mathcal{Y})$ is defined for any $\mathcal{Y} \subseteq \mathcal{X} = \{X_{v_1}, \ldots, X_{v_n}\}$),*

2. *f is associative and commutative,*

3. *the representation of $f(\mathcal{X})$ is "relatively short" with respect to that of the inputs.*

A semigroup function f can be computed efficiently on a tree T by a convergecast process. In this process, the value sent upwards by each vertex v in the tree will be the value of the function on the inputs of the vertices in its subtree T_v, namely, $f_v = f(\mathcal{Y}_v)$ where $\mathcal{Y}_v = \{X_w \mid w \in T_v\}$. An intermediate vertex v with k children $w_1, \ldots, w_k$ computes this value by receiving the values $f_{w_i} = f(\mathcal{Y}_{w_i})$, $1 \le i \le k$, from its children, and applying $f_v \leftarrow f(X_v, f_{w_1}, \ldots, f_{w_k})$. We refer to this type of convergecast process as Procedure CONVERGE(f, X).

Correctness of the computation is guaranteed by the associativity and commutativity of f. As for the complexity of the process, we have the following.

Lemma 3.4.4 *Assuming $f(\mathcal{Y})$ can be represented in $O(p)$ bits for any $\mathcal{Y} \subseteq \mathcal{X}$, the message and time complexities of the convergecast Procedure* CONVERGE *on a tree T are*

$$\mathsf{Message}(\text{CONVERGE}(f, X)) = O(np/\log n), \text{ and}$$

$$\mathsf{Time}(\text{CONVERGE}(f, X)) = O(Depth(T) \cdot p/\log n).$$

These complexities nearly match the following obvious lower bound. Call the function f *globally-sensitive* if for every input $\mathcal{X}$ and for every $v \in V$, changing the input X_v causes a change in the value of $f(\mathcal{X})$.

Lemma 3.4.5 *For any globally-sensitive function f and every n-vertex tree T, the global function computation problem on T has message complexity $\Omega(n)$ and time complexity $\Omega(Depth(T))$.*

Global computation can be performed also on a partial set of inputs. Suppose that there is only a subset W of the vertices which have an input and we wish to compute the value of the function on W. This can be done in the same way, except that vertices v with $T_v \cap W = \emptyset$ send up a "null" message, and likewise, an intermediate vertex receiving real values only from some of its children (and "null" from the others) computes the function on the values it received. In this case, we refer to the version of the convergecast process as Procedure CONVERGE(f, X, W).

Example 1: *Addition.*

Suppose that the function f represents addition. Note that if the inputs are m-bit integers, then $f(\mathcal{Y})$ can be represented in $O(m \log n)$ bits for any $\mathcal{Y} \subseteq \mathcal{X}$. Therefore, the message and time complexities of the convergecast process performed by Procedure CONVERGE($+$) on a tree T are $O(nm)$ and $O(Depth(T) \cdot m)$, respectively.   □

Example 2: *Maximum.*

As another example, the *maximum* of n elements can be computed in this fashion. (See Figure 3.5.) The message and time complexities of the convergecast process carried by Procedure CONVERGE(max) on a tree T are $O(n)$ and $O(Depth(T))$, respectively.   □

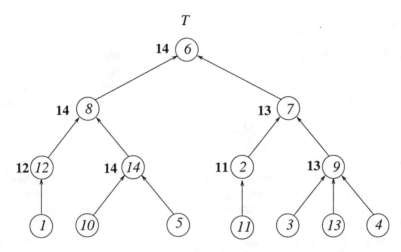

Figure 3.5: The process carried by Procedure CONVERGE(max) over the spanning tree T.

Example 3: *Logical conditions.*

The convergecast process can be applied in order to collect global knowledge from local predicates. Suppose that each vertex v holds a predicate $Pred(v)$ which may be "*True*" or "*False*." Let X_v be a bit variable set to

$$X_v = \begin{cases} 1 & \text{if } Pred(v) = \text{True}, \\ 0 & \text{otherwise.} \end{cases}$$

Then it is possible to convergecast a combined form of this information efficiently, ending up with the root knowing, for instance, whether there exists some vertex v with $Pred(v) = True$ (i.e., whether the predicate $\exists v\, Pred(v)$ holds in the network) or whether all vertices v satisfy $Pred(v) = True$ (i.e., whether $\forall v\, Pred(v)$ holds).

The former can be achieved by taking f to be the logical "or" function and performing a global convergecast computation as above. At each intermediate vertex v, the value sent by v to its parent will be a bit f_v set to 1 if and only if at least one of the vertices w in the subtree T_v rooted at v has $X_v = 1$. Consequently, the value computed by the root is 1 if and only if $\exists v\, Pred(v)$. We refer to this as Procedure CONVERGE($\bigvee, X$) or Procedure CONVERGE($\bigvee, Pred$).

Computing $\forall v\, Pred(v)$ is achievable in a similar way, by taking f to be the logical "and" function. This process is referred to as Procedure CONVERGE($\bigwedge, X$) or CONVERGE($\bigwedge, Pred$). In particular, the acknowledgement process performed by Procedure CONVERGE(Ack), as presented in Section 3.4.1, can be computed by performing Procedure CONVERGE($\bigwedge$, *Pred*) for

$$Pred(v) = \text{``}v \text{ has received the message.''}$$

(This is a rather trivial use of the logical and computation, as all inputs are 1 once defined, hence so is the output.)

The message and time complexities of this procedure on a tree T are $O(n)$ and $O(Depth(T))$, respectively.

Again, the same applies if we wish to apply our function to the inputs X_v of only a subset W of the vertices. In this case, we refer to the process corresponding to the operation *op* by Procedure CONVERGE(op, X, W). $\square$

3.4.3 Pipelined broadcasts and convergecasts

We next consider a situation in which the vertices of the network store data of a number of different types, and it is necessary to perform separate convergecast computations on each of the different data collections. For instance, suppose that each vertex in the tree stores k separate variables $X_i(v)$, $1 \le i \le k$, and we would like to compute all k maximums

$$M_i = \max_{v \in V}\{X_i(v)\}$$

and inform all vertices of the results. Clearly, for each i, it is possible to compute M_i separately, through a convergecast process performed by Procedure CONVERGE(max), and then broadcast the result on the tree. Assuming the variables hold $\log n$-bit numbers, each of those k processes requires Message(CONVERGE(max)) $= O(n)$ and Time(CONVERGE(max)) $= O(Depth(T))$. But performing all k operations sequentially, waiting for the computation of M_{i-1} to end before beginning the computation of M_i, would multiply the time complexity by a factor of k, resulting in a total of $O(k \cdot Depth(T))$ time.

A simple technique for reducing this time complexity is to *pipeline* the computations. Each leaf v starts the k processes one after another, sending $X_1(v)$ followed by $X_2(v)$ and so on. Denote by $T(v)$ the subtree of T rooted at a vertex v. Each intermediate vertex v computes each of the k partial maximums

$$M_i(v) \;=\; \max_{w \in T_v}\{X_i(w)\}$$

immediately when receiving the corresponding partial maximums from all its children and sends the values $M_i(v)$ to its parent one by one. This process is illustrated in Figure 3.6.

In the synchronous model, the algorithm can be formalized by noting that each vertex v sends the values $M_i(v)$ to its parent consecutively, at rounds $\hat{L}(v) + i$ (for $1 \le i \le k$) (as defined in Section 2.1.2). This can be proved for every i by induction on $\hat{L}(v)$, from the leaves up. We conclude the following.

Lemma 3.4.6 *In the synchronous model, computing k global semigroup functions on a tree T can be performed in $Depth(T) + k$ time.*

In the asynchronous model, we rely on the fact that messages are passed up the tree in first-in first-out order, so an intermediate vertex can match together the values of the ith type, which it receives from each of its children, and interpret them as belonging to the ith maximum computation. It is easy to verify that the complexity bounds remain the same.

Lemma 3.4.7 *In the asynchronous model, computing k global semigroup functions on a tree T can be performed in $Depth(T) + k$ time as well.*

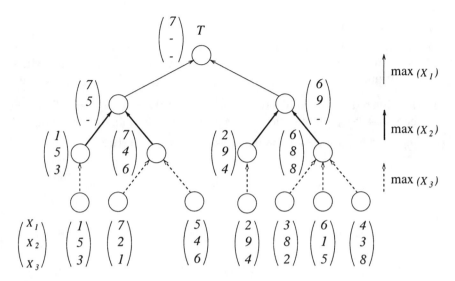

Figure 3.6: Three parallel processes of Procedure CONVERGE(max) carried over the spanning tree T. (For pictorial simplicity, this example assumes the inputs are stored only at the leaves.)

Bibliographical notes

Broadcast in computer networks was the subject of extensive studies. One early source for the study of broadcast as a basic primitive in distributed computing is [DM78].

Literature on broadcast has dealt extensively with a broad spectrum of aspects and models. Much of the research dealt with the so-called telephone model, in which communication is synchronous and a vertex can speak with only one neighbor in each round. The survey papers [HHL88, FL94] cover some of the work done in this area in recent years (also see Chapters 5.2.2 and 5.2.3 in [BG92]). A variant of the pipelined convergecast problem is studied in detail under an elaborate database setting in [T95]. Exercise 4 was suggested by [SS96].

Exercises

1. Formally prove Lemmas 3.2.1 and 3.2.3.

2. Consider a partially synchronous model in which the delay incurred by each message is between $1/4$ and 1 time unit. What can be said about the behavior of Algorithm FLOOD&ECHO in this model? In particular, how long does it take until every vertex receives the message, what is the time complexity of the algorithm and what is the depth of the spanning tree constructed by it?

3. Describe the processes resulting from applying Procedure CONVERGE(min) to the tree of Figure 3.5 and Procedure CONVERGE(+) to the tree of Figure 3.6 (with the given inputs).

4. Consider the global addition operation described in the first example in Section 3.4.2. Explain how pipelining can be used to speed up the computation, and determine the resulting time complexity.

5. (a) Give a distributed algorithm for counting the number of vertices in a rooted tree T, initiated at the root.

(b) Extend your algorithm to an arbitrary graph G.

(c) Give a distributed algorithm for counting the number of vertices in each layer of the rooted tree T separately. Analyze the time and message complexities of your algorithm.

6. (a) Describe a distributed algorithm initiated by the root of a tree T for calculating the max-level $\hat{L}(v)$ of each vertex v in the tree, and analyze its complexities.

(b) Repeat the question for the min-level $\check{L}(v)$ of the vertices.

Chapter 4

Downcasts and upcasts

Another pair of tasks that can be carried out via the process similar to (but different from) broadcast and convergecast is *downcast* and *upcast*. These tasks refer to the case where there is a possibly different item communicated between the root and each of the vertices in the tree, hence each such item needs to be treated individually and may not be combined. In this chapter we discuss the downcast and upcast operations under different settings. For simplicity, we will assume the synchronous model, although a number of the principal results described hold also for the asynchronous model. As our focus here is on message complexity, we will disallow large messages, i.e., concentrate on the synchronous $\mathcal{CONGEST}$ model.

4.1 Downcasts

We first examine the case where the root has m distinct items $\mathcal{A} = \{\mu_1, \ldots, \mu_m\}$, each destined to one specific vertex in the tree. (Each vertex in the tree may get zero or more such messages.) Clearly, both the depth of the tree and the number of distinct messages that need to be sent are potential bottlenecks, hence we have the following lower bounds.

Lemma 4.1.1

1. *Downcasting m distinct messages on T requires $\Omega(Depth(T))$ time in the worst case for every tree T.*

2. *Downcasting m distinct messages on arbitrary trees requires $\Omega(m)$ time in the worst case.*

These lower bounds can be met by the straightforward algorithm DOWNCAST. For each of its children w, the root r_0 simply sends the messages destined to the subtree rooted at w one by one on the edge (r_0, w), in an arbitrary order. Each intermediate vertex v in the tree receives at most one message at each step and passes it on towards its destination (unless the destination of the message is itself).

Lemma 4.1.2 *Algorithm* DOWNCAST *performs downcasting of m distinct messages on the tree T in time $O(m + Depth(T))$.*

Proof: The root releases at least one message per step, so it terminates by time m. The proof is completed upon noting that messages are never delayed, so a message leaving the root at time t will reach its destination at time at most $t + Depth(T)$. $\qquad\square$

4.2   Upcasts

Let us now consider the dual problem. Suppose that m data items $\mathcal{A} = \{\mu_1, \ldots, \mu_m\}$ are initially stored at some of the vertices of the tree T. Items can be replicated, namely, each item is stored in one or more vertices (and each vertex may store zero or more items). The goal is to end up with all the items stored at the root of the tree.

Note that this task is not really a "convergecast" process, since the items are sent up to the root individually. Specifically, items are "combined" only in the following limited sense: If a particular item is replicated and multiple copies of it arrive at some vertex v (from different children), then v sends only a single copy of the item to its parent.

The same bottlenecks that exist for the downcast operation apply also to upcast, hence we get the following lower bounds.

Lemma 4.2.1

1. *For every tree T, upcasting m distinct messages on T requires $\Omega(Depth(T))$ time in the worst case.*

2. *Upcasting m distinct messages on arbitrary trees requires $\Omega(m)$ time in the worst case.*

At first, it may seem that the upcast operation should be inherently more difficult than the downcast operation: intuitively, in the downcast operation the different messages "spread out" on the tree, hence they disrupt each other less and less, whereas in the upcast operation the different messages "converge" to a single spot on the tree, hence they tend to disrupt each other more and more.

It turns out, however, that this intuition is misleading. There is a simple argument that shows that the bound of Lemma 4.2.1 is theoretically feasible. Consider the dual downcast operation. By the previous subsection, this operation can be performed in time $m + Depth(T)$. Now, simply "rolling the execution tape backwards" will give us a feasible schedule for the upcast operation.

While this argument proves feasibility in principle, it does not give any specific way of scheduling the messages. When performing an upcast operation, the vertices of the tree have no information regarding the specific schedule used for the dual downcast. Despite this difficulty, we will now see that there are simple algorithms that will guarantee this optimal bound on the upcast operation.

We will look at three possible settings of assumptions regarding the given items.

4.2.1   Ranked items

It is easy to achieve the $O(m + Depth(T))$ time bound in case the items are taken from an ordered set, and each item is marked by its rank in the set (e.g., the items are given in the form of pairs (i, μ_i) such that $\mu_i \leq \mu_{i+1}$ for $1 \leq i \leq m$). In this case, we may adopt the policy of Algorithm RANKED_UPCAST, described in Figure 4.1. (For the definition of $\hat{L}(v)$ see Section 3.4.3.)

On round $\hat{L}(v) + i$ (for every $i \geq 1$) **do:**

    If the ith item, (i, μ_i), is stored locally **then** forward it to parent.

Figure 4.1: Algorithm RANKED_UPCAST (for vertex v).

For every v, let M_v denote the set of items initially stored at any vertex of T_v. By straightforward induction on $\hat{L}(v)$, we can prove the following lemma.

Lemma 4.2.2 *If the ith item is in M_v, then at the end of round $\hat{L}(v) + i - 1$ it is stored at v.*

This immediately guarantees that by time $Depth(T) + m$, all items are collected at the root.

Corollary 4.2.3 *Upcast of m ranked items on a tree T can be performed in time $Depth(T) + m$.* □

4.2.2 Ordered items

Now consider the slightly more general case where the items are still taken from an ordered set, but their ranks are not marked. Hence given two items, it is possible to compare them and decide which is the larger of the two, but it is not possible to tell the position of a particular item in the complete list just by inspecting the item. In this case, we may still make use of the ordering in order to impose some pipelining policy. The rule followed by each vertex v is that of Algorithm ORDERED_UPCAST, described in Figure 4.2.

On each round **do**:

> Forward to parent the smallest locally stored item that has not been upcast so far.

Figure 4.2: Algorithm ORDERED_UPCAST (for vertex v).

Note that this does not necessarily mean that items are upcast in nondecreasing order; a vertex may learn of smaller items after it has already forwarded some large ones.

Interestingly, under this policy it is still possible to prove Lemma 4.2.2, although the induction becomes slightly more complicated. (See Exercise 2.)

Corollary 4.2.4 *Upcast of m ordered items on a tree T can be performed in time $Depth(T) + m$.* □

4.2.3 Unordered items

Finally, let us consider the case where the items are entirely incomparable (except for identity). In this situation, the only sensible rule that one may adopt is the policy used in Algorithm UNORDERED_UPCAST, described in Figure 4.3.

On each round **do**:

> Forward to parent an *arbitrary* locally stored item that has not been upcast so far.

Figure 4.3: Algorithm UNORDERED_UPCAST (for vertex v).

In this setting, Lemma 4.2.2 no longer holds, yet the overall bound can still be proved. We need the following claim.

Lemma 4.2.5 *Consider a vertex v and an integer t. Suppose that for every $1 \leq i \leq k$, at the end of round $t + i$, v stored at least i items. Then at the end of round $t + k + 1$, v's parent w has received from v at least k items.*

Proof: By induction on i, we prove that at the end of round $t + i + 1$, v's parent w has received from v at least i items. For $i = 1$, note that by assumption, at the end of round $t + 1$, v stored at least one item. Therefore either v has already upcast an item to w or it will do so at round $t + 2$. In either case, at the end of round $t + 2$, w will have received at least one item from v.

Now suppose the claim holds up to $i - 1$ and consider i. By the inductive hypothesis, at the end of round $t + i$, w has already received at least $i - 1$ items from v. If w has actually received i items or more by that time, then we are done. So suppose by the end of round $t + i$, w has received *exactly* $i - 1$ items from v. But by assumption of the lemma, at the end of round $t + i$, v stored at least i items. Hence at least one of those items has not been upcast yet and can be upcast in round $t + i + 1$, reaching w by the end of that round. It follows that at the end of round $t + i + 1$, w has received from v at least i items, as required.   □

Lemma 4.2.6 *For every $1 \leq i \leq |M_v|$, at the end of round $\hat{L}(v) + i - 1$, at least i items are stored at v.*

Proof: Let us fix i and prove the claim by induction on $\hat{L}(v)$. For a leaf v (with $\hat{L}(v) = 0$), the claim is immediate since the entire set M_v is stored at v from the very beginning. Now suppose the claim holds for every vertex w with $\hat{L}(w) \leq \ell - 1$ and prove the claim for v with $\hat{L}(v) = \ell$.

Consider such a vertex v, and denote its children by $w_1, \ldots, w_k$. For every $1 \leq j \leq k$, let $\ell_j = \hat{L}(w_j)$, $m_j = |M_{w_j}|$ and $\gamma_j = \min\{m_j, i\}$.

Consider a child w_j of v. Note that $\ell_j \leq \ell - 1$. By the inductive hypothesis on w_j, we have that for every $1 \leq i' \leq m_j$, at the end of round $\ell_j + i' - 1$, w_j has stored at least i' items. By Lemma 4.2.5 (taking $t = \ell_j - 1$ and $k = \gamma_j$), at the end of round $(\ell_j - 1) + \gamma_j + 1$, v has already received from w_j at least γ_j items.

Now, if v has any child w_j with $m_j \geq i$ (namely, with $\gamma_j = i$), then we are done, since by the last conclusion, at the end of round $\ell_j + i$, v has already received from w_j at least i items and this round is no later than round $\ell + i - 1$.

So the remaining case is when $m_j < i$ (hence $\gamma_j = m_j$) for every child w_j. Then by the above conclusion, at the end of round $\ell + i - 1$, v has already received from each child w_j all the m_j items stored at its subtree and, consequently, v already stores all the items of M_v. Hence it stores at least i items.   □

Hence at the end of round $Depth(T) + m$, all the items are stored at the root of the tree, and we have the following corollary.

Corollary 4.2.7 *Upcast of m unordered items on a tree T can be performed in time $Depth(T) + m$.*   □

4.3   Applications

Let us now discuss some applications of the convergecast and upcast paradigms.

4.3.1   Smallest k-of-m

Consider the following example. Suppose that the elements μ_v stored at the vertices are taken out of an ordered domain $\mathcal{A}$ and that our goal is to collect the smallest k elements at the root. The global function computation scheme described above could be used to solve this problem as follows. First, find the minimum element and inform all the vertices by broadcasting it throughout the tree. Now, find the next smallest element by the same method and so on. This should take $O(kDepth(T))$ time.

An alternative and faster method would be the following. At any given moment along the execution, every vertex keeps the elements it knows of in an ordered list. In each step, each vertex sends to its parent the smallest element that hasn't been sent yet.

Recalling the definition of $\hat{L}(v)$, the max-level of a vertex v in T, we note that for each vertex v, the smallest value stored at any vertex in the subtree T_v has already reached v by round $\hat{L}(v)$; more generally, v already has the ith smallest value in T_v by round $\hat{L}(v) + i - 1$. This can be proved in a way similar to the proof of Lemma 4.2.2 in the above case of ordered items (Section 4.2.2). We conclude the following.

Lemma 4.3.1 *Upcasting the k smallest elements on a tree T can be performed in $Depth(T)$ $+ k$ time.*

4.3.2 Information gathering and dissemination

A slightly more involved task that combines a number of the above subtasks is disseminating information among the vertices of a tree. Consider the following problem. Suppose that m data items are initially stored at some of the vertices of the tree T. Items can be replicated, namely, each item is stored in one or more vertices (and each vertex may store zero or more items). The goal is to end up with each vertex knowing all the items. A natural approach for achieving this is to collect the items at the root of the tree and then broadcast them one by one.

Clearly, since broadcasting the items can be done in a pipelined fashion (i.e., releasing one item in each round), the broadcast phase can be completed within $O(m + Depth(T))$ time. By what we've seen in Section 4.2, the collecting phase can be performed by an upcast operation with a similar complexity. Hence the entire problem can be solved in time $O(m + Depth(T))$.

4.3.3 Route-disjoint matching

Our last two applications, described in this section and the next, fall under the general convergecast/upcast framework, although they do not fit precisely into the paradigms discussed above.

The following "matching" problem can be solved using the techniques discussed earlier. Suppose that we are given a network in the form of a rooted tree T (with each vertex knowing the edge leading to its parent and the edges leading to its children in T). In addition, a set of $2k$ vertices $W = \{w_1, \ldots, w_{2k}\}$ for $k \leq \lfloor n/2 \rfloor$ is initially marked in the tree. (See Figure 4.4.)

Our goal is to find (by a distributed algorithm) a matching of these vertices into pairs (w_{i_1}, w_{i_2}) for $1 \leq i \leq k$, such that the (unique) routes Υ_i connecting w_{i_1} to w_{i_2} in T are all edge-disjoint. "Finding" the matching means that each vertex in W should know the identifier of the vertex with which it is paired. (In fact, the solution technique allows us to guarantee, at the same time and communication costs, the stronger requirement that the routes Υ_i are "marked" in the network. By this we mean that each vertex $v \neq w_{i_2}$ along the route Υ_i should know which of its edges leads towards w_{i_2} on Υ_i and, similarly, each

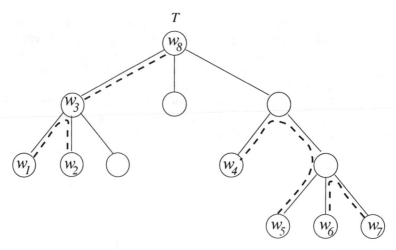

Figure 4.4: An instance of the route-disjoint matching problem and a possible solution for it.

vertex $v \neq w_{i_1}$ along Υ_i should know the edge leading from it towards w_{i_1} on Υ_i.) We have the following lemma, whose proof is left to Exercise 6.

Lemma 4.3.2

1. *For every tree T and for every set W as above, there exists an edge-disjoint matching as required.*

2. *Furthermore, this matching can be found by a distributed algorithm on T in time $O(Depth(T))$.* $\square$

4.3.4   Token distribution

The *token distribution* problem is stated as follows: n tokens (of $O(\log n)$ bits each) are initially distributed among the n vertices of the tree with no more than K at each site. Redistribute the tokens so that each processor will have exactly one token.

The limit on the token size implies that each token can be sent in a single message. Hence the cost of the entire redistribution process equals the sum of the distances traversed by the tokens in their way to their destinations. An optimal solution can be derived by using a convergecast process in order to determine, for every vertex v in the tree, the following three parameters:

1. s_u, the number of tokens in the subtree T_u,

2. n_u, the number of vertices in the subtree T_u,
   and consequently,

3. $p_u = s_u - n_u$, the (positive or negative) number of tokens that need to be transferred out of T_u.

The total number of messages required for achieving an even distribution of the tokens is at least $P = \sum_{u \neq r_0} |p_u|$. This bound can be met by an appropriate distributed algorithm, as stated in the following lemma.

Lemma 4.3.3 *There exists a distributed algorithm for performing token distribution on a tree using an optimal number of messages P and $O(n)$ time, after a preprocessing stage requiring $O(Depth(T))$ time and $O(n)$ messages.*

Bibliographical notes

Results similar to Lemma 4.1.2 and Corollary 4.2.7 hold also in much more general settings, without the tree structure. In particular, the bounds hold even when the m messages are sent from different senders to different (possibly overlapping) recipients along arbitrary shortest paths and under a wide class of conflict resolution policies (for resolving collisions in intermediate vertices between messages competing over the use of an outgoing edge), so long as these policies are consistent (namely, if μ_i is preferred over μ_j at some vertex v along their paths, then the same preference will be made whenever their paths intersect again in the future). This was first shown in [CKMP90, RVVN90] for two specific policies and was later extended to any consistent greedy policy in [MPS91].

Part 1 of Lemma 4.3.2 is due to [KR93].

Exercises

1. (a) Explain why the first lower bound of Lemma 4.1.1 is global while the second is only existential.

    (b) Characterize a subclass of trees for which the second lower bound of the lemma applies globally.

2. Prove Lemma 4.2.2 in the setting of Section 4.2.2, namely, gathering ordered items with unmarked rank. (Hint: the proof requires a double induction: on $\hat{L}(v)$ from the leaves up and on i. Also, it may help to strengthen the lemma and prove that if the ith item is in M_v, then (1) at the end of round $\hat{L}(v) + i - 1$, it is stored at v, and (2) at the end of round $\hat{L}(v) + i$, v has already upcast this item to its parent.)

3. Devise downcast and upcast algorithms analogous to those in Section 4.1 and the unordered case of Section 4.2.3 for the asynchronous model, and analyze their time complexities.

4. The following policy is proposed for solving the "smallest k-of-m" problem of Section 4.3.1:

    - At any given moment along the execution, every vertex keeps only the set of k smallest elements that it knows.

    - In each step, each vertex sends to its parent an *arbitrary* element from this set that hasn't been sent yet.

    (a) Prove that using this policy, the k smallest elements must still arrive at the root by time $O(k\,Depth(T))$.

    (b) For every integer $m \geq 1$, give an example for a tree T and an initial distribution of m elements, where $k = Depth(T) = \lceil \sqrt{m} \rceil$ and the above process takes $\Omega(m)$ steps.

5. Consider a tree-shaped distributed network connecting a number of sites of a scientific organization. Suppose that the organization is interested in measuring k parameters and towards that end it employs measuring equipment at various sites in the network. Suppose that the measurements approximate the true parameters by bounding them from above and that we are interested in finding the most accurate approximation for each of the k parameters and collecting these approximations at the root.
   Explain how this problem can be solved in $O(Depth(T) + k)$ time by fitting it into the framework of Section 3.4.3.

6. Prove Lemma 4.3.2.

7. Describe and analyze the token distribution algorithm of Section 4.3.4 (including both the preprocessing stage and the actual distribution stage), and prove Lemma 4.3.3.

Chapter 5

Tree constructions

In this chapter we discuss some basic constructions of various types of spanning trees, including *Breadth-First Search (BFS)* trees, *Depth-First Search (DFS)* trees and *Minimum-weight Spanning Trees (MST)*, and their distributed implementation.

5.1 BFS tree construction

The BFS tree of a given network with respect to a given root was defined in Section 3.2. Recall that in Section 3.3 we saw how broadcast through flooding can be used to define a spanning tree for the network. Moreover, by Lemma 3.3.2, in a synchronous network Algorithm FLOOD generates a BFS tree, and this is done with complexities Message(FLOOD) = $\Theta(|E|)$ and Time(FLOOD) = $\Theta(Diam(G))$. These complexities are asymptotically optimal for a clean network (in which vertices know nothing on the topology). This is implied by the following lower bounds on distributed BFS tree construction, which we state without proof. In Chapter 23 (Theorem 23.2.2), we will see a proof for a result similar to part 1 of the lemma concerning broadcast.

Lemma 5.1.1

1. *For every n-vertex graph $G = (V, E)$, distributed BFS tree construction in a clean network requires $\Omega(|E|)$ messages in the worst case.*

2. *For arbitrary n-vertex graphs, distributed BFS tree construction requires $\Omega(Diam)$ time in the worst case.*

In the asynchronous model, however, the tree generated by Algorithm FLOOD need not necessarily be a BFS tree. Hence in our discussion of BFS tree constructions, we shall concentrate on the asynchronous setting. As our main focus here is on the trade-offs between the time and message complexities, we will disallow large messages, i.e., concentrate on the asynchronous $\mathcal{CONGEST}$ model.

There are two basic sequential algorithms for computing a BFS tree for a given graph, known as the *Dijkstra* and *Bellman–Ford* algorithms. The two distributed algorithms we present next are in fact the respective distributed implementations of those two algorithms.

5.2   Layer-synchronized BFS construction

Let us start by describing the distributed implementation of Dijkstra's algorithm. This algorithm is based on the idea of developing the BFS tree layer by layer, from the root downwards. At each stage, the next layer is built by adding all the vertices that are adjacent to some vertex in the tree but are not yet in the tree themselves.

This algorithm is implemented in the distributed setting as follows. Let r_0 be the vertex initiating the construction. This vertex governs the process described above by originating synchronous phases, with one new layer added in each phase. These phases are signaled by a *Pulse* message which r_0 generates and broadcasts on the existing part of the tree.

Let us proceed with a more detailed description of the algorithm, denoted DIST_DIJK. Suppose that the first p phases have finished. At this stage, the algorithm has already constructed a tree T_p rooted at r_0, which is in fact a BFS tree spanning $\Gamma_p(r_0)$. In particular, each vertex in T_p knows its parent and children (if they exist), as well as its depth in the tree.

Phase $p + 1$ of Algorithm DIST_DIJK is described informally in Figure 5.1.

---

1. The root r_0 generates the message *Pulse* and broadcasts it on T_p.

2. Upon receiving the broadcast message *Pulse*, each leaf v of T_p sends an "exploration" message *Layer* to all of its neighbors except its parent.

3. A vertex w receiving an exploration message *Layer* for the first time, possibly from a number of its neighbors, picks one such neighbor v, lists it as its parent (by locally setting the variable $parent(w) \leftarrow v$) and sends back *Ack* messages to all the exploration messages (informing these neighbors also of the particular choice of parent it has just made).

   A vertex $w \in T_p$ that receives an exploration message *Layer* (evidently not for the first time) sends back *Ack* messages to all the exploration messages (informing these neighbors of the fact that it already belongs to the tree).

4. Each leaf v of T_p collects acknowledgements on its exploration messages. Whenever the *Ack* from some vertex w informs v that w has chosen it as its parent, v also lists w as its child (by adding it to its set variable $child(v)$).

5. Having received an *Ack* on all of its exploration messages, the leaf v upcasts an *Ack* to its parent in the tree. These acknowledgements are now convergecast on the tree T_p back to r_0.

6. Once the convergecast process terminates at the root, it may start the next phase.

Figure 5.1: Phase $p + 1$ of Algorithm DIST_DIJK (informal description).

A schematic description of the process is given in Figure 5.2.

One point not taken care of by the above description is termination detection. Allowing the root to detect that the tree has completed requires us to augment the convergecast *Ack* message with a bit *New*, indicating that some new vertices were added to the tree in the current phase. More specifically, a leaf vertex v sets $New(v) = 1$ in its *Ack* message to its parent if some new vertices have responded to its exploration message by joining the tree as its children. The "or" of these bits is convergecast via an invocation of Procedure CONVERGE$(\bigvee, X, \text{Leaves})$ as described in the "logical condition" example of Section 3.4.2. When some phase p ends with the root getting $New(v) = 0$ in all the *Ack* messages it

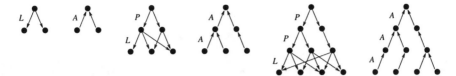

Figure 5.2: Schematic description of the first three phases in Algorithm DIST_DIJK, depicted from left to right. (Here P, L and A represent the *Pulse*, *Layer* and *Ack* message types.)

receives from its children, it may conclude that the next layer explored by the leaves in the current phase is empty, and hence the tree is complete.

The process as described is somewhat inefficient in a number of ways. For one, it is clear that certain exploration messages can be avoided. Specifically, the leaf v may have neighbors in layer $p-1$ of the tree. These neighbors are already known by v to be in the tree since they have all sent it exploration messages in the previous phase. (Thus the exploration messages are only necessary for distinguishing between neighbors in layer p and neighbors in layer $p + 1$ and for establishing the tree edges connecting layer p to layer $p + 1$.) Also, some of the acknowledgements to exploration messages can be omitted (see Exercise 1).

Analysis

By simple induction on p we prove the correctness of the algorithm.

Lemma 5.2.1 *After phase p is completed, the variable's parent and child set by the first p phases of Algorithm* DIST_DIJK *correspond to a legal BFS tree spanning $\Gamma_p(r_0)$, the p-neighborhood of r_0.*

We now estimate the time and message complexities of phase p of the algorithm. Clearly, the broadcast and convergecast stages each take p time units, and the exploration stage takes two additional time units, hence

$$\text{Time(Phase } p) = 2p + 2.$$

For analyzing the communication requirements, we need the following definition. For integer $p \geq 0$, let V_p denote the set of vertices in layer p of the tree T constructed by the algorithm. Let E_p denote the edges internal to V_p (i.e., the edges of the induced subgraph $G(V_P)$), and let $E_{p,p+1}$ denote the edges connecting V_p to V_{p+1} (see Figure 5.3).

Now, exploration messages of phase p are sent only on E_p and $E_{p,p+1}$, and only a constant number of messages is sent over each such edge (see Exercise 1). In addition, the edges of T_p (of which there are at most n) are traversed twice. In sum, we get

$$\text{Message(Phase } p) = O(n) + O(|E_p| + |E_{p,p+1}|).$$

Summing these expressions over all phases $1 \leq p \leq Diam(G)$, we get the following bounds on the time and message complexities of the entire algorithm.

$$\text{Time(DIST\_DIJK)} = \sum_p \text{Time(Phase } p) = \sum_p 2p + 2 = O(Diam^2(G)).$$

$$\text{Message(DIST\_DIJK)} = \sum_p \text{Message(Phase } p)$$

$$= \sum_p O(n) + O(|E_p| + |E_{p,p+1}|)$$

$$= O(nDiam(G) + |E|).$$

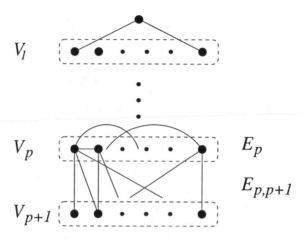

$$V_1$$

$$V_p \qquad E_p$$

$$E_{p,p+1}$$

$$V_{p+1}$$

Figure 5.3: Phase $p+1$ of Algorithm DIST_DIJK.

Lemma 5.2.2 *Algorithm* DIST_DIJK, *the distributed Dijkstra algorithm, constructs a BFS tree rooted at r_0, and its complexities are*

$$\text{Time}(\text{DIST\_DIJK}) \quad = \quad O(Diam^2(G)) \ and$$
$$\text{Message}(\text{DIST\_DIJK}) \quad = \quad O(nDiam(G) + |E|). \qquad \square$$

5.3   Update-based BFS construction

Next, we describe the distributed implementation of the algorithm of Bellman and Ford. This algorithm is based on an "optimistic" variant of the flooding algorithm. The idea is to start by running Algorithm FLOOD and constructing the tree as discussed above. This tree would be fine if communication were synchronous. In an asynchronous execution, the initial tree we end up with might not be a BFS tree. However, if that happens, then this fact will be discovered in due time as the flooding progresses by vertices which will later get messages indicating the existence of shorter paths to the root. For that purpose, each vertex v stores a variable $L(v)$ indicating its layer number, i.e., its distance from the root. Whenever a vertex v discovers such a shorter path, it will need to fix the tree by adopting its neighbor along that path as its parent and informing all its other neighbors of the improved route to the root, thus propagating the correction. It will also update its layer variable $L(v)$.

Formally, the algorithm, denoted DIST_BF, is described in Figure 5.4. Figure 5.5 describes a possible execution of Algorithm DIST_BF on a 6-vertex ring.

Analysis

In a synchronous model, the distributed Bellman–Ford algorithm DIST_BF behaves just as Algorithm FLOOD. In particular, once a vertex v sets its $L(v)$ variable to a value smaller than ∞ for the first time, this value is never changed in subsequent rounds, hence v sends messages on its outgoing edges exactly once. Consequently, the complexities of the algorithm are as follows.

Lemma 5.3.1 *In the synchronous model, the distributed Bellman–Ford algorithm* DIST_BF *constructs a BFS tree rooted at r_0, and its complexities are* $\text{Time}(\text{DIST\_BF}) = O(Diam(G))$ *and* $\text{Message}(\text{DIST\_BF}) = O(|E|)$. $\square$

1. Initially, the root sets $L(r_0) \leftarrow 0$, and all other vertices v set $L(v) \leftarrow \infty$.

2. The root sends out the message $Layer(0)$ to all its neighbors.

3. Every other vertex v reacts to incoming messages as follows:
   Upon receiving a message $Layer(d)$ from a neighbor w **do:**

   If $d + 1 < L(v)$, **then do:**
       (a) $parent(v) \leftarrow w$;
       (b) $L(v) \leftarrow d + 1$;
       (c) Send $Layer(d + 1)$ to all neighbors except w.

Figure 5.4: Algorithm DIST_BF.

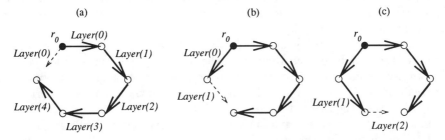

Figure 5.5: Schematic description of a possible execution of Algorithm DIST_BF on a 6-vertex ring.

Let us now turn to the asynchronous model. We claim that the algorithm correctly computes a BFS tree, and moreover, the time required by the algorithm in this model is still only $O(Diam(G))$. This follows as an immediate corollary of the following claim (which in turn is proved by straightforward induction on d).

Lemma 5.3.2 *For every $d \geq 1$, after d time units from the start of the execution, every vertex v at distance d from the root has already received a $Layer(d-1)$ message from some neighbor and, consequently, set $L(v) = d$ and chose a parent w with $L(w) = d - 1$.* $\square$

As for the message complexity, we make the following observations. The first value a vertex v ever assigns to its $L(v)$ variable is at most $n - 1$ (which is an upper bound on the length of the longest simple path in the network). Hence from that point on, v will change its $L(v)$ variable at most $n - 2$ times (each time strictly reducing its content). Whenever v assigns a new value to $L(v)$, it sends messages over its outgoing edges. Thus each vertex v sends at most $n \cdot deg(v)$ messages throughout the algorithm, and the total message complexity is thus $\mathsf{Message}(\text{DIST\_BF}) = \sum_v n \cdot deg(v) = O(n|E|)$.

Lemma 5.3.3 *In the asynchronous model, the distributed Bellman–Ford algorithm constructs a BFS tree rooted at r_0; its complexities are $\mathsf{Time}(\text{DIST\_BF}) = O(Diam(G))$ and $\mathsf{Message}(\text{DIST\_BF}) = O(n|E|)$.* $\square$

Figure 5.6 provides a comparison of the message and time complexities of the distributed BFS construction algorithms discussed above against the best known solution for the problem.

	Messages	Time
Lower bound (and synchronous model)	E	D
Dijkstra	$E + n \cdot D$	D^2
Bellman–Ford	nE	D
Best known	$E + n \log^3 n$	$D \log^3 n$

Figure 5.6: Complexity of BFS construction algorithms on a graph $G = (V, E)$ with diameter D.

5.4   Distributed DFS

DFS is a common type of search process on a graph during which one traverses all vertices, progressing only over edges. The search pattern is based on always continuing further into the graph, visiting new vertices as long as possible, and retreating from a certain region of the graph only after exhausting it.

The basic DFS algorithm operates as follows. The search starts at some origin vertex r_0. Whenever the search reaches a vertex v, the next step is decided as follows. If v has neighbors that were not yet visited, then we next visit one of them. Otherwise, we return to the vertex from which v was visited for the first time. If there is no such vertex (i.e., if v is the origin r_0), then the search terminates.

We know that this process is guaranteed to visit every vertex in the graph. Moreover, the search defines a tree, known as a DFS tree, with r_0 as the root. This is done by setting the parent of a vertex v to be the vertex w from which v was visited for the first time. The graph edges not in this tree are called "backward edges." Given appropriate data structures, the (sequential) time complexity of this algorithm is known to be $O(|E|)$.

Let us now consider a distributed implementation of this algorithm, named Algorithm DIST_DFS. This implementation is in fact sequential, i.e., it has exactly one locus of activity at any given moment. The control of the algorithm is carried via a single message (the "token") that traverses the graph in depth-first fashion. (See Figure 5.7(a).)

Note that in the distributed setting, in order for a vertex v to know whether its neighbor w still needs to be visited, it is necessary to send a message over the edge (v, w) (either querying for this information or actually moving the token along the edge to w and backtracking to v in case it is found that w has indeed been visited earlier). It follows that both the time and message complexities of this implementation are $\Theta(|E|)$. (Note, however, that an edge need not be examined from both endpoints; once the edge (v, w) is examined from v, w knows that v has already been visited.)

Now, the message complexity of the problem is clearly lower bounded by $\Omega(|E|)$ due to the need to explore every edge. In contrast, the time complexity can be improved. The idea behind the improvement is to perform the explorations of all nontree edges "for free." To do that, it is necessary to ensure that a vertex visited for the first time will know which of its neighbors have already been visited and which have not. This can be achieved by requiring each vertex v to do the following when visited for the first time:

- temporarily freeze the DFS process,

- inform all neighbors that it has been visited,

- wait for acknowledgements from all neighbors, and

- resume the DFS process.

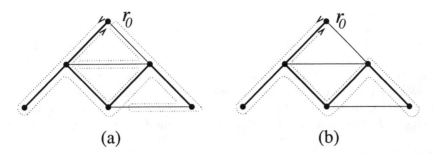

Figure 5.7: (a) A possible DFS tour starting at r_0 (marked by dotted line). The resulting DFS tree is emphasized. (b) The DFS tour obtained by avoiding traversal of nontree edges.

This ensures that when a vertex v is visited (whether for the first time or in later visits), it knows exactly which of its neighbors have already been visited and which haven't. Using this information, the center of activity can choose the next vertex to be visited to be one of the yet unvisited vertices, and if v has no such neighbors, retreat to v's parent. (See Figure 5.7(b).)

Since the additional time cost incurred during each first visit to a vertex is $O(1)$ time units, and only tree edges are traversed, the time complexity of this implementation becomes $O(n)$.

Theorem 5.4.1 *For every graph G and source r_0, Algorithm* DIST_DFS *requires* Message(DIST_DFS) $= O(|E|)$ *and* Time(DIST_DFS) $= O(n)$.

5.5 MST

Another natural parameter for evaluating spanning trees (and other subgraphs in general) is their total weight, defined as follows.

Definition 5.5.1 [Subgraph weight]: *For any subgraph $G' = (V', E')$ of a weighted graph $G = (V, E, \omega)$, we let $\omega(G')$ denote the* weight *of G', i.e.,*

$$\omega(G') = \sum_{e \in E'} \omega(e).$$

Definition 5.5.2 [MST]: *The MST, or, minimum-weight spanning tree, of G is a spanning tree T_M minimizing $\omega(T_M)$. The weight of the MST is denoted by $\omega(MST(G))$ (or simply $\omega(MST)$ when G is clear from the context).*

In the MST problem, we are given a weighted graph $G = (V, E, \omega)$ and wish to compute an MST for G. We will now discuss some basic algorithms for constructing an MST.

We assume that the edge weights are distinct and are known to the adjacent vertices. The usefulness of having distinct edge weights stems from the following known fact.

Lemma 5.5.3 *If the edge weights in the network G are all distinct, then the MST of G is unique.*

Clearly, having distinct weights is not an essential requirement, since one can always "create" such weights locally relying on the unique vertex identifiers (see Exercise 10). Conversely, as discussed in a later chapter (Section 8.1.2), in an anonymous network (see Section 1.3.2) having neither distinct edge weights nor distinct vertex identifiers, no distributed algorithm exists for computing an MST with a bounded number of messages.

As done for BFS tree construction in Lemma 5.1.1, we state without proof the following (global and existential) lower bounds on the message complexity of distributed MST construction. (The time complexity of this task is discussed in more detail in Chapter 24.)

Lemma 5.5.4

1. *For every weighted n-vertex graph $G = (V, E, \omega)$, distributed MST construction in a clean network requires $\Omega(|E|)$ messages in the worst case.*

2. *For arbitrary n-vertex graphs, distributed MST construction requires $\Omega(n \log n)$ messages in the worst case.*

The algorithms discussed in this section all rely on the following basic notions.

Definition 5.5.5 [MST fragment]: *Given a weighted graph $G = (V, E, \omega)$, a tree T in G (whose edges belong to E) is called an* MST *fragment (or simply fragment) of G if there exists an MST T_M of G such that T is a subtree of T_M.*

The edge $e = (u, w)$ is an outgoing edge *of the fragment T if exactly one of its endpoints belongs to T. The* minimum weight *outgoing edge of the fragment T is denoted $MWOE(T)$.*

The basic rule at the basis of many algorithms for MST construction, sometimes known as the *blue rule*, relies on the following well-known fact.

Lemma 5.5.6 *Consider a graph $G = (V, E, \omega)$ and a fragment T in G. Let $e = MWOE(T)$. Then $T \cup \{e\}$ is a fragment as well.*

Proof: Consider a graph G, a fragment T and an edge $e = MWOE(T)$ as in the lemma. Let T_M be an MST of G containing T. If T_M contains e, then we are done. So suppose e does not occur on T_M. As T_M is connected, there is some edge e' in T_M connecting some vertex of T to the rest of the graph. As e' is also an outgoing edge of T, necessarily $\omega(e) \leq \omega(e')$. Adding e to T_M creates a cycle going through e'. Now discarding e' from T_M yields a new (connected) tree T'_M spanning G and $\omega(T'_M) \leq \omega(T_M)$. Also, T'_M contains $T \cup \{e\}$, thus proving the lemma.   □

Lemma 5.5.6 motivates the following procedure for constructing an MST for a given graph G. Start with the individual vertices as our initial fragments and apply the following *blue rule* repeatedly until a single fragment T remains that spans all the vertices of G.

The "blue rule": Pick a fragment T and add to it the minimum-weight outgoing edge $MWOE(T)$.

Lemma 5.5.6 guarantees that after applying the above procedure, the resulting tree T is an MST for the graph G.

5.5.1   A distributed variant of Prim's algorithm

The first algorithm we describe is based on a sequential algorithm known as Prim's algorithm. This algorithm operates by designating a single vertex r_0 as the initial fragment T and repeatedly applying the blue rule to T until reaching a spanning tree of the network. By the above discussion, the resulting tree T is an MST.

This algorithm can be implemented in the distributed setting, say, in the asynchronous $\mathcal{CONGEST}$ model. It yields a distributed algorithm denoted DIST_PRIM, described next. The algorithm is initiated by the vertex r_0 and proceeds in synchronized phases with one new edge added to T in each phase. These phases are signaled by a *Pulse* message which r_0 generates and broadcasts on the current tree.

At the end of the first p phases, the algorithm has already constructed a fragment T rooted at r_0. In particular, each vertex in T knows its parent and children (if they exist). In addition, each vertex v knows, for each of its adjacent edges $e = (v, w)$, whether the other endpoint w already belongs to T. In other words, each vertex knows exactly which of its adjacent edges are outgoing edges of T and which are internal edges.

In each phase $p + 1$, the algorithm searches for the minimum weight outgoing edge $MWOE(T)$ and adds it to the tree, i.e., it applies the "blue rule." The strategy for identifying this edge involves broadcasting over the tree T and asking each vertex separately for its own minimum weight outgoing edge. The minimum weight edge is then convergecast upwards on T, towards the root, by applying Procedure CONVERGE(min) on the edge weights, i.e., each intermediate vertex first collects this information from all its children in the tree, and then passes up only the lowest-weight edge it has seen (which is therefore the lowest-weight edge in its subtree). The minimum weight outgoing edge is selected by the root to be included in the final MST and is announced throughout the tree. (See Figure 5.8.)

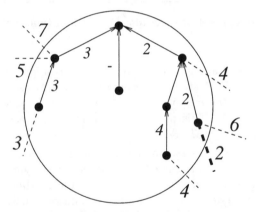

Figure 5.8: A phase of Algorithm DIST_PRIM. The number beside each (dashed) outgoing edge represents its weight. The number beside each (solid) tree edge is the weight forwarded along that edge, i.e., the minimum weight of any outgoing edge adjacent to the corresponding subtree.

Phase $p + 1$ of Algorithm DIST_PRIM is described informally in Figure 5.9.

The correctness of Algorithm DIST_PRIM follows from the correctness of the blue rule, by Lemma 5.5.6. As for the complexity of the algorithm, since the communication is carried on the MST fragment, which can be of arbitrary structure (and in particular, is not necessarily a BFS tree w.r.t. the root r_0), each phase p requires up to $O(p)$ time and communication, hence the total time and message complexities are both $O(n^2)$.

5.5.2 The synchronous GHS algorithm

The distributed variant of Prim's algorithm is inherently sequential, as it grows a single fragment. An alternative way of employing the blue rule is to grow a number of fragments

1. The root r_0 generates the message *Pulse* and broadcasts it on T. Except for the very first phase, this message also informs the vertices of T about the new vertex y and the edge $e = (x, y)$ added to the tree in the previous phase p.

2. Upon receiving the broadcast message *Pulse*, each vertex v of T connected in G by an edge $e = (v, y)$ to y marks the edge e as internal.

3. The vertex y itself probes all its neighbors, asking each of them whether or not it belongs to the tree T, and marks its adjacent edges accordingly.

4. If v is a leaf, then it next sends to its parent the tuple $\langle e, \omega(e), z_e \rangle$, where e is the lightest outgoing edge adjacent to it and z_e is its other endpoint.

5. The tuples are now convergecast on the tree T back to r_0, applying Procedure CONVERGE(min) on the edge weights. Namely, each intermediate vertex upcasts the tuple with the minimum value of $\omega(e)$ among its own tuple and the tuples it has received from its children.

6. Once the convergecast process terminates at the root, it selects the tuple $\langle e, \omega(e), z_e \rangle$ of minimum $\omega(e)$ among its own tuple and the tuples it has received from its children.
   /* This edge e is $MWOE(T)$ and will be added to T in the next phase. */

Figure 5.9: Phase $p + 1$ of Algorithm DIST_PRIM (informal description).

in parallel. Kruskal's sequential algorithm is based on this approach. Initially, each vertex forms a singleton fragment. Each step of that algorithm involves selecting the outgoing edge of minimum weight over all the fragments and adding it to the tree, thus merging the two fragments it touches into one. This process is continued until a single fragment remains, which is evidently the desired MST.

While Kruskal's algorithm grows many fragments in parallel, it is still a sequential algorithm in that each step adds a single edge, hence $n - 1$ sequential steps are needed. In the distributed setting, one may hope to be able to parallelize this idea and grow a number of fragments concurrently. Indeed, the distributed variant of Kruskal's algorithm, known as the GHS algorithm, achieves exactly that. Let us now describe a simplified version of the GHS algorithm, which works in the synchronous $\mathcal{CONGEST}$ model.

In the distributed GHS algorithm, at any given moment the vertices are partitioned into a number of *fragments* $F_1, \ldots, F_k$. Each fragment F_i is a rooted tree. (Initially, the sole vertex comprising a fragment is also its root.) Each vertex in a fragment knows its parent and children. Moreover, each fragment has an identifier (say, the identifier of its root), and each vertex knows the identifier of its fragment.

The events in the algorithm are divided into *phases*. Each phase takes as its input the fragment structure output by the previous one and outputs larger fragments. (The first phase takes as its input the singleton fragments, one per vertex.)

Let us now describe one phase. In the first part of the phase, the vertices of each fragment F cooperate to find the minimum weight outgoing edge $MWOE(F)$. It is assumed that at the beginning of the phase, each vertex knows which of its neighbors belong to the same fragment and which do not, or in other words, which of its edges are outgoing. The search for the minimum weight outgoing edge $MWOE(F)$ is carried out as in Algorithm DIST_PRIM by convergecasting the minimum weight outgoing edges over F from the leaves up.

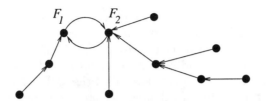

Figure 5.10: A component of the graph $\hat{G}$. All fragments in this component merge into a single fragment of the next phase. The edge $e = MWOE(F_1) = MWOE(F_2)$ is the core edge of this fragment.

Once the vertices of the fragment F have completed their search and found their minimum weight outgoing edge $e = MWOE(F)$, a *Request_to_merge* message is sent out over the edge e to the chosen fragment F' on the other side, carrying the identifier of the fragment and of the root and requesting to merge the two fragments. The two fragments then combine, possibly along with several other fragments, into a new, larger fragment.

More specifically, if the other fragment F' has also selected the same edge e as its own minimum weight outgoing edge, $e = MWOE(F')$, then the two fragments agree at that point to combine. Otherwise, the resulting merged fragment will be composed of more than just the two fragments F and F'.

The chosen edges induce a special structure over the collection of fragments. Let $\hat{F}$ denote the collection of fragments, and let $\hat{E}$ be a set of directed arcs containing the arc (F, F') for every fragment F whose minimum weight outgoing edge, $e = MWOE(F)$, leads to F'. The resulting directed graph $\hat{G} = (\hat{F}, \hat{E})$ is henceforth referred to as the *fragment forest*. The reason for this name is that $\hat{G}$ consists of a collection of connected components of the form illustrated in Figure 5.10 and formally described in the following claim.

Lemma 5.5.7 *Each connected component of $\hat{G}$ consists of a directed tree whose arcs point upwards towards the root, except that the root is not a single fragment, but rather a pair of fragments F_1, F_2 pointing at each other.*

In each connected component of the graph $\hat{G}$, all fragments are now merged into a single fragment of the next phase. This is done as follows. The edge $e = MWOE(F_1) = MWOE(F_2)$ is the core edge of this combined fragment. Assuming $e = (v_1, v_2)$ where $v_i \in F_i$ for $i = 1, 2$, the root of the combined fragment is decided to be the higher identifier vertex of v_1 and v_2, say, v_1. Note that the vertices v_1 and v_2 can identify the fact that the edge e is the chosen core edge, since *Request_to_merge* messages have been sent over it in both directions. Moreover, v_1 knows that it is the new root as its identifier, $ID(v_1)$, is smaller than that of v_2.

The new root v_1 now broadcasts a *New_fragment* announcement message throughout the combined fragment, informing all vertices of its identifier (which serves also as the identifier of the new fragment). This announcement is broadcast over the entire new combined fragment (i.e., in particular, it gets forwarded over all chosen $MWOE$ edges and thus reaches all original fragments in the connected component). Upon getting this message, each vertex updates its records concerning the identifier of its new fragment and its root and also changes the directions of its fragment edges, so that now its parent in the new fragment is the edge leading towards the new root v_1 (namely, the edge on which it has received the *New_fragment* announcement). Finally, each vertex updates its neighbors of its new fragment ID. This ensures that at the beginning of the next phase, each vertex knows which of its edges are outgoing.

This concludes the description of a single phase. In the next phase, the new fragment finds its own minimum weight outgoing edge and the entire process is repeated until all the vertices in the graph have combined themselves into one single fragment.

Let us now discuss the time and message complexities of this algorithm. Each phase involves a broadcast and convergecast step for finding the $MWOE$ of each fragment, followed by a fragment merging procedure (including neighbor update). As the size and depth of a fragment never exceed n, both the time and message complexities of the broadcast and convergecast step are $O(n)$. The fragment merging procedure also requires similar complexities, except for the very final step, in which each vertex updates its neighbors of its new fragment identifier. This last step costs $\Theta(|E|)$ messages. As the entire algorithm takes $\log n$ or fewer phases, we have the following complexity bounds for the resulting algorithm.

Lemma 5.5.8 *The distributed Algorithm GHS constructs an MST rooted at r_0, and its complexities are* Time(GHS) $= O(n \log n)$ *and* Message(GHS) $= O(|E| \log n)$. $\square$

We remark that Algorithm GHS can be modified to operate asynchronously. The difficulty that arises is that of undesirable "growth patterns" of fragments, resulting in excessive communication costs (measured in number of messages). This problem is handled by using special rules for merging fragments designed to prevent these complications. These rules are based on a "balanced data structure" approach. A *phase number* is associated with each fragment. If $phase(F) = l$ for a given fragment F, then the number of vertices in F is greater than or equal to 2^l. Initially, all fragments (singleton vertices) are at phase 0. When two fragments at phase l are combined, the resulting fragment has phase $l + 1$. Thus the total number of messages is kept to $O(n \log n)$ (although some more complex rules are needed to allow merges between fragments of unequal phases). Similarly, it is not hard to show by induction on the phase numbers that the time complexity of the algorithm is $O(n \log n)$ time units.

5.6   Faster upcasting on matroid problems

In this section we return to the upcast operation and discuss the fast distributed solution of *matroid problems* through upcasting in the synchronous $\mathcal{CONGEST}$ model. This, in turn, provides us with an alternative, and somewhat faster, algorithm for MST construction.

5.6.1   Matroid problems

Let us start with a brief presentation of matroid problems. A *subset system* is specified as a pair $\Phi = \langle \mathcal{A}, \mathcal{S} \rangle$, where $\mathcal{A}$ is a universe of m elements and $\mathcal{S}$ is a collection of subsets of $\mathcal{A}$ closed under inclusion (namely, if $A \in \mathcal{S}$ and $B \subseteq A$ then also $B \in \mathcal{S}$). The sets in $\mathcal{S}$ are called the *independent sets* of the system. The optimization problem associated with the system Φ is the following: given a weight function ω assigning nonnegative weights to the elements of $\mathcal{A}$, find the independent set of maximum total weight. This problem may be intractable in general.

A natural approach for solving the optimization problem associated with Φ is to employ a greedy approach. Two types of greedy approaches may be considered. The *best-in* greedy algorithm is based on starting with the empty set and adding at each step the heaviest element that still maintains the independence of the set. Its dual, the *worst-out* greedy algorithm, starts with the entire universe and discards at each step the lightest element whose removal still leaves us with a set containing some maximal independent set of Φ. Unfortunately, these algorithms do not necessarily yield an optimal solution.

A subset system Φ is said to be a *matroid* if it satisfies the following property.

Replacement property: If $A, B \in S$ and $|B| = |A| + 1$, then there exists some element $\mu \in B \setminus A$ such that $A \cup \{\mu\} \in S$.

(There are in fact a number of other equivalent definitions for matroids.)

One of the most well-known examples for matroids is the MST problem. As introduced above, an MST for the network G is a spanning tree T_M of minimum weight $\omega(T_M)$. Note that MST construction can be represented as a matroid problem, where the universe is the edge set of a graph, the independent sets are cycle-free subsets of edges and the maximal independent sets are the spanning trees of the graph. (The goal here is typically to find the spanning tree of *minimum* weight, rather than maximum weight, but this can still be formalized as a matroid optimization problem.)

Another fundamental example is that of vector spaces, where the universe is the collection of vectors in d-dimensional space, dependence in set of vectors is defined in the usual algebraic sense and the maximal independent sets are the bases of the space.

One important property of matroids is that both the best-in greedy algorithm and the worst-out greedy algorithm correctly solve every instance of the optimization problem associated with Φ. (In fact, these properties hold for a somewhat wider class of problems, named *greedoids*.)

The common representation of matroids is based not on explicit enumeration of the independent sets, but on a *rule*, or procedure, deciding for every given subset of $\mathcal{A}$ whether or not it is independent. Here is another well-known property of matroids that we will use later.

Lemma 5.6.1 *All maximal-cardinality independent sets of a given matroid Φ are of the same cardinality, denoted* rank(Φ).

One source of difficulty in trying to adapt the greedy algorithms for solving matroid problems in a distributed fashion is that both algorithms are inherently "global" and sequential. First, they require us to go over the elements in order of weight, and second, they require us to be able to decide, for each element, whether after eliminating it we still have an independent set of cardinality rank(Φ) in our set of remaining elements. It is therefore useful to have a variant of the greedy algorithm which is more localized in nature. Such a variant was given for the MST problem. This algorithm makes use of the so-called red rule, which is based on the following fact.

Lemma 5.6.2 *Consider an instance of the MST problem on a graph $G = (V, E, \omega)$ with a solution of (minimum) weight ω^*. Consider a spanning subgraph G' of G (with all the vertices and some of the edges), and suppose that G' still contains a spanning tree of weight ω^*. Let C be a cycle in G', and let e be the heaviest edge in C. Then $G' \setminus \{e\}$ still contains a spanning tree of weight ω^*.*

Proof: Consider a graph G', a cycle C and an edge e as in the lemma. Let T be some tree of weight ω^* in G. If T does not contain e, then T still exists in $G' \setminus \{e\}$ and we are done. Now suppose that $e \in T$. Then the removal of e disconnects T into two components T_1 and T_2. As the cut separating T_1 from T_2 contains e, it must necessarily contain also at least one more edge e' from the cycle C. Hence the tree $T' = T_1 \cup T_2 \cup \{e'\}$ is in $G' \setminus \{e\}$. The proof is completed upon observing that as e is the heaviest edge in C, $\omega(e') \le \omega(e)$ and therefore T' is no heavier than T. $\square$

This lemma leads to a localized version of the worst-out greedy algorithm, avoiding both difficulties discussed above. This localized algorithm starts with the entire graph G and repeatedly applies the *red rule* (stated next) until a spanning tree remains.

The "red rule": Pick an *arbitrary* cycle in the remaining graph, and erase the heaviest edge in that cycle.

Lemma 5.6.2 guarantees that once the process halts, the resulting tree is an MST of the graph G.

The proof of Lemma 5.6.2 relies on some specific properties of the MST problem, and therefore it is not immediately clear that a similar general red rule applies to every matroid problem. Nonetheless, it turns out that such a rule exists for all matroids.

For a dependent set B, let $\mathsf{Key}(B) = \{\mu \in B \mid B \setminus \{\mu\}$ is independent$\}$.

Lemma 5.6.3 *Consider an instance ω of the optimization problem associated with the matroid $\Phi = \langle \mathcal{A}, \mathcal{S} \rangle$ with a solution of (maximum) weight ω^*. Consider a set $A \subseteq \mathcal{A}$, and suppose that A contains an independent set of weight ω^*. Let $B \subseteq A$ be a dependent set with nonempty subset $\mathsf{Key}(B)$. Let ε be the lightest element in $\mathsf{Key}(B)$. Then $A \setminus \{\varepsilon\}$ still contains an independent set of weight ω^*.*

Proof: Call the set B *minimally dependent* if $\mathsf{Key}(B) = B$ (namely, $B \setminus \{\mu\}$ is independent for every $\mu \in B$). Consider sets A, B and an element ε as in the lemma. We first observe that without loss of generality, we may assume that B is minimally dependent. This is because otherwise it is easy to verify that B contains a minimally dependent subset B' with the same properties (containing all the elements of $\mathsf{Key}(B)$, and in particular ε). To get B' from B, repeatedly pick an element $\mu \in B$ such that $B \setminus \{\mu\}$ is still dependent and remove it from B.

Let Z be some maximal independent set of weight ω^* in A. If $\varepsilon \notin Z$, then we are done, as $Z \subseteq A \setminus \{\varepsilon\}$. Otherwise, let $Y = Z \setminus \{\varepsilon\}$, and let $D = B \setminus \{\varepsilon\}$. Clearly, D can be expanded into a maximal independent set $D' = D \cup Q$ of cardinality $\mathsf{rank}(\Phi)$. (In particular, the process of expanding D by repeatedly adding new elements that preserve independence as long as possible yields a maximal independent set D', and by Lemma 5.6.1, $|D'| = \mathsf{rank}(\Phi)$.)

We next argue that there exists some $X \subseteq Y$ such that $D'' = D \cup X$ is a maximal independent set of cardinality $\mathsf{rank}(\Phi)$. This D'' can be obtained from D by repeatedly applying the replacement rule, at each stage discarding some element of Q and replacing it by some element of Z. The replacing element cannot be ε, as $B \cup \{\varepsilon\}$ is dependent, hence it must come from Y.

Note that D'' is contained in A and that $|D''| = |Y| + 1$. By the replacement rule, there exists some element $\beta \in D'' \setminus Y$ such that $Z' = Y \cup \{\beta\}$ is an independent set. As $X \subseteq Y$, necessarily $\beta \in D \subset B$. This implies that $\omega(\beta) \geq \omega(\varepsilon)$, as ε is the lightest element in B. Hence $\omega(Z') \geq \omega(Z)$, necessitating that $\omega(Z') = \omega^*$. The claim now follows, as $Z' \subseteq A$. $\square$

We thus get a modified greedy algorithm, based on the following rule.

The "generalized red rule": Pick an *arbitrary* dependent set B with nonempty subset $\mathsf{Key}(B)$ in the remaining set A, and erase the lightest element in $\mathsf{Key}(B)$ from A.

5.6.2   A distributed algorithm for matroids

We now describe a distributed algorithm for solving a matroid optimization problem on a tree T and analyze its performance.

The pipeline algorithm

We assume that each of the elements of the set $\mathcal{A}$ is stored at some vertex of the tree T (we make no a priori assumptions on the precise distribution of the elements). In order to solve the problem, we require that the elements of the maximal-weight independent set be gathered at the root of the tree T.

A straightforward approach to solving this problem would be to upcast all the elements of $\mathcal{A}$ to the root and solve the problem locally using the greedy algorithm. However, this solution would require $O(m + Depth(T))$ time for completing the upcast stage. Our aim in this section is to derive an algorithm requiring only $O(rank(\Phi) + Depth(T))$ time.

The algorithm presented herein for the problem is a distributed implementation of the localized greedy algorithm for matroids. It is based on upcasting the elements towards the root in a careful way, attempting to eliminate as many elements as we can along the way, relying on the generalized red rule.

A description of Procedure PIPELINE is given in Figure 5.11.

---

1. Throughout the execution, each vertex v on the tree maintains a set Q of all the elements it knows of (either directly or by "learning" about from its children in the previous rounds), ordered by nonincreasing weight. Initially this set contains only the elements stored in it. It also maintains a set A (initially empty) of all the elements it has already sent up to its parent in the tree.

2. A leaf v starts sending elements upwards at pulse 0. An intermediate vertex v starts sending at the first pulse after it has received messages from all its children.

3. At each pulse i, the vertex computes the set of *eliminated elements*

$$Dep \leftarrow \{\mu \in Q \setminus A \mid A \cup \{\mu\} \text{ is dependent}\}$$

and the set of *remaining candidates*

$$RC \leftarrow Q \setminus (A \cup Dep).$$

If $RC = \emptyset$, then v sends a "terminating" message to its parent in the tree and terminates its participation in the protocol.
Else, it sends up to its parent the heaviest element μ in RC.

4. The root r_0 computes locally the solution to the problem from among the elements it hears of from its children.

Figure 5.11: Procedure PIPELINE.

5.6.3 Analysis

The analysis hinges on two main properties of the procedure. First, the elements reported by each intermediate vertex to its parent in the tree are sent in nonincreasing weight order. Second, each intermediate vertex transmits elements upwards in the tree *continuously* until it exhausts all the reportable elements from its subtree. Namely, once the set of candidates RC is empty, the vertex will learn of no more reportable elements.

Let us first make the following straightforward but crucial observation.

Lemma 5.6.4 *The elements reported by each intermediate vertex to its parent in the tree form an independent set.*

Proof: This follows immediately from the rule used by the procedure to select the next element to be transmitted upwards. □

Lemma 5.6.5 *Every vertex v starts sending messages upwards at pulse $\hat{L}(v)$.*

Proof: By straightforward induction on the tree structure, from the leaves upwards. □

The main technical lemma of the proof concerns the properties of a vertex on the tree in some round of the algorithm. Consider an intermediate vertex v at height h that has still not terminated its participation in the algorithm, at round t, for some $t \geq h$. Note that each of the children of v in the tree is of height $h - 1$ or lower, hence by Lemma 5.6.5, all of them started transmission at round $h - 1$ or earlier. Call a child *active* if it has not terminated yet (i.e., if it has sent an element to v on round $t - 1$).

Lemma 5.6.6

(a) *For each child u of v that is still active at round t, the candidate set RC examined by v at the beginning of round t contains at least one candidate element sent by u.*

(b) *If v sends to its parent an element of weight ω_0 at round t, then all of the elements v was informed of at round $t - 1$ by its active children were of weight ω_0 or smaller.*

(c) *If v sends to its parent an element of weight ω_0 at round t, then any later element it will learn of is of weight ω_0 or smaller.*

(d) *Vertex v sends elements to its parent in nonincreasing weight order.*

Proof: We prove the lemma by induction on the height of the tree, starting from the leaves upwards.

A *leaf* v has no (active or other) children, and therefore Claims (a), (b) and (c) hold vacuously. Claim (d) follows trivially from the rules of the procedure.

Let us now consider an intermediate vertex v and assume that the claims hold for each of its children. We need to prove the four claims for v. We start with Claim (a).

Let A_v be the set of m elements sent by v to its parent during the first $m = t - h$ rounds it has participated in (namely, rounds $h, \ldots, t - 1$ if $t > h$). Consider an active child u of v. Denote by A_u the set of elements sent by u to v so far (up to and including round $t - 1$). Since u was still active on round $t - 1$, it has transmitted continuously to v since round $\hat{L}(u)$, which, as discussed before, is at most $h - 1$. Therefore $|A_u| \geq m + 1$.

By Lemma 5.6.4, both A_v and A_u are independent. Hence by the replacement property there exists some element $\mu \in A_u \setminus A_v$ such that $A_v \cup \{\mu\}$ is independent. This element is therefore in RC of v, hence Claim (a) holds.

Next, we prove Claim (b) as follows. Consider any active child u of v. Let μ be the element sent by u on round $t - 1$. (Note that μ does not necessarily have to be in RC of v.) Let μ' be some element that was sent by u at some round $t' \leq t - 1$ and is still in the candidate set RC of v on round t (such an element must exist by Claim (a)). By the inductive hypothesis of Claim (d), $\omega(\mu) \leq \omega(\mu')$. By the element selection rule of vertex v, $\omega(\mu') \leq \omega_0$, and Claim (b) follows.

Next, we note that Claim (c) follows trivially from Claim (b). Finally, Claim (d) follows from Claim (c) and the element selection rule of the procedure. □

Finally, we need to argue that vertices do not terminate the algorithm prematurely.

Lemma 5.6.7 *After a vertex v has terminated its participation in the algorithm, it will learn of no more reportable elements.*

Proof: We need to argue that once the set RC becomes empty, no new candidate elements will become known to v. We prove this fact by induction on the structure of the tree, starting from the leaves upwards. The inductive step follows directly from Claim (a) of Lemma 5.6.6, which guarantees that if RC is empty on round t, none of v's children have sent it an element in round $t-1$ and hence all of them have already terminated. □

Lemma 5.6.8 *The running time of Procedure* PIPELINE *is bounded by* $O(\text{rank}(\Phi) + Depth(T))$ *and its output is a solution for the problem.*

Proof: To prove that the resulting set is a maximum-weight independent set, we need to argue that the set of elements collected at the root at the end of the upcast contains some maximum-weight independent set, despite the element eliminations performed along the way. This is shown by observing that each elimination performed by the algorithm conforms to the "generalized red rule." Indeed, whenever a vertex v places an element μ in the set Dep of eliminated elements, it knows that the set $B = A \cup \{\mu\}$ is dependent, by Lemma 5.6.4 the set A is independent, hence clearly $\mu \in \text{Key}(B)$, and by Claim (c) of Lemma 5.6.6, μ is the lightest element in B, hence also in $\text{Key}(B)$. Therefore, by Lemma 5.6.3, eliminating μ does not harm the solution.

As for the running time, the bound is derived from the following facts. First, the root of the tree receives at most $rank(\Phi)$ elements from each of its children. Second, the children send these elements to the root in a fully pipelined fashion (namely, without stopping until exhausting all the elements of which they know). Finally, the root starts getting such messages at time $Depth(T)$ at the latest. □

Example: *Smallest k-of-m revisited.*

As an example, let us reconsider the *smallest k-of-m* problem of Section 4.3.1. In fact, to make it compatible with our "maximization" representation, let us switch to the dual *largest k-of-m* problem, in which we look for the k largest elements in the set $\mathcal{A}$. The corresponding matroid is defined by setting S to contain all the subsets of the domain $\mathcal{A}$ containing k or fewer elements. (To see that this is indeed a matroid, note that it satisfies the replacement property.) It follows that Procedure PIPELINE yields an $O(k + Depth(T))$ time solution for this problem, thus providing an alternative proof for Lemma 4.3.1. □

5.6.4 An alternative MST construction algorithm

A natural application for the matroid upcast technique is for solving the MST problem. Here we assume that in addition to the (weighted) network $G = (V, E, \omega)$ itself, we are also given some spanning tree T for G, which may be used in computing an MST for G. The inputs are given as in Section 5.5, namely, each vertex initially knows only the weights of the edges incident to itself.

Despite the fact that we seek the minimum-weight solution rather than the maximum-weight one, this problem is in fact a matroid problem, so the same algorithm applies (flipping the ordering in the procedure, or redefining the edge weights by setting $\omega'(e) = \hat{W} - \omega(e)$, where $\hat{W} = \max_e\{\omega(e)\}$). As discussed earlier, the dependent sets of this matroid problem are the cycles of the graph. A cycle C is known to a vertex v in the tree T if all the vertices occurring on C belong to the subtree T_v rooted at v. Eliminating the heaviest edge in the cycle C by v amounts to applying the "red rule" w.r.t. that cycle. (See Figure 5.12.)

Thus applying Procedure PIPELINE to the MST problem yields an $O(n)$ time distributed algorithm for MST. At the end of the execution, the solution set of $n-1$ MST edges is stored at the root r_0. The root can now broadcast the entire set of MST edges to all the vertices in the graph. This can be done in a pipelined manner, as discussed in Section 3.4.3, at an additional cost of $O(Depth(T) + (n-1)) = O(n)$ time.

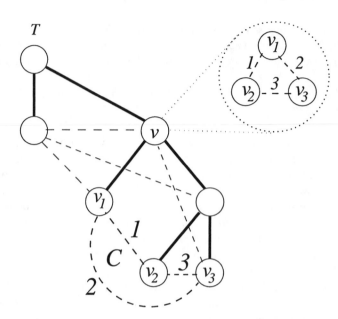

Figure 5.12: A cycle C identified locally by the vertex v. Bold edges belong to the tree T, and dashed lines represent graph edges outside T. The edge (v_2, v_3) is the heaviest on the cycle C, so v will avoid upcasting it to its parent in the tree T.

If the tree T is not available to us initially, it is possible to first construct such a tree efficiently, say, using Algorithm FLOOD of Section 3.3. This takes at most $O(Diam(G))$ additional time. Hence the resulting procedure PIPELINEMST satisfies the following.

Lemma 5.6.9 *Procedure* PIPELINEMST *constructs an MST, and its time complexity is* Time(PIPELINE(MST)) $= O(n)$.   □

Bibliographical notes

The problem of designing an asynchronous distributed algorithm for breadth first search, introduced by Gallager in [Gal82], has been studied intensively since then [Gal82, Fre85, Awe85a, Awe85c, AG85b, AG87, Awe89]. The layer-synchronized BFS construction algorithm and the update-based BFS construction algorithm are distributed implementations of the sequential algorithms of Dijkstra and Bellman and Ford, respectively (cf. [Eve79, CLR90, Gal82]). A distributed implementation of the Bellman–Ford algorithm for the weighted case and a discussion of its execution time are presented in [BG92]. The best known distributed BFS algorithm is due to [AP90b, AR92]. The time-efficient distributed DFS algorithm of Section 5.4 was introduced in [Awe85b]. The label assignment problem of Exercises 8 and 9 is treated in [FPPP00].

The MST problem, the "blue rule" and sequential algorithms for MST construction are described in most textbooks on algorithms, e.g., [CLR90, Tar83]. Kruskal's algorithm for constructing an MST is originated in [Kru56], cf. [CLR90]. The distributed MST construction algorithm GHS presented in Section 5.5 is a simplified version of the renowned algorithm of [GHS83]. Lemma 5.5.4 is also due to [GHS83]. The original GHS algorithm of [GHS83] applies also to asynchronous networks and has optimal message complexity (unlike the variant described here). The time complexity of the algorithm of [GHS83] is $O(n \log n)$, which was later improved to the existentially optimal $O(n)$ in [Awe87]. We refer the reader to [GHS83, Lyn95, AW98] for a more detailed description and discussion of the complete GHS algorithm.

The distributed algorithm of Section 5.6 for solving matroid problems, due to [Pel98], is an extension of a procedure appearing in [GKP98, KP98b] as a component in a fast distributed algorithm for computing an MST. For more on the subject of matroids see, e.g., [PS82]. Greedoids were thoroughly treated in [KL81, KL83, KL84b, KL84a]. The "red rule" and Lemma 5.6.2 appear, e.g., in [Tar83].

Exercises

1. Prove that in phase p of Dijkstra's algorithm, at most two (respectively, four) messages are sent over each edge of $E_{p,p+1}$ (resp., E_p). Show how the algorithm can be modified so that at most two messages are sent over each edge of E_p as well.

2. Prove the tightness of the message complexity analysis of Dijkstra's algorithm by establishing the following (existential) lower bound: For arbitrary integers n and $1 \leq D \leq n-1$, there exists an n-vertex, D-diameter graph $G = (V, E)$ on which the execution of Dijkstra's algorithm requires $\Omega(nD + |E|)$ messages.

3. Repeat the previous question with the additional requirement that the graph G has $|E| = O(n)$ edges.

4. Prove or disprove the following global lower bounds:

   For every n-vertex, D-diameter graph $G = (V, E)$, there exists an execution of Dijkstra's algorithm requiring

   (a) $\Omega(nD)$ messages,

   (b) $\Omega(|E|)$ messages,

   (c) $\Omega(D^2)$ time.

5. Give an example for an execution of the Bellman–Ford algorithm requiring $\Omega(n^3)$ messages.

6. Modify the Bellman–Ford algorithm so that it detects termination.

7. (a) Describe a distributed algorithm based on DFS for counting the number of vertices in the network $G = (V, E)$ and informing the outcome to all the vertices of G. The algorithm should function correctly even when invoked by a number of initiators.

   (b) What are the time and message complexities of your algorithm assuming it was invoked by K initiators?

   (c) Does the algorithm work in the asynchronous model?

8. Describe a distributed algorithm based on DFS that when invoked by a single initiator on an n-vertex anonymous network $G = (V, E)$, assigns unique labels from the range $[1, n]$ to the vertices of G.

9. In the synchronous model, give a faster ($O(Diam(G))$ time) algorithm for the label assignment problem of the previous problem.

10. Suppose that the network $G = (V, E, \omega)$ has unique vertex identifiers but the weights of different edges might be identical. Describe an algorithm allowing each vertex in the network to locally assign a new edge weight $\omega'(e)$ to each of its adjacent edges, based on its original weight and the identifiers of its endpoints, so that the resulting edge weights are distinct and consistent (i.e., the weights assigned to the edge $e = (u, w)$ by u and by w are the same).

11. Give an $O(n)$ time distributed algorithm for MST construction on an n-vertex weighted ring with a single initiator.

12. Prove Lemma 5.5.7.

13. Explain how Exercise 5 of Chapter 4 can be solved in $O(Depth(T) + k)$ time by fitting it into the framework of Section 5.6.

14. (a) Analyze the message complexity of Procedure PIPELINE of Section 5.6.

    (b) What is the resulting bound on the message complexity of the MST construction Procedure PIPELINEMST of Section 5.6.4? Take into account also the need to first construct a spanning tree for the network.

Chapter 6

Synchronizers

Algorithms for synchronous networks are easier to design, debug and test than similar algorithms for asynchronous networks. The behavior of asynchronous systems is typically harder to grasp and analyze. Consequently, it is desirable to have a uniform methodology for transforming an algorithm for synchronous networks into an algorithm for asynchronous networks. This tool will enable one to design an algorithm for a synchronous network, test it and analyze it in that simpler environment and then use the standard methodology to transform the algorithm into an asynchronous one and use it in the asynchronous network.

This general approach for handling asynchrony is known as a *synchronizer*. We will discuss several specific methods for implementing a simulation of this type and look at their complexities. Naturally, throughout this chapter we concentrate on the $\mathcal{ASYNC}$ model.

One might argue that in order to achieve a fast asynchronous algorithm,[1] it is necessary to program it directly in the environment in which it is to be run (much the same as programming in low-level languages usually yields better performance than compiling a high-level program). However, the surprising fact that in spite of the inevitable overheads involved in such a simulation, asynchronous algorithms designed in this way are sometimes more efficient than any previously known. This is mainly due to the inherent difficulty in reasoning about an asynchronous network, which sometimes makes it hard to reach an optimal solution for a problem directly in such an environment.

6.1 The synchronizer methodology

6.1.1 Underlying simulation principles

The synchronizer is intended to enable any synchronous algorithm to run on any asynchronous network. More specifically, given an algorithm Π_S written for a synchronous network and a synchronizer ν, it is possible to *combine* Π_S on top of ν to yield a protocol $\Pi_A = \nu(\Pi_S)$ that can be executed on an asynchronous network. The simulation should be *correct*, in the sense that Π_A's execution in a synchronous network should be "similar" to Π_S's execution in a synchronous network. (A more precise definition is given later on.)

The combined protocol Π_A is composed of two main components, which we hereafter refer to as the "original component" and the "synchronization component." Each of these components has its own local variables and message types at every vertex. The "original

---

[1]Henceforth we will use the term "(a)synchronous algorithm" to indicate an algorithm written for operation in an (a)synchronous network.

component" consists of the local variables and the messages of the original protocol Π_S, whereas the "synchronization component" consists of local synchronization variables and synchronization messages.

The basic ingredient of the simulation is a "pulse generator" at each processor of the network. That is, the processor v has a pulse variable P_v, and it is supposed to generate a sequence of local "clock pulses" by increasing the value of P from time to time, setting $P_v = 0, 1, 2, \ldots$. Conceptually, these pulses are supposed to simulate the ticks of the global clock in the synchronous setting. That is, under the combined protocol Π_A, each processor v is expected to perform during the time interval in which its pulse variable is set to p, precisely the actions it was supposed to perform during round p of the synchronous algorithm Π_S.

Clearly, this component *alone* will give nothing in an asynchronous environment; in order to prevent the simulation from becoming a total mess, it is essential to ensure some guarantee about the relationship between the pulse values at neighboring processors at various moments during the execution. To facilitate the discussion on this relationship, let us introduce the following terminology. Denote by $t(v, p)$ the (real, global) time in which v has increased its pulse to p. We say that v is "at pulse $P_v = p$" (or even less formally, "at pulse p") during the time interval $\tau(v, p) = [t(v, p), t(v, p+1))$.

It should be clear that in a fully asynchronous network, we cannot hope to force the processors to maintain the same pulse at all times. In fact, in all the solutions we will consider, vast gaps might be created between the pulse numbers of various processors at certain times during the execution. (See Exercise 4.) However, it is possible to enforce a weaker form of compatibility between the pulses of *neighboring* processors in the network. Specifically, we attempt to impose the following requirement on the simulation.

Pulse compatibility: If processor v sends an "original message" *MSG* to a neighbor w during its pulse $P_v = p$, then *MSG* is received at w during its pulse $P_w = p$ as well.

Let us now informally describe what we mean by correct simulation.

Definition 6.1.1 [Similar executions]: *Consider a synchronous protocol Π_S and a simulating protocol $\Pi_A = \nu(\Pi_S)$. Consider an execution $\eta^S = \eta^S(G, I)$ of Π_S in a synchronous network and a corresponding execution η^A of Π_A over an asynchronous network of the same topology G and with the same initial inputs I. The executions are said to be* similar *if for every processor v, neighbor w, original local variable X at v and integer $p \geq 0$, the following properties hold.*

1. *The value stored at X at the beginning of pulse p in execution η^A is the same as that stored at X at the beginning of round p in execution η^S.*

2. *The original messages sent by v to w during pulse p in execution η^A (if any) are the same as those sent by v to w during round p in execution η^S.*

3. *The original messages received by v from w during pulse p in execution η^A (if any) are the same as those received by v from w during round p in execution η^S.*

4. *The final output of v in execution η^A is the same as in execution η^S.*

Definition 6.1.2 [Correct simulation]: *The asynchronous protocol Π_A is said to simulate the synchronous protocol Π_S if for every network topology and for every initial input their executions are similar. The synchronizer ν is said to be* correct *if for every synchronous protocol Π_S the protocol $\Pi_A = \nu(\Pi_S)$ simulates Π_S.*

We state without proof the following claim.

Lemma 6.1.3 *If synchronizer ν guarantees pulse compatibility, then it is correct.* $\square$

6.1.2   Conceptual implementation strategy

By the above lemma, in order to ensure correct simulation, it is sufficient to impose pulse compatibility. The fundamental question one must answer is as follows: when is it permissible for a processor to increase its pulse number? A natural answer to this question is that a processor should be allowed to increase its pulse number from $p - 1$ to p once it is certain that it will not receive any more "original messages" of the algorithm Π_S sent to it by its neighbors during their pulse number $p - 1$. More formally, let us give the following definition.

Readiness property: A processor v is *ready* for pulse p, denoted $Ready(v, p)$, once it has already received all the messages of the algorithm sent to it by its neighbors during their pulse number $p - 1$.

Readiness rule: A processor v is allowed to generate its pulse p once it is finished with its required original actions for pulse $p - 1$ and $Ready(v, p)$ holds.

One should note, however, that obeying the "readiness rule" does not fully impose pulse compatibility. What it does ensure is a weaker property, namely, if processor v sends an "original message" MSG to a neighbor w during its pulse $P_v = p$, then MSG is received at w during its pulse $P_w = p'$, where $p' \leq p$. In other words, the readiness rules guarantees that a processor cannot get "messages from the past," but it still allows processors to get "messages from the future."

To see where the problem might occur, note that it is possible that v is ready for pulse p, and therefore generates pulse p, and immediately follows it up by sending a message of pulse p to its neighbor w. Yet w might still be "stuck" at pulse $p - 1$, waiting for messages of pulse $p - 1$ from some other neighbor. Moreover, suppose v knows somehow (e.g., by inspecting the properties of the simulated algorithm) that no messages are expected to reach it from its neighbors in the next five rounds. Then v is entitled to raise its pulse to $p + 5$ (performing the local computations required from it for those five pulses) and continue from there. In fact, when w receives a message from v while w is in pulse $p - 1$, it may not even be certain whether this message was sent by v during its pulse $p - 1$, or p, or some later pulse!

There are a number of ways to overcome this difficulty. Let us first discuss one approach, based on "delaying" messages that have arrived too early.

Delay rule: If a processor v receives in pulse p a message sent to it from a neighbor w during some later pulse $p' > p$ of w, then v declines consuming it and temporarily stores it in a buffer. It is allowed to process it only once it has already generated its pulse p'.

For the delay rule to be applicable, we must first ensure that a vertex receiving a message during its pulse p can know whether this message was sent during pulse p or some other pulse $p' > p$ of the sender. This can easily be achieved by attaching a "pulse number" to each message. (In fact, the specific synchronizer implementations we will discuss later guarantee that the gap between the pulse numbers of neighboring processors is never more than one, hence a single "pulse parity" bit should suffice.)

Lemma 6.1.4 *A synchronizer imposing the readiness and delay rules guarantees pulse compatibility.*   □

By Lemma 6.1.3 we get the next corollary.

Corollary 6.1.5 *If synchronizer ν imposes the readiness and delay rules, then it is correct.*   □

6.1.3   Implementation phases

The readiness property is easy to guarantee as long as we restrict our attention to synchronous algorithms with complete communication, i.e., algorithms that require every processor to send messages to every neighbor at every time pulse. The obvious problem with partial communication algorithms is that in case processor v did not send any message to its neighbor u at a certain pulse, u is obliged to wait forever for a message, as link delays in the asynchronous network are unpredictable.

The conceptual solution for this problem consists of employing two phases of communication.

Phase A: The first phase starts with every processor sending its original messages. Then, every processor receiving a message from a neighbor is required to send back an acknowledgment.

The outcome of Phase A is that every processor learns (within finite time) that all the messages it sent during a particular pulse have arrived, or that it is "safe," according to the following definition.

Safety property: We say that a processor v is *safe* with respect to pulse p, denoted $Safe(v, p)$, if all the messages it sent during pulse p have already arrived.

The following fact is immediate from the definitions.

Lemma 6.1.6 *If each neighbor w of v satisfies $Safe(v, p)$, then v satisfies $Ready(v, p+1)$.*

Consequently, a processor may generate a new pulse whenever it learns that all its neighbors are safe with respect to the current pulse. Thus the second and main phase of the synchronizer involves delivering this "safety" information.

Phase B: Apply a procedure to let each processor know when all its neighbors are safe w.r.t. pulse p.

Different synchronizer constructions all employ this two phase strategy. Moreover, they all use the same Phase A. The difference between them therefore lies entirely in the way they tackle the problem of designing the procedure for implementing Phase B.

6.1.4   Alternative conceptual implementation

The solution of delaying messages works well assuming each vertex has a sufficient number of buffers for delayed messages (specifically, one per each incoming edge). However, in some cases this option is not available. In such a case, a different approach is necessary.

A possible solution is to perform the pulse increase in two stages. The first stage, in which the pulse variable P_v is actually increased from p to $p+1$, is after v learns that $Ready(v, p+1)$.

Once this is done, v may receive messages of pulse $p+1$, but it still refrains from *sending* original messages of pulse $p+1$, since it does not know yet whether its neighbors are ready for pulse $p+1$.

Enabling property: A processor v is *enabled* for pulse p, denoted $Enabled(v, p)$, once each of its neighbors w satisfies $Ready(w, p)$.

Enabling rule: A processor v is allowed to send original messages of pulse p only once $Enabled(v, p)$ holds.

Lemma 6.1.7 *A synchronizer imposing the readiness and enabling rules guarantees pulse compatibility.*   □

Corollary 6.1.8 *If synchronizer ν imposes the readiness and enabling rules, then for a given synchronous protocol Π_S, the protocol $\Pi_A = \nu(\Pi_S)$ simulates Π_S.*   □

Consequently, a processor may start sending new messages whenever it learns that all its neighbors are ready with respect to the new pulse. Implementing this rule requires adding a third phase to the synchronizer, involving the delivery of this "readiness" information.

Phase C: Apply a procedure to let each processor know when all its neighbors are ready for pulse p.

Typically, a synchronizer can implement Phase C using precisely the same procedure it is using for implementing Phase B, so the introduction of this additional phase incurs (asymptotically) no complexity increase.

6.2   Complexity measures for synchronizers

It is clear that every synchronizer incurs some time and message costs for the synchronization of every round. We now define these costs and relate them to the cost of the resulting simulation.

A first issue to be noticed is that a synchronizer may require an initialization phase which may be needed for setting it up. We say that synchronizer ν is "up and running" once all the required data structures are set up and initialized at every vertex and each vertex has already generated the first pulse. Denote the time and message requirements of the initialization procedure setting up synchronizer ν by $\mathsf{Time}_{init}(\nu)$ and $\mathsf{Message}_{init}(\nu)$, respectively.

Let us now consider the time and message overheads added by a synchronizer ν for each pulse of the algorithm. Define $\mathsf{Message}_{pulse}(\nu)$ to be the total message cost of the synchronization messages sent by all the vertices during their pulse p. For the time delay imposed by using the synchronizer, the definition is not as clear. One natural possibility for defining the time overhead of ν is as the maximum length of a period $\tau(v,p)$ that some processor v stays in some pulse p. We refer to this parameter as the *gap* of the synchronizer ν and denote it by

$$\mathsf{Time}_{gap}(\nu) \;=\; \max_{v,p}\{t(v,p+1) - t(v,p)\}.$$

Unfortunately, this parameter turns out to be rather large for certain synchronizer constructions and therefore it does not represent the true picture concerning the rate at which the simulation progresses. Instead, we define the time overhead of a pulse as follows. For every $p \geq 0$, let $t_{\max}(p) = \max_{v \in V}\{t(v,p)\}$. Intuitively, $t_{\max}(p)$ is the time when the slowest of the processors has progressed to pulse p, or put another way, this is the earliest time by which the lowest pulse number in the network is p. We now define

$$\mathsf{Time}_{pulse}(\nu) \;=\; \max_{p \geq 0}\{t_{\max}(p+1) - t_{\max}(p)\}.$$

Clearly, an efficient synchronizer should keep these costs as low as possible, and especially the overheads per pulse, $\mathsf{Time}_{pulse}(\nu)$ and $\mathsf{Message}_{pulse}(\nu)$.

The complexities of a synchronous algorithm Π_S are related to those of the asynchronous simulation algorithm $\Pi_A = \nu(\Pi_S)$ as follows.

Lemma 6.2.1

1. $\mathsf{Message}(\Pi_A) \leq \mathsf{Message}_{init}(\nu) + \mathsf{Message}(\Pi_S) + \mathsf{Time}(\Pi_S) \cdot \mathsf{Message}_{pulse}(\nu)$,

2. $\mathsf{Time}(\Pi_A) \leq \mathsf{Time}_{init}(\nu) + \mathsf{Time}(\Pi_S) \cdot \mathsf{Time}_{pulse}(\nu)$.

Proof: First note that by the definition of similarity and correctness, if the synchronizer ν is correct, then the simulating algorithm Π_A terminates by pulse $\mathsf{Time}(\Pi_S)$. The additional message cost incurred by the synchronizer messages is at most $\mathsf{Message}_{pulse}(\nu)$ per pulse, hence the bound on $\mathsf{Message}(\Pi_A)$.

As for the time bound, by time $\mathsf{Time}_{init}(\nu)$ all processors have already generated their first pulse 0. It follows by induction that for any $p \geq 0$, by time $\mathsf{Time}_{pulse}(\nu) + p \cdot \mathsf{Time}_{pulse}(\nu)$, the slowest processor has already generated pulse p. The claim follows. $\square$

Note that Phase A does not increase the message complexity or the time complexity of the algorithm by more than a constant factor. Hence Phase B (and Phase C if used) is the one responsible for the additional time and message requirements $\mathsf{Message}_{pulse}(\nu)$ and $\mathsf{Time}_{pulse}(\nu)$.

In both Phase B and Phase C, the task that needs to be performed boils down to solving the following problem.

The neighbor update problem: Suppose that each processor in the network has two bit variables, b_v and all_v, initially set to 0. In each processor v, an external event flips the value of the bit b_v to 1 at some point. The task of each processor v is to set its all_v bit to 1 at some point after all its neighbors w already flipped to $b_w = 1$. We are interested in solving this problem as efficiently as possible, in terms of the required message complexity and the time elapsed from the time t_0 in which all bits b_v are flipped to 1, until the time t_f in which all bits all_v are set to 1 as well.

6.3   Two basic synchronizers

Synchronizers exhibit a certain trade-off between their message and time requirements. We now present two simple synchronizers, named α and β, that represent the two endpoints of this trade-off. Synchronizer α is time optimal, i.e., $\mathsf{Time}_{pulse}(\alpha) = O(1)$, but its message overhead is very large, namely, $\mathsf{Message}_{pulse}(\alpha) = O(|E|)$. On the other hand, synchronizer β achieves an optimal number of messages (i.e., $\mathsf{Message}_{pulse}(\beta) = O(n)$), but its time requirement may be high, namely, $\mathsf{Time}_{pulse}(\beta) = O(Diam(G))$. (Recall that these complexities are crucial since they represent the overhead *per pulse* of the synchronous algorithm.)

6.3.1   Synchronizer α

Our simplest construction is synchronizer α. Phase B of this synchronizer is performed directly: after the execution of pulse p, when a processor v learns that it is safe, it simply reports this fact directly to all its neighbors. Thus the behavior and complexity of this synchronizer boil down to those of an algorithm in which every processor sends messages to every neighbor in every pulse.

It is clear that this is a valid implementation of Phase B and thus implements the readiness rule. Hence if the delay rule is observed as well, then by the discussion in Section 6.1.3 and by Corollary 6.1.5 we get the following lemma.

Lemma 6.3.1 *Synchronizer α is correct.* $\square$

Let us now consider the complexities of synchronizer α. Synchronizer α can be set up by broadcasting a message from the initiating processor r_0. This can be done using the flooding algorithm (without acknowledgements) of Chapter 3. This determines the initialization costs of the synchronizer.

The message overhead of synchronizer α per pulse is clearly proportional to the number of edges, as every processor sends a message to each neighbor. Let us now consider the time overhead of α. We first note that if we look at an arbitrary processor p and consider the amount of time this processor spends on some pulse p, this time (bounded by $\mathsf{Time}_{gap}(\alpha)$) may be rather large. In fact, it is possible to devise a scenario in which this delay is as high as the network diameter.

To see how this can happen, notice that it is possible for two adjacent processors to differ by one in their pulse number. Consequently, along a chain of k processors $(v_0, v_1, \ldots, v_{k-1})$ it is possible to reach a state in which the pulse numbers form an increasing sequence $(p, p+1, \ldots, p+k-1)$. Once such a chain has formed, it may happen that processor v_i be forced to wait for i time units before processors $(v, \ldots, v_{i-1})$ have "caught up" with it and it is allowed to proceed. In particular, v_0 might have to wait for $k-1$ time units. Thus $\mathsf{Time}_{gap}(\alpha) = \Theta(Diam(G))$. (See Exercise 2.)

In contrast with the last argument, notice that when considering the tardiest pulse in the network at any given time, it takes at most a constant time until all the vertices holding this pulse number will increase it, hence $\mathsf{Time}_{pulse}(\alpha)$ is constant. Intuitively, while it is true that "the armada sails at the speed of the slowest boat," the slowest boat itself waits for nobody.

In summary we have the following complexity bounds.

Lemma 6.3.2

1. $\mathsf{Message}_{init}(\alpha) = O(|E|)$,

2. $\mathsf{Time}_{init}(\alpha) = O(Diam(G))$,

3. $\mathsf{Message}_{pulse}(\alpha) = O(|E|)$,

4. $\mathsf{Time}_{pulse}(\alpha) = O(1)$. $\quad\square$

Note that even though the message overhead of synchronizer α is very large in general, there are several natural network classes for which its behavior is asymptotically optimal. For example, note that for the class of bounded-degree networks, synchronizer α is optimal in both time and messages, since $|E| = O(n)$. This covers many common architectures proposed for parallel computing, like grids, butterflies and cube-connected cycles, rings etc. The same holds also for the class of trees and planar graphs in general.

6.3.2 Synchronizer β

For synchronizer β we assume the existence of a rooted spanning tree T in the network. After the execution of Phase A of a certain pulse p, the safety information is collected in Phase B by means of a convergecast process, invoking Procedure $\textsc{Converge}(\bigwedge, Safe(v, p))$ on the tree, namely, whenever a processor learns that it and all its descendants in the tree are safe, it reports this fact to its parent. Eventually the root learns that all the processors in the network are safe, and then it broadcasts this fact along the tree, letting the processors start a new pulse. This process is illustrated in Figure 6.1.

Again, this is clearly a valid implementation of Phase B, imposing the readiness rule. Combined with the delay rule, we get the following lemma by Corollary 6.1.5.

Lemma 6.3.3 *Synchronizer β is correct.* $\quad\square$

Since the process is carried out on the tree T, the complexities of synchronizer β are as follows.

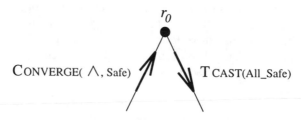

Figure 6.1: The two phases of synchronizer β.

Lemma 6.3.4

1. $\mathsf{Message}_{init}(\beta) = O(n|E|)$,

2. $\mathsf{Time}_{init}(\beta) = O(Diam(G))$,

3. $\mathsf{Message}_{pulse}(\beta) = O(n)$,

4. $\mathsf{Time}_{pulse}(\beta) = O(Diam(G))$.

Proof: To set up synchronizer β, it is necessary to construct a BFS tree in the network. This can be done using a number of distributed algorithms, for example, a distributed implementation of Dijkstra's algorithm (whose costs are $\mathsf{Time} = O(Diam^2(G))$ and $\mathsf{Message} = O(|E| + Diam(G)n)$) or the Bellman–Ford algorithm (whose costs are $\mathsf{Time} = O(Diam(G))$ and $\mathsf{Message} = O(n|E|)$).

The overhead parameters are simply the costs involved in a single "convergecast and broadcast" cycle on a tree of depth $O(Diam(G))$. □

Note that synchronizer β is optimal for bounded-diameter networks.

Bibliographical notes

The synchronization ideas behind synchronizers α and β were used implicitly in a number of distributed asynchronous algorithms, e.g., [Cha79, Jaf80, Gal82, CL85]. The general approach of using synchronizers as a unified methodology for handling asynchrony was first introduced in [Awe85a]. This paper also proposed synchronizers α and β. Alternative constructions were presented in [PU89b, AP90b]. Applications of synchronizers were studied in [Awe85c, SM86, LTC89, PU89b, AP90b].

The difficulties in the correctness of the simulation based on the readiness rule were pointed out in [LT87], and various corrections and correctness proofs were proposed in [LT87, FLS88, SS91]. The former two are based on the idea of message delaying.

Various complexity issues concerning synchronizers, including their time slowdown and memory overheads, were studied further in [CGZ86, AS88, ER88, ER90, ER95, RS94, SS93b, SS93a]. Synchronization in the presence of faults was discussed in [APSPS92, HS94].

Exercises

1. Prove Lemmas 6.1.4 and 6.1.7.

2. (a) Design a scenario realizing $\mathsf{Time}_{gap}(\alpha) = \Omega(Diam(G))$, i.e., in which some processor is forced to wait for time $\Omega(Diam(G))$ until it can increase its pulse number.

   (b) Prove that this is the worst possible case.

3. Establish the maximum possible value for $\mathsf{Time}_{gap}(\beta)$ and prove it.

4. Consider a 15-processor asynchronous network with processors $0, \ldots, 14$. The processors constantly run a synchronizer. Let v and v' be two processors in the network, and suppose that at a certain moment, the pulse counter at v shows $p = 27$. What is the range of possible pulse numbers at v' in each of the following cases:

   (a) The network is a ring (with the processors arranged according to their numbers), v is processor number 11, v' is processor number 2 and the synchronizer used is α.

   (b) The network is a full balanced binary tree (4 levels), v is the root, v' is one of the leaves and the synchronizer used is β.

   (c) The same as in (b), except both v and v' are leaves.

5. What are the message and time complexities of the asynchronous broadcast algorithms $\alpha(\text{FLOOD})$ and $\beta(\text{FLOOD})$ resulting from combining the synchronous Algorithm FLOOD on top of synchronizers α and β, respectively?

6. Consider a model combining the $\mathcal{ASYNC}$ and $\mathcal{LOCAL}$ models, that is, with asynchronous communication but allowing arbitrarily large messages. Which synchronizer type is preferable in this model? Justify your answer.

Chapter 7

Vertex coloring

Symmetry-breaking techniques play a major role in distributed network algorithms. Various computational tasks require the cooperation of many processors in the network, but prohibit certain processor pairs (or larger groups) from operating simultaneously. For example, in certain cases it may be prohibited for neighboring processors to act concurrently. This may require us to find a way to efficiently schedule processor groups under such prohibition rules. The task that needs to be solved towards constructing such a schedule can be formalized as a *vertex coloring* or *maximal independent set (MIS)* problem. Efficient MIS construction techniques can also help in decomposing the network into clusters of low diameter, which is often very useful in designing and implementing distributed divide-and-conquer algorithms.

In other situations, it may be required to apply an even stricter schedule, allowing at most one processor to act at any given time. This may arise, for example, in situations where the computation involves access to a critical section. A preliminary task on the way to constructing such a schedule is to have an algorithm for selecting the *first* processor to be scheduled. This task is often referred to as *leader election*.

These seemingly simple tasks become rather problematic in the distributed setting. The reason is that in a distributed network, all processors may be a priori alike, and in many cases they may start the computation from the same initial state and execute the same local protocol. In other words, the "view" of the system from the various processors may be symmetric. In such a situation, it becomes difficult to "break" the symmetry and enable different processors to be scheduled differently. Indeed, in certain settings this may even prove impossible, as we shall see later on.

In this chapter and the next we concentrate on two symmetry breaking tasks of "localized" nature, namely, coloring and MIS. (Note that leader election is more global in nature.) Throughout both chapters we concentrate on the synchronous, simultaneous wakeup, congestion-free, $\mathcal{LOCAL}$ model.

7.1 The coloring problem

The vertex coloring problem is defined as follows.

Definition 7.1.1 [Vertex coloring]: *A legal vertex coloring for a graph $F = (V, E)$ is an assignment of a color φ_v to each vertex v, such that any two adjacent vertices have a different color, i.e., $\varphi_v \neq \varphi_w$ for every $(v, w) \in E$.*

The vertex coloring problem is the problem of associating a legal coloring with a given graph.

Recall that by our assumption that each vertex v has a unique $O(\log n)$ bit identifier $ID(v)$, the coloring problem is essentially solved as the identifiers form a legal coloring by n colors. However, the typical goal is to obtain a coloring with as few colors as possible. In particular, defining the *chromatic number* of a graph G, denoted $\chi(G)$, as the minimum number of colors that can be used to legally color the vertices of G, a natural question involves achieving colorings that use close to $\chi(G)$ colors. In this section we discuss a number of distributed coloring algorithms.

7.2   A basic palette reduction procedure

Let us start by describing a simple procedure for reducing the number of colors in a given legal coloring by m colors. This procedure is based on the well-known sequential recoloring technique, and hence it is rather slow, and reduces the number of colors by one in each step. Later on we will describe faster reduction methods.

Let $\Delta = \Delta(G)$, the maximum vertex degree in G. The reduction is based on the observation that the set of neighbors of a given vertex can utilize at most Δ distinct colors, and therefore a palette of $\Delta + 1$ colors should always suffice for a vertex to find a "free" color. As this basic rule repeatedly appears in subsequent algorithms, it is convenient to define it as a basic procedure $\text{FIRST\_FREE}(W, \mathcal{P})$, defined for a set of colors $\mathcal{P}$ and a set of vertices W (see Figure 7.1).

---

1. Let c be the smallest color in the palette $\mathcal{P}$
   that is currently not used by any of the vertices in W.

2. Return (c).

Figure 7.1: Procedure $\text{FIRST\_FREE}(W, \mathcal{P})$.

We only apply this procedure in cases when it is known that such a free color exists. One particular palette typically used is $\mathcal{P}_m = \{1, \dots, m\}$ for $m \geq 1$.

The palette reduction Procedure REDUCE is described in Figure 7.2.

For round $i = 1$ through $m - \Delta + 1$ **do**:

1. $j \leftarrow i + \Delta + 1$ $/* \ \Delta + 2 \leq j \leq m \ */$.

2. **If** v's original color is $\varphi_v = j$, **then do**:

   (a) $\varphi_v \leftarrow \text{FIRST\_FREE}(\Gamma(v), \mathcal{P}_{\Delta+1})$.

   (b) Inform all neighbors of this choice.

Figure 7.2: Procedure REDUCE(m) (code for vertex v).

Lemma 7.2.1 *Procedure* REDUCE *produces a legal coloring of the network G with $\Delta + 1$ colors, and* $\text{Time}(\text{REDUCE}(m)) = m - \Delta + 1$.

Proof: The time bound is trivial, and it remains to prove correctness. Consider iteration i of the procedure. First, as argued earlier, a vertex v recoloring itself in the current iteration will always succeed in finding an available (nonconflicting) color, since it has at most Δ neighbors, and a $(\Delta + 1)$-color palette to choose from. Now, the color selection rule ensures that v's choice does not conflict with any of the vertices that recolored themselves in earlier iterations or with vertices originally colored by 1 through $\Delta + 1$. Furthermore, its new color does not conflict with choices made by other vertices in the current iteration, since all of these vertices are mutually nonadjacent (by the legality of the original coloring φ). Hence the new coloring is legal. □

7.3 3-coloring trees and bounded-degree graphs

Let us next describe an algorithm for coloring the vertices of a tree T with three colors in time $O(\log^* n)$. (Recall that $\log^* n$ is the minimum number of log-taking operations required to get n down to 2 or less, i.e., $\log^* n = \min\{i \mid \log^{(i)} n \leq 2\}$, where $\log^{(1)} n = \log n$ and $\log^{(i+1)} n = \log(\log^{(i)} n)$.)

We first give a 6-coloring algorithm for trees called Algorithm 6-COLOR. The idea of this and subsequent algorithms is to look at colors as bit strings and attempt to reduce the number of bits used for the colors. This approach clearly yields faster palette reduction than the basic procedure REDUCE, as even reducing the number of bits by one will halve the color space.

Denote the number of bits in φ_v by $|\varphi_v|$, and let $\varphi_v[i]$ denote the ith bit in the bit string representing φ_v.

The idea behind Algorithm 6-COLOR is to produce a new legal coloring for a vertex v from the current one, φ_v, by finding an index $1 \leq i \leq |\varphi_v|$ in which v's color differs from its parent's and setting the new color to be i concatenated with the bit $\varphi_v[i]$. (The root picks, say, the first bit.) This rule guarantees that neighbors will have different new colors and that the bit representation of the new coloring is of length roughly logarithmic of that of the previous coloring.

Algorithm 6-COLOR is described in Figure 7.3.

---

1. Let $\varphi_v \leftarrow ID(v)$.

2. **Repeat:**

    (a) $\ell \leftarrow |\varphi_v|$.
    (b) **If** v is the root, **then** set $I \leftarrow 0$
        else set $I \leftarrow \min\{i \mid \varphi_v[I] \neq \varphi_{parent(v)}[I]\}$.
    (c) Set $\varphi_v \leftarrow \langle I; \varphi_v[I] \rangle$.
    (d) Inform all children of this choice.

3. **until** $|\varphi_v| = \ell$.

Figure 7.3: Algorithm 6-COLOR(T) (code for vertex v).

Figure 7.4 illustrates the recoloring rule applied by Algorithm 6-COLOR(T).

Lemma 7.3.1 *In each iteration, Procedure* 6-COLOR *produces a legal coloring.*

Proof: Consider some iteration of the algorithm, and consider two neighboring vertices v, w in the tree, where without loss of generality $v = parent(w)$. Let I and J be the indices picked by v and w, respectively, in Step 2b of the algorithm. If $I \neq J$, then the new colors selected by v and w differ in their first component. On the other hand, if $I = J$, then the

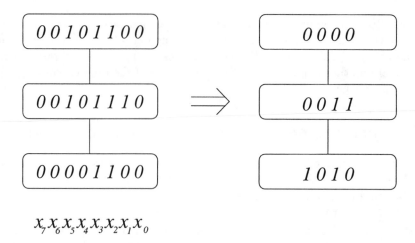

$$X_7 X_6 X_5 X_4 X_3 X_2 X_1 X_0$$

Figure 7.4: An example for the recoloring rule applied by Algorithm 6-COLOR(T).

rule applied in Step 2b ensures that the new colors differ in their second component, namely, $\varphi_v[I] \neq \varphi_w[J]$.   □

Let K_i denote the number of bits in the color representation after the ith iteration. ($K_0 = K = O(\log n)$ is the number of bits in the original ID coloring.) Note that $K_{i+1} = \lceil \log K_i \rceil + 1$. Therefore the second coloring will be of roughly $\log \log n$ bits, the third of roughly $\log^{(3)} n$ bits, and more generally we have the following lemmas.

Lemma 7.3.2 $K_{i+1} < K_i$ as long as $K_i \geq 4$.   □

Lemma 7.3.3 $K_i \leq \lceil \log^{(i)} K \rceil + 2$ for every i satisfying $\log^{(i)} K \geq 2$.   □

Lemma 7.3.4 The final coloring consists of six colors.

Proof: By the last two lemmas, for the final iteration i we have $K_i = K_{i-1} \leq 3$. Therefore in the final coloring there are at most three choices for an index to a bit in the $(i-1)$st coloring and two choices for the value of that bit. This gives a total of six possible colors.   □

We now show how to reduce the number of colors from 6 to 3 in three additional steps. A *shift down* operation on a given legal coloring of a tree (Procedure SHIFT_DOWN) is described in Figure 7.5 and illustrated in Figure 7.6.

Concurrently at all vertices:

  Recolor each nonroot vertex by the color of its parent.
  Color the root by a new color (different from its current one).

Figure 7.5: Procedure SHIFT_DOWN.

Lemma 7.3.5 The shift down operation preserves coloring legality. Moreover, in the resulting coloring, siblings (namely, children of the same vertex) are monochromatic.

Proof: Since the colors of the original coloring φ are shifted down, two neighboring vertices v, w where $v = parent(w)$ are recolored by $\varphi_{parent(v)}$ and φ_v, which are different since φ

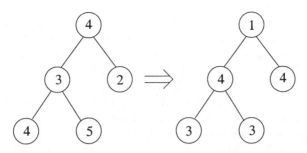

Figure 7.6: An example for the shift down operation.

was legal. (If v is the root, then the new colors are x and φ_v, where x is some color different from φ_v.) Also, all children of some vertex v get the same new color φ_v.   □

Assuming the six remaining colors are 1–6, the final three palette reduction steps involve cancelling colors 4, 5 and 6, one at a time. This is done by Algorithm SIX2THREE, described in Figure 7.7 and illustrated in Figure 7.8.

For $x \in \{4, 5, 6\}$ **do:**   /* Cancel color x */

1. Perform Procedure SHIFT_DOWN on the current coloring.

2. Each vertex v colored x selects a new color by applying
   $\varphi_v \leftarrow$ FIRST_FREE$(\Gamma(v), \mathcal{P}_3)$.
   /* Choose a new color from among $\{1, 2, 3\}$ not used by any of the neighbors. */

Figure 7.7: Algorithm SIX2THREE.

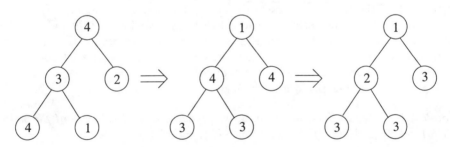

Figure 7.8: Example: Discarding the color 4.

Lemma 7.3.6 *Each color cancelling step in Algorithm* SIX2THREE *produces a legal coloring.*

Proof: First note that each vertex colored x will find an available color from the set $\{1, 2, 3\}$, since by Lemma 7.3.5 at most two of these colors are occupied, one by its parent and one by its children. Second, note that recoloring the x colored vertices simultaneously creates no problem since they are all mutually nonadjacent.   □

Theorem 7.3.7 *There exists a deterministic distributed algorithm for coloring trees with three colors in time* $O(\log^* n)$.   □

Finally, we note that the above algorithm can be extended into an algorithm for coloring an arbitrary graph G of bounded degree (i.e., constant $\Delta(G)$) with $\Delta + 1$ colors in time $O(\log^* n)$. Consider the following variant of Algorithm 6-COLOR. In each iteration i, vertex v selects *for each* of its d neighbors w an index I_w such that $\varphi_v[I_w] \neq \varphi_w[I_w]$. Then, the new color is set to be $\langle I_{w_1}; \varphi_v[I_{w_1}]; \ldots; I_{w_d}; \varphi_v[I_{w_d}] \rangle$.

This reduction step is clearly legality preserving by an extension of the proof of Lemma 7.3.1. As to the progress rate, a K-bit coloring goes down to a $\Delta(\lceil \log K \rceil + 1)$ bit one, hence for constant Δ the entire process will again take $\log^* n$ steps, ending with a 2Δ-bit coloring. This coloring uses up to $2^{2\Delta}$ different colors, but again, for constant Δ, this can be reduced to a $(\Delta + 1)$-coloring in $2^{2\Delta} = O(1)$ time using Procedure REDUCE of Section 7.2. Hence we conclude the following theorem.

Theorem 7.3.8 *There exists a deterministic distributed algorithm for coloring arbitrary bounded-degree graphs with $\Delta + 1$ colors in time $O(\log^* n)$.*   □

For graphs of unbounded degree, the above algorithm still works, but yields a coloring with a number of colors that is exponential in Δ, or using Procedure REDUCE, a $(\Delta + 1)$-coloring in time $O(\log^* n + 2^{2\Delta})$.

7.4 $(\Delta + 1)$-coloring for arbitrary graphs

Let us now describe an algorithm for coloring an arbitrary graph of maximum degree Δ with $\Delta + 1$ colors in $O(\Delta \log n)$ time. The algorithm is based on a recursive procedure RECURSECOLOR(x), where x is a binary string of up to K bits. Let $U_x \subseteq V$ denote the collection of (up to $2^{K-|x|}$) vertices whose ID ends with the suffix x. The procedure is applied to a set U_x and returns with a coloring of the vertices of U_x with $\Delta + 1$ colors.

The procedure RECURSECOLOR(x) operates as follows. If $|x| = K$, then it returns, say, the color 0. Otherwise, it separates the set U_x into two sets, U_{0x} and U_{1x}, and recursively computes a $(\Delta + 1)$-coloring for each of them by invoking RECURSECOLOR$(0x)$ and RECURSECOLOR$(1x)$. To remove conflicts between the two colorings, the procedure then alters the colors of the vertices of U_{1x}, color by color, as in Procedure REDUCE. A formal description of Procedure RECURSECOLOR is given in Figure 7.9.

Letting λ denote the empty word, we make the following claim.

Lemma 7.4.1 *Procedure* RECURSECOLOR(λ) *produces a legal coloring of the network G with $\Delta + 1$ colors, and* Time(RECURSECOLOR(λ)) $= O(\Delta \log n)$.

Proof: To establish the correctness of the coloring, we prove by induction on the length of the string x handed to the procedure as parameter (starting with $|x| = K$) that RECURSECOLOR(x) produces a legal $(\Delta+1)$-coloring for the vertices of $G(U_x)$, the subgraph induced by U_x. The base case is immediate, and the general case follows similarly to the proof of Lemma 7.2.1. Consider the execution of RECURSECOLOR(x). First note that the coloring assigned to U_{0x} is legal (by the inductive assumption) and does not change later on. As for the vertices of U_{1x}, note that as before, a vertex v recoloring itself in some iteration i, via the FIRST_FREE operation, will always succeed in finding an available (nonconflicting) color. Moreover, v's choice does not conflict with any of the vertices of U_{1x} that recolored themselves in earlier iterations or with vertices of U_{0x}. It also does not conflict with choices made by other vertices in the current iteration, since all of these vertices are mutually non-adjacent (by the legality of the coloring generated by RECURSECOLOR$(1x)$ to the set U_{1x}). Hence the new coloring is legal.

1. Let $ID(v) = a_1 a_2 \ldots a_K$.

2. Set $\ell \leftarrow |x|$.

3. If $\ell = K$, then set $\varphi_v \leftarrow 0$ and **Return**.   /* singleton $U_x = \{v\}$ */

4. Set $b \leftarrow a_{K-\ell}$.

5. $\varphi_v \leftarrow \text{RECURSECOLOR}(bx)$.

6. If $b = 1$, then do:

> **For** round $i = 1$ through $\Delta + 1$ do:
>> If $\varphi_v = i$, then do:
>>> (a) $\varphi_v \leftarrow \text{FIRST\_FREE}(\Gamma(v), \mathcal{P}_{\Delta+1})$.
>>> (b) Inform all neighbors of this choice.

Figure 7.9: Procedure $\text{RECURSECOLOR}(x)$ (code for vertex v).

As for the time bound, it follows from the fact that each level of the recursion requires $\Delta + 1$ time units and there are $K = O(\log n)$ levels.   □

7.5   A lower bound for 3-coloring the ring

We conclude this section by presenting a lower bound of $\Omega(\log^* n)$ on the time required to color the n-vertex ring by three colors. Together with Theorem 7.3.8, this implies a tight bound of $\Theta(\log^* n)$ on the time required for 3-coloring the ring.

The lower bound applies even under rather strong assumptions. In particular, we may assume the congestion-free (time-oriented) $\mathcal{LOCAL}$ model, i.e., synchronous communication, simultaneous start, free local computation and unlimited-size messages. Moreover, we assume that the identifiers are taken from the range $\{1, \ldots, n\}$, i.e., they form an arbitrary permutation. (Clearly, if the identifiers are assumed to occur in order, then optimal coloring in 2 or 3 colors can be achieved with no communication at all.) The proof we present applies to deterministic algorithms, but the result itself can be extended to randomized algorithms as well.

Under the $\mathcal{LOCAL}$ model, after t time units a vertex v can know everything known to any other vertex in its t-neighborhood. In particular, given no inputs but the vertex identifiers, these t steps can be used to let each vertex v learn the topology (including identifiers) of $\Gamma_t(v)$. On a ring, v ends up with a $(2t+1)$-tuple $(x_1, \ldots, x_{2t+1})$ from the set $W_{2t+1,n}$, where

$$W_{s,n} = \{(x_1, \ldots, x_s) \mid 1 \le x_i \le n, \ x_i \ne x_j\}$$

with $x_{t+1} = ID(v)$ and with x_t and x_{t+2} being the identifiers of its two neighbors, etc. (See Figure 7.10.)

Hence without loss of generality, it is possible to assume that any deterministic $t(n)$-step algorithm Π_t for coloring the ring in $c_{\max}$ colors operates according to the following 2-phase policy:

1. For t rounds, collect and pass on topological information. At the end of this phase, each vertex v holds a $(2t+1)$-tuple $\zeta(v) \in W_{2t+1,n}$.

2. Select $\varphi_v \leftarrow \tilde{\varphi}_\Pi(\zeta(v))$, where $\tilde{\varphi}_\Pi : W_{2t+1,n} \mapsto \{1, \ldots, c_{\max}\}$ is the *coloring function* of the algorithm Π_t.

Define the graph $B_{s,n} = (W_{s,n}, E_{s,n})$, where the edge set $E_{s,n}$ contains all the edges of the form $((x_1, x_2, \ldots, x_s), (x_2, \ldots, x_s, x_{s+1}))$ satisfying $x_1 \neq x_{s+1}$. Intuitively, two s-tuples of $W_{s,n}$ are connected in $B_{s,n}$ if they may occur as the tuples corresponding to two neighboring vertices in some ID-assignment for the ring.

Lemma 7.5.1 *If Algorithm Π_t produces a legal coloring for any n-vertex ring, then $\tilde{\varphi}_\Pi$ defines a legal coloring for $B_{2t+1,n}$.*

Proof: Suppose $\tilde{\varphi}_\Pi$ is not a legal coloring for $B_{2t+1,n}$, i.e., there exist two neighboring vertices $\zeta = (x_1, x_2, \ldots, x_{2t+1})$ and $\zeta' = (x_2, \ldots, x_s, x_{2t+2})$ in $B_{2t+1,n}$ such that $\tilde{\varphi}(\zeta) = \tilde{\varphi}(\zeta')$. Consider the n-vertex ring with ID-assignment as in Figure 7.11. Then algorithm Π will color the vertices v and w by colors $\tilde{\varphi}(\zeta)$ and $\tilde{\varphi}(\zeta')$, respectively, thus yielding an illegal coloring for the ring, which is a contradiction. $\square$

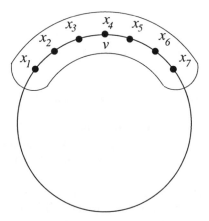

Figure 7.10: The topological information collected at vertex v after 3 rounds: the identifiers $(x_1, \ldots, x_7)$.

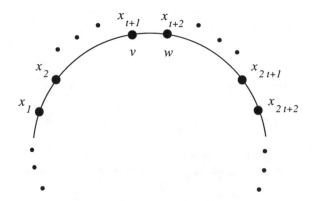

Figure 7.11: An ID-assignment leading to an inconsistent coloring of the ring.

Corollary 7.5.2 *If the n-vertex ring can be colored in t rounds using $c_{\max}$ colors, then* $\chi(B_{2t+1,n}) \leq c_{\max}.$

Based on this corollary, it is possible to immediately derive an $\Omega(n)$ lower bound on the time required to 2-color the (even length) ring.

Theorem 7.5.3 *Any deterministic distributed algorithm for coloring the (2n)-vertex ring with two colors requires at least $n-1$ rounds.*

Proof: By Corollary 7.5.2, the existence of such an algorithm that works in t time units implies that $\chi(B_{2t+1,2n}) \leq 2$, which in turn means that $B_{2t+1,n}$ is bipartite. Thus to prove the theorem it suffices to show that for $t \leq n-2$, the graph $B_{2t+1,2n}$ contains a cycle of odd length (thus prohibiting it from being bipartite). One such cycle (of length $2t+3$) is given in Figure 7.12.   □

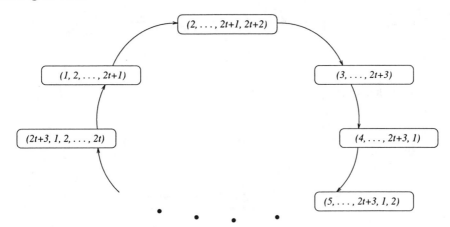

Figure 7.12: An odd-length cycle in $B_{2t+1,2n}$ for $t \leq n-2$.

Returning to 3-coloring, we next prove the following lemma.

Lemma 7.5.4 $\chi(B_{2t+1,n}) \geq \log^{(2t)} n.$

To prove the lemma, we define a family of directed graphs $\tilde{B}_{s,n} = (\tilde{W}_{s,n}, \tilde{E}_{s,n})$, where

$$\tilde{W}_{s,n} = \{(x_1, \ldots, x_s) \mid 1 \leq x_1 < \cdots < x_s \leq n\}$$

and the arc set $\tilde{E}_{s,n}$ contains all the arcs of the form (ζ, ζ') for $\zeta = (x_1, x_2, \ldots, x_s)$ and $\zeta' = (x_2, \ldots, x_s, x_{s+1})$ in $\tilde{W}_{s,n}$. Note that the undirected version of $\tilde{B}_{s,n}$ is a subgraph of $B_{s,n}$, and therefore we have the next lemma.

Lemma 7.5.5 $\chi(\tilde{B}_{s,n}) \leq \chi(B_{s,n}).$

Therefore in order to prove Lemma 7.5.4, it suffices to bound $\chi(\tilde{B}_{2t+1,n})$ from below. In order to derive such a lower bound, we first describe a recursive representation for the directed graphs $\tilde{B}$, based on the concept of a *line graph*.

Definition 7.5.6 [Line graph]: *Given a directed graph $H = (U, F)$, the line graph of H, denoted $\mathcal{DL}(H)$, is a directed graph whose vertices are the arcs of F and in which there is an arc directed from e to e' (for $e, e' \in F$) iff in H, e' starts at the vertex in which e ends.*

Lemma 7.5.7

1. $\tilde{B}_{1,n}$ *is the complete directed graph on n vertices (with every two vertices connected by one arc in each direction).*

2. $\tilde{B}_{s+1,n} = \mathcal{DL}(\tilde{B}_{s,n})$.

Proof: The first claim is immediate from the definition. The second claim is proved in a straightforward manner by establishing an appropriate isomorphism between $\tilde{B}_{s+1,n}$ and $\mathcal{DL}(\tilde{B}_{s,n})$. Consider the vertex e of $\mathcal{DL}(\tilde{B}_{s,n})$. Recall that e is an arc of $\tilde{B}_{s,n}$, say, connecting $(x_1, \ldots, x_s)$ to $(x_2, \ldots, x_{s+1})$. Then map e to the vertex $(x_1, \ldots, x_s, x_{s+1})$ of $\tilde{B}_{s+1,n}$. It is now straightforward to verify that this mapping preserves the adjacency relation (see Figure 7.13). □

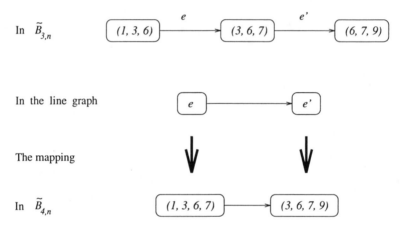

Figure 7.13: An example for the mapping from $\mathcal{DL}(\tilde{B}_{3,n})$ into $\tilde{B}_{4,n}$.

This relationship allows us to use the following lemma relating the chromatic number of a graph to that of its line graph.

Lemma 7.5.8 *For every directed graph H, $\chi(\mathcal{DL}(H)) \geq \log(\chi(H))$.*

Proof: Let $k = \chi(\mathcal{DL}(H))$, and consider a k-coloring $\hat{\varphi}$ of $\mathcal{DL}(H)$. The function $\hat{\varphi}$ can be thought of as an edge coloring for H, with the property that if e' starts at the vertex in which e ends, then $\hat{\varphi}(e') \neq \hat{\varphi}(e)$. Such a coloring can be used to create a 2^k-coloring $\tilde{\varphi}$ for H by setting the color of a vertex v to be the set $\varphi_v = \{\hat{\varphi}(e) \mid e \text{ ends in } v\}$.

Clearly, there are at most 2^k colors used by $\tilde{\varphi}$. To see that the coloring is legal, note that if v and w are neighbors in H, then there exists an edge e leading (without loss of generality) from v to w and then $\hat{\varphi}(e)$ occurs in φ_w but not in $\hat{\varphi}(v)$ (since its being in $\hat{\varphi}(v)$ as well would imply the existence of an edge e' entering v such that $\hat{\varphi}(e') = \hat{\varphi}(e)$, violating the legality of $\hat{\varphi}$ as an edge coloring of H).

It follows that $\chi(H) \leq 2^k$, proving the claim. □

Lemma 7.5.9 $\chi(\tilde{B}_{s,n}) \geq \log^{(s-1)} n.$

Proof: By straightforward induction on s, relying on Lemma 7.5.7 and Lemma 7.5.8. □

We can now complete the proof as follows.

Proof of Lemma 7.5.4: The proof is immediate from Lemmas 7.5.5 and 7.5.9. □

Theorem 7.5.10 *Any deterministic distributed algorithm for coloring the n-vertex ring with three colors requires at least $\frac{1}{2}(\log^* n - 1)$ rounds.*

Proof: By Lemma 7.5.4 and Corollary 7.5.2, if Π is an algorithm as stated in the theorem and requires t rounds, then $\log^{(2t)} n \leq \chi(B_{2t+1,n}) \leq 3$, hence $2t \geq \log^* n - 1$. $\quad\square$

Bibliographical notes

The 3-coloring algorithm of Section 7.3 is a generalization of the solution of [CV86] for simple chains, taken from [GP87] (see also [Plo88]). The $\Omega(\log^* n)$ lower bound for 3-coloring the ring (or computing an MIS on it) is due to [Lin92]. This lower bound was also extended to randomized algorithms in [Nao91, Lin92].

An algorithm for producing a Δ^2-coloring of an arbitrary graph of maximum degree Δ, yielding also a $(\Delta+1)$-coloring in time $O(\log^* n + \Delta^2)$, is presented in [Lin92]. The algorithm of Section 7.4 is an adaptation of the algorithm of [GPS88] presented in [AGLP89]. Results on distributed edge coloring can be found in [PS92a, PS95, DP95].

Exercises

1. Devise a coloring algorithm for trees which operates in one time unit and uses as few colors as possible.

2. Modify the 3-coloring algorithm of Section 7.3 into a 3-coloring algorithm for the ring.

3. How many vertices and edges does the graph $B_{s,n}$ of Section 7.5 contain?

4. Is the graph $\tilde{B}_{s,n}$ acyclic?

5. Let Π be a correct coloring algorithm for the n-vertex ring, which operates in one time unit. What lower bound can be deduced (from the results of Section 7.5) on the number of colors it must use?

6. What is the smallest n for which the lower bound of Theorem 7.5.10 on 3-coloring is greater than 1?

Chapter 8

Maximal independent sets (MIS)

In this chapter we turn to the second "localized" symmetry breaking task of MIS. As in the previous chapter, we assume the synchronous, simultaneous wakeup, congestion-free, $\mathcal{LOCAL}$ model.

8.1 Basic distributed MIS algorithms

The selection of an MIS in a given graph is a very well studied graph-algorithmic problem. It also serves as a basic building block in many distributed algorithms.

Definition 8.1.1 [MIS]: *An* independent set *is a set of vertices $U \subseteq V$, no two of which are adjacent. An independent set is* maximal *if no vertex can be added to it without violating its independence.*

The MIS problem is the problem of computing a maximal independent set for a given graph.

8.1.1 Sequential greedy MIS construction

The well-known sequential algorithm for selecting an MIS operates in a greedy fashion, as follows. We maintain a set U of vertices that have not been considered so far (initially containing all vertices) and an independent subset M of the vertices (initially empty). While U is nonempty, we repeat the following. We pick an arbitrary vertex $v \in U$ and add it to M. At the same time, we remove from U the vertex v itself and every vertex adjacent to it. A formal description of Algorithm GREEDY_MIS is given in Figure 8.1.

It is easy to see that M is independent throughout the process and, moreover, once U is exhausted, M forms an MIS. Algorithm GREEDY_MIS has linear ($O(|E|)$) time complexity (assuming an appropriate data structure for representing the graph).

In case the algorithm always picks the vertex with the largest identifier available, the resulting MIS is the *lexicographically first* one, sometimes denoted LEXMIS (see Figure 8.2). The problem of computing the LEXMIS is known to be complete for PTIME.

It is worth noting that in contrast to the MIS problem, the related problem of finding a *maximum* size independent set is notoriously hard. Not only is it NP-hard, but it is also known to be rather difficult to approximate.

Set $U \leftarrow V$, $M \leftarrow \emptyset$.

While $U \neq \emptyset$ **do**:

   1. Pick an arbitrary vertex $v \in U$.

   2. Set $U \leftarrow U - \Gamma(v)$.

   3. Set $M \leftarrow M \cup \{v\}$.

Figure 8.1: Algorithm GREEDY_MIS.

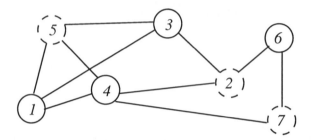

Figure 8.2: For the depicted graph, the lexicographically first MIS consists of the (dashed) vertices $\{7, 5, 2\}$, selected in this order.

8.1.2   Distributed implementation

In the distributed setting, the outcome of an MIS computation is marked by a special Boolean variable $\hat{b}$ stored at each of the vertices; a vertex joining the MIS sets $\hat{b}$ to 1 and a vertex not joining the MIS sets $\hat{b} = 0$. (Initially, say $\hat{b} = -1$.)

The basic greedy sequential algorithm for MIS has a straightforward distributed implementation, based on a depth-first tour of the graph, denoted Algorithm MIS_{DFS}. This implementation is in fact sequential, i.e., it has exactly one locus of activity at any given moment. The control of the algorithm is carried via a single message (the token) that traverses the graph in depth-first fashion as described in Section 5.4. As this token goes along, it marks vertices as either belonging to the MIS or excluded from it. Specifically, whenever the token reaches an unmarked vertex, it adds it to the MIS (by setting $\hat{b}$ to 1) and marks its neighbors as excluded. This distributed implementation of the sequential algorithm has the following complexities.

Lemma 8.1.2 Message(MIS_{DFS}) $= O(|E|)$ *and* Time(MIS_{DFS}) $= O(n)$.

The sequential variant of the greedy algorithm that yields a LEXMIS seems harder to implement in a distributed setting, since vertices of consecutive identifiers might reside far apart in the network. Perhaps surprisingly (given the PTIME-completeness of this problem), it is possible to give it a distributed solution by departing from the sequential mode and attempting to decide membership in the MIS in a number of places concurrently. The idea is based on the observation that a vertex v should decide to join the MIS precisely if all its neighbors with a larger identifier have decided not to join. This allows us to localize the decision process. The resulting algorithm, named Algorithm MIS_{RANK}, is formally described in Figure 8.3. Procedure JOIN is given in Figure 8.4.

The complexities of this algorithm in the worst case are still no better than the sequential performance.

---

1. Invoke Procedure JOIN.

2. **On** getting a message $Decided(1)$ from a neighbor w **do:**

   (a) Set $\hat{b} \leftarrow 0$.

   (b) Send $Decided(0)$ to all neighbors.

3. **On** getting a message $Decided(0)$ from a neighbor w **do:**
   Invoke Procedure JOIN.

Figure 8.3: Algorithm $\mathrm{MIS_{RANK}}$ (code for vertex v).

If every neighbor w of v with a larger identifier has decided $\hat{b}(w) = 0$, then **do:**

1. Set $\hat{b} \leftarrow 1$.

2. Send $Decided(1)$ to all neighbors.

Figure 8.4: Procedure JOIN (code for vertex v).

Lemma 8.1.3 Message($\mathrm{MIS_{RANK}}$) $= O(|E|)$ and Time($\mathrm{MIS_{RANK}}$) $= O(n)$.

Let us remark that Algorithm $\mathrm{MIS_{RANK}}$ relies on the existence of distinct identifiers to the vertices. Algorithm $\mathrm{MIS_{DFS}}$ does not require that, but does rely on the assumption that the execution starts at a single unique processor. We note the following observation.

Lemma 8.1.4 *There is no deterministic algorithm for computing an MIS on an anonymous ring network, assuming all vertices wake up simultaneously.*

Proof Sketch: In the absence of any inputs, the assumptions of the claim imply that all processors start the execution at precisely the same state. Due to the symmetry of the topology, it is possible to prove for any deterministic protocol, by induction on the round number t, that in round t all processors send and receive the same messages and, subsequently, that at the end of round t, all processors are still at the same state. Hence if the algorithm ever terminates, it does so with all vertices having the same value in their $\hat{b}$ variable (namely, either $\hat{b} = -1$ or $\hat{b} = 0$ or $\hat{b} = 1$). $\square$

8.2 Reducing coloring to MIS

In this section we discuss the relationship between coloring and MIS computation. Clearly, each color class in a legal coloring is an independent set in itself. However, none might be maximal. Nevertheless, we now show that coloring can be reduced to MIS. This is achieved by a procedure very similar to Procedure REDUCE, named Procedure COLOR2MIS and presented in Figure 8.5.

Lemma 8.2.1 *Procedure* COLOR2MIS *constructs an MIS for G in time m.*

Proof: To see that the constructed set is independent, note that a vertex v joining the MIS in iteration i cannot be adjacent to any vertex that has joined the MIS in earlier iterations and is not adjacent to any other vertex currently trying to join (since they belong to the same color class). To see that the set is maximal, note that if it is possible to add some

---

For round $i = 1$ through m **do:**

  If v's original color is $\varphi_v = i$, **then do:**

    If None of v's neighbors has joined the MIS yet, **then do:**

      1. Decide $\hat{b} \leftarrow 1$ (join the MIS).

      2. Inform all neighbors of this choice.

    Else decide $\hat{b} \leftarrow 0$.

Figure 8.5: Procedure COLOR2MIS(m) (code for vertex v).

vertex v to the set resulting from the procedure, and this vertex is colored i in the given coloring, then in iteration i, the decision made by v not to join the MIS was erroneous. The time analysis is immediate. □

Corollary 8.2.2 *Given a coloring algorithm that colors every graph G with $f(G)$ colors in time $T(G)$, it is possible to construct an MIS for G in time $T(G) + f(G)$.* □

By Theorems 7.3.7 and 7.3.8 and Lemma 7.4.1 we get the following corollaries.

Corollary 8.2.3 *There exists a deterministic distributed MIS algorithm for trees and for bounded-degree graphs with time complexity $O(\log^* n)$.* □

Corollary 8.2.4 *There exists a deterministic distributed MIS algorithm for arbitrary graphs with time complexity $O(\Delta(G) \log n)$.* □

On the other hand, By Theorem 7.5.10 we get a complementing lower bound.

Theorem 8.2.5 *Any deterministic distributed MIS algorithm for the n-vertex ring requires at least $\frac{1}{2}(\log^* n - 3)$ rounds.*

Proof: In light of Theorem 7.5.10, it suffices to show that given an MIS for the ring, it is possible to 3-color the ring in one more round. This holds under the assumption that the edges of the ring are oriented in a consistent manner, that is, each vertex identifies its two edges as going "left" and "right" and the edge $e = (v, w)$ is marked as going "left" by precisely one of its two endpoints. Under this assumption, the ring is 3-colored as follows.

1. Each vertex in the MIS colors itself 1 and sends the message "2" to its neighbor on the left.

2. A vertex not in the MIS colors itself 2 if it gets a message "2", otherwise it colors itself 3.

It is straightforward to verify that this process, illustrated in Figure 8.6, yields a valid 3-coloring of the ring, based on the fact that the MIS vertices are spaced 2 or 3 places apart around the ring.

In case the assumption of consistent orientation cannot be made, the above 3-coloring protocol clearly fails (see Exercise 4). There are two cases to consider. If the network is anonymous, then 3-coloring is impossible (see Exercise 6). In contrast, if the vertices are equipped with distinct identifiers, then it is still possible to 3-color the ring in a single round (see Exercise 5), so the lower bound for MIS remains the same. □

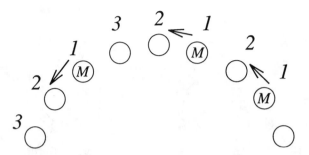

Figure 8.6: 3-coloring the ring given an MIS.

8.3 Constructing small dominating sets on trees

A dominating set in a graph is defined as follows.

Definition 8.3.1 [Dominating set]: *A set M of vertices in a graph $G = (V, E)$ is said to* dominate *the graph if every vertex in $V \setminus M$ has a neighbor in M or, alternatively, if $dist(v, M) \leq 1$ for every $v \in V$.*

In this section we present a procedure SMALL_DOM_SET for computing a small dominating set on a given tree. The procedure makes use of a sub-procedure for computing an MIS set in the tree.

Our goal is as follows. Given an n-vertex rooted tree $T = (V, E)$, find a set of vertices $M \subseteq V$ such that

1. M dominates V and

2. $|M| \leq n/2$.

Furthermore, we would like this procedure to be amenable to a fast dis tributed implementation.

The procedure is based on the following. Denote by $\check{L}_i$ the set of tree vertices at min-level i (as defined in Section 2.1.2),

$$\check{L}_i = \{v \mid \check{L}(v) = i\}.$$

Procedure SMALL_DOM_SET for computing a dominating set M on a tree T is presented next, in Figure 8.7.

---

1. Mark the vertices of T with min-level numbers $\check{L}(v) = 0, 1, 2$.

2. Select an MIS, Q, in the set R of unmarked vertices.

3. $M \leftarrow Q \cup \check{L}_1$.

Figure 8.7: Procedure SMALL_DOM_SET.

A pictorial example is given in Figure 8.8.

The fact that Procedure SMALL_DOM_SET produces a dominating set is established by the following lemma.

Lemma 8.3.2 *Let M be the outcome of Procedure SMALL_DOM_SET on the tree T. Then for every vertex $v \notin M$ there exists an adjacent vertex $v' \in M$.*

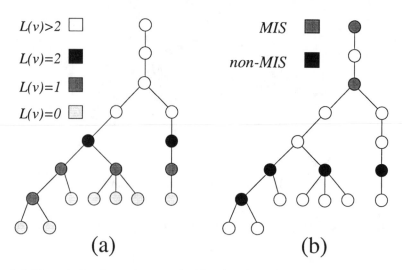

Figure 8.8: (a) The min-level numbers marked by the algorithm on a given tree T; (b) a small dominating set M on the tree T.

Proof: Partition V into $\check{L}_0 \cup \check{L}_1 \cup \check{L}_2 \cup R$. The set M output by Procedure SMALL_DOM_SET is composed of $Q \cup \check{L}_1$. Now, by choice of Q, it dominates each vertex of $R \setminus Q$. Also, each vertex of $\check{L}_0 \cup \check{L}_2$ has a neighbor in $\check{L}_1$. $\square$

The "smallness" of the resulting dominating set is guaranteed by the following lemma.

Lemma 8.3.3 $|M| \le n/2$.

Proof: By construction, $M = \check{L}_1 \cup Q$. It is clear that $|\check{L}_1| \le |\check{L}_0|$, and hence

$$|\check{L}_1| \le \frac{|\check{L}_0 \cup \check{L}_1|}{2} . \tag{8.1}$$

We now claim that

$$|Q| \le \frac{|R \cup \check{L}_2|}{2} . \tag{8.2}$$

This can be proved by selecting for every $v \in Q$ a *distinct* match $\omega(v) \in (R \cup \check{L}_2) - Q$, thus establishing that $|R \cup \check{L}_2| \ge 2 \cdot |Q|$. The matching is done as follows: Pick $\omega(v)$ to be an arbitrary child of v (by definition, vertices in Q always have children in $R \cup \check{L}_2$). Distinctness is guaranteed by the fact that each vertex in the tree has a unique parent.

It now follows from (8.1) and (8.2) that

$$|M| = |Q \cup \check{L}_1| \le \frac{|R \cup \check{L}_2|}{2} + \frac{|\check{L}_0 \cup \check{L}_1|}{2} = \frac{n}{2} . \quad \square$$

For the complexity analysis, it is important to note that although the min-level numbers $\check{L}(v)$ are defined for every vertex v in the tree, only the vertices belonging to the first three min-levels, $\check{L}_0$, $\check{L}_1$ and $\check{L}_2$, are actually marked. This is doable in constant time, hence by Corollary 8.2.3 we have the following result.

Corollary 8.3.4 *There exists a deterministic distributed algorithm for constructing a small dominating set on trees with time complexity $O(\log^* n)$.* $\square$

8.4 Randomized distributed MIS algorithm

This section presents a simple and elegant randomized distributed algorithm for the MIS problem, called Algorithm RAND_MIS. This algorithm is analyzed assuming the congestion-free $\mathcal{LOCAL}$ model, namely, allowing an arbitrary-size message to be sent over an edge in one time unit.

Similar to a number of centralized or parallel randomized algorithms for MIS, our algorithm is based on the following simple paradigm. The algorithm operates in synchronous rounds grouped into phases. At the end of each phase, some vertices mark themselves (permanently) as belonging to the MIS, by setting $\hat{b}$ to 1, and some others mark themselves (permanently) out of the MIS, by setting $\hat{b}$ to 0. The decision is based on a random choice made by the vertices. The decided vertices also erase themselves from the graph. The remaining set of undecided vertices, U, induces a subgraph $G(U)$ on which the next phase is performed. This process is continued until all vertices have made their final decision.

One point of difference concerns the probability $p(v)$ with which each vertex elects to attempt to join the MIS at each phase. A choice often made in centralized or parallel variants of this algorithm is to rely on the maximum degree in G and set this probability to $1/\Delta(G)$. This choice is not available to us in the distributed setting though since the exact value of $\Delta(G)$ is unknown to the vertices, and computing it in a distributed fashion may require $\Omega(Diam(G))$ time.

Fortunately, due to the highly local nature of the problem, it turns out that it suffices to "locally approximate" the choice of Δ, replacing it at each vertex v by the local maximum degree in its 2-neighborhood. Formally, for a vertex $v \in V$, let $D_G(v)$ denote the maximal vertex degree in $\Gamma_2(v)$,

$$D_G(v) = \max_{w \in \Gamma_2(v)} \{deg_G(w)\}.$$

Let us now describe a single phase of Algorithm RAND_MIS, starting with a set U of undecided vertices, and a graph $H = G(U)$. It is assumed that at the beginning of the phase, each vertex knows which of its neighbors are in U (i.e., have not decided yet). The number of these neighbors is $deg_H(v)$. Also, initially $\hat{b}(v) = -1$ for every $v \in U$. A vertex $v \in U$ performs the following five steps (each composed of a "compute; send; receive" cycle). The operation of the phase is described in Figure 8.9. As mentioned, these phases are repeated until all vertices have decided. (In fact, each vertex may stop participating in the process as early as possible, i.e., it is no longer required to send or receive any messages pertaining to the MIS selection once it has decided.)

Analysis

The fact that the algorithm is correct, namely, that it constructs an MIS once all the vertices terminate, is easy to prove (see Exercise 9). Isolated vertices are taken care of deterministically, so we need only consider vertices of degree 1 or higher. In particular, we consider only phases in which $\Delta(H) \geq 1$.

Consider a given phase of the algorithm. Let us define the following two events. The event $\mathcal{E}(u, w)$, defined for two neighboring vertices u and w, is that w has drawn $b(w) = 1$, u has drawn $b(u) = 0$ and every other neighbor v of u and w has drawn $b(v) = 0$ as well. (See Figure 8.10.) (Note that the outcome of this event is that u decides 0 and w decides 1.)

- Step 0:
  If $deg_H(v) = 0$, then set $\hat{b}(v) \leftarrow 1$ and halt.   /* v is isolated */

- Steps 1,2:
  Send $deg_H(v)$ to all neighbors at distance 1 or 2.
  Receive $deg_H(w)$ of all neighbors at distance 1 or 2.

- Step 3:
  Compute $D_H(v)$ as the maximum of these neighbor degrees, and set

  $$p(v) \;\leftarrow\; \frac{1}{D_H(v) + 1} \;.$$

  Draw uniformly at random a bit $b(v)$ with probability $p(v)$ for setting $b(v) \leftarrow 1$.
  Send $b(v)$ to all neighbors (at distance 1).
  Receive $b(w)$ from all neighbors w.

- Step 4:
  If $b(v) = 1$, **then do**:

  1. **If** all neighbors w have drawn $b(w) = 0$, **then** set $\hat{b}(v) \leftarrow 1$.
                              /* decide 1 */
     Else remain **undecided**.   /* at least one neighbor w has drawn $b(w) = 1$
     */

  2. Send $\hat{b}(v)$ to all neighbors.   /* inform your decision */
     Receive $\hat{b}(w)$ from all neighbors w.

- Step 5:
  If at least one neighbor w has decided $\hat{b}(w) = 1$,
              /* note that necessarily $b(v) = 0$ */
  then set $\hat{b}(v) \leftarrow 0$.   /* decide 0 */
  Send $\hat{b}(v)$ to all neighbors.
  Receive $\hat{b}(w)$ from all neighbors w.

Figure 8.9: Algorithm RAND_MIS (single phase).

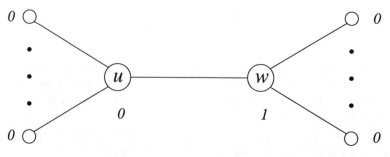

Figure 8.10: The event $\mathcal{E}(u, w)$.

The event $\mathcal{E}(u)$ is that u has drawn $b(u) = 0$, one of its neighbors w has drawn $b(w) = 1$ and every other neighbor v of u and w has drawn $b(v) = 0$ as well. (Note that the outcome of this event is that u decides 0 and exactly one of its neighbors decides 1.) Clearly,

$$\mathcal{E}(u) = \bigcup_{w \in \Gamma(u)} \mathcal{E}(u, w).$$

Since the events $\mathcal{E}(u, w)$ and $\mathcal{E}(u, w')$ are disjoint for $w \neq w'$,

$$\mathbb{P}(\mathcal{E}(u)) = \sum_{w \in \Gamma(u)} \mathbb{P}(\mathcal{E}(u, w)). \tag{8.3}$$

Fix $\epsilon = (4e^4)^{-1}$. (Here e denotes the base of the natural log.)

Lemma 8.4.1 *For every vertex u such that $deg_H(u) \geq \Delta(H)/2$ at the beginning of the phase,*

$$\mathbb{P}(\mathcal{E}(u)) \geq \epsilon.$$

Proof: Consider a vertex u as specified in the lemma. For every neighbor w of u, let us denote $Z_w = \Gamma(u) \cup \Gamma(w) \setminus \{w\}$. Note that

$$\mathbb{P}(\mathcal{E}(u, w)) = p(w) \prod_{z \in Z_w} \left(1 - p(z)\right) = \frac{1}{D_H(w) + 1} \prod_{z \in Z_w} \left(1 - \frac{1}{D_H(z) + 1}\right).$$

Note also that $D_H(w) \leq \Delta(H)$ and that $D_H(z) \geq deg_H(u) \geq \Delta(H)/2$ for every $z \in Z_w$. Consequently,

$$\mathbb{P}(\mathcal{E}(u, w)) \geq \frac{1}{\Delta(H) + 1} \left(1 - \frac{1}{\Delta(H)/2 + 1}\right)^{|Z_w|}$$

$$\geq \frac{1}{\Delta(H) + 1} \left(1 - \frac{1}{\Delta(H)/2 + 1}\right)^{2\Delta(H) - 1}.$$

For (integer) $\Delta(H) \geq 1$ we get

$$\mathbb{P}(\mathcal{E}(u, w)) \geq \frac{1}{\Delta(H) + 1} \cdot \frac{1}{e^4}.$$

It follows from Equation (8.3) that

$$\mathbb{P}(\mathcal{E}(u)) \geq deg_H(u) \cdot \frac{1}{\Delta(H) + 1} \cdot \frac{1}{e^4} \geq \frac{1}{4e^4} = \epsilon. \qquad \square$$

For the time analysis, let us define the following notation. For every phase t, let U_t denote the set of vertices that at round t are still undecided, and let $G_t = G(U_t)$ denote their induced subgraph. Let $M_i(t)$ denote the set of vertices that belong to U_t and their degree in G_t is no smaller than $n/2^i$. Let $K = \frac{3 \log n}{\epsilon}$. We break the execution into "super phases" of K phases each and focus on the status of vertices at the rounds $t_i = iK$. Consider the sequence of events $\mathcal{E}_i$ for $i \geq 0$, where $\mathcal{E}_i$ is the event that $M_i(t_i) = \emptyset$. (Note that the event $\mathcal{E}_0$ holds trivially in every execution.)

Lemma 8.4.2 $\mathbb{P}(\mathcal{E}_{i+1} | \mathcal{E}_i) \geq 1 - \frac{1}{n^2}$ *for every $i \geq 0$.*

Proof: Assume that event $\mathcal{E}_i$ holds, namely, the set $M_i(t_i)$ is empty at time $t_i = iK$. We show that under this assumption, denoting by $\bar{\mathcal{E}}$ the event complementing $\mathcal{E}$, $\mathbb{P}(\bar{\mathcal{E}}_{i+1}) \leq \frac{1}{n^2}$.

It follows from the assumption $\mathcal{E}_i$ that the subgraph G_{t_i} induced by the set U_{t_i} has $\Delta(G_{t_i}) < n/2^i$. Since vertex degrees can only decrease during the MIS selection process, the same holds for any later time $t \geq t_i$.

Supposing $\bar{\mathcal{E}}_{i+1}$, consider a vertex $v \in M_{i+1}(t_{i+1})$. We prove that during the $(i + 1)$st super phase, this v was expected to leave the set U at every phase t with probability at least ϵ. For this, we first need to show that v satisfies the premise of Lemma 8.4.1 in each of these phases. Indeed, this vertex has degree $deg_{G_{t_{i+1}}}(v) \geq n/2^{i+1}$, and again, its degrees in earlier induced subgraphs could only be larger, hence $deg_{G_t}(v) \geq n/2^{i+1}$ for every $t \leq t_{i+1}$. It follows that at any time $t_i \leq t \leq t_i + K$, the vertex v belonged to $M_{i+1}(t)$ and, moreover, it satisfied $deg_{G_t}(v) \geq \Delta(G_t)/2$.

By Lemma 8.4.1, in each phase t between $t_i + 1$ and t_{i+1}, $\mathbb{P}(\mathcal{E}(v)) \geq \epsilon$, implying that with probability at least ϵ, v leaves the set U in round t, i.e., $v \notin M_{i+1}(t + 1)$. Since the trials in different rounds are independent, we have that for every $v \in M_{i+1}(t_i)$ and every $j \geq 1$, $\mathbb{P}(v \in M_{i+1}(t_i + j)) \leq (1 - \epsilon)^j$, and hence

$$\mathbb{P}(v \in M_{i+1}(t_i + K)) \ \leq \ (1 - \epsilon)^{3 \log n/\epsilon} \ \leq \ \frac{1}{n^3} \ .$$

It follows that, assuming $\mathcal{E}_i$,

$$\mathbb{P}(M_{i+1}(t_{i+1}) \neq \emptyset) \ \leq \ \frac{1}{n^2} \ ,$$

implying the lemma.   □

Lemma 8.4.3 *With probability at least $1 - 1/n$, all processors decide by time $O(\log^2 n)$.*

Proof: Let $\ell = \lceil \log n \rceil$, denote $\mathcal{E} = \bigcap_{1 \leq i \leq \ell} \mathcal{E}_i$ and let P denote the probability that all vertices have decided by time t_ℓ. Then

$$P \ \geq \ \mathbb{P}(M_i(t_\ell) = \emptyset \ \forall 1 \leq i \leq \ell) \ \geq \ \mathbb{P}(\mathcal{E}).$$

Note that $\bar{\mathcal{E}}$ can be decomposed into *disjoint* events as

$$\bar{\mathcal{E}} \ = \ \bar{\mathcal{E}}_1 \ \cup \ (\bar{\mathcal{E}}_2 \cap \mathcal{E}_1) \ \cup \ (\bar{\mathcal{E}}_3 \cap \mathcal{E}_2 \cap \mathcal{E}_1) \ \cdots \ \cup \ (\bar{\mathcal{E}}_\ell \cap \mathcal{E}_{\ell-1} \cap \cdots \cap \mathcal{E}_1),$$

so

$$
\begin{aligned}
1 - P \ &\leq \ \mathbb{P}(\bar{\mathcal{E}}) \\
&= \ \mathbb{P}(\bar{\mathcal{E}}_1) + \mathbb{P}(\bar{\mathcal{E}}_2 \cap \mathcal{E}_1) + \mathbb{P}(\bar{\mathcal{E}}_3 \cap \mathcal{E}_2 \cap \mathcal{E}_1) + \cdots + \mathbb{P}(\bar{\mathcal{E}}_\ell \cap \mathcal{E}_{\ell-1} \cap \cdots \cap \mathcal{E}_1) \\
&\leq \ \mathbb{P}(\bar{\mathcal{E}}_1) + \mathbb{P}(\bar{\mathcal{E}}_2 \cap \mathcal{E}_1) + \cdots + \mathbb{P}(\bar{\mathcal{E}}_\ell \cap \mathcal{E}_{\ell-1}).
\end{aligned}
$$

Recalling that $\mathbb{P}(\mathcal{E}_1 \mid \mathcal{E}_2) = \mathbb{P}(\mathcal{E}_1 \cap \mathcal{E}_2)/\mathbb{P}(\mathcal{E}_2) \geq \mathbb{P}(\mathcal{E}_1 \cap \mathcal{E}_2)$, we have

$$1 - P \ \leq \ \mathbb{P}(\bar{\mathcal{E}}_1 \mid \mathcal{E}_0) + \mathbb{P}(\bar{\mathcal{E}}_2 \mid \mathcal{E}_1) + \cdots + \mathbb{P}(\bar{\mathcal{E}}_\ell \mid \mathcal{E}_{\ell-1}).$$

By Lemma 8.4.2 it follows that $1 - P \leq \ell/n^2 \leq 1/n$, implying the lemma.   □

Corollary 8.4.4 *There exists a randomized distributed MIS algorithm for arbitrary graphs that halts in time $O(\log^2 n)$ with probability at least $1 - 1/n$.*   □

8.5   PRAM-based deterministic MIS algorithm

In Section 8.1 we considered deterministic distributed algorithms for MIS computation based on simulating the basic sequential algorithm for the problem. A natural option is to consider simulating *parallel* algorithms for the problem in the distributed setting. In particular, the MIS problem has deterministic parallel algorithms in the PRAM model that work in time polylog(n). (One such algorithm is obtained by derandomizing a randomized PRAM algorithm, which is rather similar to the one presented above.) Unfortunately, the PRAM model requires (potential) communication between all processors in every time step, which means that a simulation of a PRAM algorithm on the network must incur a slowdown proportional to the diameter of the network, $Diam(G)$. Thus the parallel deterministic MIS algorithm for the PRAM model implies the existence of a distributed variant whose time complexity is $O(Diam(G) \cdot \text{polylog}(n))$. We will not describe here any of the details involved in the resulting deterministic algorithm, Algorithm PRAM_MIS, and its distributed implementation, but state its complexity.

Lemma 8.5.1 *There exists a deterministic distributed algorithm (PRAM_MIS) for constructing an MIS on arbitrary graphs, with time complexity $O(Diam(G) \log^2 n)$.*   □

Bibliographical notes

The fact that LEXMIS is complete for PTIME is due to [Coo83]. An elegant randomized PRAM algorithm for the MIS problem is presented in [Lub86]. It requires a linear number of processors and runs in time $O(\log^2 n)$. This algorithm is directly implementable in a distributed setting, but its analysis is nontrivial. The randomized algorithm presented in Section 8.4 is a simple variant of (the distributed version of) the algorithm of [Lub86], which admits a somewhat simpler analysis. The main difference is that the original algorithm uses a simpler rule for choosing the bit $b(v)$. Specifically, the bit is set to 1 with probability $1/deg_G(v)$, hence $D_G(v)$ need not be computed. (Yet a third variant exists in which the probability used is $1/\Delta(G)$. This variant is even easier to analyze, but its distributed implementation is clearly more problematic, since computing $\Delta(G)$ is rather time consuming.)

   In addition to the randomized algorithm, a simple *deterministic* PRAM algorithm for the MIS problem is also given in [Lub86]. This algorithm is obtained from the randomized algorithm through derandomization and places the problem in the class NC^2. (See, e.g., [KR90]. The problem was placed in NC earlier in [KW84].) The distributed deterministic MIS algorithm PRAM_MIS of Section 8.5 is based on simulating this algorithm in the network.

Exercises

1. Show a graph and an ID-assignment for which Algorithm MIS$_{\text{RANK}}$ is faster than Algorithm MIS$_{\text{DFS}}$. Is there an example in the converse direction?

2. Prove that the time bound cannot be improved to $O(Diam(G))$ in Lemma 8.1.3.

3. Consider a path graph G with vertex IDs taken to be a random permutation of $\{1, \ldots, n\}$. Prove that in this case

$$\text{Time}(\text{MIS}_{\text{RANK}}) \leq c \log n / \log \log n$$

for a constant $c > 0$ with probability at least $1 - 1/n$.

4. Show that the algorithm given in the proof of Theorem 8.2.5 might fail if the ring does not enjoy a consistent orientation.

5. Prove that on a (nonanonymous) ring without a consistent orientation, it is possible to deterministically 3-color the vertices in a single round given an MIS.

6. Prove that on an anonymous ring without a consistent orientation, it is impossible to deterministically 3-color the vertices even given an MIS.

7. On an anonymous ring with a consistent orientation, is it possible to deterministically 3-color the vertices given an MIS?

8. Give deterministic algorithms for selecting an MIS and 3-coloring on anonymous rings without consistent orientation, assuming a designated leader vertex is given. Does this contradict Exercise 6? Why?

9. Prove that the randomized MIS algorithm of Section 8.4 yields an MIS once all the vertices terminate.

10. What could go wrong if the randomized MIS algorithm of Section 8.4 is modified to define the selected probabilities as $p(v) \leftarrow 1/D_H(v)$? (Note that isolated vertices cause no problem, given Step 0 of the protocol.)

11. Consider the randomized MIS algorithm of Section 8.4.

   (a) What is the maximal message size in the algorithm? What is the message complexity of the algorithm?

   (b) Modify the protocol so that the maximal message size becomes $O(\log n)$. What is the resulting message complexity of the algorithm?

12. (a) Show that in every planar graph, at least $n/7$ of the vertices have degree at most 6.

   (b) Relying on this fact, devise an iterative MIS algorithm for planar graphs with time complexity $O(\log n \log^* n)$.

   (c) Devise a similar algorithm for coloring planar graphs with as few colors as possible (this can be done with $O(1)$ colors).

13. Extend the algorithms of the previous exercise to the class of n-vertex graphs $G = (V, E)$ with a linear number of edges, $|E| = O(n)$.

Chapter 9

Message routing

9.1 The routing problem

Routing messages between pairs of processors is a primary activity of any distributed network of processors. The mechanism responsible for performing this activity in the network
is a subsystem called a *routing scheme*. This mechanism consists of a collection of message
forwarding protocols and information tables and can be invoked at any origin processor and
be required to deliver a message, or a stream of messages, to some destination processor.
The quality of the routing scheme is pivotal to the overall performance of the network, and
the design of efficient routing schemes was the subject of much recent study.

In this chapter we consider one common type of routing method, known as "store and
forward" packet routing, although the ideas presented are applicable to other types as well.
A store and forward routing scheme is based on handling each message individually, by
forwarding it from the sender to the destination through a chain of intermediate vertices.
Each of these intermediate sites stores the message locally, decides on the next edge on
which to forward the message and places the message in the queue of outgoing messages
associated with that edge.

Routing schemes

Let us now give a more precise definition for the structure and operation of a routing scheme.
A *routing scheme RS* for an n-processor network $G = (V, E)$ is a mechanism specifying for
each pair of vertices $u, v \in V$ a path in the network connecting u to v. In particular, it
has to specify, in each step along the way, the *header* attached to the message and the *port*
through which it needs to be transmitted.

As mentioned above, the routing scheme is composed of data structures and message
forwarding protocols. Let us next describe these two aspects more formally. For that
purpose, we first define the following two notions. First, the routing scheme requires us to
refer to vertices by special *routing labels*, i.e., it makes use of a labeling assignment *Label*
on v. We use

$$\texttt{Labels} \ = \ (Label(v_1), \ldots, Label(v_n))$$

to denote the vector of labels assigned to the n vertices of the network. Second, we will
formally denote the collection of *allowable message headers* by $\texttt{Headers}$.

Note that in principle, the scheme may use the unique fixed identifiers assigned to the
processors on the hardware level as routing labels. An opposite alternative would be to allow

the users responsible to the processors at the various sites to select their own meaningful routing labels by themselves. We will discuss the particular choice made here later on.

Data structures: The data structures required for maintaining a routing scheme are composed of the following three types of functions. Each vertex v stores one function of each type.

1. An *initial header function*, $I_v :$ Labels $\rightarrow$ Headers,

2. a *header function*, $H_v :$ Headers $\rightarrow$ Headers, and

3. a *port function*, $F_v :$ Headers $\rightarrow [1, deg_G(v)]$.

Forwarding protocol: The routing scheme is used for routing messages in the following way. First, let us consider the originator of a message. Suppose the vertex u wishes to send a message MSG to a destination v whose label is $Label(v)$. Then u has to perform the following two steps:

(1) Prepare a header h and attach it to the message. Such a header typically consists of (all or portions of) the destination's label, $Label(v)$, plus some additional routing information. It is computed using the initial header function I_u, i.e., by setting $h = I_u(v)$.

(2) Decide on the exit port i and load the message onto this port. This port is determined by consulting the port function F_u, i.e., by setting $i = F_u(h)$.

Now let's consider the actions of an intermediate vertex along the route of the message. Suppose that a message MSG with a header h' arrives at some vertex w. The first thing that w has to do is to read h' and check whether it is the final destination of MSG. If so, the routing process ends. Otherwise, w has to forward the message further. To this end, w has to perform the following two steps:

(1) Prepare a new header h for the message and replace the old header h' attached to the message by the new one. The new header is computed using the header function H_w, i.e., by setting $h = H_w(h')$.

(2) Compute the exit port i and load the message onto this port. This is again done by using the port function and setting $i = F_w(h)$.

For every pair of vertices u, v, the scheme RS implicitly specifies a *route*

$$\Upsilon(RS, u, v) \;=\; (u = w_1, w_2, \ldots, w_j = v),$$

consisting of the vertices through which a message passes from origin u to destination v. We denote the length of this path by $|\Upsilon(RS, u, v)|$. An obvious necessary requirement of any routing scheme is that for every pair of vertices u, v, the route defined in this way indeed reaches v. (In Chapter 26 we will discuss routing schemes based on defining several *partial routing schemes*, which are schemes that specify a successful route only for *some* pairs of vertices in the network, and combining these partial schemes together using a trial and error strategy.)

9.2   Shortest paths routing

In order to be able to evaluate the performance of a routing scheme, it is necessary to quantify the quality of the routes it produces. A major factor in evaluating the efficiency of a routing scheme is the delivery speed of messages. A good routing scheme should be able to estimate the expected delays along different paths and select the better paths for its use. Unfortunately, these delays change dynamically and are not fixed over time. Consequently, the most significant feature of an adaptive routing scheme is its ability to sense changes in the traffic distribution and the load conditions throughout the network and modify the routes accordingly, so that messages in transition avoid congested or disconnected areas of the network. The fact that makes the problem notoriously difficult is that the decisions made by the routing scheme itself directly affect future congestion, and hence delays, on the routes, or in other words, the routing scheme itself creates a feedback reaction in the network.

Typically, the routing subsystem of the network performs periodic updates in the routing scheme. Such an update operation involves two main steps. First, it is necessary to collect some information about the network state, like processor and link operational status, current queue loads and expected traffic loads. The collected data is used to compute the new edge weights. The next step involves deciding on the new routes and setting up the information tables accordingly. In the framework of this text, we do not concern ourselves with precisely how the link costs are determined. Rather, we concentrate on the second step of setting up a routing scheme once the costs of using each edge are determined.

This adaptive approach to routing imposes several inherent requirements on the routing schemes. In particular, since the entire approach revolves on the ability to compute and attach *varying* costs to the edges, it follows that our routing schemes cannot be restricted to unweighted graphs, but rather must be able to handle arbitrary edge costs (as well as arbitrary network topologies).

Let us now formalize the notion of routing efficiency using edge weights. The cost of using a link e is represented via the weight function $\omega(e)$ associated with e, reflecting the estimated link delay for a message transmitted over that link. In accordance with our earlier definitions, the cost of routing a message along a given path is simply the sum of the costs of the transmissions performed during the routing. Also, we denote the cost of routing a message from u to v by the scheme RS by $\mathsf{Comm}(RS, u, v)$. Intuitively, this communication cost can be thought of as represented by the weighted length of the *route* produced by the scheme, $|\Upsilon(RS, u, v)|$. This interpretation may be misleading though, as more sophisticated schemes may be doing things other than just forwarding the message directly, e.g., consult certain databases for routing information and so on, and the costs of these steps should be taken into account as well.

Many common routing schemes insist on always routing messages along shortest paths, given the link weights. We refer to routing schemes imposing this natural requirement as *shortest path routing* schemes.

Designing a shortest path routing scheme is composed of two components, namely,

(a) computing the shortest routes and

(b) storing information at the different network sites enabling the processors to use these routes for message routing.

The task of computing the shortest paths given the edge weights, and subsequently changing the paths whenever these weights change, can be performed using a dynamic variant of the shortest paths (Bellman–Ford style) algorithm discussed in Chapter 5. This algorithm was presented for the unweighted case, but it can easily be modified to handle the weighted case as well. It is also clear that this algorithm is suitable for online, dynamic implementation in which the processors continuously modify the selected shortest paths as the edge weights change over time. We shall not discuss this variant of the problem any further, although a fair number of variants (with different properties) were discussed in the literature.

Storing the routes: Full tables routing schemes

As for the second component, perhaps the most straightforward and commonly used approach for implementing a shortest-paths routing scheme is the *full tables* routing scheme, denoted by FTR, which operates as follows.

Data structures: Store a complete routing table in each vertex v in the network. Given an n-processor network G, a full tables scheme for G is constructed by specifying the port functions it uses. The port function F_v, stored at the vertex v, is specified as a complete table of $n-1$ entries, with one entry for each of the $n-1$ possible destinations $u \neq v$, listing the exit port to be used for forwarding a message to u. (See Figure 9.1.) The pointers with respect to a fixed destination u are set up in such a way that they form a tree of shortest paths from the vertex u, based on the edge costs.

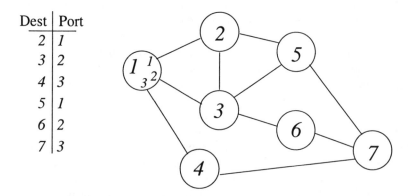

Figure 9.1: An example network with a possible routing table for vertex 1 in it.

Forwarding protocol: Whenever a vertex u needs to forward a message MSG to a destination v whose label is $Label(v)$, it decides on the exit port i to be used by consulting the entry corresponding to i in the table F_u.

This approach guarantees shortest routes and hence optimal communication cost, namely, $\mathsf{Comm}(RS, u, v) = |\Upsilon(RS, u, v)| = dist_G(u, v)$.

9.3   Compact routing

The two distinctive characteristics of (shortest-paths) full tables routing schemes are optimal route efficiency on the one hand and high memory costs on the other. We now consider a more general class of solutions, allowing also sub-optimal (i.e., nonshortest) routes. The motivation behind such solutions is that generating and using them may potentially demand substantially less of the network memory resources.

While message delivery speed is the most dominant performance parameter the routing scheme design should take into account, the space used for the routing tables is also a significant consideration. There are a number of reasons for minimizing the memory requirements of a routing scheme. The task of routing is usually performed by a special-purpose processor which may have limited resources. Furthermore, it is usually desirable that the routing tables be kept in fast memory (e.g., a "cache") in order to expedite message traffic, and such memory is usually more expensive. Also, we do not want memory requirements to grow fast with the size of the network, since it means that the incorporation of new vertices to the network requires adding hardware to all the vertices in the network. It is therefore interesting to search for routing schemes that involve small communication cost and have low space requirements.

9.3.1 Quality measures

In order to enable us to evaluate and compare schemes of this type, we need to define appropriate quality measures. The efficiency of a route provided by the routing scheme RS is measured in terms of its *dilation factor*, which in this context takes the meaning of the ratio between the communication cost of routing a message from the origin u to the destination v using the scheme, $\mathsf{Comm}(RS, u, v)$, and the cheapest possible cost for passing a message from this origin to this destination, namely, $dist(u, v)$. The dilation of the scheme is the maximum such ratio over all possible origin-destination pairs. Formally, we make the following definition.

Definition 9.3.1 [Routing dilation]: *Given a routing scheme RS for an n-processor network $G = (V, E)$, we say that RS dilates the path from u to v (for every $u, v \in V$) by*

$$\mathsf{Dilation}(RS, u, v) \;=\; \frac{\mathsf{Comm}(RS, u, v)}{dist(u, v)} .$$

Define the maximum dilation factor *of the routing scheme RS on the network G to be*

$$\mathsf{Dilation}(RS, G) \;=\; \max_{u, v \in V} \{\mathsf{Dilation}(RS, u, v)\}.$$

Let us now turn to the memory requirements of the routing schemes under consideration. Formally speaking, it suffices to use the definitions of Chapter 2, but to make it more concrete, let us spell out the definition for a routing scheme.

Definition 9.3.2 [Memory requirement]: *The* memory requirement *of a vertex v labeled $Label(v)$ under the routing scheme RS, denoted $\mathsf{Mem}(v, RS)$, is the number of memory bits required to store the label $Label(v)$ and the functions I_v, H_v and F_v in the local memory of the processor. The* total memory requirement *of the routing scheme RS is*

$$\mathsf{Mem}(RS) \;=\; \sum_{v \in V} \mathsf{Mem}(v, RS).$$

In many routing schemes, different vertices may play different roles and require different amounts of space. For instance, some vertices may be designated as *communication centers*, while others may just happen to be the crossing point of many routes which are maintained by the scheme. Such vertices may be required to store more information than others and consequently should be equipped with additional memory in advance.

When the routing scheme is static, and tailored to the availability of appropriate resources at specific vertices in advance, this creates no problems and in fact may help to yield routing schemes with low *total* memory requirements. However, in a dynamic routing scheme, vertices may be required to change roles from time to time. Ideally, it is preferable if these roles can be assigned to vertices on the basis of the current system load status, depending on the present edge costs. In other words, it is desirable in principle to allow any vertex to play any role in the scheme. This forces *every* vertex to have sufficient memory for performing the *most demanding* role in the scheme, rendering the bound on average (or total) space meaningless.

Therefore we will strive to achieve schemes ensuring *balanced* memory requirements, i.e., guaranteeing a bound on the *worst-case* (rather than average or total) memory requirements of each vertex.

Definition 9.3.3 [Maximal memory requirement]: *The* maximal memory requirement *of the routing scheme RS is*

$$\mathsf{Max\_Mem}(RS) \;=\; \max_{v \in V}\{\mathsf{Mem}(v, RS)\}.$$

In view of the two performance parameters discussed above, one basic goal in large-scale communication networks is the design of routing schemes that produce efficient routes and have low memory requirements. We will define the concept of a *routing strategy* as formalizing the idea of a methodology for producing routing schemes for every network.

Definition 9.3.4 [Routing strategy]: *A* routing strategy *is an algorithm that computes a routing scheme RS for every given (weighted) network $G = (V, E, \omega)$. A routing strategy has dilation factor κ if for every network G it produces a scheme RS such that $\mathsf{Dilation}(RS, G) \le \kappa$. The memory requirement of a routing strategy (as a function of n) is the maximum, over all n-vertex networks, of the memory requirements of the routing schemes it produces.*

9.3.2   Two basic solutions

To illustrate the cost measures defined above, let us look at two extreme types of routing schemes. The first type is a routing scheme based on *flooding*. In this scheme, instead of forwarding a message along a shortest path, the origin simply broadcasts it throughout the entire network. Clearly, this scheme (which does not exactly fit into the formal framework of Section 9.1) requires no routing tables, hence it needs minimal ($O(\log n)$ bit) memory requirements. On the other hand, the communication cost of such a scheme may be significantly higher than optimal, since instead of using just one path, we may be using many (possibly expensive) links. Thus the dilation factor is unbounded.

As an extreme opposite, consider the FTR scheme discussed in the previous section. This scheme uses shortest routes, and hence is communication-optimal (namely, $\mathsf{Dilation}(FTR, G) = 1$ for every network G). On the other hand, the disadvantage of the FTR scheme is that it may be too expensive for large systems, since it requires each vertex to store a very large routing table (of $\Theta(n \log n)$ memory bits).

Thus these two example strategies set two extreme endpoints of a possible trade-off between communication cost and memory requirements.

Note that a shortest-paths routing scheme can sometimes be achieved in a rather straightforward manner and at near-optimal costs. This holds in many simple cases and specifically when the network is unweighted (i.e., all edge costs are assumed to be 1) and its topology is simple.

Example: *The unweighted ring.*

Consider the unit cost n-vertex ring. A shortest-paths routing scheme can be implemented on the ring in a straightforward way by labeling the vertices consecutively with labels $0, \ldots, n-1$ and routing from i to j along the shorter of the two ring segments connecting them (which can be easily inferred from the labels i, j). This clearly yields dilation 1 (optimal routes) and requires only $2 \log n$ memory bits per vertex (i.e., each vertex needs to store its own label and n).   □

9.3.3 Name-based routing schemes

At this point, it may be useful to pause for a moment and discuss the need for the *routing labels* component of our routing schemes. Our definition of a routing scheme allows the scheme to impose a routing label on each of the vertices of the network, and the processors are required to use these labels for routing purposes. Two alternatives were mentioned earlier. A potentially simpler approach is to rely on the pre-existing processor identifiers supplied by the hardware level. The second, more "user-friendly" approach would be to attempt to design the scheme in such a way that it allows the sender of a message to refer to the destination by its *name*, where site names may be chosen by each of the sites for themselves. The difficulty with these two approaches is that it might be much harder to devise a routing scheme if it is required to support such "name-based" mailing. The imposed routing labels are thus intended to serve as a means of introducing some order into the site name domain and to reflect the "geographical" structure of the network to some extent. Exploiting the labels to capture information on the network topology (and, specifically, on the location of each site within the network) may be used to support more efficient routing. We may think of this latter form of address specification as a "geography-based" mailing system.

To illustrate this point, suppose that the vertices of a ring are given arbitrary identifiers (say, by taking some permutation of $\{1, \ldots, n\}$) and the routing scheme is required to allow "name-based" mailing. It is easy to see that if the routing scheme is additionally required to achieve a dilation factor of 1, then it is forced to use a full routing table at each vertex, hence its maximal memory complexity (per vertex) is $\Omega(n \log n)$. (See Exercise 3.) Interestingly, constant dilation can be achieved with minimal memory requirements per vertex. (See Exercise 4.)

Of course, user-friendliness is a highly desirable feature and, usually, a higher level software system should provide this necessary abstraction and allow users to use more meaningful site names. Elaborate "name server" mechanisms must then be employed in order to bridge between the external (user defined) and internal (system defined) routing labels.

9.4 Deadlock-free routing

We conclude this chapter with a discussion of another fundamental issue concerning the routing problem, namely, *deadlocks*, and their avoidance using *deadlock-free routing schemes*. Overcoming store-and-forward deadlocks is one of the major problems in the design of routing protocols for communication networks. Informally, a store-and-forward deadlock occurs at some set N of vertices when all the buffers of these vertices are full and each of the messages occupying these buffers needs to be forwarded to some other vertex in the set N. Clearly, then, all of these messages are locked in a vicious circle, since the only way to forward a message is to have a free buffer in the next vertex on its route and the only way to release a buffer is to forward the message currently occupying it. (See Figure 9.2.) Avoidance or fast resolution of such store-and-forward deadlocks is essential for efficient utilization of available network resources.

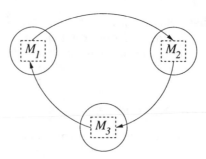

Figure 9.2: An example for a store-and-forward deadlock.

9.4.1   The buffer-class approach

In this section we concentrate on one approach to deadlock prevention known as the *buffer-class* approach. This approach involves solutions based on dividing the buffer pool into buffer classes and utilizing these classes so as to prevent cyclic waiting chains. Some of these solutions are based on restricting the family of allowed routes in order to avoid deadlocks.

In order to discuss routing at this level, we need to extend the definition of a routing scheme so that it specifies, for a given header of a message MSG currently stored at the vertex v and directed to vertex u, not only the *exit port* to be used (hence the neighbor to which it should be passed), but also the specific buffer $B_i(w)$ into which the message will be placed at w. The routing decision may possibly rely on the buffer $B_j(v)$ in which the message is currently placed at v. In fact, such a scheme may be allowed to include also *internal* routing steps, in which the message is passed from one buffer to another in the same vertex v. Consequently, the description of a route should be expanded to detail not only the identifiers of the intermediate vertices, $(u = w_1, w_2, \ldots, w_j = v)$, but also the buffers used along the way, $(B_{i_1}(w_1), \ldots, B_{i_j}(w_j))$. We refer to this expanded version of a routing scheme as a *buffer-routing scheme* and denote it by RS^B.

In order to formalize this approach, let us define the concept of the *buffer graph* corresponding to a given buffer-routing scheme RS^B. Suppose that each vertex v has k buffers, denoted $B_1(v), \ldots, B_k(v)$. The graph $\mathcal{B}(RS^B) = (V_{\mathcal{B}}, E_{\mathcal{B}})$ is a directed graph defined as follows. Its vertices are the buffers in the network

$$V_{\mathcal{B}} \;=\; \{B_i(v) \mid v \in V,\ 1 \le i \le k\}.$$

The edge set $E_{\mathcal{B}}$ contains a directed edge from B to B' iff there is a route in RS^B in which a message is moved from B to B' in one of the steps along the route.

Buffers are often considered in the literature as grouped into classes, with the collection of buffers $\{B_i(v) \mid v \in V\}$ referred to as the *i*th *buffer class*.

The major observation on which this approach is based is the following.

Lemma 9.4.1 *If the graph* $\mathcal{B}(RS^B)$ *is acyclic, then the routing scheme* RS^B *is deadlock-free.*   □

Rather than developing specific strategies for designing deadlock-free buffer-routing schemes, a promising alternative would be to come up with a general technique of starting with a known routing scheme RS and expanding its specification into a buffer-routing scheme RS^B in such a way that the resulting scheme is guaranteed to be deadlock-free. In view of Lemma 9.4.1, one particular way of doing so would be to ensure that the corresponding buffer graph is acyclic. We next describe two general methods for transforming routing schemes into deadlock-free buffer-routing schemes.

9.4.2 Individual buffer-routing

Let RS be a shortest-paths routing scheme for the network $G = (V, E)$, where $V = \{v_1, \ldots, v_n\}$. Fix $k = n$ (i.e., each vertex v will have n buffers $B_i(v)$ for $1 \leq i \leq n$). Expand RS into RS^B by requiring a message whose destination is vertex v_i to use buffer $B_i(w)$ in every vertex w along its route. In other words, all messages directed at v_i will travel in "private" buffers dedicated to v_i.

The fact that the routes of RS use shortest paths ensures the following.

Lemma 9.4.2 *The resulting buffer graph $\mathcal{B}$ is acyclic.* □

Corollary 9.4.3 *The individual routing scheme is deadlock-free.* □

9.4.3 Increasing class buffer-routing

We now describe another general method for transforming routing schemes into deadlock-free buffer-routing schemes, with slightly better buffer utilization. Let RS be a shortest-paths routing scheme for the network G. Fix $k = Diam(G) + 1$. Note that for every $u, v \in V$, the route

$$\Upsilon(RS, u, v) = (u = w_1, w_2, \ldots, w_j = v)$$

consists of at most $Diam(G)$ links. Expand RS into RS^B by requiring a message originated at vertex v to start its way in buffer $B_1(v)$, and for every transition from u to w along its route, if the message is stored at $B_i(u)$ in u, then it must enter $B_{i+1}(w)$ in w. In other words, the buffers visited by any message routed on the network must belong to strictly increasing classes.

Note that the expansion is valid in the sense that it defines a legal entry buffer for every message transition, given the bound of $Diam(G)$ on the number of buffers needed for the longest route. We make the following observation.

Lemma 9.4.4 *The resulting buffer graph $\mathcal{B}$ is acyclic.* □

Corollary 9.4.5 *The increasing class routing scheme is deadlock-free.* □

Bibliographical notes

Extensive and thorough treatment of routing, distributed shortest-path computation and topology update can be found in a fair number of sources, including [Tan81, BG92, Lyn95, Tel94]. Those treatments cover a host of aspects not dealt with here, such as dynamic variants, fault-tolerance and fault recovery, guaranteeing various other desirable properties and so on.

Deadlock-free routing has also been extensively studied in the literature. Some deadlock-free routing schemes include [G81, Gop85, MS80, GMS77, Sch91]. The general concept of relying on buffer classes for preventing cyclic waiting chains has been used in [Gop85, MS80, TU81, BC89]

Exercises

1. Is it possible, using our definition of a routing scheme, that the same scheme may be used for two different (nonisomorphic) n-vertex networks? What if the routing scheme is also required to yield shortest routes? Prove your answers.

2. Describe an optimal routing scheme RS (with Dilation(RS) = 1 and Max_Mem(RS) = $O(\log n)$) for the unweighted $\sqrt{n}$ by $\sqrt{n}$ 2-dimensional n-vertex grid and for the unweighted d-dimensional n-vertex hypercube (for $n = 2^d$).

3. Prove that for an n-vertex unweighted ring with arbitrary vertex identifiers, any name-based routing scheme RS achieving Dilation(RS) = 1 must have Max_Mem(RS) = $\Omega(n)$.

4. (a) Describe a name-based routing scheme RS for the n-vertex unweighted ring with arbitrary vertex identifiers that achieves Dilation(RS) = $O(1)$ using only Max_Mem(RS) = $O(\log n)$.

   (b) Modify your scheme so that it applies also to a weighted ring (with arbitrary edge weights), and analyze the increase in memory requirements.

5. Describe a name-based routing scheme RS for the unweighted $\sqrt{n}$ by $\sqrt{n}$ 2-dimensional n-vertex grid with arbitrary vertex identifiers that uses only Max_Mem(RS) = $O(\log n)$ and guarantees Comm(RS, u, v) = $O(dist^2(u, v))$.

6. Prove Lemmas 9.4.1, 9.4.2 and 9.4.4.

Chapter 10

Local queries and local resource finding

10.1 Local queries

Distributed systems often make use of *directory servers*, enabling the storage and retrieval of global information in the network. The main activity of such a directory is to make data generated by some processors available to all other processors. In this chapter we examine a number of examples for such directories.

10.1.1 Single-shot local queries

As a motivating example, let us consider the problem of responding to queries regarding the value of a certain function on some data stored by the processors of the network. Specifically, we focus on cases where the data sought by a query is of a *local* nature. This can be formalized as follows.

Definition 10.1.1 [ρ-local query]: *Suppose that each vertex v in the network stores a variable X_v containing some data. A ρ-local query issued by some vertex u is of the form* $\text{QUERY}(f, \rho, u)$, *and its response should be the value of the function f on the data values of the vertices in the ρ-neighborhood of u, $f(\mathcal{X}_\rho(u))$, where $\mathcal{X}_\rho(u) = \{X_v \mid v \in \Gamma_\rho(u)\}$.*

In case f is a semigroup function (as defined in Section 3.4.2), such as maximum or addition, this query can be answered by a two phase algorithm. The first phase constructs a BFS tree $BFS_\rho(u)$ for the subgraph induced by $\Gamma_\rho(u)$. In the synchronous model, this can be done using flooding restricted to distance ρ. In the asynchronous model, we can use a variant of Algorithm DIST_DIJK described in Section 5.2, again restricted to depth ρ. Namely, the algorithm will perform exactly ρ phases, thus growing the first ρ layers of the BFS tree around u, and then terminate. The second phase convergecasts the value of f on the tree back to u using Procedure CONVERGE(f, X).

The time complexity of this algorithm for answering ρ-local queries is $O(\rho)$ in the synchronous model and $O(\rho^2)$ in the asynchronous model. The cost of constructing the BFS clearly dominates the message complexity of the algorithm and it depends on the number of vertices and edges in the subgraph induced by $\Gamma_\rho(u)$, which in the worst case may be $\Omega(n)$ and $\Omega(|E|)$, respectively.

For an arbitrary function, it may be necessary to collect the inputs X_v of all vertices $v \in \Gamma_\rho(u)$ to u and compute the function locally. The costs are still dominated by the BFS construction costs.

10.1.2   Repeated local queries

Let us now turn to the more interesting "dynamic" variant of the problem in which the data stored at the vertices may change from time to time and, occasionally, some vertex u issues the query QUERY(f, ρ, u), which must be answered on the basis of the *current* data values of the vertices in its ρ-neighborhood.

There are a number of ways to handle this case, depending on the characteristics of the specific situation and, in particular, the relative frequency of data changes versus queries. For illustrative purposes, let us consider the following three representative policies which demonstrate a certain trade-off between the message complexities of queries and of the update process performed whenever data values change (by invoking an UPDATE operation), as well as their memory requirements.

Update-free policy

Clearly, the solutions outlined above for the single-shot case apply for the dynamic case as well. However, notice that in the dynamic case, the BFS construction phase should in fact be performed only once. Moreover, a single BFS tree $BFS(v)$, spanning the entire network, suffices for every vertex v, provided that the layers are clearly "marked" in the sense that each vertex w knows its layer on $BFS(v)$ (i.e., its distance from v) for every v.

The construction of $BFS(v)$ can be done either as a preprocessing stage or upon the very first query issued by v. An even more conservative approach would be to construct $BFS(v)$ gradually, so that after a number of queries by v, the deepest being to depth ρ, the BFS tree around v is already constructed to depth ρ and every subsequent query to a larger depth $\rho' > \rho$ will cause the expansion of the tree to depth ρ'.

Data structures: A tree $BFS(v)$ is constructed in the network for every vertex v.

Query protocol: A query QUERY(f, ρ, v) originated by v is answered by a round of broadcast and convergecast to depth ρ on $BFS(v)$.

Assuming a preconstructed BFS tree, the time complexity of the solution for semigroup functions is $O(\rho)$ and the message complexity is $O(|\Gamma_\rho(u)|)$ (which in the worst-case could be as bad as $\Omega(n)$). For an arbitrary function, the cost of upcasting the inputs of all vertices in $\Gamma_\rho(u)$ to u is $O(|\Gamma_\rho(u)|)$ time and messages in the worst case.

Define the memory requirement of a policy as the total number of memory bits it uses in the processors of the network. Let us assume that the data items X_v require at most B bits each.

Lemma 10.1.2 *Under the update-free policy for ρ-local queries, the time and message complexities of the QUERY operation are $O(n)$ and the time and message complexities of the UPDATE(X_v) operation are 0. The memory requirements of the policy are $O(n \cdot B)$.*

The above approach to solving the problem makes no special effort to exploit the fact that queries are repeated. We therefore refer to this policy as the *update-free* policy. The other two policies presented next are based on a different and rather natural approach, namely, to organize the data in special distributed data structures in order to make the computation more efficient.

Full updates policy

A special case of the problem occurs when the data is *nearly static*, namely, vertices change their data values relatively rarely. In such a case, the efficiency of queries is more significant than that of updates, which makes it reasonable to apply the *full updates* policy.

Data structures: The data structures stored under this policy depend on whether ρ is assumed to be fixed or not.

    Fixed ρ: A tree $BFS_\rho(v)$ is constructed in the network for every vertex v. In addition, for every vertex u, all the data items of the set $\mathcal{X}_\rho(u)$ are stored at u.

    Arbitrary ρ: The same as fixed ρ, except with ρ set to $Diam(G)$. Namely, a tree $BFS(v)$ is constructed for every vertex v and every vertex u stores the data items of all the vertices.

Query protocol: Answer queries locally.

Update protocol: Again, the protocol depends on whether ρ is fixed or not.

    Fixed ρ: Whenever some value X_v changes, the vertex v must update all vertices u in its ρ-neighborhood $\Gamma_\rho(v)$, by broadcasting the updated X_v over the tree $BFS_\rho(v)$.

    Arbitrary ρ: The same as fixed ρ, except with ρ set to $Diam(G)$.

    The extensive update policy incurs high communication overheads, but on the other hand it allows queries to be processed locally with no communication costs at all. This approach is also expensive memorywise, as in the worst-case it may require each vertex to store $\Omega(n)$ data items.

Lemma 10.1.3 *Under the full updates policy for ρ-local queries, the time and message complexities of the* QUERY *operation are 0 and the time and message complexities of the* UPDATE(X_v) *operation are* $O(n)$. *The memory requirements of the policy are* $O(n^2 \cdot B)$.

Centralized policy

Finally, the *centralized* policy is based on using a single vertex r_0 as a central directory.

Data structures: All data items X_v are stored at r_0.

Query protocol: A query QUERY(f, ρ, v) originated by v is answered by forwarding it to r_0 and getting back the reply.

Update protocol: Whenever some value X_v changes, the vertex v updates r_0.

Lemma 10.1.4 *Under the centralized policy for ρ-local queries, the time and message complexities of both operations are* $O(Diam(G))$. *The memory requirements of the policy are* $O(n \cdot B)$.

10.2   Local resource finding

10.2.1   The problem

Our next example concerns an application system one may call "distributed yellow pages," or "distributed matchmaker," which deals with resource finding in a distributed network. Suppose that the network sites host a collection of "resources" (or "servers") of various types, which come in fixed units. Suppose also that the network hosts a collection of "clients," each residing at some vertex. From time to time, the client in a certain site needs to use a unit (or several units) of a certain type of resource. After the resource is used, it may be released back to the global pool. The matchmaking system has to provide means for enabling prospective clients in need of some service (or resource) to locate the whereabouts of available servers (or resource units) of the appropriate type. Towards that end, the system may establish a *distributed directory* for storing information that may enable efficient searches by the clients and contain a *resource controller* component, which is an algorithm for keeping track of and allocating services (or resource units).

In this setting, too, locality issues may play a key role. When a processor needs a resource unit, it may in many cases find an available unit in many different locations in the network. However, in many natural applications, it is advantageous if the client is able to get the resources it needs from *nearby* locations (subject to availability constraints). Hence our problem is to attempt to ensure the property that nearby servers are considered before distant ones are brought up, and thus the resource controller finds the closest, or one of the closest, available servers. We refer to this variant of the problem as *local resource finding*.

This locality requirement is desirable mainly in the common situation in which the cost of the service depends on the distance between the server and the client. To motivate this point, let us consider two examples. First, suppose that the resource in question is disk storage space. Each site has a fixed size disk, and each processor occasionally needs to store some data files. If it doesn't have local space, it is forced to store its data in a disk residing at some other site. Once the file is stored, it is not transferred (until erased by the user processor). Thus every access to the file requires the user processor to communicate with the storing site. Consequently, it is desirable that the file is stored at the nearest location currently having free disk space.

As a second example consider the task of load balancing. The processors at the different sites may be occupied in running various (system or user-generated) processes. At the same time, some other processors may be idle. From time to time, a new process is spawned at some site. If the local processor is busy, it is necessary to find another processor which is currently idle. Once the process is allocated to a processor, it is not reallocated any further. Thus in order to minimize the cost of communication between the parent (spawning) process and the child (spawned) processes, it is again desirable that the new process is scheduled to run on the nearest available processor.

10.2.2   Formal statement and relevant parameters

Let us formalize the problem for a single type of resource. Every vertex stores, at any given moment, a certain number of resource units. However, as we shall only be interested in whether a particular vertex has any available resources or not, let us model the two situations by associating with every vertex v a *free* bit $F(v)$, set to 1 iff v currently has at least one free resource unit:

$$F(v) = \begin{cases} 1 & \text{if } v \text{ currently has at least one resource unit,} \\ 0 & \text{otherwise.} \end{cases}$$

At any given moment, the configuration of the system is specified by the set of free bits

$$\bar{F} = \{F(v) \mid v \in V\}.$$

A *resource controller* is a distributed algorithm supporting the FIND operation. The instruction FIND(v) can be issued from any vertex v in the network. In response to this instruction, the controller should assign v a free resource unit, from any other (but preferably a nearby) vertex in the network, and inform v of the location of this unit.

In order to perform its role efficiently, the resource controller may include also a *maintenance component* whose task is to maintain a reasonably coherent picture of the current distribution of resources in the network. For that purpose, whenever a vertex v flips its $F(v)$ bit, that vertex is required to issue an UPDATE(v, b) operation indicating that now $F(v) = b$. The maintenance unit may make use of this information in order to update its directories.

For simplicity, we concentrate solely on sequential accesses, that is, we assume that a FIND or UPDATE request is issued only after the controller has completed handling the previous one. Clearly, in order for any solution to be practical, it is required that it handle also concurrent accesses. In fact, the constructions described here can be extended to the concurrent case as well, but we will not discuss this issue.

We now define one central parameter of the problem, dictated by the current configuration.

Definition 10.2.1 [κ-dilated controller]: *Let $D_{server}(v)$ denote the distance from v to the nearest available server, or resource unit:*

$$D_{server}(v) = \min\{dist(v, w) \mid F(w) = 1, \ w \in V\}.$$

A resource controller is called κ-dilated if whenever the instruction FIND(v) is issued from a vertex v, the free resource unit assigned to v by the controller is at distance at most $\kappa \cdot D_{server}(v)$ from v.

Our problem is thus to design an κ-dilated resource controller that is as efficient as possible in the message complexity required for the FIND and UPDATE operations, denoted Message(FIND(v)) and Message(UPDATE(v)), respectively.

10.2.3 Exact solution

We first note that this problem can be reduced to the local query problem, yielding a *query-based* resource controller. This controller operates as follows. The variable X_v stored at each vertex v is set to

$$X_v = \begin{cases} \{ID(v)\} & \text{if } F(v) = 1, \\ \emptyset & \text{otherwise.} \end{cases}$$

The semigroup function f is defined as

$$f(\mathcal{X}_\rho(v)) = \begin{cases} \min\{\bigcup_{v \in \Gamma_\rho(v)} X_v\} & \text{if } \bigvee_{v \in \Gamma_\rho(v)} F(v) = 1, \\ \text{``failure''} & \text{otherwise.} \end{cases}$$

When a processor v wishes to locate the closest resource unit, it successively invokes the query QUERY(f, ρ, v) for range values $\rho = 1, 2, \ldots$ and so on, until reaching the first value of ρ for which the answer is not "failure."

A seemingly more efficient approach would be to perform a binary search on the range of possible ρ values in order to find the minimal value of ρ for which the search does not fail. However, this might prove more expensive in case the complexity of the ρ-local query algorithm chosen for the task is strongly affected by ρ. For instance, some of our query algorithms had complexities depending on the size of the ρ-neighborhood $\Gamma_\rho(v)$. If these neighborhoods grow rapidly with ρ, then a sequential search may be cheaper than a binary search in case the answer is eventually found at some small ρ value.

Hence, every policy for handling local queries should in principle work here as well. However, since local resource finding is an important special case, it may be interesting to obtain better solutions for it than those discussed in the previous section.

10.2.4   Three policies revisited

Let us reconsider the three policies discussed in the previous section. All three policies are easily adapted to the context of resource allocation, yielding a 1-dilated resource controller.

Update-free resource controller

Under the update-free policy, servers do nothing, but clients are required to exhaustively search the network.

Lemma 10.2.2 *The update-free resource controller is 1-dilated. The time and message complexities of its* FIND(v) *operation are* $O(n)$, *and the time and message complexities of its* UPDATE(v, b) *operation are 0. The memory requirements of the policy are* $O(n)$.

Full updates resource controller

Under the full updates policy, each vertex maintains an accurate picture of the network topology and the current distribution of available resource units in it. This requires servers to broadcast an update message throughout the network whenever their status changes (namely, their free bit F flips from 0 to 1 or vice versa). Again, updates are expensive, but clients are allowed to perform searches locally (although they still need to access the resource directly in any case, hence they must pay at least $D_{\text{server}}(v)$).

Lemma 10.2.3 *The full updates resource controller is 1-dilated. The time and message complexities of its* FIND(v) *operation are* $D_{server}(v)$, *and the time and message complexities of its* UPDATE(v, b) *operation are* $O(n)$. *The memory requirements of the policy are* $O(n^2)$.

Centralized resource controller

Using a central directory at a single vertex r_0, updated and consulted by every server and client, yields the following properties.

Lemma 10.2.4 *The centralized resource controller is 1-dilated. The time and message complexities of both operations are* $O(Diam(G))$. *The memory requirements of the policy are* $O(n)$.

10.2.5   The global matching paradigm

The paradigm of *distributed matchmaking* was proposed for establishing connection between clients and servers in a distributed system. Intuitively, a matchmaking system is a specification of rendezvous locations in the network, enabling users to locate and communicate with one another.

Definition 10.2.5 [Global matching]: *The basic components of the global matching construct are two sets of vertices, a* read set Read$(v) \subseteq V$ *and a* write set Write$(v) \subseteq V$, *defined for every vertex* $v \in V$.
  The collection of sets

$$\mathcal{RW} = \{\, \text{Read}(v),\ \text{Write}(v) \mid v \in V \,\}$$

is a global matching *if the read set of a vertex intersects the write set of every other vertex, i.e.,* Write$(v) \bigcap$ Read$(u) \neq \emptyset$ *for all* $v, u \in V$.

We observe that the previous three solutions for local resource finding can be thought of as special cases of global matching structures. This is done by interpreting those solutions as assigning each vertex v a read set and a write set as follows.

The update-free resource controller: Assign, for every vertex v,

$$\text{Read}(v) = V \quad \text{and} \quad \text{Write}(v) = \{v\} \, .$$

The full-updates resource controller: Assign, for every vertex v,

$$\text{Read}(v) = \{v\} \quad \text{and} \quad \text{Write}(v) = V \, .$$

The centralized controller: Assign, for every vertex v,

$$\text{Read}(v) = \text{Write}(v) = \{r_0\} \, .$$

More elaborate global matching schemes will be discussed later on, in Chapter 27.

Bibliographical notes

Directories occur in distributed systems in a wide variety of forms. Typical examples are name servers and topology databases in communication networks, bulletin boards, resource allocation managers, etc. [LEH85, MV88]. Several different approaches to distributed data structures appear in the literature. The survey paper [HR88] covers a representative sample of previous research efforts on distributed data allocation strategies. Most of these strategies treat the case of site-independent data, in which there is no significance to the question of the specific placement of each individual data item, and accessibility is measured in absolute, global terms. Complexity aspects of data structures in such a setting were treated in [Pel89a, Pel91, GP91].

Some work has been done on dependencies among the different data items or attributes. Accordingly, vertical and horizontal data partitioning methods were developed for placing data in optimal ways, relying on the relative affinity between data records and attributes (see [HR88]).

A variety of types of resource allocation problems in distributed networks have been dealt with in the literature (cf. [AAPS96, ADD82, Man86]). Most of those problems do not take the locality issue into account. The resource finding problem discussed here was studied in [MV88] (under the name "distributed matchmaking") and the solutions presented in Section 10.2.4 are presented in that paper along with a number of combinatorial results concerning the problem.

Exercises

1. Give an upper bound on the message complexity of the algorithm given in Section 10.1.1 for ρ-local query computation on a semigroup function f, in case the graph at hand is bounded-degree, with maximum degree Δ.

2. Consider a dynamic local query algorithm as in Section 10.1.2. Suppose that the algorithm only has to support ρ-local queries for $\rho \leq \rho_0$ for some fixed integer $\rho_0 \geq 1$. Suppose further that the stream of updates and queries entering the system consists of a p-fraction of updates and a $(1-p)$-fraction of queries for some fixed $0 < p < 1$. For which values of p is the full-update policy preferable to the update-free policy in terms of the total expected message complexity?

3. Devise an $O(1)$-dilated resource controller for the n-vertex unweighted ring with $\text{Message}(\text{UPDATE}(v)) = 0$ and $\text{Message}(\text{FIND}(v)) = O(D_{\text{server}}(v))$.

Part II

Locality-preserving representations

Chapter 11

Clustered representations:
Clusters, covers and partitions

We now temporarily put aside distributed network algorithms and turn to discussing LP-graph representations. We begin this part by focusing on the first type of LP-representations, namely, cluster-based representations. Later, in Chapters 15–18 we turn to skeletal representations, and finally, in Chapter 19 we discuss also a third type of network representation, based on vertex labelings.

This chapter introduces the basic concepts of locality-preserving clustered representations and presents the terminology and notation used throughout the discussion of those representations and their properties.

11.1   The graph model

We consider an arbitrary weighted graph $G = (V, E, \omega)$, where V is the set of vertices, $E \subseteq V \times V$ is the set of edges and $\omega : E \to R^+$ is a *weight* function, assigning a nonnegative weight $\omega(e)$ to every edge $e \in E$. The weights are assumed to satisfy the triangle inequality. Usually, this causes no loss of generality, since an edge whose weight exceeds that of some alternate path connecting its two endpoints can be replaced by that path for many practical purposes. We may occasionally restrict ourselves to unweighted graphs by assuming that $\omega(e) = 1$ for every edge $e \in E$. Such a graph is denoted $G = (V, E)$. We usually denote $n = |V|$. When discussing an unspecified graph G', we may refer to its vertex and edge sets by $V(G')$ and $E(G')$, respectively.

11.2   Clusters, covers and partitions

11.2.1   Clusters

Clusters are naturally the most basic concept in our discussion of locality-preserving clustered representations of graphs. A cluster is essentially a collection of vertices in the graph. However, we are also interested in the topological connections among the vertices in the cluster. Given a set of vertices $S \subseteq V$, let $G(S)$ denote the subgraph induced by S in G, namely, $G(S) = (S, E')$, where E' consists of all the edges of G whose endpoints both belong to S. In what follows we may sometimes interchange S with its induced subgraph $G(S)$.

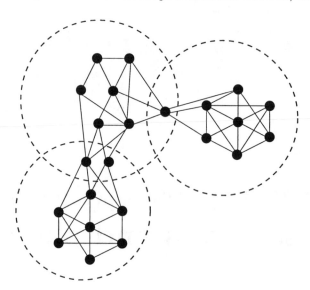

Figure 11.1: A graph $G = (V, E)$ and a cover for it.

Definition 11.2.1 [Cluster]: *A cluster is a subset of vertices $S \subseteq V$ in G, such that the subgraph $G(S)$ induced by it is connected.*

We use clusters and clustering techniques in order to represent the original graph in useful ways. Naturally, we would like these representations to capture the inherent locality relationships in the graph. Therefore it is useful for our purposes to think of clusters as not just any connected subgraphs, but ones typically composed of all (or at least many) vertices in a certain region of the graph. For example, suppose we would like to find a useful representation for the 2-dimensional grid. Although a path is technically a cluster, a representation based on the collection of all row-paths and all column-paths in the grid will usually be unsatisfactory for our purposes, and we shall typically prefer to use a representation based on square subgrids.

11.2.2   Covers and partitions

The basic graph representations we consider are composed of collections of clusters with certain useful properties. Throughout we denote clusters by capital P, Q, R, etc. and collections of clusters by calligraphic type, $\mathcal{P}, \mathcal{Q}, \mathcal{R}$, etc. For a collection $\mathcal{S}$ of clusters, let $\bigcup \mathcal{S}$ denote $\bigcup_{S \in \mathcal{S}} S$.

Definition 11.2.2 [Cover]: *A cover of the graph $G = (V, E, \omega)$ is a collection of clusters $\mathcal{S} = \{S_1, \ldots, S_m\}$ that contain all the vertices of the graph, i.e., such that $\bigcup \mathcal{S} = V$.*

Definition 11.2.3 [Partition]: *A partial partition of G is a collection of disjoint clusters $\mathcal{S} = \{S_1, \ldots, S_m\}$, i.e., with the property that $S \cap S' = \emptyset$ for every $S, S' \in \mathcal{S}$.*

A partition of G is a collection of clusters $\mathcal{S}$ that is both a cover and a partial partition. Figures 11.1 and 11.2 illustrate a cover and a partition for a given graph G, respectively.

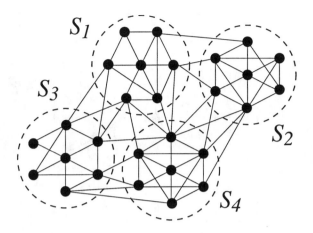

Figure 11.2: A graph $G = (V, E)$ and a partition for it.

11.2.3 Evaluation criteria

There are two basic types of qualitative criteria that are of interest for cluster design. The first type involves criteria for measuring the *locality level* of the clusters, while the second type of criteria applies to a collection of clusters and attempts to capture the *sparsity level* of the clusters in the collection. These qualitative criteria have concrete technical manifestations in terms of parameters for evaluating cluster-based representations. In particular, the locality level of a cluster is usually measured by its radius (and sometimes by its size, or "volume"). There are several plausible definitions for the parameter of cover sparsity (or overlap), usually relying on the *degrees* of vertices or clusters in either the cover, the graph itself or the induced cluster graph.

An important property of the parameters of locality and sparsity is that they tend to go opposite ways. Indeed, many of the representations discussed hereafter exhibit a trade-off between the two parameters: better sparsity typically implies worse locality and vice versa.

We next give more precise definitions for these parameters.

11.3 Locality measures and neighborhoods

11.3.1 Cluster radius and diameter

The locality level of a cluster is usually measured by distance parameters. In particular, cluster radii and diameters are defined based on their induced subgraph.

Definition 11.3.1 [Cluster radius and diameter]: *For a vertex $v \in S$, we define the radius of S w.r.t. v as in the induced subgraph $G(S)$, namely,*

$$Rad(v, S) = Rad(v, G(S)) = \max_{w \in S}\{dist_{G(S)}(v, w)\}.$$

Similarly we use $Rad(S)$ and $Diam(S)$ as a shorthand for $Rad(G(S))$ and $Diam(G(S))$.
Given a collection of clusters $\mathcal{S}$, let $Diam(\mathcal{S}) = \max_i\{Diam(S_i)\}$ and $Rad(\mathcal{S}) = \max_i\{Rad(S_i)\}$.

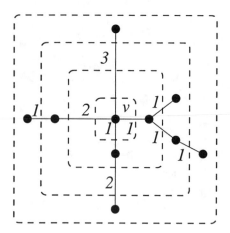

Figure 11.3: The neighborhoods $\Gamma_0(v)$, $\Gamma_1(v)$, $\Gamma_2(v)$ and $\Gamma_3(v)$ of a vertex v in a weighted graph.

11.3.2   Neighborhoods

In light of our approach to measuring cluster locality, one of the most natural and useful types of clusters are vertex neighborhoods. However, it is important to note that in weighted graphs, there are (at least) two distinct notions of neighborhoods. In particular, note that the notion of ρ-neighborhoods as defined in Section 2.1.2 applies also to weighted graphs, with distances defined in the weighted sense, but in this setting it no longer corresponds to the natural interpretation which holds in the unweighted case. See, for example, Figure 11.3.

Hereafter, we reserve the notation $\Gamma_\rho(v)$ in the sense of the formal definition of Section 2.1.2, with weighted distances. In the few cases where we need to speak about ρ-neighborhoods in the unweighted sense, this will be explicitly stated and we will use the notation $\Gamma_\rho^{un}(v)$, representing the set of vertices at *unweighted* distance ρ or less from v.

In order to be able to handle covers, it is convenient to extend the concept of ρ-neighborhoods to *sets* of vertices as well.

Definition 11.3.2 [ρ-neighborhood cover]: *Given a subset of vertices $W \subseteq V$, the ρ-neighborhood cover of W is the collection of ρ-neighborhoods of the vertices of W, denoted*

$$\hat{\Gamma}_\rho(W) \;=\; \{\Gamma_\rho(v) \mid v \in W\}.$$

In particular, $\hat{\Gamma}_0(V)$ is the partition of G into singleton clusters,

$$\hat{\Gamma}_0(V) \;=\; \{\{v\} \mid v \in V\}.$$

(Later on we sometimes abuse notation by substituting v for $\Gamma_0(v)$ and W for $\hat{\Gamma}_0(W)$.)

11.4   Sparsity measures

11.4.1   Cover sparsity

We use the following measures for the sparsity (or overlap) of a cover $\mathcal{S}$.

Definition 11.4.1 [Maximum degree]: *For every vertex $v \in V$, let $deg_S(v)$ denote the number of occurrences of v in clusters $S \in \mathcal{S}$, i.e., the degree of v in the hypergraph $(V, \mathcal{S})$. The* maximum degree *of a cover $\mathcal{S}$ is defined as*

$$\Delta^C(\mathcal{S}) = \max_{v \in V} \{deg_S(v)\}.$$

In a sense, this measure captures the extent of the overlaps existing between the clusters in the given cover.

In some applications, one may be interested in the average overlap rather than the maximum.

Definition 11.4.2 [Average degree]: *The* average degree *of a cover $\mathcal{S}$ is defined as*

$$\bar{\Delta}(\mathcal{S}) = \frac{1}{n} \cdot \sum_{v \in V} deg_S(v) = \frac{1}{n} \cdot \sum_{S \in \mathcal{S}} |S|.$$

11.4.2 Partition sparsity

For partitions, namely, covers consisting of disjoint clusters, the interaction between clusters involves no *direct* overlap, hence the degree parameter is inappropriate. Instead, we may be interested in several different parameters, based on the neighborhood relations among clusters, or between clusters and individual vertices outside them.

In order to talk about adjacency relations among the clusters of a partition $\mathcal{S}$ in a graph $G = (V, E)$, it is convenient to "contract" each cluster into a single vertex and look at the resulting auxiliary "cluster graph" (either uniting parallel edges or considering the resulting graph as a multigraph). Formally, let the *cluster graph* of $\mathcal{S}$ with respect to G be the (unweighted) graph

$$\tilde{G}(\mathcal{S}) = (\mathcal{S}, \tilde{E}),$$

where

$$\tilde{E} = \{(S, S') \mid S, S' \in \mathcal{S}, \text{ and } G \text{ contains an edge } (u, v) \text{ for } u \in S \text{ and } v \in S'\}.$$

The edges of $\tilde{E}$ are often referred to as *intercluster edges*.

Example: *Cluster graph.*

The cluster graph $\tilde{G}(\mathcal{S})$ for the partition $\mathcal{S}$ from Figure 11.2 is given in Figure 11.4. $\quad\square$

Definition 11.4.3 [Vertex- and cluster-neighborhood]: *Given a partition $\mathcal{S}$, a cluster $S \in \mathcal{S}$ and an integer $\rho \geq 0$, let us define the ρ-vertex-neighborhood of S as the union of the ρ-neighborhoods of the vertices in S,*

$$\Gamma_\rho^v(S, G) = \bigcup_{v \in S} \Gamma_\rho(v, G),$$

and the ρ-cluster-neighborhood of S as the ρ-neighborhood of S in the cluster graph $\tilde{G}(\mathcal{S})$,

$$\Gamma_\rho^c(S, G) = \Gamma_\rho(S, \tilde{G}(\mathcal{S})).$$

Figure 11.5 illustrates the vertex-neighborhood and the cluster-neighborhood of the cluster S_3 in the partition $\mathcal{S}$ from Figure 11.2.

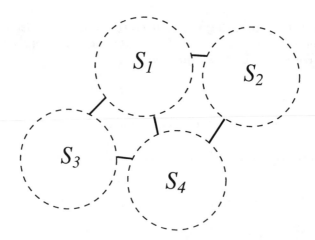

Figure 11.4: The cluster graph $\tilde{G}(\mathcal{S})$ corresponding to the partition $\mathcal{S}$ from Figure 11.2.

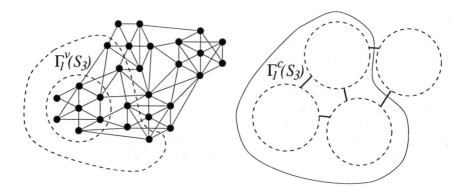

Figure 11.5: The vertex-neighborhood and the cluster-neighborhood of the cluster S_3 in the partition $\mathcal{S}$ from Figure 11.2.

Now, to estimate overlaps we employ the following measures.

Definition 11.4.4 [Vertex- and cluster-degree]:   *The maximum and average vertex-degree and cluster-degree of the partition $\mathcal{S}$ are defined, based on the various 1-neighborhood notions presented earlier, as*

$$\Delta^C_v(\mathcal{S}) = \max_{S \in \mathcal{S}}\left\{\frac{|\Gamma^v(S)|}{|S|}\right\}, \qquad \bar{\Delta}_v(\mathcal{S}) = \frac{1}{n} \cdot \sum_{S \in \mathcal{S}} |\Gamma^v(S)|,$$

$$\Delta^C_c(\mathcal{S}) = \max_{S \in \mathcal{S}}\left\{\frac{|\Gamma^c(S)|}{|S|}\right\}, \qquad \bar{\Delta}_c(\mathcal{S}) = \frac{1}{n} \cdot \sum_{S \in \mathcal{S}} |\Gamma^c(S)|.$$

In particular, note that $|\tilde{E}| = \frac{1}{2}\sum_{S \in \mathcal{S}}(|\Gamma^c(S)| - 1) \approx n\bar{\Delta}_c(\mathcal{S})/2$ or, in other words, optimizing $\bar{\Delta}_c(\mathcal{S})$ is equivalent (up to a constant) to optimizing the number of intercluster edges in the partition.

One may wonder at this point why $\Delta^C_v(\mathcal{S})$, for instance, is defined as normalized by cluster size, rather than as simply $\Delta^C_v(\mathcal{S}) = \max_{S \in \mathcal{S}}\{|\Gamma^v(S)|\}$. As usual, the answer is a mixture of "this turns out to be useful in various applications" and "the parameter's behavior becomes uninteresting otherwise." (See, for example, Exercise 4 in Chapter 13.)

Let us remark that our version of a cluster graph is unweighted (even when the original graph G was weighted). In fact, most of the techniques introduced later for constructing useful partitions of a given graph (with the exception of Chapter 18) apply to unweighted graphs only.

11.5   Example: A basic construction

Before we proceed, let us illustrate the concepts discussed so far by describing a simple basic construction for a sparse partition for a given unweighted graph $G = (V, E)$ and parameter $\kappa \geq 1$. The goal of the construction is to produce a partition $\mathcal{S}$ with clusters of radius at most κ and with a small number of intercluster edges (i.e., with low $\bar{\Delta}_c(\mathcal{S})$). The construction exhibits a trade-off between the parameter κ and the resulting sparsity, which is typical of virtually all of our later constructions.

The general structure of Algorithm BASIC_PART(G, κ) is as follows. The algorithm operates in iterations, with each iteration constructing one cluster. The iteration begins by arbitrarily picking a vertex v from V and growing the cluster by adding layers around it, one layer at a time (see Figure 11.6). The vertices added to the cluster S are subsequently discarded from V. The merging process is carried out repeatedly until reaching the required sparsity condition, namely, until the next iteration increases the number of vertices merged into S by a factor of less than $n^{1/\kappa}$. The algorithm then adds the resulting cluster S to the output collection $\mathcal{S}$, and then a new iteration is started. These iterations proceed until V is exhausted. The algorithm then outputs the set $\mathcal{S}$.

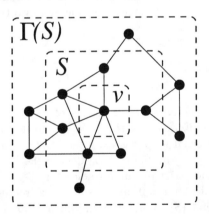

Figure 11.6: A layer-merging step in the iteration of Algorithm BASIC_PART constructing cluster S.

A formal description of the algorithm is given in Figure 11.7.

Theorem 11.5.1 [Partition]: *Given an n-vertex unweighted graph $G = (V, E)$ and an integer $\kappa \geq 1$, Algorithm BASIC_PART constructs a partition $\mathcal{S}$ that satisfies the following properties:*

(1) $\text{Rad}(\mathcal{S}) \leq \kappa - 1$, and

(2) The cluster graph $\tilde{G}(\mathcal{S})$ has at most $n^{1+1/\kappa}$ intercluster edges (or, $\bar{\Delta}_c(\mathcal{S}) \leq n^{1/\kappa}$).

Set $S \leftarrow \emptyset$.

While $V \neq \emptyset$ **do:**

    1. Select an arbitrary vertex $v \in V$.

    2. Set $S \leftarrow \{v\}$.

    3. **While** $|\Gamma^v(S)| > n^{1/\kappa}|S|$ **do:**

        Set $S \leftarrow \Gamma(S)$.

    End-while

    4. Set $\mathcal{S} \leftarrow \mathcal{S} \cup \{S\}$ and $V \leftarrow V - S$.

End-while
Output $(\mathcal{S})$.

Figure 11.7: Algorithm BASIC_PART(G, κ).

Proof: First note that every set S added to $\mathcal{S}$ is a (connected) cluster. Moreover, the clusters generated by the procedure are clearly disjoint, as the procedure erases from V every vertex added to the cluster under construction, so this vertex cannot be added to another cluster in the future.

Property (2) is now derived as follows. It is immediate from the termination condition of the internal loop that the resulting set S satisfies $|\Gamma^v(S)| \leq n^{1/\kappa}|S|$. Therefore the number of intercluster edges touching S is at most $n^{1/\kappa}|S|$. This number can only decrease as a result of later iterations, as adjacent vertices get merged into the same clusters. Thus

$$|\tilde{E}| \leq \sum_{S \in \mathcal{S}} n^{1/\kappa}|S| = n^{1+1/\kappa},$$

which proves Property (2).

Finally, we analyze the increase in the radius of clusters in the cover and establish Property (1). Consider some iteration of the main loop of the algorithm, and let J denote the number of times the internal loop was executed. Denote the set S constructed on the ith internal iteration ($1 \leq i \leq J$) by S_i. (Let S_0 denote the initial set $S = \{v\}$.) Note that $|S_i| \geq n^{i/\kappa}$ for $0 \leq i \leq J$ and strict inequality holds for $i \geq 1$. This is shown by induction on i: The claim is immediate for $i = 0$; and assuming correctness for $i - 1 \geq 0$, the claim for i is proved by noting that $|S_i| > n^{1/\kappa}|S_{i-1}|$, which follows directly from the fact that the termination condition of the internal loop was not met.

It follows that $J \leq \kappa - 1$, since otherwise the cardinality of the cluster S would exceed n.

Finally, we note that $Rad(v, S_i) = i$ for every $0 \leq i \leq J$. This follows from the fact that S_0 is composed of a single vertex, and for $1 \leq i \leq J$, we add one layer, so $Rad(v, S_i)$ increases by exactly 1.

Combining the last two observations, we conclude that $Rad(S_J) \leq \kappa - 1$, which completes the proof of Property (1) of the theorem.   □

In many applications, it is necessary not only to construct the partition, but also to assign a representative intercluster edge between any two adjacent clusters, thus defining the cluster graph $\tilde{G}$. In most cases, these intercluster edges can be selected arbitrarily in a straightforward way.

11.6 Some additional variants

Let us finally define some additional variants of the concepts discussed earlier, which will be needed later on.

11.6.1 Separated partial partitions

For partial partitions we are sometimes interested in the *separation* between the clusters.

Definition 11.6.1 [Separation]: *The* separation *of a partial partition S is defined as the minimal distance between any two clusters in S,*

$$\mathrm{Sep}(S) \;=\; \min_{\substack{S,S' \in S \\ S \neq S'}} \Big\{ dist_G(S,S') \Big\}.$$

When $\mathrm{Sep}(S) = s$ we may also say that S is s-separated.

Figure 11.8 illustrates a 2-separated partial partition. Note that in an unweighted or weighted normalized graph (where the smallest edge weight is set to be 1), $\mathrm{Sep}(S)$ is guaranteed to be at least 1 for any partial partition S.

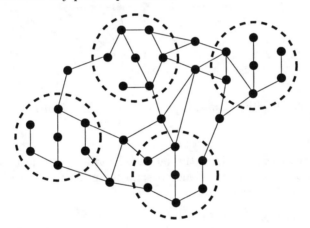

Figure 11.8: A 2-separated partial partition.

11.6.2 Coarsening

The clustering algorithms presented later on for constructing covers are based on the central idea of *coarsening*.

Definition 11.6.2 [Coarsening]: *Given two covers $S = \{S_1, \dots, S_p\}$ and $T = \{T_1, \dots, T_q\}$, we say that T* coarsens *S if the clusters of S are fully subsumed in those of T, i.e., for every $S_i \in S$ there exists a $T_j \in T$ such that $S_i \subseteq T_j$. We refer to the ratio between the respective radii of S and T clusters, $Rad(T)/Rad(S)$, as the* radius ratio *of the coarsening.*

Intuitively, if the cover T coarsens the cover S, then in an algorithm based on the clusters of S, it is possible to use T to functionally replace S. Coarsening is useful when we have a cover S that meets our algorithmic needs but has high cluster overlaps. In such a case, it is possible to coarsen S by merging some of its clusters together. The result is a coarsening cover T that has larger clusters and, we hope, better sparsity. Of course, the

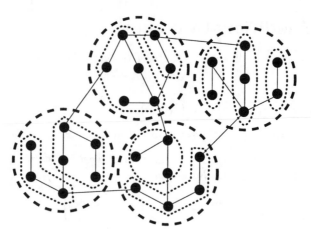

Figure 11.9: A coarsening partition.

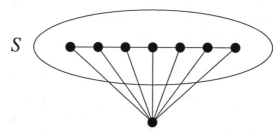

Figure 11.10: A cluster S with $Diam(S)=6$, $Rad(S)=3$, $WDiam(S)=2$ and $WRad(S)=2$.

price for this improved sparsity is in the increased radii of the clusters of T. Later, we present algorithms for coarsening a given cover, attempting to improve its sparsity while maintaining a relatively low radius ratio.

Example: *Coarsening cover/partition.*

The cover depicted in Figure 11.1 coarsens the initial cover $\hat{\Gamma}_0(V)$ (namely, the set of vertices V). Similarly, the partition in Figure 11.2 coarsens $\hat{\Gamma}_0(V)$. Depicted in Figure 11.9 are two partitions, one coarsening the other.   □

11.6.3   Weak clusters

In some cases, we may be interested in a weaker notion of a cluster, allowing disconnected subgraphs to be considered as clusters. This immediately yields also weaker notions of covers and partitions. For example, a weak partition is a partition of the vertices into (not necessarily connected) clusters.

In order to handle weak clusters, it is necessary to generalize the notion of cluster radii and define it based on distances *in the entire graph G*, rather than in the subgraph induced by the cluster. This leads to the following definition of *weak diameters*.

Definition 11.6.3 [Weak radius and diameter]:   *For a vertex $v \in S$, we define the weak radius of S w.r.t. v as the maximal distance in G from v to any other vertex of S, namely,*

$$WRad(v, S) \; = \; WRad(v, G(S)) \; = \; \max_{w \in S}\{dist_G(v, w)\}.$$

We denote

$$WRad(S) \;=\; \min_{v \in S}\{WRad(v, S)\}.$$

The weak diameter $WDiam(S)$ *of a cluster S is defined similarly. Given a collection of clusters $\mathcal{S}$, let $WDiam(\mathcal{S}) = \max_i\{WDiam(S_i)\}$ and $WRad(\mathcal{S}) = \max_i\{WRad(S_i)\}$.*

Note that the center determining $WRad(S)$ must be a vertex of S. These definitions are illustrated in Figure 11.10.

Bibliographical notes

The definitions presented in this chapter mostly follow [AP90c]. The basic partition construction of Section 11.5 is due to [Awe85a], where the concept of sparse partitions was introduced for the first time. Exercise 2 can be found, e.g., in [KP98b].

Exercises

1. Consider an n-vertex planar unweighted graph $G = (V, E)$.

   (a) Prove that the average degree of the 1-neighborhood cover of G satisfies $\bar{\Delta}(\hat{\Gamma}_1(V)) = O(1)$.

   (b) Show that a similar claim cannot hold for the maximum degree of the cover (specifically, give an example of a planar graph G for which $\Delta^C(\hat{\Gamma}_1(V)) = \Omega(n)$).

   (c) Prove or disprove a claim similar to Exercise 1a for the 2-neighborhood cover of G.

   (d) Prove that if G has a partition into m clusters, then this partition has only $O(m)$ intercluster edges.

2. Prove that for every unweighted n-vertex graph G and every integer $k \geq 1$, there exists a partition of G into at most $O(n/k)$ connected clusters of radius at most k.

3. Use Exercises 1d and 2 to state and prove a variant of the Partition Theorem 11.5.1 with better bounds for planar graphs. Demonstrate (via an example) that your bounds are the best possible.

4. When Algorithm BASIC_PART completes the construction of some cluster S, it is guaranteed that $|\Gamma^v(S)| > n^{1/\kappa}|S|$. Yet Theorem 11.5.1 only provides a bound for the *average* cluster degree of the resulting partition $\mathcal{S}$ and makes no claim on $\Delta^C{}_c(\mathcal{S})$. Explain why.

5. Modify Algorithm BASIC_PART so that in addition to the constructed partition, it also selects an edge set $\breve{E}$ as follows. Initially set $\breve{E}$ to $\emptyset$. Whenever completing the construction of a cluster S, for every neighboring vertex $v \in \Gamma^v(S)$, select one edge connecting v to some neighbor w in S and place it in $\breve{E}$. Prove that the resulting set $\breve{E}$ is of cardinality at most $n^{1+1/\kappa}$.

6. Suppose that in the previous exercise we took into the set $\breve{E}$ *every* edge $e = (v, w) \in E$ connecting vertices $v \in S$ and $w \notin S$.

   (a) Explain why the bound on the cardinality of $\breve{E}$ no longer holds.

   (b) Give a variant of the algorithm guaranteeing that the resulting set $\breve{E}$ satisfies $|\breve{E}| \leq |E|/2$ and the resulting bound on the cluster radii is $O(\log n)$.

Chapter 12

Sparse covers

12.1 Basic goals

This section presents several algorithms for constructing covers with various desirable properties. The clustering algorithms used for this purpose are based on the central idea of *coarsening* and share the following overall structure. We are given some initial cover S, dictated by the application (i.e., exhibiting the appropriate locality level required for this application). This will usually be some natural cover, for instance, the neighborhood cover $\hat{\Gamma}_\rho$ for some ρ. This cover has the desired radius properties, but is not necessarily sparse (i.e., it may have large overlaps). Our goal is to construct, via repeated cluster merging, a *coarsening* cover $\mathcal{T}$ (subsuming each original cluster in some new one) with relatively low overlaps, without paying too much in increased cluster radii.

The inherent trade-off between overlaps and radii, dictating most of the trade-offs in the applications presented later on, is that lower overlap implies higher radius ratio and vice versa. As in the simple example construction presented in Section 11.5, this trade-off is of the following typical shape: guaranteeing $O(n^{1/\kappa})$ average overlap necessitates $\Omega(\kappa)$ (multiplicative) radius increase in the worst case for every fixed κ. We later present some lower bounds, implying that these trade-offs are nearly tight.

12.2 Low average-degree covers

In this section we present a simple algorithm named Av_Cover for constructing covers with low *average* degree. The way this algorithm operates is typical of several other algorithms presented later on, although those may involve more complex variations on the same theme.

12.2.1 Algorithm Av_Cover

The general structure of Algorithm Av_Cover is as follows. The algorithm operates in iterations. Each iteration constructs one output cluster $Z \in \mathcal{T}$ by merging together some clusters of S. The iteration begins by arbitrarily picking a cluster S_0 in S and designating it as the *kernel* of a cluster to be constructed next. The cluster is then repeatedly merged with intersecting clusters from S. This is done in a layered fashion, adding one layer at a time. The clusters of S added to Z are subsequently discarded from S. At each stage, the original cluster is viewed as the internal kernel Y of the resulting cluster Z. (See Figure 12.1.) The merging process is carried out repeatedly until reaching a certain sparsity

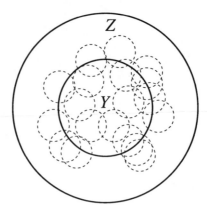

Figure 12.1: The structure of a cluster Z. The dashed circles represent clusters of the initial cover $\mathcal{S}$.

$\mathcal{T} \leftarrow \emptyset$.

While $\mathcal{S} \neq \emptyset$ **do:**

    1. Select an arbitrary cluster $S_0 \in \mathcal{S}$.   /* seed of built cluster */

    2. $Z \leftarrow S_0$.

    3. **Repeat**   /* merge cluster layers around Z */

        (a) $Y \leftarrow Z$.

        (b) $\mathcal{Z} \leftarrow \{S \mid S \in \mathcal{S},\ S \cap Y \neq \emptyset\}$.

        (c) $Z \leftarrow \bigcup_{S \in \mathcal{Z}} S$.

    until $|Z| \leq n^{1/\kappa}|Y|$.

    4. $\mathcal{S} \leftarrow \mathcal{S} - \mathcal{Z}$.

    5. $\mathcal{T} \leftarrow \mathcal{T} \cup \{Z\}$.

End-while

Output $(\mathcal{T})$.

Figure 12.2: Algorithm AV_COVER(G, κ).

condition (specifically, until the next iteration increases the number of vertices merged into Z by a factor of less than $n^{1/\kappa}$). The algorithm then adds the resulting cluster Z to the output collection $\mathcal{T}$, and then a new iteration is started. These iterations proceed until $\mathcal{S}$ is exhausted. The algorithm then outputs the set $\mathcal{T}$.

A formal description of the algorithm is given in Figure 12.2.

12.2.2   Analysis

Theorem 12.2.1 [Average cover]: *Given a weighted graph $G = (V, E, \omega)$, $|V| = n$, a cover $\mathcal{S}$ and an integer $\kappa \geq 1$, Algorithm AV_COVER constructs a cover $\mathcal{T}$ that satisfies the following properties:*

(1) T coarsens S,

(2) $Rad(T) \leq (2\kappa + 1)Rad(S)$, and

(3) $\bar{\Delta}(T) \leq n^{1/\kappa}$.

Proof: First let us note that since the elements of S at the beginning of the procedure are clusters (i.e., their induced graphs are connected), the construction process guarantees that every set Z added to T is a cluster. The fact that T coarsens S (Property (1)) now holds directly from the construction, noting that each of the original clusters in S is covered by some cluster $Z \in T$ constructed during the execution of the algorithm.

Consider the collection C of kernels Y corresponding to the clusters Z generated by our algorithm throughout its execution. We now claim the following.

Lemma 12.2.2 *The kernels in C are mutually disjoint.*

Proof: Suppose, seeking to establish a contradiction, that there is a vertex v such that $v \in Y \cap Y'$. Without loss of generality suppose that Y was created in an earlier iteration than Y'. Since $v \in Y'$, there must be a cluster S' such that $v \in S'$ and S' was still in S when the algorithm started constructing Y'. But every such cluster S' satisfies $S' \cap Y \neq \emptyset$, and therefore the final construction step creating the collection Z from Y should have added S' into Z and eliminated it from S; this is a contradiction. $\square$

In view of the above lemma, the output collection T and the corresponding collection of kernels C look as in Figure 12.3.

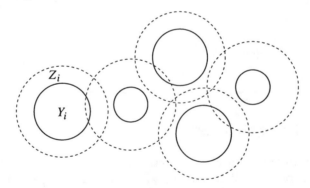

Figure 12.3: The output collection T of Algorithm AV_COVER (dashed clusters) and the corresponding kernels (solid lines).

Property (3) is now derived as follows. It is immediate from the termination condition of the internal loop that the resulting pair Y, Z satisfies $|Z| \leq n^{1/\kappa}|Y|$. Therefore, using Lemma 12.2.2,

$$\sum_{Z} |Z| \leq \sum_{Y} n^{1/\kappa}|Y| \leq n^{1/\kappa} \cdot n = n^{1+1/\kappa},$$

which proves Property (3).

Finally, we analyze the increase in the radius of clusters in the cover and establish Property (2). Consider some iteration of the main loop of Algorithm AV_COVER in Figure 12.2, starting with the selection of some cluster $S \in S$. Let J denote the number of times the internal loop was executed. Denote the initial sets Z and Z by Z_0, and Z_0, respectively. Denote the set Z (respectively, Z, Y) constructed on the ith internal iteration ($1 \leq i \leq J$) by Z_i (resp., Z_i, Y_i). Note that for $1 \leq i \leq J$, $Y_i = Z_{i-1}$, Z_i is constructed on the basis of Y_i and $Z_i = \bigcup_{S \in Z_i} S$. We proceed with the following two claims.

Lemma 12.2.3 $|Z_i| \geq n^{i/\kappa}$ *for every* $0 \leq i \leq J - 1$, *and strict inequality holds for* $i \geq 1$.

Proof: The proof is by induction on i. The claim is immediate for $i = 0$. Assuming the claim for $i - 1 \geq 0$, it remains to prove that $|Z_i| > n^{1/\kappa}|Z_{i-1}|$, which follows directly from the fact that the termination condition of the internal loop was not met.   □

Lemma 12.2.4 *For every* $1 \leq i \leq J$, $Rad(Y_i) \leq (2i - 1)Rad(\mathcal{S})$.

Proof: The proof follows by straightforward induction on i. The base case is immediate since $Y_1 = S \in \mathcal{S}$. The inductive step follows from the fact that for $2 \leq i \leq J$, $Rad(Y_i) = Rad(Z_{i-1}) \leq Rad(Y_{i-1}) + 2Rad(\mathcal{S})$, since Z_{i-1} is created from Y_{i-1} by adding into it all $\mathcal{S}$ clusters intersecting it and $Y_i = Z_{i-1}$ is simply a merge of all the clusters in $\mathcal{Z}_{i-1}$.   □

It follows from Lemma 12.2.3 that $J \leq \kappa$, and hence by Lemma 12.2.4 we have that $Rad(Y_J) \leq (2\kappa - 1)Rad(\mathcal{S})$, hence $Rad(Z_J) \leq (2\kappa + 1)Rad(\mathcal{S})$, which completes the proof of Property (2) of the theorem.   □

In many of our later applications, the initial cover to be coarsened is the ρ-neighborhood cover for some parameter ρ. For such covers, the Average Cover Theorem 12.2.1 implies the following result.

Corollary 12.2.5 *Given a weighted graph* $G = (V, E, \omega)$, $|V| = n$, *and integers* $\kappa, \rho \geq 1$, *it is possible to construct a cover* $\mathcal{T} = \mathcal{T}_{\rho,\kappa}$ *that satisfies the following properties:*

(1) $\mathcal{T}$ *coarsens* $\hat{\Gamma}_\rho(V)$,

(2) $Rad(\mathcal{T}) \leq (2\kappa + 1)\rho$, *and*

(3) $\bar{\Delta}(\mathcal{T}) \leq n^{1/\kappa}$.

12.3   Partial partitions

Before dealing with the problem of constructing a cover with low *maximal* degree, let us consider the simpler problem of constructing a *partial partition*, which we later use as a building block.

The input of this problem is a graph $G = (V, E, \omega)$, $|V| = n$, a collection of (possibly overlapping) clusters $\mathcal{R}$ and an integer $\kappa \geq 1$. The output consists of a partial partition, i.e., a collection of *disjoint* clusters, $\mathcal{DT}$, that subsume a subset $\mathcal{DR} \subseteq \mathcal{R}$ of the original clusters. The goal is to subsume "many" clusters of $\mathcal{R}$ while maintaining the radii of the output clusters in $\mathcal{DT}$ relatively small. We next describe a procedure PART achieving this goal.

12.3.1   Procedure PART

The general structure of Procedure PART$(\mathcal{R}, \kappa)$ is similar to that of Algorithm AV_COVER. It starts by setting $\mathcal{U}$, the collection of *unprocessed* clusters, to equal $\mathcal{R}$. The procedure operates in iterations. Each iteration is similar to the corresponding iteration of Algorithm AV_COVER, with the following differences. First, throughout the process, the procedure also keeps the "unmerged" collections $\mathcal{Y}$ and $\mathcal{Z}$ containing the original $\mathcal{R}$ clusters merged into Y and Z.

Second, the sparsity condition used for terminating the iterative process is different. Specifically, the condition now concerns the relative sizes of $\mathcal{Z}$ and $\mathcal{Y}$ (i.e., the number of *original clusters* "captured" by the merging process), rather than the sizes of Z and Y (i.e., the number of *vertices* captured). Formally, the iterative process terminates when the next iteration increases the number of clusters merged into $\mathcal{Z}$ by a factor of less than $|\mathcal{R}|^{1/\kappa}$.

The main difference, compared to Algorithm Av_COVER, is that while the procedure discards the cluster Z as before, it does not take the entire cluster Z into the output collection $\mathcal{DT}$, but only its *kernel* Y. The fact that each newly formed cluster consists of only the kernel Y, and not the entire cluster Z, means that each selected cluster Y has an additional "external layer" of $\mathcal{R}$ clusters around it. (See Figure 12.3.) The role of this external layer is to act as a "protective barrier" shielding the generated cluster Y and providing the desired disjointness between the different clusters Y added to $\mathcal{DT}$.

At the end of the iterative process, when Y is completed, every cluster in the collection $\mathcal{Y}$ is added to $\mathcal{DR}$ and every cluster in the collection $\mathcal{Z}$ is removed from $\mathcal{U}$. Then a new iteration is started. These iterations proceed until $\mathcal{U}$ is exhausted. The procedure then outputs the sets $\mathcal{DR}$ and $\mathcal{DT}$.

Note that each of the original clusters in $\mathcal{DR}$ is covered by some cluster $Y \in \mathcal{DT}$ constructed during the execution of the procedure. However, some original $\mathcal{R}$ clusters are thrown out of consideration without being subsumed by any cluster in $\mathcal{DT}$; these are precisely the clusters merged into some external layer $\mathcal{Z} - \mathcal{Y}$. Therefore there may be clusters left in $\mathcal{R}$ after the main algorithm removes the elements of $\mathcal{DR}$. This is why a single application of Procedure PART is not enough for constructing a *cover* and the cover construction algorithm of Section 12.4 requires many invocation phases.

Procedure PART is formally described in Figure 12.4.

$\mathcal{U} \leftarrow \mathcal{R}$; $\mathcal{DT} \leftarrow \emptyset$; $\mathcal{DR} \leftarrow \emptyset$.
While $\mathcal{U} \neq \emptyset$ **do:**

1. Select an arbitrary cluster $S_0 \in \mathcal{U}$.   /* seed of built cluster */

2. $\mathcal{Z} \leftarrow \{S_0\}$; $Z \leftarrow S_0$.

3. **Repeat** /* merge cluster layers around Z */

    (a) $\mathcal{Y} \leftarrow \mathcal{Z}$; $Y \leftarrow Z$.
    (b) $\mathcal{Z} \leftarrow \{S \mid S \in \mathcal{U}, \ S \cap Y \neq \emptyset\}$.
    (c) $Z \leftarrow \bigcup_{S \in \mathcal{Z}} S$.

    until $|\mathcal{Z}| \leq |\mathcal{R}|^{1/\kappa} |\mathcal{Y}|$.

4. $\mathcal{U} \leftarrow \mathcal{U} - \mathcal{Z}$.

5. $\mathcal{DT} \leftarrow \mathcal{DT} \cup \{Y\}$.

6. $\mathcal{DR} \leftarrow \mathcal{DR} \cup \mathcal{Y}$.

End-while
Output $(\mathcal{DR}, \mathcal{DT})$.

Figure 12.4: Procedure PART$(\mathcal{R}, \kappa)$.

12.3.2   Analysis

The properties of Procedure PART are summarized by the following lemma, whose proof follows the lines of the Average Cover Theorem 12.2.1 above.

Lemma 12.3.1 *Given a weighted graph $G = (V, E, \omega)$, $|V| = n$, a collection of clusters $\mathcal{R}$ and an integer κ, the collections $\mathcal{DT}$ and $\mathcal{DR}$ constructed by Procedure PART$(\mathcal{R}, \kappa)$ satisfy the following properties:*

(1) $\mathcal{DT}$ coarsens $\mathcal{DR}$,

(2) $\mathcal{DT}$ is a partial partition, i.e., $Y \cap Y' = \emptyset$ for every $Y, Y' \in \mathcal{DT}$,

(3) $|\mathcal{DR}| \geq |\mathcal{R}|^{1-1/\kappa}$, and

(4) $Rad(\mathcal{DT}) \leq (2\kappa - 1)Rad(\mathcal{R})$.   □

12.3.3   Constructing s-separated partial partitions

Another useful variant of the partial partition problem involves constructing an s-separated partial partition covering "many" ρ-neighborhoods. The construction described next applies only to neighborhood covers, i.e., the initial collection of clusters to be subsumed, $\mathcal{R}$, is a subset of $\hat{\Gamma}_\rho(V)$:

$$\mathcal{R} = \{\Gamma_\rho(v) \mid v \in R\}$$

for some subset $R \subseteq V$.

The algorithm for this problem is based on a variant of Procedure PART. To obtain the desired separation s, we use a Procedure SEP_PART(R, s, ρ, G, κ), that does the following. The procedure first constructs a modified collection $\mathcal{R}'$ of neighborhood clusters of radius $\rho' = \rho + s/2$ corresponding to the given $\mathcal{R}$, namely,

$$\mathcal{R}' = \{\Gamma_{\rho'}(v) \mid v \in R\}.$$

It then applies Procedure PART to the new initial collection $\mathcal{R}'$. This results in a partial partition $\mathcal{DT}'$ and a collection $\mathcal{DR}'$ of subsumed neighborhoods. Next, the partial partition $\mathcal{DT}'$ is transformed into the desired $\mathcal{DT}$ as follows. Each output cluster $T' \in \mathcal{DT}'$ is "shrunk" into a cluster T by eliminating from T' the vertices that are closer to its border than $s/2$, setting

$$T = \{v \in T' \mid dist_G(v, V - T') \geq s/2\}.$$

Finally, we let $\mathcal{DR} \subseteq \mathcal{R}$ be the collection of input neighborhoods corresponding to $\mathcal{DR}'$.

The procedure is formally described in Figure 12.5.

Lemma 12.3.2 *Given a weighted graph $G = (V, E, \omega)$, $|V| = n$, a collection of ρ-neighborhoods $\mathcal{R} = \{\Gamma_\rho(v) \mid v \in R\}$ and integers s, κ, the collections $\mathcal{DT}$ and $\mathcal{DR}$ constructed by the above algorithm satisfy the following properties:*

(1) $\mathcal{DT}$ coarsens $\mathcal{DR}$,

(2) $\mathcal{DT}$ is an s-separated partial partition,

(3) $|\mathcal{DR}| \geq |\mathcal{R}|^{1-1/\kappa}$, and

(4) $Rad(\mathcal{DT}) \leq (2\kappa - 1)\rho + \kappa s$.

---

1. Set $\rho' \leftarrow \rho + s/2$.

2. Set $\mathcal{R}' \leftarrow \{\Gamma_{\rho'}(v) \mid v \in R\}$.

3. $(\mathcal{DR}', \mathcal{DT}') \leftarrow \text{PART}(\mathcal{R}', \kappa)$.

   /* Transform the partial partition $\mathcal{DT}'$ into $\mathcal{DT}$ */

4. **For** every output cluster $T' \in \mathcal{DT}'$ **do:**

   (a) Set $T \leftarrow \{v \in T' \mid dist_G(v, V - T') \geq s/2\}$.

   (b) Add T to $\mathcal{DT}$.

5. Let $\mathcal{DR} \leftarrow \{\Gamma_{\rho}(v) \mid \Gamma_{\rho'}(v) \in \mathcal{DR}'\}$.

6. **Output** $(\mathcal{DR}, \mathcal{DT})$.

Figure 12.5: Procedure SEP_PART(R, s, ρ, G, κ).

Proof: By Lemma 12.3.1, the output $\mathcal{DT}'$ of Procedure PART on $\mathcal{R}'$ is a partial partition. Since $\mathcal{DT}$ is obtained from $\mathcal{DT}'$ by shrinking each cluster to within $s/2$ of its previous perimeter, it is easy to verify that the outcome $\mathcal{DT}$ is an s-separated partial partition, thus establishing Property (2). The radius bounds of Property (4) also follow from Property (4) of Lemma 12.3.1 and the choice of ρ'.

We now claim that whenever a cluster $T' \in \mathcal{DT}'$ subsumes an ρ'-neighborhood cluster $\Gamma_{\rho'}(v) \in \mathcal{DR}'$, the corresponding cluster $T \in \mathcal{DT}$ constructed by the algorithm subsumes the input ρ-neighborhood cluster $\Gamma_{\rho}(v) \in \mathcal{DR}$. Suppose that this does not hold, namely, there is a vertex $w \in \Gamma_{\rho}(v)$ that is not taken into T. By the construction of T, necessarily $dist_G(w, V - T') < s/2$. This means that there exists a vertex $z \in V - T'$ such that $dist_G(w, z) < s/2$. But then, z is included in $\Gamma_{\rho'}(v)$, hence $z \in T'$ (since T' subsumes $\Gamma_{\rho'}(v)$); this is a contradiction.

Properties (1) and (3) now follow as well. $\square$

12.4 Low maximum-degree covers

The problem of constructing a cover with low *maximal* degree is somewhat more involved than that of bounding the average degree. This problem is handled by reducing it to the subproblem of constructing a partial partition, discussed in Section 12.3. We now describe algorithm MAX_COVER for the construction of a sparse coarsening cover with low maximum degree.

12.4.1 Algorithm MAX_COVER

The construction is based on covering the clusters of $\mathcal{S}$ by a number of partial partitions using Procedure PART and then merging all these partial partitions to yield the desired cover.

The input to the algorithm is a graph $G = (V, E, \omega)$, $|V| = n$, a cover $\mathcal{S}$ and an integer $\kappa \geq 1$. The output collection of cover clusters, $\mathcal{T}$, is initially empty. The algorithm maintains the set of "remaining" clusters $\mathcal{R}$. These are the clusters not yet subsumed by the constructed cover. Initially $\mathcal{R} = \mathcal{S}$, and the algorithm terminates once $\mathcal{R} = \emptyset$. The algorithm operates in at most $\kappa |\mathcal{S}|^{1/\kappa}$ phases. Each phase consists of the activation of the procedure PART($\mathcal{R}, \kappa$), which constructs a partial partition $\mathcal{DT}$ coarsening some of the clusters of $\mathcal{R}$. The algorithm then adds this subcollection of output clusters to $\mathcal{T}$ and removes the set of subsumed original clusters $\mathcal{DR}$ from $\mathcal{R}$.

Intuitively, the fact that the collection of clusters $\mathcal{DT}$ constructed by the procedure is a partial partition, namely, consists of *disjoint* clusters, ensures that each phase contributes at most *one* to the degree of each vertex in the output cover $\mathcal{T}$.

Algorithm MAX_COVER is formally described in Figure 12.6.

$\mathcal{R} \leftarrow \mathcal{S}$; $\mathcal{T} \leftarrow \emptyset$.
Repeat

    1. $(\mathcal{DR}, \mathcal{DT}) \leftarrow$ PART($\mathcal{R}, \kappa$).

    2. $\mathcal{T} \leftarrow \mathcal{T} \cup \mathcal{DT}$.

    3. $\mathcal{R} \leftarrow \mathcal{R} \setminus \mathcal{DR}$.

until $\mathcal{R} = \emptyset$.
Output ($\mathcal{T}$).

Figure 12.6: Algorithm MAX_COVER($G, \mathcal{S}, \kappa$).

12.4.2   Analysis

Theorem 12.4.1 [Maximum cover]: *Given a weighted graph $G = (V, E, \omega)$, $|V| = n$, a cover $\mathcal{S}$ and an integer $\kappa \geq 1$, Algorithm MAX_COVER constructs a cover $\mathcal{T}$ that satisfies the following properties:*

(1) $\mathcal{T}$ coarsens $\mathcal{S}$,

(2) $Rad(\mathcal{T}) \leq (2\kappa - 1)Rad(\mathcal{S})$, and

(3) $\Delta^C(\mathcal{T}) \leq 2\kappa|\mathcal{S}|^{1/\kappa}$.

Proof: Let $\mathcal{R}^i$ denote the contents of the set $\mathcal{R}$ at the beginning of phase i, and let $r_i = |\mathcal{R}^i|$. Let $\mathcal{DT}^i$ denote the collection $\mathcal{DT}$ added to $\mathcal{T}$ at the end of phase i, and let $\mathcal{DR}^i$ be the set $\mathcal{DR}$ removed from $\mathcal{R}$ at the end of phase i.

The fact that $\mathcal{T}$ coarsens $\mathcal{S}$ (Property (1)) follows from the fact that $\mathcal{T} = \bigcup_i \mathcal{DT}^i$, $\mathcal{S} = \bigcup_i \mathcal{DR}^i$ and, by Property (1) of Lemma 12.3.1, $\mathcal{DT}^i$ coarsens $\mathcal{DR}^i$ for every i. Property (2) follows directly from Property (4) of Lemma 12.3.1. It remains to prove Property (3). This property relies on the fact that by Property (2) of Lemma 12.3.1, each vertex v participates in at most one cluster in each collection $\mathcal{DT}^i$. Therefore it remains to bound the number of phases performed by the algorithm. This bound relies on the following observations. By Property (3) of Lemma 12.3.1, in every phase i, at least $|\mathcal{DR}^i| \geq |\mathcal{R}^i|^{1-1/\kappa}$ clusters of $\mathcal{R}^i$ are removed from the set $\mathcal{R}^i$, i.e., $r_{i+1} \leq r_i - r_i^{1-1/\kappa}$.

Lemma 12.4.2 *Consider the recurrence relation $x_{i+1} = x_i - x_i^\epsilon$ for $0 < \epsilon < 1$. Let $f(n)$ denote the least index i such that $x_i \leq 1$ given $x_0 = n$. Then $f(n) < ((1 - \epsilon) \ln 2)^{-1} n^{1-\epsilon}$.* $\square$

Consequently, since $r_0 = |\mathcal{S}|$, $\mathcal{S}$ is exhausted after no more than $\frac{\kappa}{\ln 2}|\mathcal{S}|^{1/\kappa}$ phases of Algorithm MAX_COVER, and hence $\Delta^C(\mathcal{T}) \leq 2\kappa|\mathcal{S}|^{1/\kappa}$. This completes the proof of the Maximum Cover Theorem 12.4.1. $\square$

Let us remark that it is possible to replace the degree bound of Property (2) with $O(\kappa \cdot n^{1/\kappa})$. This requires a slightly more complex algorithm and analysis. In most of our applications there is no real difference, as $|S| = n$. We also mention that this result is close to optimal in some cases, as implied from the lower bound of Theorem 16.2.4.

Again, we will be interested in applying Algorithm MAX_COVER for initial neighborhood covers, and in this case we have the following result.

Corollary 12.4.3 *Given a weighted graph $G = (V, E, \omega)$, $|V| = n$, and integers $\kappa, \rho \geq 1$, it is possible to construct a cover $\mathcal{T} = \mathcal{T}_{\rho,\kappa}$ that satisfies the following properties:*

(1) $\mathcal{T}$ coarsens $\hat{\Gamma}_\rho(V)$,

(2) $Rad(\mathcal{T}) \leq (2\kappa - 1)\rho$, and

(3) $\Delta^C(\mathcal{T}) \leq 2\kappa \cdot n^{1/\kappa}$.

A naive implementation of Algorithm MAX_COVER as described here requires $O(n^3)$ steps, and its straightforward distributed implementation has a similar communication cost. In Chapter 21 we discuss more efficient (sequential and distributed) construction algorithms.

Example: *Neighborhood coarsening on the grid.*
Consider the 19×19 8-way grid $G_{19} = (V, E)$, $V = \{(i, j) \mid 1 \leq i, j \leq 19\}$, with each vertex connected to its (up to) eight neighbors (see Figure 12.7(a)). This network has $n = 361$ vertices. Assume all edges have unit cost. Then $\Gamma_1(v)$ (resp., $\Gamma_2(v)$) consists of the 3×3 (resp., 5×5) subgrid centered at v (with the obvious modifications for vertices on the borders of the grid). For example, Figure 12.7(a) describes also the 1-neighborhood $\Gamma_1(3, 3)$ and the 2-neighborhood $\Gamma_2(7, 7)$.

Now consider the initial cover $S = \hat{\Gamma}_2(V)$. Note that in this cover, each vertex occurs in at most 25 clusters. Given a parameter κ, our purpose is to find a cover $\mathcal{T}$ that coarsens S such that the radius of clusters in $\mathcal{T}$ is at most $(2\kappa - 1)Rad(S)$ and the number of $\mathcal{T}$ clusters in which any particular vertex occurs is at most $\lfloor \kappa|S|^{1/\kappa}\rfloor$. For $\kappa = 2$, S itself satisfies the requirements, since the desired bound on the number of occurrences is $\lfloor 2\sqrt{361}\rfloor = 38$. For $\kappa = 3$, we need to find a coarsening cover $\mathcal{T}$ such that $Rad(\mathcal{T}) \leq (2 \cdot 3 - 1)Rad(S) = 10$ and the number of $\mathcal{T}$ clusters in which any particular vertex occurs is at most $\lfloor 3 \cdot 361^{1/3}\rfloor = 21$. A possible solution, depicted by the four ovals in Figure 12.7(b), is

$$\mathcal{T} = \{\Gamma_6(6i + 1, 6j + 1) \mid 1 \leq i, j \leq 2\}.$$

Note that this cover easily meets the requirement on the number of occurrences and, furthermore, its radius is only 6. □

12.4.3 Covers based on s-separated partial partitions

The cover generated by Algorithm MAX_COVER is composed of a number of "layers" of partial partitions, each subsuming some of the input clusters. Later on we may be interested in the construction of a cover coarsening the neighborhood cover $\hat{\Gamma}_\rho(V)$ in which the partial partitions are well separated. This can be achieved by using Procedure SEP_PART of Section 12.3.3 as a substitute for Procedure PART in Algorithm MAX_COVER. Relying on Lemma 12.3.2, this yields the following.

Theorem 12.4.4 *Given a weighted graph $G = (V, E, \omega)$, $|V| = n$, and integers $\rho, s, \kappa \geq 1$, it is possible to construct a cover $\mathcal{T}$ that satisfies the following properties:*

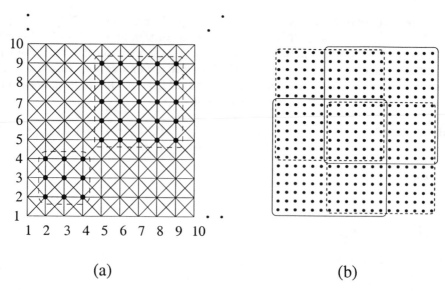

(a)   (b)

Figure 12.7: (a) The lower left corner of the 19×19 8-way grid G_{19}, and the neighborhoods $\Gamma_1(3,3)$ and $\Gamma_2(7,7)$. (b) The cover $\mathcal{T}$ for $\hat{\Gamma}_2(V)$ on G_{19}.

(1) $\mathcal{T}$ coarsens $\hat{\Gamma}_\rho(V)$,

(2) $Rad(\mathcal{T}) \leq (2\kappa - 1)\rho + \kappa s$,

(3) $\Delta^C(\mathcal{T}) \leq 2\kappa \cdot n^{1/\kappa}$, and

(4) each of the $\Delta^C(\mathcal{T})$ layers of partial partitions composing the cover $\mathcal{T}$ is s-separated.   □

Bibliographical notes

General covers (with cluster overlaps) were introduced in [Pel89b] and given improved constructions in [AP92, Pel93]. Other types of covers were also used in the literature. For instance, covers based on fixed-cardinality clusters (discussed in Section 14.4) were used in [ABLP90, ABLP89].

The cover coarsening algorithms presented in this chapter are taken from [Pel89b, AP90c, AP92]. The lower bounds presented were established in [AP90c] and were based on lower bounds for spanners in [PU89b].

Exercises

1. Prove Lemmas 12.3.1 and 12.4.2.

2. Modify Algorithm MAX_COVER and its analysis to yield a version of the Maximum Cover Theorem 12.4.1 in which the degree bound of Property (2) is replaced with $O(\kappa \cdot n^{1/\kappa})$.

3. Consider a vertex-weighted graph $G = (V, E, \hat{\omega})$ where a nonnegative weight $\hat{\omega}(v)$ is assigned to every $v \in V$. For a set of vertices $S \subseteq V$, let $\hat{\omega}(S) = \sum_{v \in S} \hat{\omega}(v)$. Denote the *total weight* of the vertices by $W = \hat{\omega}(V)$. For a cover $\mathcal{S}$, let $\hat{\omega}(\mathcal{S}) = \sum_{D \in \mathcal{S}} \hat{\omega}(S)$, and define the *average weighted degree* of $\mathcal{S}$ as $\bar{\Delta}_{\hat{\omega}}(\mathcal{T}) = \hat{\omega}(\mathcal{S})/W$. Describe and analyze a modified variant of Algorithm AV_COVER yielding a version of the Average

Cover Theorem 12.2.1 in which Property (2) is replaced with a bound of $O(\mathcal{W}^{1/\kappa})$ on the average weighted degree of the coarsening cover $\mathcal{T}$.

4. Consider an execution of Procedure PART. For each iteration i of the main loop, let Z_i be the final cluster generated by the procedure and let Y_i be its kernel, taken into the output cover $\mathcal{DT} = \{Y_1, \ldots, Y_q\}$. Prove the following two properties.

   (a) There are no two iterations i, j such that both $Y_i \cap Z_j \neq \emptyset$ and $Y_j \cap Z_i \neq \emptyset$.

   (b) There is no "cycle of nonempty intersections," namely, there are no t iterations $i_0, i_1, \ldots, i_{t-1}$ such that $Y_{i_j} \cap Z_{i_{j+1 \bmod t}} \neq \emptyset$ for every $0 \leq j \leq t-1$.

Chapter 13

Sparse partitions

This chapter presents some algorithms for coarsening a given partition $\mathcal{S}$ of a given unweighted graph G. While the general picture emerging from the results presented next is similar to that of the previous chapter concerning covers, it turns out that for some of the sparsity measures we use, the problem is somewhat harder and we do not always get optimal bounds on the radius-sparsity trade-off.

13.1 Low average-degree partitions

13.1.1 The average cluster-degree partition algorithm Av_PART$_c$

Let us first consider the cluster-degree measure, defined in Section 11.4.2. It turns out that a minor modification of Algorithm Av_COVER from Figure 12.2 yields Algorithm Av_PART$_c$ for coarsening a given partition of an unweighted graph by a partition with low average cluster-degree. The algorithm is depicted in Figure 13.1. Essentially, the iterative process of cluster construction has to be modified so as to take into account the fact that the clusters of $\mathcal{S}$ do not overlap and sparsity is measured by the number of neighboring clusters. Consequently, the next layer merged to the current cluster Y to form the next cluster Z, composed of all clusters $S \in \mathcal{S}$ that are *adjacent* to Y (rather than intersecting it). Also, the cluster taken as the subsuming cluster into the output partition is Y rather than Z, and the input clusters eliminated from $\mathcal{S}$ are those merged into Y.

We thus have the following theorem.

Theorem 13.1.1 *Given an unweighted graph $G = (V, E)$, $|V| = n$, a partition $\mathcal{S}$ and an integer $\kappa \geq 1$, Algorithm* Av_PART$_c$ *constructs a partition $\mathcal{T}$ that satisfies the following properties:*

(1) $\mathcal{T}$ coarsens $\mathcal{S}$,

(2) $Rad(\mathcal{T}) \leq (2\kappa + 1)Rad(\mathcal{S})$, and

(3) $\bar{\Delta}_c(\mathcal{T}) = O(n^{1/\kappa})$. □

13.1.2 The average vertex-degree partition algorithm Av_PART$_v$

The situation is harder with the vertex-degree measure (again defined in Section 11.4.2). We may try to devise a simple variant of Algorithm Av_COVER for this problem as follows.

$\mathcal{T} \leftarrow \emptyset.$
While $\mathcal{S} \neq \emptyset$ **do:**

  1. Select an arbitrary cluster $S_0 \in \mathcal{S}$.

  2. $\mathcal{Z} \leftarrow \{S_0\}; \quad Z \leftarrow S_0.$

  3. **Repeat**

     (a) $\mathcal{Y} \leftarrow \mathcal{Z}; \quad Y \leftarrow Z.$
     (b) $\mathcal{Z} \leftarrow \bigcup_{S \in \mathcal{Y}} \Gamma^c(S).$
     (c) $Z \leftarrow \bigcup_{S \in \mathcal{Z}} S.$

    until $|Z| \leq n^{1/\kappa}|Y|.$

  4. $\mathcal{S} \leftarrow \mathcal{S} - \mathcal{Y}.$

  5. $\mathcal{T} \leftarrow \mathcal{T} \cup \{Y\}.$

End-while
Output $(\mathcal{T}).$

Figure 13.1: Algorithm Av_Part_c.

Consider an input partition $\mathcal{S}$, and let $\hat{\mathcal{S}} = \{\Gamma^v(S) \mid S \in \mathcal{S}\}$. Then $\hat{\mathcal{S}}$ is a cover and $\bar{\Delta}(\hat{\mathcal{S}}) = \bar{\Delta}_v(\mathcal{S})$. This suggests the approach of applying the algorithm for covers, Av_Cover, to $\hat{\mathcal{S}}$ while "tracing" its operations and "mimicking" them on the original partition $\mathcal{S}$.

Unfortunately, this idea runs into difficulties due to the fact that the clusters created through merges specified in this way are not necessarily connected. In order to demonstrate where such a problem might occur, consider two clusters $S_1, S_2 \in \mathcal{S}$, and let $\hat{S}_1, \hat{S}_2 \in \hat{\mathcal{S}}$ be the corresponding neighborhoods (see Figure 13.2). Suppose that there exists a vertex $v \in \hat{S}_1 \cap \hat{S}_2$ and in some stage of the application of algorithm GV to $\hat{\mathcal{S}}$, $\hat{S}_1$ and $\hat{S}_2$ are merged into a new output cluster $\hat{T}_1$. Tracing this operation on $\mathcal{S}$ requires us to merge S_1 and S_2 into T_1. However, it might be the case that S_1 and S_2 are not even neighboring each other, so the subgraph induced by their union is disconnected. This might happen, for instance, if there exists another cluster S_3 containing v and the cluster $\hat{S}_3$ corresponding to S_3 has been merged earlier into a different output cluster $\hat{T}_3$.

Thus the algorithm Av_Part_v obtained in this way solves a weaker problem in which the output clusters are allowed to be disconnected and cluster radii are measured in the weak sense of Section 11.6.3. We refer to this problem as the problem of "weak partitions" with low average vertex-degree. By mimicking also the proof of the Average Cover Theorem 12.2.1 we establish the following theorem.

Theorem 13.1.2 *Given an unweighted graph* $G = (V, E)$, $|V| = n$, *a partition* $\mathcal{S}$ *and an integer* $\kappa \geq 1$, *Algorithm* Av_Part_v *constructs a weak partition* $\mathcal{T}$ *that satisfies the following properties:*

(1) $\mathcal{T}$ *coarsens* $\mathcal{S}$,

(2) $WRad(\mathcal{T}) \leq (2\kappa + 1)Rad(\mathcal{S})$, *and*

(3) $\bar{\Delta}_v(\mathcal{T}) = O(n^{1/\kappa})$. $\quad \square$

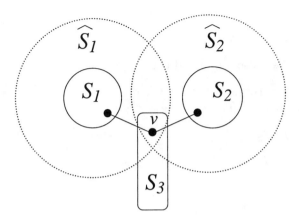

Figure 13.2: Clusters S_1 and S_2.

13.2 Low maximum-degree partitions

In this section, we discuss algorithms for the construction of sparse coarsening partitions according to the maximum vertex- and cluster-degree measures. These algorithms are differently structured. They proceed in phases, where each phase attempts to handle *many* clusters in parallel. We start with a partition S. In each phase, the clusters of the current partition are merged to form larger clusters, thus creating a new partition. This is repeated until reaching a satisfactory partition.

13.2.1 The maximum vertex-degree partition algorithm MAX_PART$_v$

We present a maximum vertex-degree partition algorithm named MAX_PART$_v$. This is the only algorithm in which our trade-off deviates considerably from the known lower bound, in that the radius ratio is exponential in κ.

We need the following definitions. We say that a cluster $S \in \mathcal{S}$ is *bad* if $|\Gamma^v(S)| > n^{1/\kappa}|S|$. We use the auxiliary cluster graph $\tilde{G}(\mathcal{S}) = (\mathcal{S}, \tilde{E})$ representing the adjacency relations among clusters, as defined earlier (Section 11.4.2). Each phase of the algorithm is based on constructing the cluster graph $\tilde{G}$, selecting a maximal 3-independent set from among the *bad* clusters (i.e., consisting of clusters at $dist_{\tilde{G}} = 3$ of each other) and merging all the other clusters around the selected ones. The definition of bad clusters, coupled with the merging process, guarantees that the minimum cardinality of clusters grows by a factor of $n^{1/\kappa}$ in each phase, hence there are at most κ phases, hence the bound on the radius ratio. The algorithm is presented in Figure 13.3.

Theorem 13.2.1 *Given an unweighted graph $G = (V, E)$, $|V| = n$, a partition $\mathcal{S}$ and an integer $\kappa \geq 1$, Algorithm MAX_PART$_v$ constructs a coarsening partition $\mathcal{T}$ that satisfies the following properties:*

(1) $Rad(\mathcal{T}) \leq 2 \cdot 5^\kappa \cdot Rad(\mathcal{S})$, and

(2) $\Delta^C{}_v(\mathcal{T}) = O(n^{1/\kappa})$.

Proof: It is obvious from the definition of $\Delta^C{}_v$ that upon termination of the algorithm, the bound on the maximum vertex-degree is met, as no bad clusters are left in $\mathcal{T}$. It remains to verify correctness and determine a bound on the radius increase of the clusters.

Set $\mathcal{T} \leftarrow \mathcal{S}$.
While there are bad clusters in $\mathcal{T}$ **do:**

1. Compute $\mathcal{B}$, the collection of bad clusters in $\mathcal{T}$.

2. Select a maximal subset $\mathcal{C} = \{T_1, \ldots, T_k\} \subseteq \mathcal{B}$
   such that for every $T_i, T_j \in \mathcal{C}$, $dist_{\tilde{G}(\mathcal{T})}(T_i, T_j) \geq 3$.

3. **For** $j = 1$ to k **do:**

   (a) Set $\mathcal{R}_j \leftarrow \{T_j\} \cup \{T \mid T \in \mathcal{T}, dist_{\tilde{G}(\mathcal{T})}(T, T_j) = 1\}$.
   (b) Set $\mathcal{T} \leftarrow \mathcal{T} \setminus \mathcal{R}_j$.

4. **For** $j = 1$ to k **do:**

   (a) Set $\mathcal{R}_j \leftarrow \{T \mid T \in \mathcal{T}, dist_{\tilde{G}(\mathcal{T})}(T, T_j) = 2\}$.
   (b) Set $\mathcal{T} \leftarrow \mathcal{T} \setminus \mathcal{R}_j$.

5. Set $\mathcal{T} \leftarrow \{\bigcup \mathcal{R}_1, \ldots, \bigcup \mathcal{R}_k\}$.

End-while

Figure 13.3: Algorithm MAX_PART$_v$.

Denote the collection $\mathcal{T}$ created by the ith iteration of the main loop by $\mathcal{T}_i$. The input partition $\mathcal{S}$ is denoted $\mathcal{T}_0$. Let $\mathcal{B}_i$ denote the subcollection of bad clusters created from $\mathcal{T}_i$ in step 1.

Lemma 13.2.2 *For every i, the resulting collection $\mathcal{T}_i$ is a partition of G.*

Proof: The proof follows by induction on i. The case $i = 0$ is immediate. Now assume that $\mathcal{T}_{i-1}$ is a partition and consider the ith iteration. We need to show that for every set $\mathcal{R}_j$ constructed by the algorithm, $\bigcup \mathcal{R}_j$ is a cluster. Clearly, steps 3 and 4 create clusters, since they merge existing clusters around a central cluster. The claim that the clusters in $\mathcal{T}_i$ contain all vertices of V follows from the fact that $\mathcal{T}_{i-1}$ is a partition and every cluster in it was merged into $\mathcal{T}_i$. $\square$

Lemma 13.2.3 *For every $i \geq 0$, $|\mathcal{B}_i| \leq n^{1-i/\kappa}$ and $Rad(\mathcal{T}_i) \leq 5^i \cdot Rad(\mathcal{S}) + (5^i - 1)/2$.*

Proof: The proof follows by induction on i. The claims are immediate for $i = 0$. Assuming the claim for $i - 1$, it remains to prove that

$$|\mathcal{B}_i| \leq n^{-1/\kappa} |\mathcal{B}_{i-1}| \tag{13.1}$$

and

$$Rad(\mathcal{T}_i) \leq 5 \cdot Rad(\mathcal{T}_{i-1}) + 2 . \tag{13.2}$$

Inequality (13.1) follows from the observations that every cluster of $\mathcal{B}_{i-1}$ is merged in the ith iteration and every collection $\mathcal{R}_j$ consists of at least $n^{1/\kappa}$ bad clusters from $\mathcal{B}_{i-1}$ and that good clusters remain good. Inequality (13.2) follows from the fact that each collection $\mathcal{R}_j$ is concentrated around a single cluster T_j in the sense that every old cluster from $\mathcal{T}_{i-1}$ merged into $\mathcal{R}_j$ neighbors either T_j or some other cluster neighboring T_j. The two inequalities, in turn, imply the claims of the lemma for i. $\square$

The first claim of the lemma implies that the main loop is performed for at most κ iterations. The second claim implies that

$$Rad(\mathcal{T}_\kappa) \leq 5^\kappa(Rad(\mathcal{S}) + 1/2) \leq 2 \cdot 5^\kappa \cdot Rad(\mathcal{S}).$$

This establishes Property (1) and completes the proof of the theorem. $\square$

13.2.2 The maximum cluster-degree partition algorithm MAX_PART$_c$

We next describe a maximum cluster-degree partition algorithm MAX_PART$_c$. The polynomial bound obtained for the radius ratio here is the result of the weaker sparsity criterion.

The algorithm MAX_PART$_c$ is similar in spirit to Algorithm MAX_PART$_v$, although both the code and the proof are more involved. Algorithm MAX_PART$_c$ again proceeds in phases, each merging the clusters of the current partition into larger clusters, thus creating a new partition. The main change compared to MAX_PART$_v$ is in the definition of badness, which now relies on cluster-neighborhoods rather than vertex-neighborhoods. That is, we say that a cluster $S \in \mathcal{S}$ is *bad* if $|\Gamma^c(S)| > n^{1/\kappa}|S|$. We use the same definitions of the auxiliary graph $\tilde{G}$ and the $dist_{\tilde{G}}$ distances as in the previous algorithm MAX_PART$_v$. The fact that this algorithm guarantees a polynomial radius ratio stems from its stricter criterion for cluster "badness," which guarantees that the cardinality of clusters at least squares in each phase, hence the number of phases is at most $\log \kappa$, in contrast with the κ phases of algorithm MAX_PART$_v$.

The algorithm MAX_PART$_c$ is presented in Figure 13.4.

Theorem 13.2.4 *Given an unweighted graph* $G = (V, E)$, $|V| = n$, *a partition* $\mathcal{S}$ *and an integer* $\kappa \geq 1$, *Algorithm* MAX_PART$_c$ *constructs a coarsening partition* $\mathcal{T}$ *that satisfies the following properties:*

(1) $Rad(\mathcal{T}) \leq 2 \cdot \kappa^{\log 5} Rad(\mathcal{S})$, *and*

(2) $\Delta^C{}_c(\mathcal{T}) = O(n^{1/\kappa})$.

Proof: Denote the collections $\mathcal{S}, \mathcal{T}$ created by the end of the ith iteration of the main loop by $\mathcal{S}_i, \mathcal{T}_i$. The input partition $\mathcal{S}$ is denoted $\mathcal{S}_0$. Let $\mathcal{B}_i, \mathcal{C}_i, \mathcal{H}_i, \mathcal{A}_i, \mathcal{G}_i$ denote the subcollections $\mathcal{B}, \mathcal{C}, \mathcal{H}, \mathcal{A}, \mathcal{G}$ computed in steps 1, 2, 3 of the ith iteration. Denote $s_i = \min_{A \in \mathcal{S}_i}\{|A|\}$. We first need to argue that the algorithm computes a partition and does not get stuck (in step (7a)).

Lemma 13.2.5 *For every* $i \geq 0$, *the resulting collection* $\mathcal{S}_i \cup \mathcal{T}_i$ *is a partition of* G.

Proof: The proof follows by induction on i. The case $i = 0$ is immediate. Now assume that $\mathcal{A}_{i-1}$ is a partition and consider the ith iteration. We need to show that for every set $\mathcal{R}_j$ constructed by the algorithm, $\bigcup \mathcal{R}_j$ is a cluster. Clearly, the sets $\mathcal{R}_1, \ldots, \mathcal{R}_k$ created in step 5 form clusters. In step 6, each iteration of the internal loop picks a collection $\mathcal{R}_j$ formed around a bad cluster $A_j \in \mathcal{B}$ and adds clusters at distance 2 from A_j. To verify connectivity, one should make sure that whenever a cluster A at distance 2 from A_j is added to $\mathcal{R}_j$, some bridging cluster (i.e., cluster A' such that $dist_{\tilde{G}(\mathcal{A})}(A_j, A') = 1$ and $dist_{\tilde{G}(\mathcal{A})}(A, A') = 1$) is also included. In fact, this is necessarily so for *every* bridging cluster A', because $dist_{\tilde{G}(\mathcal{A})}(A_j, A') = 1$, and the choice of $\mathcal{C}$ implies that $dist_{\tilde{G}(\mathcal{A})}(A_i, A') \geq 2$ for every $i \neq j$, so A' must have been added to $\mathcal{R}_j$ in step 5.

Set $\mathcal{T} \leftarrow \emptyset$.
While there are bad clusters in $\mathcal{T}$ **do**:

1. Compute $\mathcal{B}$, the collection of bad clusters in $\mathcal{T}$.

2. Set $\mathcal{H} \leftarrow \{S \in \mathcal{S} \setminus \mathcal{B} \mid \Gamma^c(S) \cap \mathcal{B} \neq \emptyset\}$.

3. Set $\mathcal{A} \leftarrow \mathcal{B} \cup \mathcal{H}, \mathcal{G} \leftarrow \mathcal{S} \setminus \mathcal{A}, \mathcal{T} \leftarrow \mathcal{T} \cup \mathcal{G}$.

4. Select a maximal subset $\mathcal{C} = \{A_1, \ldots, A_p\} \subseteq \mathcal{B}$
   such that for every $A_i, A_j \in \mathcal{C}, dist_{\tilde{G}(\mathcal{A})}(A_i, A_j) \geq 3$.

5. **For** $j = 1$ to p **do**:

   (a) Set $\mathcal{R}_j \leftarrow \{A_j\} \cup \{A \mid A \in \mathcal{A}, dist_{\tilde{G}(\mathcal{A})}(A, A_j) = 1\}$.

   (b) Set $\mathcal{A} \leftarrow \mathcal{A} - \mathcal{R}_j$.

6. **For** $j = 1$ to p **do**:

   (a) Set $\mathcal{R}_j \leftarrow \{A \mid A \in \mathcal{A}, dist_{\tilde{G}(\mathcal{A})}(A, A_j) = 2\}$.

   (b) Set $\mathcal{A} \leftarrow \mathcal{A} - \mathcal{R}_j$.

7. **For** every $A \in \mathcal{H} \cap \mathcal{A}$ **do**:

   (a) Select some $\mathcal{R}_j$ such that $dist_{\tilde{G}(\mathcal{A})}(A, \mathcal{R}_j) = 1$.

   (b) Set $\mathcal{R}_j \leftarrow \mathcal{R}_j \cup \{A\}$.

   (c) Set $\mathcal{A} \leftarrow \mathcal{A} \setminus \{A\}$.

8. Set $\mathcal{S} \leftarrow \{\bigcup \mathcal{R}_1, \ldots, \bigcup \mathcal{R}_p\}$.

End-while
Set $\mathcal{T} \leftarrow \mathcal{T} \cup \mathcal{S}$.

Figure 13.4: Algorithm MAX_PART$_c$.

Finally, inspection of the algorithm reveals that every cluster of $\mathcal{A}_{i-1}$ is merged into exactly one cluster of $\mathcal{A}_i$, since it is removed from $\mathcal{A}$ immediately upon being added into some $\mathcal{R}_j$. Hence $\mathcal{A}_i$ is a partition. $\square$

Lemma 13.2.6 *For every* $i \geq 1$, $s_i \geq n^{2^{i-1}/\kappa}$.

Proof: Note that $s_0 \geq 1$. The claim now follows by induction on i, once proving that $s_i \geq n^{1/\kappa} \cdot s_{i-1}^2$. This follows from the following two observations. First, every cluster of $\mathcal{A}_{i-1}$ is merged in the ith iteration, since every such cluster is at $dist_{\tilde{G}(\mathcal{A})} = 2$ from some cluster in the maximal $\mathcal{C}_{i-1}$. Second, for every A_j and for every $A \in \Gamma^c(A_j)$, the cluster A is included in $\mathcal{R}_j$, so $\bigcup \Gamma^c(A_j) \subseteq \bigcup \mathcal{R}_j$, and therefore by the fact that A_j is bad,

$$\left| \bigcup \mathcal{R}_j \right| \geq \sum_{A \in \Gamma^c(A_j)} |A| \geq n^{1/\kappa} \cdot s_{i-1}^2. \qquad \square$$

This lemma implies that the main loop is performed for at most $\log \kappa$ iterations. Similarly to Lemma 13.2.3 we prove the next lemma.

Lemma 13.2.7 $Rad(\mathcal{A}_i) \leq 5^i \cdot Rad(\mathcal{S}) + (5^i - 1)/2.$

This implies that $Rad(\mathcal{T})/Rad(\mathcal{S}) \leq 2 \cdot 5^{\log \kappa} = 2 \cdot \kappa^{\log 5}$ and thus establishes Property (1) and completes the proof of the theorem. □

13.3 Other types of partitions

The basic idea behind our partitioning algorithms can also be applied to construct other types of partitions, bounding parameters other than the vertex-degree or the cluster-degree. Let us illustrate this point by considering the following variant of the problem, extending Exercise 6 of Chapter 11. Consider an unweighted graph $G = (V, E)$, $|V| = n$, and a partition $\mathcal{S}$. Let E_{in} denote the set of E edges whose endpoints ended up in the same cluster of $\mathcal{S}$, and let E_{out} denote the set of E edges whose endpoints ended up in different clusters of $\mathcal{S}$. We may sometimes wish to construct a partition minimizing E_{out}. In particular, given some parameter $x \geq 1$, we may wish to ensure that $|E_{out}| \leq |E|/x$. (Note that this goal is different from that of minimizing the number of intercluster edges in the cluster graph representing $\mathcal{S}$; two distinct E edges connecting the same two clusters $S, S' \in \mathcal{S}$, but with different endpoints, are counted twice in E_{out}, whereas they contribute only one to the count of intercluster edges in the cluster graph.) This task is achievable by essentially the same gradual "cluster growing" process, only with a different termination rule: after constructing a new layer for a cluster C, we count the number of edges in the set $E_{out}(C)$ of E_{out} edges that connect the current cluster C to the new layer, and the size of the set $E_{in}(C)$ of edges added to E_{in} by C, and halt once the ratio $|E_{out}(C)|/|E_{in}(C)|$ is no greater than $1/x$. The details of the resulting algorithm, named AV_PART$_e$, are left to Exercise 5. We thus have the following theorem.

Theorem 13.3.1 *Given an unweighted graph $G = (V, E)$, $|V| = n$, and a parameter $x \geq 1$, it is possible to construct a partition $\mathcal{T}$ that satisfies the following properties:*

(1) $Rad(\mathcal{T}) \leq x \ln |E|$, and

(2) $|E_{out}| \leq |E|/x.$ □

It should be clear that by using slightly more elaborate termination rules, it is possible to enforce *combinations* of a number of desirable conditions. For example, it is possible to devise an algorithm for constructing a partition guaranteeing both low average cluster degree and low $|E_{out}|$ simultaneously (see Exercise 7).

Bibliographical notes

The average cluster-degree partition of Section 13.1.1 is based on a natural extension of the algorithm of Section 11.5. The average vertex-degree weak partition of Section 13.1.2 is sketched in [Pel89b]. The maximum vertex-degree and cluster-degree partitions of Sections 13.2.1 and 13.2.2 are from [Pel89b] and [AP90c], respectively. Variants of partitioning algorithms optimizing different parameters were used in [AP90a, AKPW95, ABCP93].

Exercises

1. Prove Theorems 13.1.1 and 13.1.2.

2. What might go wrong if algorithm AV_PART$_c$ is applied to a *weighted* graph G? In particular, would it yield a result analogous to Theorem 13.1.1?

3. ($*$) Design an algorithm for the low average vertex-degree partition problem with connected clusters and strong radius bounds.

4. Suppose we change the definition of $\Delta^C{}_c$ to $\Delta^C{}_c(\mathcal{S}) = \max_{S \in \mathcal{S}}\{|\Gamma^c(S)|\}$ (i.e., we no longer normalize the neighborhood size by $|S|$). Show that under such a definition, any radius/degree trade-off similar to Theorem 13.2.4 must be much worse. (Specifically, show that for any $\kappa \geq 1$, there exist a graph G and an initial partition $\mathcal{S}$ such that any coarsening partition $\mathcal{T}$ satisfying $Rad(\mathcal{T}) \leq \kappa \cdot Rad(\mathcal{S})$ will have $\Delta^C{}_c(\mathcal{T}) = \Omega(n/\kappa)$.)

5. Complete the details of Algorithm Av_PART$_e$ of Section 13.3, and prove Theorem 13.3.1.

6. Show that for the family of planar graphs, Theorem 13.3.1 can be strengthened by guaranteeing an improved radius bound of $Rad(\mathcal{T}) \leq cx$ for constant $c > 0$.

7. Devise an algorithm for constructing a partition guaranteeing both low average cluster degree and low $|E_{out}|$.

8. Establish a *weighted* analog of Theorem 13.3.1 by providing an algorithm that, given a weighted graph $G = (V, E, \omega)$, $W = \omega(E) = \sum_{e \in E} \omega(e)$, and a parameter $x \geq 1$, constructs a partition $\mathcal{T}$ satisfying (1) $Rad(\mathcal{T}) = O(x \ln W)$ and (2) $\omega(E_{out}) \leq W/x$.

Chapter 14

Related graph representations

This chapter introduces a number of locality-preserving graph representations related to partitions and covers and discusses their main properties.

14.1 Hierarchical cover constructions

In many of the known applications for sparse covers, it is necessary to have available a *collection* of covers with varying locality levels. More specifically, it is usually convenient to have covers coarsening the ρ_i-neighborhoods of vertices for some increasing sequence of radii ρ_i, typically $\rho_i = 2^i$. We refer to the resulting collection as a *hierarchy* of covers, $(\mathcal{S}_i)_{i \geq 1}$, where each $\mathcal{S}_i$ is an appropriately selected sparse cover coarsening the ρ_i-neighborhood cover $\hat{\Gamma}_{\rho_i}(V)$.

It turns out that for many applications based on cover hierarchies, there need to be no structural relations between the covers generated on different levels of the hierarchy; rather, the hierarchy can be composed of a collection of independent, unrelated covers. In some special cases, however, this is inadequate and it is necessary to ensure that each cover is a *refinement* of the cover on the next level up the hierarchy. More precisely, the required property is that a cluster in a higher level is composed of an (exact) *union* of clusters in the level below it. We refer to a hierarchy of covers enjoying this property as a *refinement hierarchy*.

14.1.1 The refinement hierarchy

Our approach for constructing a refinement hierarchy is based on first constructing a hierarchy of *pivot vertices* in the network and then defining a corresponding hierarchy of covers on top of it, with higher-level pivots controlling higher-level clusters (i.e., larger regions of the network). The construction is parameterized by a fixed integer $\kappa \geq 1$. Fix $\vartheta = 6\kappa$, and let $\Lambda_\vartheta = \lceil \log_\vartheta Diam(G) \rceil$. The hierarchy consists of $\Lambda_\vartheta + 1$ levels, numbered 0 through Λ_ϑ. In each level i, the graph is covered by clusters (namely, connected subgraphs) of radius ϑ^{i+1}, each managed by a pivot vertex.

We denote the collection of level i pivots by $\mathcal{P}_i$. We refer to the level i cluster associated with the pivot p as $T_i(p)$. The collection of clusters corresponding to $\mathcal{P}_i$ is denoted by

$$\mathcal{T}_i = \{T_i(p) \mid p \in \mathcal{P}_i\}.$$

For every i, each pivot $p \in \mathcal{P}_{i+1}$ has a collection of *subordinate* level i pivots, denoted $\mathrm{Sub}_i(p)$. This collection consists of all level i pivots whose territory is contained in that of p, i.e.,

$$\text{Sub}_i(p) = \{p' \in \mathcal{P}_i \mid T_i(p') \subseteq T_{i+1}(p)\}.$$

We refer to p as the *supervisor* of the pivots in $\text{Sub}_i(p)$. Subsequently, for a pivot $p \in \mathcal{P}_i$, we define

$$\text{Super}_{i+1}(p) = \{p' \in \mathcal{P}_{i+1} \mid T_i(p) \subseteq T_{i+1}(p')\}.$$

The pivot collections and the corresponding clusters are selected so as to form a refinement hierarchy, defined as follows.

Definition 14.1.1 [Refinement hierarchy]: *Given a weighted graph $G = (V, E, \omega)$ and a parameter $\kappa \geq 1$, a* refinement hierarchy *is a collection of covers and pivot sets*

$$\{(\mathcal{P}_i, T_i) \mid 0 \leq i \leq \Lambda\}$$

that satisfy the following requirements.

(H1) For every $p \in \mathcal{P}_i$, $T_i(p) = \bigcup_{p' \in \text{Sub}_{i-1}(p)} T_{i-1}(p')$.

(H2) Every cluster $T \in T_i$ contains at least one neighborhood $\Gamma_{\vartheta^i}(v)$ for some $v \in V$.

(H3) T_i subsumes $\hat{\Gamma}_{\vartheta^i}(V)$,

(H4) $\text{Rad}(T_i) \leq \vartheta^{i+1}$,

(H5) $\Delta^C(T_i) = O(\kappa \cdot n^{1/\kappa})$.

Of these requirements, (H1) is the one guaranteeing the desired refinement relationships between successive levels in the hierarchy.

14.1.2 Constructing a refinement hierarchy

Let us now describe how to construct a refinement hierarchy $\mathcal{RH}_\kappa$ for a given parameter $\kappa \geq 1$. In level 0, every vertex is a pivot and it manages only itself. For $i \geq 1$, level i of the hierarchy is constructed by constructing an initial cover $\mathcal{S}_i$ of the graph in a particular way and then constructing a cover T_i from $\mathcal{S}_i$ by applying the Maximum Cover Theorem 12.4.1 with parameter κ. A detailed description of Algorithm H_COVER for constructing the refinement hierarchy $\mathcal{RH}_\kappa$ is given in Figure 14.1.

14.1.3 Properties

Lemma 14.1.2 *The hierarchy constructed by Algorithm H_COVER is a refinement hierarchy, namely, it satisfies Properties (H1)–(H5) above.*

Proof: Property (H1) is proved as follows. Consider some cluster $T_i(p) \in T_i$. The $\supseteq$ inclusion is immediate from the definition of $\text{Sub}_i(p)$. So it is necessary to prove that

$$T_i(p) \subseteq \bigcup_{p' \in \text{Sub}_{i-1}(p)} T_{i-1}(p').$$

First note that by construction, every cluster $S_v \in \mathcal{S}_i$ is the union of some clusters of T_{i-1}. Next, by the Maximum Cover Theorem 12.4.1, $T_i(p)$ is the union of some clusters of $\mathcal{S}_i$. Hence $T_i(p)$ is the union of some clusters of T_{i-1}. The pivots of each of these clusters are in the set $\text{Sub}_{i-1}(p)$, hence the claim follows.

Property (H2) follows from the fact that every cluster $T_i(p) \in T_i$ contains at least one cluster $S_v \in \mathcal{S}_i$, which in turn contains $\Gamma_{\vartheta^i}(v)$.

For level $i = 0$ do:

   1. Set $\mathcal{P}_0 \leftarrow V$.

   2. Set $T_0(v) \leftarrow \{v\}$ for every v.

   3. Set $\mathcal{T}_0 \leftarrow \{T_0(v) \mid v \in V\}$.

For level $i = 1$ to Λ_ϑ do:

   1. /* Construct an initial cover $\mathcal{S}_i$ of the graph */
      For every vertex v do:

      (a) Let
$$\mathcal{F}_{i-1}(v) \leftarrow \{T \in \mathcal{T}_{i-1} \mid T \cap \Gamma_{\vartheta^i}(v) \neq \emptyset\}.$$

      (b) Let $S_v \leftarrow \bigcup_{T \in \mathcal{F}_{i-1}(v)} T$.

      (c) Let $\mathcal{S}_i \leftarrow \{S_v \mid v \in V\}$.

   2. Construct a cover $\mathcal{T}_i$ from $\mathcal{S}_i$ by applying the Maximum Cover Theorem 12.4.1 with parameter κ.

   3. Select a center vertex in each cluster $T \in \mathcal{T}_i$ and appoint it as the pivot $p(T)$.

   4. Set $\mathcal{P}_i \leftarrow \{p(T) \mid T \in \mathcal{T}_i\}$.

Figure 14.1: Algorithm H_COVER.

Property (H3) follows from the transitivity of the subsuming relation, since $\mathcal{S}_i$ subsumes $\hat{\Gamma}_{\vartheta^i}(V)$ by definition, and by Property (1) of Theorem 12.4.1, $\mathcal{T}_i$ subsumes $\mathcal{S}_i$.

Property (H4) is proved by induction on i. It holds trivially for $i = 0$. Now assume the property for $\mathcal{T}_{i-1}$ and consider level i ($i \geq 1$). By the definition of $\mathcal{S}_i$, each cluster $S_v \in \mathcal{S}_i$ has radius $Rad(S_v) \leq \vartheta^i + 2Rad(\mathcal{T}_{i-1})$. By the assumption on $\mathcal{T}_{i-1}$, it follows that $Rad(\mathcal{S}_i) \leq 3\vartheta^i$. It now follows from Property (2) of the Maximum Cover Theorem 12.4.1 that

$$Rad(\mathcal{T}_i) \leq (2\kappa - 1)Rad(\mathcal{S}_i) \leq 6\kappa \cdot \vartheta^i = \vartheta^{i+1}.$$

Property (H5) follows directly from Property (3) of Theorem 12.4.1. $\qquad\square$

14.2 Network decomposition

Another type of network representation introduced next is *network decomposition*. The importance of the concept lies in the fact that a decomposition can be used for designing deterministic distributed algorithms for problems like coloring and MIS with low overheads (depending on the parameters of the decomposition). This representation is defined as follows.

Definition 14.2.1 [(d, c)-decomposition]: *Consider a partition $\mathcal{S}$ of a weighted graph $G = (V, E)$. Then $\mathcal{S}$ is a (d, c)-decomposition of the graph G if*

- *the maximum radius of a cluster in G is $Rad(\mathcal{S}) \leq d$, and*

- *the chromatic number of the cluster graph $\tilde{G}(\mathcal{S})$ is $\chi(\tilde{G}(\mathcal{S})) \leq c$.*

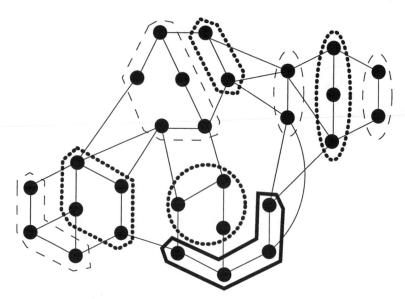

Figure 14.2: A graph and a $(2,3)$-decomposition for it.

Figure 14.2 depicts a graph with a $(2,3)$-decomposition.

Example: *Decompositions for planar graphs.*

It follows from the celebrated four-color theorem that every planar graph has a $(1,4)$-decomposition.   □

14.2.1   Decomposition algorithm DECOMP

An efficient network decomposition can be obtained by Algorithm DECOMP, described next. The algorithm involves multiple applications of Procedure SEP_PART from Section 12.3.3 (Figure 12.5), handling a different graph in each invocation. Hence we will consider the input graph to be a parameter of the procedure.

Algorithm DECOMP operates as follows. In the first iteration, construct a 2-separated partial partition for $\mathcal{R} = \hat{\Gamma}_0(V)$ (or simply V). Assign color 1 to all the output clusters, and delete them from the graph. On the next iteration, continue with the graph induced by the remaining vertices. Repeat these iterations until no more vertices remain.

Note that the resulting Algorithm DECOMP is quite similar to Algorithm AV_COVER. One difference is that the procedure used there was PART (i.e., the guaranteed separation was 1). Separation 2 is necessary in order to guarantee that all the output clusters of a single iteration can be colored by a single color. Another difference is that in Algorithm AV_COVER, all applications of the partial partition procedure are on the original graph. This results in possible overlaps between clusters constructed in different iterations. Here, in contrast, the procedure is applied in each iteration to the graph $G(R)$ induced by the remaining vertices, hence all clusters generated throughout all iterations are disjoint. (Note that in later iterations, this induced graph may be disconnected. In such a case, each connected component is partitioned separately.)

A formal description of Algorithm DECOMP is given in Figure 14.3.

```
Set i ← 1.
Set R ← V.
Repeat

    1. (DR, DT) ← SEP_PART(R, 2, 0, G(R), κ).

    2. T ← T ∪ DT.

    3. Color the clusters of DT by color i.

    4. Erase the vertices in DR from R.

    5. i ← i + 1.

until R = ∅.
Output (T).
```

Figure 14.3: Algorithm DECOMP(G, κ).

14.2.2 Properties

The decomposition algorithm DECOMP establishes the following theorem.

Theorem 14.2.2 [Decomposition]: *For every weighted graph $G = (V, E, \omega)$, $|V| = n$, for all $\kappa \geq 1$ Algorithm DECOMP constructs an $(O(\kappa), O(\kappa n^{1/\kappa}))$-decomposition.*

Proof: Let us first note that the final collection T is a partition, since each collection DT generated by Procedure SEP_PART is a partial partition, and vertices participating in the output collection DT of a particular iteration are subsequently removed from the graph.

Since starting an iteration with a set R results with a set DR of size $|DR| = \Omega(|R|^{1-1/\kappa})$, the process continues for only $O(\kappa n^{1/\kappa})$ iterations (see proof of the Maximum Cover Theorem 12.4.1). Hence we end up with $O(\kappa n^{1/\kappa})$ colors and each cluster has $O(\kappa)$ diameter. □

Picking $\kappa = \log n$, we achieve the following corollary.

Corollary 14.2.3 *For every weighted graph $G = (V, E, \omega)$, $|V| = n$, it is possible to construct an $(O(\log n), O(\log n))$-decomposition.*

Later on (in Section 21.1 and Chapter 22) we discuss also the issue of fast distributed algorithms for constructing decompositions. The application of these algorithms to the problems of distributed coloring and MIS computation is discussed further in Section 25.2.

14.3   Regional matchings

A convenient "high-level" abstraction based on covers that has proved extremely useful in several applications is the *regional matching*. This paradigm is similar in principle to the *global matching* discussed in Section 10.2.5. Our focus on locality leads naturally to the introduction of a localized variant of the match-making paradigm. In this section we introduce the concept of a regional matching geared towards this goal.

The basic components of our construction are the same as in a global matching, namely, a "read set" Read$(v) \subseteq V$ and a "write set" Write$(v) \subseteq V$ for every vertex $v \in V$. The resulting collection of sets

$$\mathcal{RW} = \{ \text{Read}(v), \text{Write}(v) \mid v \in V \}$$

is an ρ-*regional matching* if the read set of a vertex intersects the write set of every other vertex within distance ρ from it. More formally, we state the following definition.

Definition 14.3.1 [ρ-regional matching]: *The collection $\mathcal{RW}$ is an ρ-regional matching (for some integer $\rho \geq 1$) if for all $v, u \in V$,*

$$dist(u, v) \leq \rho \quad \Rightarrow \quad \texttt{Write}(v) \bigcap \texttt{Read}(u) \neq \emptyset.$$

The relevant parameters of a regional matching are its *radius*, which is the maximal distance from a vertex to any other vertex in its read or write set, and its *degree*, which is the maximal number of vertices in any read or write set. It is convenient to evaluate the radii of the sets by looking at their *stretch*, or ratio, with respect to ρ. Formally, for any m-regional matching $\mathcal{RW}$ define the following four parameters:

$$\Delta_{write}(\mathcal{RW}) = \max_{v \in V}\{|\texttt{Write}(v)|\},$$

$$\texttt{Str}_{write}(\mathcal{RW}) = \frac{1}{\rho} \cdot \max_{u,v \in V}\{dist(u, v) \mid u \in \texttt{Write}(v)\},$$

$$\Delta_{read}(\mathcal{RW}) = \max_{v \in V}\{|\texttt{Read}(v)|\},$$

$$\texttt{Str}_{read}(\mathcal{RW}) = \frac{1}{\rho} \cdot \max_{u,v \in V}\{dist(u, v) \mid u \in \texttt{Read}(v)\}.$$

Again, there appears to be a trade-off between the degree and radius parameters, making simultaneous minimization of both of them a nontrivial task. We next describe how by using Algorithm MAX_COVER it is possible to construct a regional matching with reasonably low radius and degree.

14.3.1   Regional matching construction

Algorithm REG_MATCH for constructing a regional matching $\mathcal{RW}_{\rho,\kappa}$ given the graph G and the integers $\kappa, \rho \geq 1$ is presented in Figure 14.4.

---

1. Set $\mathcal{S} = \hat{\Gamma}_\rho(V)$.

2. Construct a coarsening cover $\mathcal{T}$ for $\mathcal{S}$, as in the Maximum Cover Theorem 12.4.1, using Algorithm MAX_COVER.

3. **For** each cluster $T \in \mathcal{T}$ **do:**
   Select a center vertex $r(T)$ of $G(T)$ (in the graph-theoretic sense of Section 2.1.2).

4. Select for every vertex v a cluster $T_v \in \mathcal{T}$ such that $\Gamma_\rho(v) \subseteq T_v$.

5. Set $\texttt{Write}(v) \leftarrow \{r(T) \mid v \in T\}$,
   $\texttt{Read}(v) \leftarrow \{r(T_v)\}$.

Figure 14.4: Algorithm REG_MATCH.

Note that step 4, involving the selection of a cluster $T_v \in \mathcal{T}$ such that $\Gamma_\rho(v) \subseteq T_v$, can always be performed since $\mathcal{T}$ coarsens $\hat{\Gamma}_\rho(V)$, so at least one such cluster must exist for every vertex v.

14.3.2 Properties

Bounds on $\mathtt{Str}_{write}$, Δ_{write}, $\mathtt{Str}_{read}$ and Δ_{read} are provided directly from the Maximum Cover Theorem 12.4.1, noting that $|\mathcal{S}| = |\hat{\Gamma}_\rho(V)| = n$. We need to argue that the defined collection of sets meets our requirements.

Lemma 14.3.2 *The set $\mathcal{RW}_{\rho,\kappa}$ constructed by Algorithm REG_MATCH is an ρ-regional matching.*

Proof: Consider two processors u, v such that $dist(u, v) \leq \rho$. Let T_v be the cluster such that $\mathtt{Read}(v) = \{r(T_v)\}$. By definition, $u \in \Gamma_\rho(v)$. Hence $\Gamma_\rho(v) \subseteq T_v$ implies $u \in T_v$; therefore $r(T_v) \in \mathtt{Write}(u)$, so $\mathtt{Read}(u) \cap \mathtt{Write}(v) \neq \emptyset$. $\square$

This establishes the following theorem.

Theorem 14.3.3 [Regional matching]: *For every weighted graph $G = (V, E, \omega)$, $|V| = n$, and all $\rho, \kappa \geq 1$, it is possible to construct a ρ-regional matching $\mathcal{RW}_{\rho,\kappa}$ with*

$$
\begin{aligned}
\Delta_{read}(\mathcal{RW}_{\rho,\kappa}) &= 1, \\
\Delta_{write}(\mathcal{RW}_{\rho,\kappa}) &\leq 2\kappa \cdot n^{1/\kappa}, \\
\mathtt{Str}_{read}(\mathcal{RW}_{\rho,\kappa}) &\leq 2\kappa + 1, \\
\mathtt{Str}_{write}(\mathcal{RW}_{\rho,\kappa}) &\leq 2\kappa + 1. \quad \square
\end{aligned}
$$

By taking $\kappa = \log n$, we get the following useful form of regional matchings.

Corollary 14.3.4 *For every weighted graph $G = (V, E, \omega)$, $|V| = n$, and all $\rho \geq 1$, it is possible to construct a ρ-regional matching $\mathcal{RW}_\rho$ with*

$$
\begin{aligned}
\Delta_{read}(\mathcal{RW}_\rho) &= 1, \\
\Delta_{write}(\mathcal{RW}_\rho) &= O(\log n), \\
\mathtt{Str}_{read}(\mathcal{RW}_\rho) &= O(\log n), \\
\mathtt{Str}_{write}(\mathcal{RW}_\rho) &= O(\log n). \quad \square
\end{aligned}
$$

Later on, in Section 16.2, we discuss some lower bounds on the trade-offs between radius and degree for regional matchings.

14.4 Cardinality-based clusters

In estimating the locality level of clusters, it is possible to rely on parameters other than radius. In particular, it is possible to define a notion of neighborhoods based on size. The *size-neighborhood* of a vertex $v \in V$, with respect to a parameter $j \geq 1$, is a collection of the j nearest vertices to v, breaking ties consistently. For concreteness, order the vertices of S by increasing distance from v, breaking ties by increasing vertex names. Hence $x \prec_v y$ if either $dist(x, v) < dist(y, v)$ or both $dist(x, v) = dist(y, v)$ and $x < y$. Then $\Gamma^s(v, j)$ contains the first j vertices according to the order $\prec_v$. A size-neighborhood can also be restricted to some specific subset of vertices S from which the first j neighbors are picked.

The basic facts regarding neighborhoods that make them useful are the following.

Lemma 14.4.1 *For every weighted graph $G = (V, E, \omega)$, for every vertex $w \in V$,*

1. *if $w \in \Gamma^s(v, j)$, then $dist(v, w) \leq Rad(v, \Gamma^s(v, j))$,*

2. *if $w \notin \Gamma^s(v, j)$, then $dist(v, w) \geq Rad(v, \Gamma^s(v, j))$.*

The crucial consistency (or monotonicity) property maintained by this structure of neighborhoods is the following (see Figure 14.5(a)).

Lemma 14.4.2 *For every weighted graph $G = (V, E, \omega)$ and $v, u, x \in V$, if $v \in \Gamma^s(u, j)$ and x occurs on some shortest path connecting u and v, then also $v \in \Gamma^s(x, j)$.*

Proof: The proof follows by contradiction. Assume that $w \notin \Gamma^s(x, j)$. We claim that for every vertex z, if $z \in \Gamma^s(x, j)$, then $z \in \Gamma^s(v, j)$. In order to prove this it suffices to show that every $z \in \Gamma^s(x, j)$ satisfies $z \prec_v w$, since w is included in $\Gamma^s(v, j)$. Consider some $z \in \Gamma^s(x, j)$. By the triangle inequality,

$$dist(v, z) \leq dist(v, x) + dist(x, z).$$

By Lemma 14.4.1, $dist(x, z) \leq dist(x, w)$. Since x is on a shortest path from v to w, $dist(v, w) = dist(v, x) + dist(x, w)$. Put together,

$$dist(v, z) \leq dist(v, w).$$

There are two cases to consider. If $dist(v, z) < dist(v, w)$, then the claim is immediate. Now suppose $dist(v, z) = dist(v, w)$, then necessarily $dist(x, z) = dist(x, w)$, too. Since $w \notin \Gamma^s(x, j)$ and $z \in \Gamma^s(x, j)$, by definition $z \prec_x w$, so $z < w$. Therefore $z \prec_v w$. It follows from our claim that $\Gamma^s(x, j) \subseteq \Gamma^s(v, j)$, and since both are of size j, $\Gamma^s(x, j) = \Gamma^s(v, j)$. But $w \in \Gamma^s(v, j) - \Gamma^s(x, j)$; this is a contradiction.   □

Size-neighborhoods also satisfy the following form of "triangle inequality" (see Figure 14.5(b)).

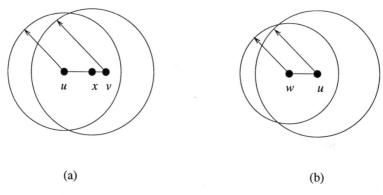

(a)   (b)

Figure 14.5: Properties of size-neighborhoods.

Lemma 14.4.3 *For every two vertices $u, w \in V$ and integer $1 \leq j \leq n$,*

$$Rad(u, \Gamma^s(u, j)) \leq Rad(w, \Gamma^s(w, j)) + dist(u, w).$$

Proof: The proof follows by contradiction, relying on the fact that $|\Gamma^s(u, j)| = |\Gamma^s(w, j)| = j$.   □

This modified version of neighborhoods is complemented with a different concept of "covers." Instead of covering neighborhoods with coarsening clusters, the idea is to select a small set $\mathcal{P}$ of "representative" vertices, such that each neighborhood is represented by at least one member of $\mathcal{P}$. The pivot selection process has to guarantee that pivots are well distributed and properly "cover" the neighborhoods in the network. The problem of selecting a minimal size set $\mathcal{P}$ of representatives (which can be formalized as a "hitting set" or "set cover" problem) is of course NP-hard, but relatively efficient (greedy deterministic or randomized) approximation algorithms exist for it.

Bibliographical notes

Network decomposition was defined in [AGLP89] and later studied in several papers, e.g., [LS91c, ABCP92a, ABCP92b, ABCP93, PS92b, PS95, Cow94]. The decomposition Theorem 14.2.2 is due to [LS91c]. Decompositions and their connection to the related notion of cut covers were also studied in [PRS94].

The concept of distributed match-making was introduced and studied in [MV88, KV88], as discussed in Chapter 10. The matchmaking functions of [MV88] are somewhat different from regional matchings. In particular, they do not have any distance limitation and they insist on having exactly one element in each intersection.

Regional matchings were defined, applied and studied in [AP90c, AP91, KS91, AP95]. Exercises 1 and 3 are due to [KS91], and Exercise 5 is due to [HP00].

Cardinality-based neighborhoods were introduced in [ABLP90]. The basic lemmas concerning their properties, namely, Lemma 14.4.1 and Lemma 14.4.2, appear there and are based on [Lov75]. This type of cluster was applied in [ABLP90, ABLP89] for the design of routing schemes with compact routing tables, discussed at length in Chapter 26. Somewhat related are approximation algorithms for selecting network representatives, or centers, discussed in several places, e.g., [Lov75, Chv79, HS84, HS86, ABLP89, BP91, BKP92].

Exercises

1. Consider the graph $G = (V, E)$, where $V = \{0, 1, \ldots, 99\}$ and $E = E_1 \cup E_2$, with

$$
\begin{aligned}
E_1 &= \{(v, v + i \bmod 100) \mid v \in V, \ i = 1, 2, 3, 4\}, \\
E_2 &= \{(v, v + 10i + 5 \bmod 100) \mid v \in V, \ i = 0, 1, \ldots, 9\}.
\end{aligned}
$$

Find a $(1, 2)$-decomposition for G.

2. Show that the degree bounds in Corollary 14.3.4 can be reversed, yielding a ρ-regional matching $\mathcal{RW}_\rho$ with $\Delta_{read}(\mathcal{RW}_\rho) = O(\log n)$ and $\Delta_{write}(\mathcal{RW}_\rho) = 1$.

3. Given a tree T and an integer ρ, show how to construct a ρ-regional matching $\mathcal{RW}$ on T with $\Delta_{write}(\mathcal{RW})$, $\Delta_{read}(\mathcal{RW})$, $\mathtt{Str}_{write}(\mathcal{RW})$ and $\mathtt{Str}_{read}(\mathcal{RW})$ all bounded above by 2.

4. Given a 2-dimensional grid G and an integer ρ, show how to construct a ρ-regional matching $\mathcal{RW}$ on G with $\Delta_{write}(\mathcal{RW}), \Delta_{read}(\mathcal{RW}) \leq 9$ and $\mathtt{Str}_{write}(\mathcal{RW})$, $\mathtt{Str}_{read}(\mathcal{RW}) = O(1)$. Generalize your construction to k-dimensional grids for constant k. (The degree bound may depend on k.)

5. Given a 2-dimensional Euclidean graph G (where the vertices are points in the plane and distances are taken in the usual L_2 norm) and an integer ρ, show how to construct a ρ-regional matching $\mathcal{RW}$ on G with $\Delta_{write}(\mathcal{RW}), \Delta_{read}(\mathcal{RW}) = O(1)$ and $\mathtt{Str}_{write}(\mathcal{RW}), \mathtt{Str}_{read}(\mathcal{RW}) = O(1)$.

6. For $\rho = 1, 2$, show that every graph G with maximal degree Δ has a ρ-regional matching $\mathcal{RW}$ with $\Delta_{write}(\mathcal{RW}), \Delta_{read}(\mathcal{RW}) \leq \Delta + 1$ and $\mathtt{Str}_{write}(\mathcal{RW}), \mathtt{Str}_{read}(\mathcal{RW}) \leq 1$.

7. Consider the following construction for a regional matching. Given a set of vertices $X \subseteq V$, let $\mathtt{Write}(v) = X$ and $\mathtt{Read}(v) = \{near(v, X)\}$ for every vertex v, where $near(v)$ is the nearest vertex to v in X.

(a) Prove that the resulting collection $\mathcal{RW}_X$ of read and write sets is a matching (i.e., a $Diam(G)$-regional matching).

(b) Show that for every n-vertex unweighted graph $G = (V, E)$, it is possible to select a set X of $O(\sqrt{n})$ vertices such that $\mathcal{RW}_X$ satisfies $\text{Str}_{read}(\mathcal{RW}_X) = O(\sqrt{n})$. (Hint: Use Exercise 2.)

(c) Prove that the above is (existentially) the best possible, i.e., show that for every $n \geq 1$ there exists an n-vertex unweighted graph $G = (V, E)$ such that $\text{Str}_{read}(\mathcal{RW}_X) = \Omega(\sqrt{n})$ for every set $X \subseteq V$ of size $|X| = O(\sqrt{n})$.

(d) What (global and existential) upper and lower bounds can be given on $\text{Str}_{write}(\mathcal{RW}_X)$ in general? Prove your answer.

Chapter 15

Skeletal representations: Spanning trees, tree covers and spanners

The representations discussed so far were all of a different nature from the graph itself: rather than a collection of edges, they were based on collections of clusters, pairs of sets or hierarchies of the above.

In the remainder of Part II, we consider *skeletal representations*, namely, representations based on sparse subgraphs of the network itself. As we shall see, a sparse skeletal representation may be useful as a substitution for using the entire network in various applications.

15.1 Representation types and relevant parameters

We consider two kinds of skeletal representations. The representations of the first type are called *spanners*. These are connected subgraphs spanning all the vertices of the network. The most common special case of a spanner is a *spanning tree* of the graph, and we define and discuss spanning trees with various desirable properties.

The second type of skeletal representations we consider involves a collection of subgraphs, which collectively cover the entire network. In particular, we introduce and discuss the notion of a *tree cover*, which is a collection of trees covering the network.

In all cases, we are mostly interested in representations that preserve the locality properties of the original network or, in other words, approximately preserve distances (up to some ratio). Naturally, there are close connections between these skeletal representations and the cover-based representations we've seen earlier, and we discuss these connections at length as we go along.

15.1.1 Locality and sparsity

The two basic types of qualitative criteria we focused on for cluster design, namely, locality and sparsity, reappear when we discuss skeletal representations, although their technical manifestation and parameters are somewhat different. Another point of similarity is that, just as happened with clustered representations, here too the parameters of locality and sparsity tend to go opposite ways and reveal similar trade-offs.

For now, let us focus on spanners, i.e., representations based on a single spanning subgraph. The appropriate measures for collections of subgraphs is discussed in Section 15.5.

Locality measures

Roughly speaking, the extent to which a skeletal representation preserves locality is measured by its *stretch*, namely, the changes in intervertex distances imposed by using it. This gives rise to the following more formal definition.

Definition 15.1.1 [Stretch]: *Given a weighted graph $G = (V, E, \omega)$ and a spanning subgraph $G' = (V, E')$ of G such that $E' \subseteq E$, we define the following parameters. For a distinguished root vertex $r_0 \in V$, define the* root-stretch *(or simply the* stretch*) of G' with respect to r_0 as*

$$\text{Stretch}(G', r_0) = \max_{v \in V} \left\{ \frac{dist_{G'}(r_0, v)}{dist_G(r_0, v)} \right\}.$$

The stretch factor *of G' is*

$$\text{Stretch}(G') = \max_{u, w \in V} \left\{ \frac{dist_{G'}(u, w)}{dist_G(u, w)} \right\}.$$

Note that the stretch factor of a spanning subgraph G' equals the maximal root-stretch over all possible roots r_0, i.e.,

$$\text{Stretch}(G') = \max_{r_0 \in V} \{ \text{Stretch}(G', r_0) \}.$$

Sparsity measures

There are two plausible technical measures for the sparsity parameter of a spanner $G' = (V', E')$ of a weighted graph $G = (V, E, \omega)$. The first relies on the *size* of the spanner G', which is simply the number of edges it contains, $|E'|$. The second measure is its *total weight*, $\omega(G')$, as defined in Section 5.5.

15.1.2   Size and girth

There is an interesting connection between the size of a graph and its girth. The *girth* of a graph G, denoted $Girth(G)$, is the minimum unweighted length (number of edges) of a cycle in G. (A single edge is not considered a cycle of length 2, so $Girth(G) \geq 3$ for every G.) In several places later on, we make use of the following known result in extremal graph theory, which provides near-tight bounds on the relationships between the girth of a graph and the number of edges it contains.

Lemma 15.1.2

1. *For every integer $r \geq 3$ and n-vertex, m-edge graph $G = (V, E)$ with $Girth(G) \geq r$, $m \leq n^{1+2/(r-2)} + n$.*

2. *For every integer $r \geq 3$, there exist (infinitely many) n-vertex, m-edge graphs $G = (V, E)$ with $Girth(G) \geq r$ and $m \geq \frac{1}{4}n^{1+1/r}$.* $\square$

15.2   Global skeletal representations: Spanning trees

For many graph problems, it is convenient to simplify the representation of a given graph $G = (V, E, \omega)$ by ignoring the entire set of graph edges and representing the graph by means of a *spanning tree*, namely, a tree $T = (V, E')$ containing all the vertices of G, where $E' \subseteq E$. Such representations lead to simpler algorithms and improved complexities for certain problems. In this section we review some common types of spanning trees with some additional desirable properties.

15.2.1 Basic types of spanning trees

Earlier we discussed three specific types of useful spanning trees, namely, the *BFS tree*, the *MST* and the *DFS tree*. Let us now define an additional type of spanning tree that has proved very useful for several applications in distributed computing, as well as in other areas of computer science. This class of spanning trees extends the BFS tree to weighted graphs and attempts to optimize distances with respect to a specific vertex in the network.

Definition 15.2.1 [Shortest path spanning tree]: *The* shortest path spanning tree, *or* SPT, *of G with respect to a given root r_0 is a spanning tree T_S with the property that for every other vertex $v \neq r_0$, the path leading from r_0 to v in the tree is the shortest possible, or in other words,* $\text{Stretch}(T_S, r_0) = 1$.

For all four types of trees, there are well-known (sequential as well as distributed) algorithms for constructing them.

15.2.2 Controlling tree degrees

Another parameter of relevance to skeletal representations involves vertex degrees. Let $deg_G(v)$ denote the degree of v, i.e., the number of edges incident to it in the graph G. Also, let $\Delta(G)$ denote the maximal vertex degree in the graph,

$$\Delta(G) = \max_{v \in V}\{deg_G(v)\}.$$

In general for spanning trees for a given network, the degrees may be arbitrarily high, which is sometimes undesirable. Consequently, it may be useful to be able to bound these degrees. This can be done by replacing the original tree T with a *virtual tree S* embedded in the original one, with the same set of vertices and with the same root but with a different set of edges, so that the degrees of S are bounded using some parameter m. We next present an algorithm for getting rid of high degrees in this way. Algorithm TREE_EMBED is presented in Figure 15.1.

Figure 15.2 depicts a tree T and the corresponding virtual tree S.

The following theorem establishes the properties of the embedded virtual tree constructed by Algorithm TREE_EMBED.

Theorem 15.2.2 [Degree bounding]: *For any rooted weighted tree T and integer $m \geq 2$, the embedded virtual tree S constructed by Algorithm TREE_EMBED satisfies the following properties.*

(1) $\Delta(S) \leq 2m$,

(2) each edge of S corresponds to a path of length at most two in T, and

(3) $Depth_S(v) \leq (2\log_m \Delta(T) - 1) \cdot Depth_T(v)$ for every vertex v.

For every vertex v in the tree T **do:**

1. Let d_0 be v's degree.
   Let v's children be $v_0, \cdots, v_{d_0-1}$, ordered in nondecreasing order of depth.

2. **For** every $0 \leq i \leq m - 1$ **do:**
   Make v the parent of v_i in the tree S, just as in T.

3. **For** every $m \leq i \leq d_0 - 1$ **do:**

   (a) Set $j \leftarrow \lfloor i/m \rfloor - 1$.
   (b) Make v_j the parent of v_i in the tree S.

Figure 15.1: Algorithm TREE_EMBED(T).

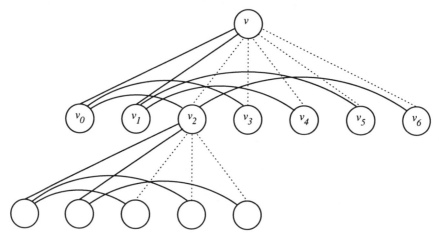

Figure 15.2: A tree T (dotted edges) and the corresponding virtual tree S (solid edges) for $m = 2$.

Proof: Clearly, the resulting collection of edges forms a tree spanning all the vertices of T. Furthermore, every vertex in the new tree S will have at most $2m$ children, including up to m of its closest children and up to m of its siblings in original tree T. This proves property (1) of the theorem. Since a path to a sibling consists of two edges in T, Property (2) follows as well.

To prove Property (3) of the theorem, it is sufficient to show that for any vertices u, v such that u is a child of v in T,

$$dist_S(u, v) \leq (2\log_m \Delta(T) - 1) \cdot dist_T(u, v). \tag{15.1}$$

Indeed, summing Equation (15.1) over a path from v to the root yields Property (3).

To prove Equation (15.1), consider a path P from v to u in S. Since all vertices on that path, except for the last one, are lower-ranked siblings of u, it can be represented as

$$P = (v, v_{i_1}, \ldots, v_{i_q})$$

such that $u = v_{i_q}$. Since $i_{j+1} = \lfloor i_j/m \rfloor - 1$, it follows that the length of the path is at most $q \leq \log_m \Delta(T)$. Recall that children are ranked by their distance, and thus $dist_T(v, v_j) \leq$

$dist_T(v, v_q)$ for $j \leq q$. Observe that the edge $(v_{i_j}, v_{i_{j+1}})$ in S is implemented by a path $(v_{i_j}, v, v_{i_{j+1}})$ in T. Thus,

$$dist_S(v_{i_j}, v_{i_{j+1}}) = dist_T(v_{i_j}, v) + dist_T(v, v_{i_{j+1}}) \leq 2dist_T(v_{i_q}, v) = 2dist_T(u, v).$$

Also,

$$dist_S(v, v_{i_1}) = dist_T(v, v_{i_1}) \leq dist_T(v, u).$$

It follows that the path P consists of at most q edges, $q - 1$ of them of length at most $2dist_T(v, u)$ and one of length at most $dist_T(v, u)$. This completes the proof. □

15.3 Minimum total distance trees

Another type of spanning trees, which we look at next, can be thought of as a variant of the shortest-paths tree that attempts to optimize the *sum* of the distances between *all* vertex pairs in the network.

Definition 15.3.1 [Minimum total distance tree]: *For a subgraph G' spanning the graph $G = (V, E)$, let* $\mathtt{Tot\_D}(G')$ *denote the sum of the distances between any two vertices in G', namely,*

$$\mathtt{Tot\_D}(G') = \sum_{u,v \in V} dist_{G'}(u, v).$$

The minimum total distance tree, or MTDT, of G is a spanning tree T_D minimizing $\mathtt{Tot\_D}(T)$ *over all spanning trees T of G.*

Unfortunately, unlike the situation with BFS, DFS, MST and SPT, we have no efficient procedure for calculating the MTDT of a given graph. In fact, this problem is known to be NP-hard. On the bright side, there is a simple approximation algorithm for the problem whose outcome is a tree T whose cost $\mathtt{Tot\_D}(T)$ is at most twice the optimal. In fact, we next show that there always exists a vertex w in the graph G such that the SPT of G w.r.t. w provides such an approximation.

Lemma 15.3.2 *For every n-vertex instance of the MTDT problem, there is a vertex $w \in V$ such that the SPT of G w.r.t. w, T, satisfies* $\mathtt{Tot\_D}(T) \leq 2\mathtt{Tot\_D}(T^*)$.

Proof: Let T^* be the MTDT of the graph G. Let $p_u = \sum_{v \in V} dist_T(u, v)$ denote the sum of the distances from u to the rest of the vertices in G. Clearly,

$$\mathtt{Tot\_D}(T^*) \geq \sum_{u \in V} p_u.$$

Let w be the vertex with minimum p_w. Then

$$p_w \leq \mathtt{Tot\_D}(T^*)/n.$$

Now let T be a shortest path tree rooted at w. We claim that this tree achieves the desired approximation. Indeed,

$$\mathtt{Tot\_D}(T) = \sum_{u,v \in V} dist_T(u, v) \leq \sum_{u,v \in V} (dist_T(u, w) + dist_T(w, v))$$

$$\leq (n-1) \sum_{u \in V} dist_T(u, w) + (n-1) \sum_{v \in V} dist_T(w, v)$$

$$\leq 2(n-1) \cdot p_w \leq 2\mathtt{Tot\_D}(T^*). \quad □$$

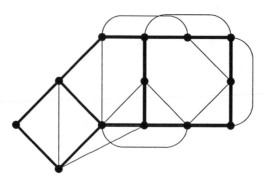

Figure 15.3: A graph and a 2-spanner for it (spanner edges are highlighted).

15.4   Proximity-preserving spanners

As discussed earlier, the best known type of spanners are spanning trees of various sorts. The one most relevant to our discussion of preserving locality is the shortest path tree T_S defined above. This tree preserves the distances in the graph with respect to its root r_0, i.e., it achieves $\texttt{Stretch}(T_S, r_0) = 1$. However, it clearly fails to preserve distances with respect to pairs of vertices not involving the root (or in other words, to bound $\texttt{Stretch}(T_S)$). In fact, it is easy to construct examples in which two neighboring vertices in the graph find themselves at distance $2Depth(T_S)$ of each other in the shortest path tree T_S (as happens, for instance, on the unit-weight ring).

General (nontree) spanners are motivated by this inadequacy of shortest path trees. Actually, they can be thought of intuitively as a relaxation of the concept of a spanning tree, allowing the spanning subgraph to have cycles, in order to provide us with a skeletal representation that is approximately faithful to the original structure and its locality properties. Specifically, a κ-*spanner* of a graph G is a spanning subgraph that approximately maintains the distances between pairs of vertices up to factor κ. More formally, we have the following definition.

Definition 15.4.1 [κ-spanner]: *Given a weighted graph $G = (V, E, \omega)$, we say that the subgraph $G' = (V, E')$ (where $E' \subseteq E$) is a κ-spanner of G if $\texttt{Stretch}(G') \leq \kappa$.*

Example: *2-spanner.*

Figures 15.3 and 15.4 depict an unweighted graph G and a possible 2-spanner for the graph. $\square$

In many applications, one is mainly interested in finding sparse spanners with small stretch factor. In particular, a family $\mathcal{F}$ of graphs is said to have a near-optimal spanner if for every n-vertex graph $G \in \mathcal{F}$ there is an $O(1)$-spanner with $O(n)$ edges. An example is the family of complete graphs, as depicted in Figure 15.4. Our focus in the next chapter is on the construction of sparse spanners for various graph families. Although *size* is our main sparsity parameter, we are also interested in optimizing the *weight* of our spanners, and the issue is further developed in Chapter 17.

Compared to the partition and cover based representations described earlier, or the tree covers described next, spanners seem to capture less of the structural information that can be extracted from the network. Their range of applicability may therefore seem somewhat

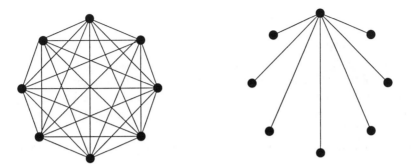

Figure 15.4: A graph and a 2-spanner for it.

limited in comparison. Nonetheless, it turns out (as seen in Chapter 23, for example) that this structure is sufficient to capture all the necessary information and yield considerable reductions in complexity for certain applications, while being somewhat simpler conceptually than those other structures.

15.5 Tree covers

Let us now turn our attention to the second type of skeletal representations mentioned earlier, namely, ones based on a *collection* of subgraphs. In fact, we only consider such representations in their simplest form, i.e., as collections of trees.

A *tree cover* for a graph G is a collection of trees in the graph containing all vertices of G. Intuitively, a tree cover captures locality by obeying the following property: for every two vertices that are not too far apart in the graph, the tree cover should contain a tree common to both on which their distance is close to optimal. Naturally, it is desirable that the tree cover also be sparse (or have low overlaps). Formally, we have the following definition.

Definition 15.5.1 [ρ-tree cover]: *Given a weighted graph $G = (V, E, \omega)$, a ρ-tree cover, or a tree cover for $\hat{\Gamma}_\rho(V)$, is a collection TC of trees in G with the property that for every vertex $v \in V$, there is a tree $T \in TC$ that spans its entire ρ-neighborhood, namely,*

$$\Gamma_\rho(v) \subseteq V(T).$$

The depth *of a tree cover TC is*

$$Depth(TC) = \max_{T \in TC}\{Depth(T)\},$$

the maximum degree *of TC is*

$$\Delta^{TC}(TC) = \max_{T \in TC}\{\Delta(T)\}$$

and the overlap *of TC is the maximum, over all vertices v, of the number of different trees containing v,*

$$\texttt{Overlap}(TC) = \max_{v \in V}\{|\{T \in TC \mid v \in V(T)\}|\}.$$

Note that a tree cover TC associates with each vertex v a tree T spanning its ρ-neighborhood. Hereafter, we refer to this tree T as the *home-tree* of v and denote it by *home*(v). (In case there are several appropriate trees, we select one arbitrarily.)

15.5.1   Tree cover construction

Again, our maximum degree cover Algorithm MAX_COVER can be used to construct an efficient tree cover $\mathcal{TC}_{\kappa,\rho}$ for a given graph G and parameters $\kappa, \rho \geq 1$, where efficiency is defined with respect to the *Depth* and Overlap measures. This is done by starting from the ρ-neighborhood cover of G, coarsening it appropriately and then selecting a spanning tree for each cluster. Formally, the collection $\mathcal{TC}_{\kappa,\rho}$ is constructed by Algorithm TREE_COVER, presented in Figure 15.5.

Figure 15.6 depicts a possible tree cover corresponding to the cover of Figure 11.1.

Example: *Cover for the grid.*

The grid G_{19} described earlier (Figure 12.7(a)) has diameter 18. Fix the parameter $\kappa = 3$, and consider the cover selected for $\hat{\Gamma}_2(V)$. This cover may be $\mathcal{T}$ of the example from Section 12.2, and the tree collection $\mathcal{TC}_{3,2}$ consists of four shortest-path trees, each spanning one of the four clusters depicted in Figure 12.7(b). A possible tree for such a cluster is given in Figure 15.7.   □

---

1. Set $\mathcal{S} \leftarrow \hat{\Gamma}_\rho(V)$.

2. Construct a coarsening cover $\mathcal{R}$ for $\mathcal{S}$ as in the Maximum Cover Theorem 12.4.1, using Algorithm MAX_COVER with parameter κ.

3. **For** each cluster $R \in \mathcal{R}$ **do:**
   Select a shortest-path tree $T(R)$ rooted at some center of R and spanning R.

4. Set $\mathcal{TC}_{\kappa,\rho} \leftarrow \{T(R) \mid R \in \mathcal{R}\}$.

Figure 15.5: Algorithm TREE_COVER(G, κ, ρ).

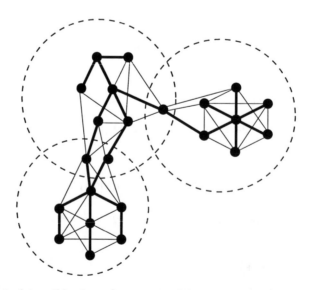

Figure 15.6: A possible tree cover corresponding to the cover of Figure 11.1.

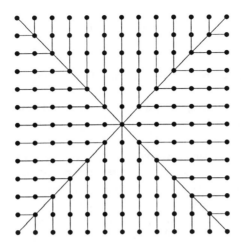

Figure 15.7: A shortest-path spanning tree for a cluster of the cover T on the grid G_{19}.

15.5.2   Properties

The properties of this construction yield the following theorem.

Theorem 15.5.2 [Tree cover]: *For every weighted graph $G = (V, E, \omega)$, $|V| = n$ and integers $\kappa, \rho \geq 1$, Algorithm* TREE_COVER *constructs a ρ-tree cover $TC = TC_{\kappa,\rho}$ for G with $Depth(TC) \leq (2\kappa - 1)\rho$ and $\mathtt{Overlap}(TC) \leq \lceil 2\kappa \cdot n^{1/\kappa} \rceil$.*

Proof: Given G and integers $\kappa, \rho \geq 1$, let $TC = TC_{\kappa,\rho}$ be the tree collection constructed for G using Algorithm TREE_COVER. Let us first prove that TC is a ρ-tree cover. Consider a vertex $v \in V$. By the fact that the cover $\mathcal{R}$ coarsens $\mathcal{S}$, there is a cluster $R \in \mathcal{R}$ such that $\Gamma_\rho(v) \subseteq R$. Consequently, the tree $T(R) \in TC$ spans the entire ρ-neighborhood $\Gamma_\rho(v)$.

The bound on $Depth(TC)$, the maximal depth of the trees in the constructed collection, follows from the radius bound on the clusters of the cover $\mathcal{R}$, guaranteed by Property (1) of the Maximum Cover Theorem 12.4.1 and the fact that these trees are shortest-path trees. Likewise, the bound on $\mathtt{Overlap}(TC)$, the maximal number of trees containing any vertex, follows from the degree bound on the cover $\mathcal{R}$ (Property (2) of Theorem 12.4.1), noting that $|\mathcal{S}| = n$. $\square$

Relying on the Tree Cover Theorem 15.5.2 and the Degree Bounding Theorem 15.2.2, and taking $m = n^{1/\kappa}$, we conclude the following.

Theorem 15.5.3 [Balanced tree cover]: *For every weighted graph $G = (V, E, \omega)$, $|V| = n$ and integers $\kappa, \rho \geq 1$, it is possible to construct a (virtual) ρ-tree cover $TC = TC_{\kappa,\rho}$ for G with $Depth(TC) \leq (2\kappa - 1)^2 \rho$, $\mathtt{Overlap}(TC) \leq \lceil 2\kappa \cdot n^{1/\kappa} \rceil$ and $\Delta^{TC}(TC) \leq 2n^{1/\kappa}$.* $\square$

The role of tree covers, and their relationship to cluster-based covers, becomes clear by looking at the construction of Algorithm TREE_COVER. Essentially, a tree cover TC constructed for a given cluster-based cover $\mathcal{S}$ serves as a way to "materialize" $\mathcal{S}$ in an efficient way. In fact, whenever we use covers in our applications (e.g., in Chapter 26), we shall actually be using the corresponding tree cover.

Bibliographical notes

The well-known sequential SPT construction algorithms of Dijkstra and of Bellman and Ford are described in many sources, cf. [Eve79, CLR90]. These algorithms are in fact applicable in more general settings. For instance, both algorithms apply to weighted, directed graphs. Detailed expositions of the sequential DFS algorithm and its history can be found in [Eve79, CLR90].

Lemma 15.1.2 is presented in [Bol78], and the Degree Bounding Theorem 15.2.2 is taken from [ABLP89].

The NP-hardness of computing the MTDT of a graph is due to [JLR78], and the ratio 2 approximation algorithm is due to [Won80]. This type of tree is studied further in [Pel97, PR98, PR99a].

The initial motivation for studying spanners for general graphs came from the problem of constructing network synchronizers; spanners were introduced in [PU89b] as a tool for constructing synchronizers and were later studied in various contexts. More generally, spanners appear to be the underlying graph structure in a number of constructions in distributed systems and communication networks. Applications of spanners in the setting of distributed computing are developed further in Chapters 23 and 25.

It is interesting to note that spanners are also relevant in other contexts than communication networks. For instance, they show up in biology, in the process of reconstructing phylogenetic trees from matrices, whose entries represent genetic distances among various living species [BD86]. In the area of robotics and computational geometry, spanners have been considered in the Euclidean setting, assuming that the vertices of the graph are points in space and the edges are line segments connecting pairs of points (cf. [Che86, DFS87, ADDJ90] and the references therein).

Moreover, the notion of spanners appears in other forms in the literature. Efficient embeddings of graphs in graphs are considered in [BCLR86] with the ultimate goal of selecting a *universal network* as the underlying topology of a universal parallel machine. One of the parameters studied is the *dilation* of the embedding, which is similar to our stretch factor. The dilation of embedding a network G in a network H has immediate implication on the time delay incurred by simulating G on a universal machine based on H. There, however, the subgraph of H onto which G is embedded need not be a subgraph of G. Moreover, the major size consideration in [BCLR86] is the size of the universal network H, and not the number of edges of H needed to embed G.

The construction and usage of tree covers was implicit in several papers, e.g., [AP92], but the concept was introduced explicitly for the first time in [AKP91]. Exercise 4 is due to [HP00].

The concept of spanners was later generalized into questions of approximating metric spaces by simpler metric spaces and questions of low-distortion embeddings in low-dimensional spaces [LLR95, RR95, Bar96b].

Exercises

1. (a) State and prove tight (existential) upper and lower bounds on $\text{Tot\_D}(G')$, the sum of the distances in a subgraph G' spanning an unweighted n-vertex graph G, for any G and G', as a function of n, $|E|$ and $Diam(G)$.

   (b) Give examples establishing the tightness of the bounds stated in part (a).

2. (a) Describe an algorithm for constructing the MTDT T for an n-vertex weighted ring.

   (b) Bound the resulting $\text{Tot\_D}(T)$ in the unweighted case (i.e., where all the weights of the ring edges are 1).

   (c) Construct an MTDT T for the 2-dimensional $n \times n$ unweighted grid, and estimate the resulting $\text{Tot\_D}(T)$.

3. Suppose that G_1 is a κ_1-spanner of G and G_2 is a κ_2-spanner of G_1. What can be said about G_2 as a spanner of G?

4. Given a 2-dimensional Euclidean graph G (where the vertices are points in the plane and distances are in the L_2 norm) and an integer ρ, show how to construct a ρ-tree cover $\mathcal{TC}$ on G with $Depth(\mathcal{TC}) = O(\rho)$, $\texttt{Overlap}(\mathcal{TC}) = O(1)$ and $\Delta^{TC}(\mathcal{TC}) = O(1)$.

5. (a) Show that for any rooted weighted tree T and integer $\kappa \geq 2$, there exists an embedded virtual tree s satisfying the following properties: (1) $\Delta(S) \leq 2n^{1/\kappa}$, (2) each edge of S corresponds to a path of length at most two in T, and (3) $Depth_S(v) \leq (2\kappa - 1) \cdot Depth_T(v)$ for every vertex v.

   (b) Use this fact to prove Theorem 15.5.3.

Chapter 16

Sparse spanners for unweighted graphs

In this chapter we discuss some upper and lower bounds concerning the existence and efficient constructability of sparse spanners for general unweighted graphs, as well as examples of various specific families of unweighted graphs, including chordal graphs and hypercubes.

16.1 Sparse spanners for arbitrary graphs

This section deals with sparse spanners for unweighted graphs of arbitrary topology. The following lemma gives an equivalent, and sometimes more convenient to use, formulation of the definition of κ-spanners in case the graph is unweighted.

Lemma 16.1.1 *For an unweighted graph* $G = (V, E)$, *the subgraph* $G' = (V, E')$ *is a* κ-*spanner of* G *iff for every* $(u, v) \in E$, *dist*$_{G'}(u, v) \leq \kappa$. ☐

16.1.1 Constructing a spanner for unweighted graphs

Let us first present a method of constructing a sparse $O(\kappa)$-spanner $G' = (V, E')$ for an arbitrary unweighted graph $G = (V, E)$ using the basic partition algorithm BASIC_PART of Section 11.5. The construction is performed using Algorithm UNWEIGHTED_SPAN, presented in Figure 16.1.

Example: *Spanner construction for a general graph.*

The partition given for the cover $\hat{\Gamma}_0(V)$ of the graph $G = (V, E)$ from Figure 11.2 yields several possible spanners, one of which is depicted in Figure 16.2 below. ☐

16.1.2 Analysis

Theorem 16.1.2 [Sparse spanner]: *For every unweighted n-vertex graph G and for every* $\kappa \geq 1$, *Algorithm* UNWEIGHTED_SPAN *constructs an* $O(\kappa)$-*spanner with at most* $n^{1+1/\kappa}$ *edges.*

Proof: Given a graph G and an integer κ, let G' be the subgraph constructed using Algorithm UNWEIGHTED_SPAN. Let us first estimate the number of edges in G'. Since $\mathcal{T}$ is a partition of V, there are clearly less than n edges belonging to trees constructed for the

1. Construct a partition T as in the Partition Theorem 11.5.1 using Algorithm BASIC_PART.

2. **For** every cluster $T_i \in T$ **do:**
   Construct a single-source, shortest-paths spanning tree rooted at some center c_i of T_i.

3. Set $E' \leftarrow \bigcup_{T_i \in T} E(T_i)$.

4. **For** every pair of neighboring clusters T_i, T_j **do:**
   /* the edge (T_i, T_j) occurs in the cluster graph $\tilde{G}(T)$ */

   (a) Select a single intercluster edge e_{ij} of G connecting vertices in these two clusters.

   (b) $E' \leftarrow E' \cup \{e_{ij}\}$.

Figure 16.1: Algorithm UNWEIGHTED_SPAN(G, κ).

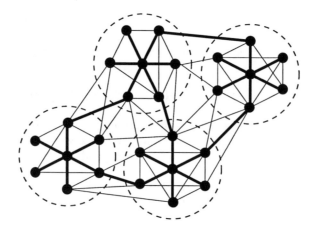

Figure 16.2: A possible spanner (in bold edges) for the graph $G = (V, E)$ from Figure 11.2 based on the partition given there for $\hat{\Gamma}_0(V)$.

clusters of T. Also, by the Partition Theorem 11.5.1 the total number of intercluster edges in E' does not exceed $n^{1+1/\kappa}$.

Finally, we have to verify that the resulting subgraph G' indeed has stretch factor $\text{Stretch}(G') \leq 4\kappa - 3$. Consider an edge $e = (u, w)$ in G, and suppose that u belongs to the cluster T_i and w belongs to T_j. The radius of each cluster in the partition is at most $r = \kappa - 1$. If $i = j$, then the path from u to w through c_i is of length at most $2r = 2\kappa - 2$. Otherwise, there is a path going from u to c_i (in at most r steps), from c_i through e_{ij} to c_j (in at most $r + 1 + r$ steps) and from c_j to w (in at most r steps), so the total length is at most $4r + 1 = 4\kappa - 3$. (See Figure 16.3.) $\square$

Fixing $\kappa = \log n$ we get the following corollary.

Corollary 16.1.3 *For every unweighted n-vertex graph $G = (V, E)$ there exists a (polynomial-time constructible) $O(\log n)$-spanner with $O(n)$ edges.* $\square$

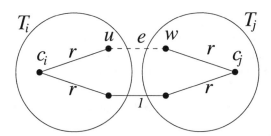

Figure 16.3: A (dashed) edge $e = (u, w)$ connecting vertices in different clusters, and an alternative path provided by the spanner of Algorithm UNWEIGHTED_SPAN.

16.2   Lower bounds

Virtually all of the constructions of LP-representations shown so far exhibit the same fundamental trade-off between locality and sparsity. Let us now turn our attention to the question of lower bounds for these trade-offs. We start by giving a lower bound on the size-stretch trade-off for spanners, demonstrating that for some graphs, the best possible improvements are only a constant factor from the construction of the Spanner Theorem 16.1.2.

Definition 16.2.1 [Nonspannability]: *The graph G is κ-nonspannable if the only κ-spanner of G is G itself.*

Lemma 16.2.2 *For every $\kappa \geq 1$, every unweighted graph $G = (V, E)$ with $Girth(G) \geq \kappa+2$ is κ-nonspannable.*

Proof: The existence of another spanner G', with some edge $(u, v) \in E$ omitted, would imply the existence of an alternative path Υ of length κ connecting u to v (see Figure 16.4), which together with the edge (u, v) constitutes a cycle of length $\kappa + 1 < Girth(G)$, which is a contradiction.   □

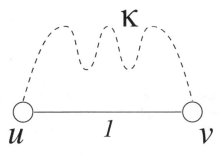

Figure 16.4: The edge e (solid) and the path Υ replacing it in the spanner (dashed).

Combining the last lemma with the second claim of Lemma 15.1.2, we get the following (existential) lower bound.

Theorem 16.2.3 *For every $\kappa \geq 3$, there exist (infinitely many) unweighted n-vertex graphs $G = (V, E)$ for which every $(\kappa - 2)$-spanner requires $\Omega(n^{1+1/\kappa})$ edges.*   □

It should be stated that more efficient clustering algorithms translate directly into better spanner constructions (with the obvious relationships between the corresponding parameters) by the construction method of Algorithm UNWEIGHTED_SPAN. This enables us to use the lower bound on spanners (Theorem 16.2.3) in order to deduce similar (existential) lower bounds for the coarsening cover problem. These lower bounds are claimed for the simplest setting, i.e., using an unweighted graph G and an initial cover $\hat{\Gamma}_1(V)$ or partition $\hat{\Gamma}_0(V)$ $(= \{\{v\} \mid v \in V\})$, although they hold for other settings as well.

Theorem 16.2.4 *For every $\kappa \geq 3$, there exist (infinitely many) unweighted n-vertex graphs $G = (V, E)$ for which*

(a) for every cover $\mathcal{T}$ coarsening $\hat{\Gamma}_1(V)$, if $Rad(\mathcal{T}) \leq \kappa$, then $\bar{\Delta}(\mathcal{T}) = \Omega(n^{1/\kappa})$;

(b) for every partition $\mathcal{T}$ coarsening $\hat{\Gamma}_0(V)$, if $Rad(\mathcal{T}) \leq \kappa$, then $\bar{\Delta}_c(\mathcal{T}) = \Omega(n^{1/\kappa})$.   ☐

These bounds clearly imply similar bounds for the average vertex-degree *partition* problem of Section 13.1, as well as for all *maximum* degree problems. The radius-chromatic number trade-off for network decomposition, presented in the decomposition Theorem 14.2.2, is also optimal within a factor of κ.

A lower bound on the trade-off between radius and degree for ρ-regional matchings on arbitrary graphs can be deduced in a similar way. First note the following fact.

Lemma 16.2.5 *Given an arbitrary unweighted graph $G = (V, E)$ and a ρ-regional matching $\mathcal{RW}$ on G, it is possible to construct a $\rho \cdot (\mathtt{Str}_{read}(\mathcal{RW}) + \mathtt{Str}_{write}(\mathcal{RW}))$-spanner G' for G with size no greater than $n \cdot (\Delta_{write}(\mathcal{RW}) \cdot \mathtt{Str}_{write}(\mathcal{RW}) + \Delta_{read}(\mathcal{RW}) \cdot \mathtt{Str}_{read}(\mathcal{RW}))$.*

Proof: The spanner G' is constructed as follows. Start by constructing, for each vertex u in the graph, a shortest path tree $T_R(u)$ connecting it to all the vertices in its read set $\mathtt{Read}(u)$ and a similar tree $T_W(u)$ connecting it to its write set $\mathtt{Write}(u)$. Take the spanner G' to be the union of all these $2n$ trees.

Note that for every two adjacent vertices v, u in G, necessarily $\mathtt{Read}(v) \cap \mathtt{Write}(u) \neq \emptyset$, and therefore there exists a vertex w occurring on both $T_R(v)$ and $T_W(u)$. Since the depths of these trees are bounded by $\rho \cdot \mathtt{Str}_{read}(\mathcal{RW})$ and $\rho \cdot \mathtt{Str}_{write}(\mathcal{RW})$, respectively, it follows that

$$dist_{G'}(u, v) \leq \rho \cdot (\mathtt{Str}_{read}(\mathcal{RW}) + \mathtt{Str}_{write}(\mathcal{RW})).$$

Lemma 16.1.1 implies the desired bound on the stretch factor of G'.

Noting that for an unweighted graph G, each tree $T_R(u)$ (resp., $T_W(u)$) consists of at most $\Delta_{read}(\mathcal{RW}) \cdot \mathtt{Str}_{read}(\mathcal{RW})$ (resp., $\Delta_{read}(\mathcal{RW}) \cdot \mathtt{Str}_{read}(\mathcal{RW})$) edges, the bound on the spanner's number of edges follows.   ☐

This lemma, combined with Theorem 16.2.3, has the following immediate implication.

Corollary 16.2.6 *For every $\kappa \geq 1$, there exist (infinitely many) unweighted n-vertex graphs $G = (V, E)$ for which the following holds. For every ρ-regional matching $\mathcal{RW}$ on G, if $\mathtt{Str}_{read}(\mathcal{RW})$ and $\mathtt{Str}_{write}(\mathcal{RW})$ are bounded by κ, then $\Delta_{write}(\mathcal{RW}) + \Delta_{read}(\mathcal{RW}) = \Omega(n^{1/(2\rho\kappa+2)}/\kappa)$.*   ☐

In particular, for constant ρ, this implies that on these graphs, any regional matching with constant radius must have read or write sets of cardinality $\Omega(n^\epsilon)$ for fixed $\epsilon > 0$. For the hypercube, in contrast, a similar statement is known for ρ-regional matchings with arbitrary ρ.

16.3   Examples

The upper and lower bounds of the Spanner Theorem 16.1.2 and Theorem 16.2.3 depict
a picture of the behavior of κ-spanners as a function of κ that conforms to what we may
expect: the larger κ, the sparser the resulting spanner may be. As may also be expected, for
various restricted graph families one can do appreciably better than is implied by the lower
bound of Theorem 16.2.3. Clearly, every class of graphs with $O(n)$ edges has a near-optimal
spanner, as in such a class each graph G can be taken as its own 1-spanner. This covers
various graph topologies commonly used for communication networks, including bounded-
degree and planar graphs (e.g., rings, grids, trees, butterflies and cube-connected cycles).
   Likewise, for bounded-diameter graphs, any rooted shortest-paths tree will do as a near-
optimal spanner. Thus the problem remains interesting only for graph classes in between.
   In this section we consider two graph families belonging to this intermediate range,
namely, the unweighted hypercubes and the unweighted chordal graphs. Interestingly, both
families exhibit the same phenomenon as the class of all graphs, although in both classes
the trade-off converges towards an optimal number of edges for a small constant stretch
factor κ.

16.3.1   Spanners for the hypercube

As a first interesting example, let us consider spanners for the family of m-dimensional
hypercubes. The hypercube of dimension m, $H_m = (V_m, E_m)$, is defined by $V_m = \{0,1\}^m$
and

$$E_m = \{(x,y) \mid x,y \in V_m, \ x \text{ and } y \text{ differ in exactly one bit}\}.$$

The network has $|V_m| = 2^m$ vertices, $|E_m| = m \cdot 2^{m-1}$ edges and diameter m. (Figure 16.5
depicts the 4-dimensional cube.)

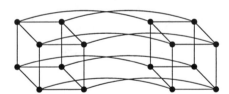

Figure 16.5: The 4-dimensional cube.

   It is useful to interpret the structure of the hypercube using the notion of graph product.
The *Cartesian product* of two graphs $G_1 = (V_1, E_1)$ and $G_2 = (V_2, E_2)$, denoted $G_1 \times G_2$, is
defined as

$$G_1 \times G_2 = (V_1 \times V_2, E),$$

where

$$\begin{aligned} E = \ & \{((\langle u_1, v_1 \rangle, \langle u_2, v_2 \rangle)) \mid (u_1 = u_2 \text{ and } (v_1, v_2) \in E_2) \text{ or} \\ & (v_1 = v_2 \text{ and } (u_1, u_2) \in E_1)\}. \end{aligned}$$

Hence $G_1 \times G_2$ is constructed by substituting a copy of G_2 for each vertex in G_1 and drawing
in edges between corresponding vertices of adjacent copies.
   The hypercube H_m can now be viewed as the Cartesian product graph $H_m = H_{m-k} \times H_k$
for any $0 \leq k \leq m$. Later, we make use of this characterization of the cube.

Since the m-dimensional cube has girth 4 for $m \geq 2$, Lemma 16.2.2 implies the following.

Lemma 16.3.1 *For every $m \geq 1$, the m-dimensional hypercube H_m is 2-non-spannable.*

Nevertheless, sparse 3-spanners do exist for the hypercube. Specifically, we now show how to construct a 3-spanner for the hypercube H_m with a linear ($O(2^m)$) number of edges. Recall that a *dominating set* for a graph G (defined in Section 8.3) is a subset U of vertices with the property that for every vertex v of G, U contains either v itself or some neighbor of v.

Lemma 16.3.2 *For every $m \geq 1$, the m-cube has a dominating set of at most $\frac{2^{m+1}}{m}$ vertices.*

Proof: Let us first consider the case of $m = 2^r - 1$ for some $r \geq 1$. To construct dominating sets, we make use of the notion of a Hamming code. For any integer r, the Hamming code $HC(r)$ consists of *code words* of length $2^r - 1$. The *distance* between two words is the number of positions in which the two words differ. An important fact about Hamming codes is that they have minimum distance 3; that is, no two code words have distance less than 3.

Now, let the *neighborhood* of a code word be that word plus all words of distance 1. Then in $HC(r)$, all neighborhoods have 2^r members. No word can be in the neighborhood of two code words or else those code words would be of distance 2.

The last fact we need about Hamming codes is that $HC(r)$ has exactly 2^{2^r-1-r} members. The number of words in the neighborhood of some code word of $HC(r)$ is thus $2^r \times 2^{2^r-1-r}$ or $2^{2^r-1} = 2^m$. Thus $HC(r)$ is a dominating set for the hypercube H_{2^r-1}. As argued above,

$$|HC(r)| = \frac{2^m}{m+1} < \frac{2^{m+1}}{m}.$$

Now consider an arbitrary $m \geq 1$. Let r be the integer satisfying $2^r - 1 \leq m < 2^{r+1} - 1$, and let $d = 2^r - 1$. Note that $m/2 \leq d$. Let U_d be a dominating set for the d-cube. View the m-cube as the Cartesian product $H_m = H_{m-d} \times H_d$, and let

$$U = \{\langle x, y \rangle \mid x \in V_{m-d}, \, y \in U_d\},$$

where V_{m-d} is the set of vertices of H_{m-d}. Clearly U is a dominating set for the m-cube and its size is

$$2^{m-d}|U_d| = 2^{m-d}\frac{2^d}{d+1} = \frac{2^m}{d+1} < \frac{2^{m+1}}{m}. \qquad \square$$

We finally construct a spanner for the m-cube. The cases $m = 1, 2$ can easily be verified directly, so assume $m \geq 3$. The construction uses dominating sets for some of the subcubes of our hypercube. Consider an m-cube H_m, and let $p = \lfloor \frac{m}{2} \rfloor$ and $q = \lceil \frac{m}{2} \rceil$. View H_m as the Cartesian product $H_p \times H_q$. Let U_1 and U_2 be minimum-size dominating sets for H_p and H_q, respectively.

We define the subgraph $G' = (V_m, E')$ by choosing the following sets of edges:

1. Every edge $(\langle x, y \rangle, \langle x, y' \rangle)$ s.t. $\langle y, y' \rangle \in E_q$ and $y' \in U_2$.

2. Every edge $(\langle x, y \rangle, \langle x', y \rangle)$ s.t. $\langle x, x' \rangle \in E_p$ and $x' \in U_1$.

3. Every edge $(\langle x, y \rangle, \langle x, y' \rangle)$ s.t. $\langle y, y' \rangle \in E_q$ and $x \in U_1$.

4. Every edge $(\langle x, y \rangle, \langle x', y \rangle)$ s.t. $\langle x, x' \rangle \in E_p$ and $y \in U_2$.

Lemma 16.3.3 *G' has fewer than $7 \cdot 2^m$ edges.*

Proof: By the previous lemma, $|U_1| \leq \frac{2^{p+1}}{p}$ and $|U_2| \leq \frac{2^{q+1}}{q}$. Therefore the number of edges $(y, y') \in E_q$ with $y' \in U_2$ is at most $q|U_2| \leq 2^{q+1}$, and so the number of edges of the first type is at most $2^p 2^{q+1} = 2^{m+1}$. Similarly, the number of edges of the second type is at most 2^{m+1}. For the third type we get the bound

$$|U_1| \cdot |E_q| \leq \frac{2^{p+1}}{p} \cdot q \cdot 2^{q-1} = \frac{q}{p} \cdot 2^m,$$

and similarly for the fourth type there are at most $|U_2| \cdot |E_p| \leq \frac{p}{q} \cdot 2^m$ edges. (This simple counting ignores multiple occurrences of certain edges in the various types, which in fact implies a slightly smaller bound.) Since $m \geq 3$, $\frac{p}{q} + \frac{q}{p} < 3$, so overall we get a bound of fewer than $7 \cdot 2^m$ edges (or $6 \cdot 2^m$ for even m). □

Lemma 16.3.4 G' *is a 3-spanner of the m-cube.*

Proof: Consider two neighboring vertices u, v in H_m. Let $u = \langle x, y \rangle$, where $x \in \{0,1\}^p$. Then either $v = \langle x, y' \rangle$ for some neighbor y' of y in H_q or $v = \langle x', y \rangle$ for some neighbor x' of x in H_p. Suppose the first case holds. If $x \in U_1$, then G' contains the edge (u, v) itself (type 3). Otherwise, G' contains the following edges (see Figure 16.6).

1. $e_1 = (\langle x, y \rangle, \langle x', y \rangle)$ for some $x' \in U_1$ (type 2).

2. $e_2 = (\langle x', y \rangle, \langle x', y' \rangle)$ (type 3).

3. $e_3 = (\langle x', y' \rangle, \langle x, y' \rangle)$ (type 2).

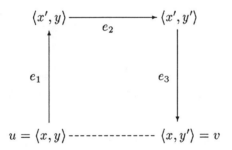

Figure 16.6: A path of length 3 substituting for the edge (u, v) (dashed) in the spanner for the hypercube.

These three edges constitute a path of length 3 in G' connecting u and v. The second case is handled similarly, using edges of types 1 and 4. □

Theorem 16.3.5 *For every $m \geq 1$, the m-cube has a 3-spanner of fewer than $7 \cdot 2^m$ edges.* □

16.3.2   Spanners for chordal graphs

A graph is *chordal* if it contains no induced cycles of length greater than 3, i.e., for every cycle C of length 4 or more in G, the subgraph induced by the vertices of C contains at least one more edge (forming a *chord* on the cycle C). A graph is *split* if its vertices can be partitioned into two sets X and Y such that X induces a clique (namely, a complete subgraph) and

Y is an independent set (namely, a set whose members are mutually nonadjacent). It is easy to verify that every split graph is chordal. Every connected chordal graph is either a tree or has girth 3; furthermore, any connected induced subgraph of a chordal graph is also chordal, so a lower bound similar to Theorem 16.2.3 does not apply.

We begin this section by showing that for every unweighted n-vertex chordal graph there exists a 2-spanner with $O(n^{1.5})$ edges and that there are infinitely many unweighted n-vertex chordal graphs (in fact, split graphs) for which every 2-spanner requires $\Omega(n^{1.5})$ edges. However, the situation changes drastically when allowing a slight increase in the stretch factor. We prove that for every unweighted n-vertex chordal graph there exists a 3-spanner with $O(n \log n)$ edges. It is also the case that every such graph has a 5-spanner with $O(n)$ edges, although we will not show that here.

Star spanners

Given a graph $G = (V, E)$, a clique $K \subseteq V$ and a vertex $v_K \in K$, a *star* is the tree $Star(K, v_K) = (K, E_K)$, where

$$E_K = \{(v_K, v) \mid v \in K, v \neq v_K\}.$$

The vertex v_K is said to be the *root* of the clique.

Let $\mathcal{K}(G)$ be the collection of maximal cliques in a given graph $G = (V, E)$. A *root assignment* $r_0 : \mathcal{K}(G) \mapsto V$ is a function assigning to every clique $K \in \mathcal{K}(G)$ a vertex $r_0(K) \in K$.

A *star spanner* of G is the graph $Star(G, r_0)$ obtained by merging together all the star spanners for $\mathcal{K}(G)$, under the given root assignment r_0, i.e.,

$$Star(G, r_0) = \bigcup_{K \in \mathcal{K}(G)} Star(K, r_0(K)).$$

Note that every root assignment r_0 uniquely determines a star spanner for G.

Lemma 16.3.6 *Every star spanner $Star(G, r_0)$ for G has stretch factor* $\texttt{Stretch}(Star(G, r_0))$ $= 2$.

Proof: Consider any edge $(u, v) \in E$. This edge belongs to some maximal clique K of G. If u or v is $r_0(K)$, then (u, v) is in the edge set of the star spanner, since it belongs to $Star(K, r_0(K))$. Otherwise, both edges $(r_0(K), u)$ and $(r_0(K), v)$ are in the edge set. In both cases $dist_{Star(K, r_0(K))}(u, v) \leq 2$, and the claim follows by Lemma 16.1.1. □

2-spanners for chordal graphs

Consider an n-vertex chordal graph $G = (V, E)$. G can have at most n maximal cliques. We now describe how to select the root assignment for G so that the resulting star spanner $Star(G, r_0) = (V, E')$ has $O(n^{1.5})$ edges.

Start with the set $\mathcal{K} = \mathcal{K}(G)$ containing all maximal cliques of G ($|\mathcal{K}| \leq n$) and $E' = \emptyset$. Let $deg_{\mathcal{K}}(v)$ denote the number of cliques $K \in \mathcal{K}$ such that $v \in K$. Select the assignment r_0 in two phases.

The first phase consists of iteratively executing the following loop.
While there is a vertex v such that $deg_{\mathcal{K}}(v) \geq \sqrt{n}$ **do:**

- For every $K \in \mathcal{K}$ s.t. $v \in K$, select v as $r_0(K)$, add E_K to E' (removing duplicate edges) and remove K from $\mathcal{K}$.

In the second phase, the selection of the vertices $r_0(K)$ for the remaining cliques $K \in \mathcal{K}$ is completed arbitrarily.

Lemma 16.3.7 *The star spanner $Star(G, r_0) = (V, E')$ corresponding to the root assignment selected by the above algorithm has $O(n^{1.5})$ edges.*

Proof: Each iteration of the first phase reduces $|\mathcal{K}|$ by at least $\sqrt{n}$, so the number of iterations is at most $|\mathcal{K}|/\sqrt{n} \leq \sqrt{n}$. Also, each such iteration augments E' by no more than n edges, namely, (some of) the edges adjacent to the vertex v. Hence by the end of this phase, E' contains at most $n^{1.5}$ edges.

When the first phase ends, the remaining collection $\mathcal{K}$ satisfies $deg_{\mathcal{K}}(v) < \sqrt{n}$ for every $v \in V$. Therefore the number of edges added in this phase is bounded by $\sum_{K \in \mathcal{K}}(|K| - 1) < \sum_{v \in V} deg_{\mathcal{K}}(v) < n^{1.5}$. Thus at the end of the process $|E'| \leq O(n^{1.5})$. $\square$

Theorem 16.3.8 *For every n-vertex chordal graph there exists a 2-spanner with $O(n^{1.5})$ edges.* $\square$

This result is complemented by a matching lower bound.

Theorem 16.3.9 *There exist (infinitely many) n-vertex chordal graphs for which every 2-spanner requires $\Omega(n^{1.5})$ edges.*

Proof Sketch: Let q be any prime, and let $m = q^2 + q + 1$ and $n = 2m$. Construct a set of $2m$ vertices by letting $\mathcal{P} = \{p_i \mid 1 \leq i \leq m\}$, $\mathcal{W} = \{w_i \mid 1 \leq i \leq m\}$ and $V = \mathcal{P} \cup \mathcal{W}$. A finite projective plane of order q over the set of points $\mathcal{P}$ is composed of a collection of lines $\mathcal{L} = \{L_i \mid 1 \leq i \leq m\}$, where each line L_i is a set of q distinct points in $\mathcal{P}$ with the following properties:

1. every two points are common to exactly one line, and

2. every two lines share exactly one point.

It is known that finite projective planes of order q exist for every prime q with m chosen as above (cf. [Hal86]). Construct a split graph $G = (V, E)$ as follows. For every $1 \leq i \leq m$ connect $w_i \in \mathcal{W}$ to all the vertices $p \in L_i$ and make $\mathcal{P}$ into a clique (see Figure 16.7).

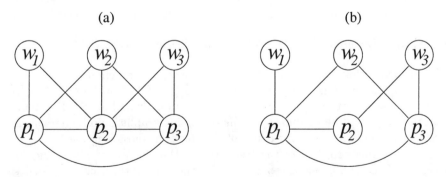

Figure 16.7: (a) The split graph G for $q = 1$. (b) A possible 2-spanner for G.

Let E_c denote the set of "crossing" edges in G (i.e., edges (p, w) such that $p \in \mathcal{P}$ and $w \in \mathcal{W}$). Note that $|E_c| = m(q+1)$ since $|L_i| = q + 1$ for every $1 \leq i \leq m$. Consider a 2-spanner $G' = (V, E')$ for G. For every crossing edge $(p, w) \in E_c$, G' has to include either

(p, w) or $(p, p'), (p', w)$ for some $p' \in \mathcal{P}$. To complete the proof, we now claim (Exercise 5) that G' must contain a distinct edge for each crossing edge in E_c, which implies that overall,

$$|E'| \geq |E_c| = q^3 + 2q^2 + 2q + 1 = \Omega(n^{1.5}). \qquad \Box$$

3-spanners for chordal graphs

The 3-spanner construction for chordal graphs is based on the following separator theorem.

Theorem 16.3.10 *Every n-vertex chordal graph G contains a maximal clique C such that if the vertices in C are deleted from G, every connected component in the graph induced by any remaining vertices is of size at most $n/2$.* $\quad \Box$

An $O(|E|)$-time algorithm for finding a separating clique C satisfying the conditions of the theorem is also known.

We now describe an algorithm to construct a 3-spanner for a chordal graph $G = (V, E)$. We begin by partitioning G into separating cliques recursively, using Theorem 16.3.10, and constructing a logical tree of cliques, corresponding to the recursive partition. This is done as follows.

- Find a maximal separating clique C for G as prescribed in Theorem 16.3.10.

- Suppose C partitions the rest of G into connected components $\{G_1, \ldots, G_r\}$.

- For each G_i, construct a partitioning tree $T(G_i)$ recursively.

- Construct $T(G)$ by taking C to be the root and connecting the root of each tree $T(G_i)$ as a child of C.

The vertices of the final tree $T(G)$ represent a certain collection of disjoint cliques $\{C_1, \ldots, C_q\}$ that cover the entire graph.

The spanner G' contains two disjoint sets of edges E_1 and E_2. The set of edges E_1 includes a star-spanner based on the maximal separating cliques we chose with some arbitrary root assignment. The set E_2 is constructed as follows. Consider a clique C_i represented in the tree. For every vertex v in C_i, and for every other clique C_j, if v has neighbors in C_j, then select one such neighbor, denoted $w(v, C_j)$, and put the edge $(v, w(v, C_j))$ in E_2.

Lemma 16.3.11 *The graph $G' = (V, E_1 \cup E_2)$ has $O(n \log n)$ edges.*

Proof: Since each vertex occurs in exactly one of the separating cliques, $|E_1| < n$.

Let us next consider some properties of the tree $T(G)$. The depth of $T(G)$ corresponds to the maximal number of recursion levels in the partition algorithm. By Theorem 16.3.10, in each partitioning step the cardinality of the remaining graphs is no larger than half that of the previous graph. Therefore the depth of the tree is at most $\log_2 n + 1$.

Another interesting property of the tree $T(G)$ is that for every edge (u, v) in G, if v belongs to a clique C_i and u belongs to a clique C_j, then one of these cliques is a descendent of the other in the tree. This is because for two cliques C_i and C_i that have no descendence relationship in the tree, the clique C_k that is their lowest common ancestor in the tree separates the vertices of C_i and C_j, hence no edge is possible between them.

As a direct consequence of these properties, a vertex $v \in C_i$ can have edges to at most $\log n$ other cliques above it in the tree. Hence this vertex may contribute at most $\log n$ upward edges to E_2, so $|E_2| \leq n \log_2 n$. $\quad \Box$

Lemma 16.3.12 *The subgraph $G' = (V, E_1 \cup E_2)$ has stretch factor $\mathtt{Stretch}(G') = 3$.*

Proof: Consider an arbitrary edge $(u, v) \in E$. If both endpoints u, v are in the same separating clique, then the edge can be replaced by a path consisting of at most 2 edges of E_1 as in the proof of Lemma 16.3.6.

Now suppose the endpoints of (u, v) are not in the same separating clique, i.e., u and v belong to some separating cliques C_i and C_j, respectively. As u has neighbors in C_j (particularly, v), there is some neighbor $w(u, C_j)$ such that the edge connecting it to u was added to E_2. Even if $w(u, C_j) \neq v$, G' contains a path of at most 2 edges in E_1 from $w(u, C_j)$ to v, which completes the proof. $\square$

Theorem 16.3.13 *For every n-vertex chordal graph there exists a 3-spanner with $O(n \log n)$ edges.* $\square$

16.4 Directed variants

The situation for directed graphs is generally harder than for undirected ones in the sense that sparse spanners for general directed graphs do not always exist. The NP-completeness result is naturally extended to this case. It is also clear that there are n-vertex, $\Omega(n^2)$-edge directed graphs that have at most one directed path between any two vertices (e.g., the complete bipartite graph (X, Y, E) with $|X| = |Y| = n/2$ and with all edges directed from X to Y), and for such graphs, no subgraph is a spanner. Moreover, the following lower bound implies that for any fixed $\kappa \geq 1$ there are infinitely many dense graphs with high (strong) edge-connectivity for which one cannot do any better than taking the entire graph as its own κ-spanner.

Lemma 16.4.1 *For every $\kappa \geq 1$ and $n \geq \kappa$ there exists an n-vertex directed unweighted graph G with $\Omega(n^2/\kappa^2)$ edges and $O(n/\kappa^2)$ directed edge-connectivity which is κ-non-spannable.* $\square$

Theorem 16.4.2 *For every $\kappa \geq 1$ there are infinitely many n-vertex directed graphs for which every κ-spanner requires $\Omega(n^2/\kappa^2)$ edges.* $\square$

Bibliographical notes

The Spanner Theorem 16.1.2 is given in [PS89]. Note that this theorem does not guarantee any nontrivial result for small stretch values (due to the constant hidden in the guaranteed stretch, the smallest value of κ for which the theorem provides a meaningful result is $\kappa = 9$). Nonetheless, better results can be shown for smaller values. In particular, it is known that every graph has a 3-spanner with $O(n^{3/2} \log n)$ edges [DHZ96]. Exercise 3 is due to [HZ96].

The results concerning spanners for classes of unweighted graphs are from [PS89], including the constructions for chordal graphs, Exercise 6 and the claims concerning directed graphs. For some basic facts regarding chordal graphs used here see [Gol80]. Theorem 16.3.10 is due to [GRE84] as is the $O(|E|)$-time algorithm associated with it.

The example of the hypercube is from [PU89b]. This construction was later improved to fewer than $4n$ edges in [DZ99], which also established a lower bound of $3n/2 - o(1)$ on the minimum number of edges in any 3-spanner for the hypercube.

Additional material on Hamming codes, and codes in general, can be found in numerous textbooks, e.g., [Hil86]. Spanners for other specific graph classes were studied in [RL95, LS91b, Cai91, CK94, CC95b, CC95a, HP97a, HP97b].

The notion of *additive* spanners is introduced in [LS91a, LS93a]. These are spanners with additive, rather than multiplicative, stretch factor (referred to as *delay*). Low additive stretch and low-degree spanners were studied for various graph families. For 2-dimensional grids, since the degree is 4 it makes sense to focus on either spanners of maximum degree 2 or spanners with low average degree. In [LS95] it was shown that for graphs of maximum degree $\Delta = 3$, a delay of $\Theta(\sqrt{x})$ is necessary and sufficient. As for average degree bounds, in [LS93a] it is shown how to construct low average degree spanners with only constant delay. Spanners with delay kx but near-optimal average degrees are constructed in [LS93b]. For the d-dimensional grid, it is relatively easy to give spanners with maximum degree $\Delta = 4$ and constant delay (of the form $(1+1/k)d+k+c$ for fixed k, c) [LS96], which is asymptotically optimal. As for $\Delta = 3$, a construction with delay $5d + 4$ is given in [LS96]. Results for X-trees and pyramids were obtained in [RL95, LS93a, LS95]. In particular, degree-4 spanners of delay 1 for the X-tree are presented in [LS93a]. Focusing on degree-3 spanners, it is shown in [LS95] that $\Omega(x)$ delay is necessary and constructions with delay $x/k + O(k)$ are given (for fixed k). For the pyramid, maximum degree 7 (resp., 6) yields spanners with delay 1 (resp., 2) [LS93a, LS95]. Insisting on maximum degree $\Delta \leq 5$ necessitates delay $\Omega(x)$, and delay $x/k + O(k)$ (for fixed k) is achievable for $\Delta = 5$ [LS95]. Also, degree 4 (resp., 3) spanners with delay $2x$ (resp., $6x$) are constructible [LS95]. More generally, it was shown in [DHZ96] that every graph has a 2-additive spanner with $O(n^{3/2} \log n)$ edges (Exercise 7) and a 4-additive spanner with $O(n^{4/3} \log n)$ edges.

The problem of finding many edge-disjoint spanners in a given graph was studied in [LLP$^+$99].

In [KS91], a stronger lower bound than Corollary 16.2.6 is proved on the trade-off between radius and degree for ρ-regional matchings on the hypercube.

Rather than general constructions guaranteeing some prescribed bound, one may ask the associated optimization problem, namely, is there an algorithm that given a graph G and $\kappa > 1$ returns a minimum size κ-spanner for G. This problem was shown to be NP-hard for $\kappa = 2$ in [PS89], relying on the hardness of the Edge Dominating Set problem for bipartite graphs (problem (GT2) in [GJ79]). Later, this result was extended to every integer κ in [Cai94]. The problem is NP-hard even if the graph G is known to be chordal, but it becomes linear in $|E|$ (for $\kappa \geq 3$) if we restrict attention to the class of interval graphs [MR96, VRM$^+$97]. NP-completeness in the planar case was studied in [BH97].

An approximation algorithm of logarithmic ratio was given for the case of $\kappa = 2$ [KP94] and was later generalized in [Kor98, EP99]. The problem of approximating the minimum degree 2-spanner was considered in [KP98a]. The hardness of approximating spanner problems is studied in [Kor98, EP00a, EP00b].

Exercises

1. Prove Lemma 16.1.1.

2. Prove or disprove the following "weighted analog" of Lemma 16.1.1:

   For a weighted graph $G = (V, E, \omega)$, the subgraph $G' = (V, E', \omega)$ is a κ-*spanner* of G iff for every $e = (u, v) \in E$, $dist_{G'}(u, v) \leq \kappa \cdot \omega(e)$.

3. Modify the spanner construction of Section 16.1 as follows. Instead of picking a single intercluster edge for every pair of neighboring clusters in the partition, add to the spanner the entire set $\check{E}$ defined in Exercise 5 of Chapter 11. Show that the resulting subgraph is a $(2\kappa - 1)$-spanner for G and that its size is still $O(n^{1+1/\kappa})$.

4. (a) Show that bipartite graphs are 2-nonspannable.

    (b) Suppose that a given bipartite graph G is $(2\kappa - 1)$-nonspannable for some integer $\kappa \geq 1$. Show that G is also 2κ-nonspannable.

5. Complete the proof of Theorem 16.3.9.

6. ($*$) Prove that every n-vertex chordal graph G has a polynomial-time constructible 5-spanner with $O(n)$ edges.

7. ($*$) Show that every n-vertex graph G has a 2-additive spanner H (namely, such that $dist_H(u, w) \leq dist_G(u, w) + 2$ for every $u, w \in G$) with $O(n^{3/2} \log n)$ edges.

Chapter 17

Light-weight spanners

In Section 15.2 we discussed the representation of graphs by spanning trees and mentioned two types of trees, namely, the MST and the SPT. These trees optimize the total weight and the root-stretch of the tree, respectively. The problem addressed here is how to handle situations in which it is desirable to have a spanning tree enjoying both low weight *and* stretch simultaneously. The same need may arise with any of our other types of locality-preserving skeletal representations. In this chapter we discuss possible modifications to our earlier constructions that lead to light-weight spanning subgraphs.

17.1 Light, low-stretch trees

17.1.1 MST, SPT and SLT

Suppose that we are given a weighted graph G and need to construct a spanning tree T achieving near optimal performance in both the root stretch and the weight measures. Ideally, it would be best if it were possible to use either an SPT or an MST for this purpose. Unfortunately, it turns out that the weight and stretch requirements are sometimes contradictory. In particular, in an n-vertex graph, the weight of an SPT T_S might be up to n times as large as that of an MST, i.e., $\omega(T_S) = \Omega(n \cdot \omega(MST))$. Analogously, the depth of an MST T_M with respect to a given root r might be up to n times as high as that of an SPT, i.e., $\text{Stretch}(T_M, r) = \Omega(n)$.

Example: *Depth/weight anomalies.*

In the weighted graph G shown in Figure 17.1, the weight of the shortest path tree with respect to the root 1 is $\omega(T_S) = (n-1)W$, whereas $\omega(MST) = W + n - 2$, yielding a ratio approaching $n - 1$ as W tends to infinity. In contrast, in the weighted graph G shown in Figure 17.2, the depth of the minimum weight tree T_M is $Depth(T_M) = 1 + (n-2)(1-\epsilon)$, whereas $Depth(T_S) = 1$, yielding a ratio approaching $n - 1$ as ϵ tends to zero. □

A possible approach to overcoming this problem is to attempt to construct a tree simultaneously approximating both an SPT and an MST, i.e., optimizing $\text{Stretch}(T)$ and $\omega(T)$ simultaneously.

Definition 17.1.1 [Shallow-light tree]: *A shallow-light tree (or SLT) for a weighted graph $G = (V, E, \omega)$ and a root vertex r_0 is a spanning tree T with constant weight ratio and root-stretch, i.e., such that $\text{Stretch}(T, r_0)$ and $\omega(T)/\omega(MST)$ are both bounded by a constant.*

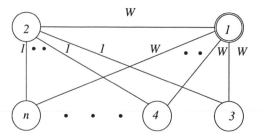

Figure 17.1: A weighted graph G for which $\omega(T_S)/\omega(T_M)$ tends to $n-1$ as W increases.

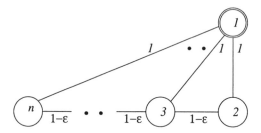

Figure 17.2: A weighted graph G for which $Depth(T_M)/Depth(T_S)$ tends to $n-1$ as ϵ decreases.

We now show that SLTs are effectively constructible for every graph G and root r_0 with small constant bounds on the root-stretch $\texttt{Stretch}(T, r_0)$ and the weight ratio $\omega(T)/\omega(MST)$.

17.1.2   The SLT algorithm

This section describes an algorithm named $\mathrm{SLT}(r_0, \theta)$ for constructing an SLT with respect to the root r_0 for an arbitrary weighted graph G. The basic idea is to rely on the existence of trees that optimize each of the two parameters separately. We therefore approach the problem by constructing a shortest path tree and an MST for the graph and using cut-and-paste methods for combining them into a satisfactory tree. The algorithm employs a parameter $\theta > 0$ controlling the trade-off between the quality of the approximation of root-stretch and weight ratio.

For every subgraph G' of G, and for every two vertices $u, v \in V$, let $\hat{\Upsilon}(u, v, G')$ denote some arbitrary path of length $dist_{G'}(u, v)$ connecting u and v in G'.

At the outset of the algorithm, we construct an MST T_M for the entire graph G and preprocess it for further use throughout the rest of the algorithm. Specifically, given a special root vertex r_0 in G, we create a "path-version" L of T_M starting at r_0, corresponding to a tour of the tree. Formally, we apply Procedure TOUR_MST, described in Figure 17.3. Figure 17.4 depicts a possible tree T_M, the resulting path L and the corresponding matching ν.

The algorithm then proceeds as follows. In addition to the MST, we also construct an SPT T_S for G, rooted at the intended root r_0. We use this tree in order to construct "shortcuts" on the path L in order to improve its root-stretch. For that purpose, we first identify "break-points" B_i on the path L by scanning it from left to right according to the following rules.

---

1. Construct an MST T_M for G.

2. Traverse T_M in a DFS fashion, starting from r_0.

   Denote by $\nu(i)$ $(0 \leq i \leq 2(n-1))$ the vertex visited by the tour in its ith step $(\nu(0) = r_0)$.

3. Construct the "path-version" L of T_M, which is a weighted $(2n-1)$-vertex path containing vertices $0, 1, \ldots, 2n-2$, where a vertex i on the path corresponds to $\nu(i)$.

4. **For** every edge $e = (i, i+1)$ on the path L **do:**
        Set $\omega(e) \leftarrow \omega(\nu(i), \nu(i+1))$.   /* the weight of the corresponding edge in G. */

5. **Output** (T_M, L).

Figure 17.3: Procedure $\text{TOUR\_MST}(r_0)$.

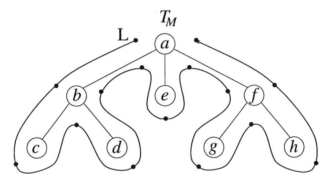

$$i = 0\text{-}1\text{-}2\text{-}3\text{-}4\text{-}5\text{-}6\text{-}7\text{-}8\text{-}9\text{-}10\text{-}11\text{-}12\text{-}13\text{-}14$$

$$\nu(i) = a \quad b \quad c \quad b \quad d \quad b \quad a \quad e \quad a \quad f \quad g \quad f \quad h \quad f \quad a$$

Figure 17.4: A tree T_M, the resulting path L and the corresponding matching ν.

1. Break-point B_1 is vertex 0 on the path L.

2. Break-point B_{i+1} is the first point to the right of B_i such that

$$dist_L(B_i, B_{i+1}) > \theta \cdot dist_{T_S}(r_0, \nu(B_{i+1})).$$

Intuitively, the current point under examination, say, x, is selected as a new break-point B_{i+1} whenever the best path from the root r_0 to x (composed of the "shortcut" from r_0 to the last break-point B_i plus the segment of L from B_i to x) becomes "too expensive," meaning, specifically, that the distance from B_i to x in L exceeds that in T_S by a factor of at least θ.

Next, create a subgraph G' of G by taking T_M and adding $\hat{\Upsilon}(r_0, \nu(B_i), T_S)$ for all break-points B_i, $i > 1$. Finally, construct a shortest path tree T rooted at r_0 in the resulting graph G'. This tree is our output.

Algorithm $\text{SLT}(r_0, \theta)$ is presented formally in Figure 17.5. In the algorithm, T denotes the set of edges selected to the shallow-light spanning tree and X, Y are pointers to vertices

1. $(T_M, L) \leftarrow \text{TOUR\_MST}(r_0)$.

2. Construct a shortest path tree T_S rooted at r_0 for G.

3. $E' \leftarrow T_M$.

4. $X \leftarrow 0$.   /* First break-point, B_1 */

5. $Y \leftarrow 0$.   /* candidate for next break-point */
   /* Scan for break points */

6. **Repeat**

   (a) **Repeat** $Y \leftarrow Y + 1$ **until** $dist_L(X, Y) > \theta \cdot dist_{T_S}(r_0, \nu(Y))$.
       /* Y is the next break-point, B_{i+1} */
   (b) $E' \leftarrow E' \bigcup \hat{\Upsilon}(r_0, \nu(Y), T_S)$.
   (c) $X \leftarrow Y$.

   until $Y = n$.

7. Construct a shortest path tree T in $G' = (V, E')$.

8. **Output** (T).

Figure 17.5: Algorithm SLT(r_0, θ).

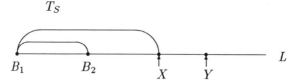

Figure 17.6: An example run of Algorithm SLT.

on the path L during the scan. (The break-points are used implicitly to define the segments of T_S added to the tree, but are not required explicitly in the code.) An illustration for a possible execution of the algorithm is given in Figure 17.6.

17.1.3   Analysis

The following two lemmas establish bounds on the stretch and weight of the tree T constructed by the tree algorithm.

Lemma 17.1.2 *The tree T constructed by the algorithm satisfies*

$$\omega(T) \leq (1 + 2/\theta) \cdot \omega(MST).$$

Proof: The tree T is a subgraph of G', created by adding the paths $\hat{\Upsilon}(r_0, \nu(B_i), T_S)$ for $i > 1$ to T_M. Therefore

$$\omega(T) \leq \omega(G') = \omega(T_M) + \sum_{i>1} \omega(\hat{\Upsilon}(r_0, \nu(B_i), T_S)).$$

But by choice of the break-points B_i, for $i > 1$

$$\omega(\hat{\Upsilon}(r_0, \nu(B_i), T_S)) \; = \; dist_{T_S}(r_0, \nu(B_i)) \; < \; \frac{1}{\theta} \cdot dist_L(B_{i-1}, B_i),$$

hence

$$\sum_{i>1} \omega(\hat{\Upsilon}(r_0, \nu(B_i), T_S)) \; < \; \frac{1}{\theta} \sum_{i>1} dist_L(B_{i-1}, B_i) \; \leq \; \frac{1}{\theta} \cdot \omega(L).$$

Observe that in the tour through the tree forming the path L, each tree edge is traversed exactly twice. Hence the total weight of the path is twice the total weight of the MST T_M, i.e., $\omega(L) = 2 \cdot \omega(T_M)$. Hence

$$\sum_{i>1} \omega(\hat{\Upsilon}(r_0, \nu(B_i), T_S)) \; < \; \frac{2}{\theta} \cdot \omega(T_M),$$

and thus $\omega(T) \leq (1 + \frac{2}{\theta})\omega(T_M)$.   □

Lemma 17.1.3 *The tree T constructed by the algorithm satisfies* $\mathtt{Stretch}(T, r_0) \leq 1 + 2\theta$.

Proof: Consider an arbitrary vertex $x \in V$. We need to show that

$$dist_T(r_0, x) \; \leq \; (2\theta + 1)dist_{T_S}(r_0, x).$$

Since T is a shortest-paths tree w.r.t. r_0 in G', it suffices to bound $dist_{G'}(r_0, x)$. Let j denote the point corresponding to x on the path L, i.e., $\nu(j) = x$. Suppose that $B_i \leq j < B_{i+1}$, i.e., j occurs on the path L between B_i and B_{i+1} for some i. The entire path $\hat{\Upsilon}(r_0, \nu(B_i), T_S)$ is included in G', and hence $dist_{G'}(r_0, \nu(B_i)) = dist_{T_S}(r_0, \nu(B_i))$. Also, since G' contains all of L, necessarily $dist_{G'}(\nu(B_i), x) \leq dist_L(B_i, j)$. Combining these two path segments (see Figure 17.7), it follows that

$$dist_{G'}(r_0, x) \; \leq \; dist_{T_S}(r_0, \nu(B_i)) + dist_L(B_i, j). \tag{17.1}$$

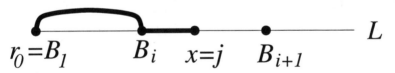

$$r_0 = B_1 \qquad\qquad B_i \quad x = j \quad B_{i+1} \qquad\qquad L$$

Figure 17.7: The combined path $r_0 \rightarrow \nu(B_i) \rightarrow x$ in G' (bold). The first segment is $\hat{\Upsilon}(r_0, \nu(B_i), T_S)$.

Also, since T_S is a shortest path tree with respect to r_0,

$$dist_{T_S}(r_0, \nu(B_i)) \; \leq \; dist_{T_S}(r_0, x) + dist_L(j, B_i), \tag{17.2}$$

hence combining Equations (17.1) and (17.2), we get

$$dist_{G'}(r_0, x) \; \leq \; dist_{T_S}(r_0, x) + 2 \cdot dist_L(j, B_i). \tag{17.3}$$

If $j = B_i$, then we are done. Otherwise, by the fact that j was not selected as the $(i+1)$st break-point, necessarily

$$dist_L(B_i, j) \; \leq \; \theta \cdot dist_{T_S}(r_0, x).$$

Put together with Equation (17.3), we get that $dist_{G'}(r_0, x) \leq (2\theta + 1)dist_{T_S}(r_0, x)$, as required.   □

Combining the above two lemmas, we establish the following theorem.

Theorem 17.1.4 [SLT]: *For every weighted graph $G = (V, E, \omega)$ and vertex r_0 there exists a spanning tree T with constant root-stretch $\mathtt{Stretch}(T, r_0)$ and weight ratio $\omega(T)/\omega(MST)$.*

17.2   Light, sparse, low-stretch spanners

All the spanner constructions described in Chapter 16 concerned unweighted graphs. Clearly, the question of sparse spanners is relevant also for weighted graphs. Moreover, for such graphs it is natural to search for representations that are not only sparse in the number of edges, but also *light* in their total weight.

17.2.1   A tree-cover based algorithm

Let us first mention that using the Tree Cover Theorem 15.5.2 in a straightforward manner, it is possible to derive a result similar to the Spanner Theorem 16.1.2 for weighted graphs, although with an additional logarithmic factor based on the edge weights. The construction is achieved by Algorithm WEIGHTED_SPAN, described in Figure 17.8.

---

1. **For** every $1 \leq i \leq \Lambda$ **do:**
    Construct a 2^i-tree-cover $\mathcal{TC}_{\kappa,2^i}$ for G as in the Tree Cover Theorem 15.5.2.

2. Set E' to be the union of all edges in the trees of these covers

3. **Output** $(G' = (V, E'))$.

Figure 17.8: Algorithm WEIGHTED_SPAN(G, κ).

Lemma 17.2.1 *The subgraph G' constructed by Algorithm WEIGHTED_SPAN(G, κ) has stretch factor $\mathtt{Stretch}(G') \leq 4\kappa - 2$.*

Proof: Consider an arbitrary pair of vertices $x, y \in V$. Suppose that

$$2^{i-1} \ < \ dist_G(x, y) \ \leq \ 2^i.$$

By definition, the tree cover $\mathcal{TC}_{\kappa,2^i}$ constructed for the graph contains a tree T such that $\Gamma_{2^i}(x) \subseteq V(T)$. Hence both $x, y \in V(T)$. By the Tree Cover Theorem 15.5.2, $Depth(T) \leq (2\kappa - 1) \cdot 2^i$. Consequently, the tree T provides a path of length at most $2 \cdot (2\kappa - 1) \cdot 2^i \leq (4\kappa - 2) \cdot dist(x, y)$ connecting x and y in the spanner G'. $\square$

Lemma 17.2.2 *The size of the spanner G' is $O(\Lambda \cdot \kappa \cdot n^{1+1/\kappa})$.*

Proof: The number of edges in G' is bounded from above by

$$|E'| \ \leq \ \sum_{i=1}^{\Lambda} \sum_{T \in \mathcal{TC}_{\kappa,2^i}} |E(T)|$$

$$< \ \sum_{i=1}^{\Lambda} \sum_{T \in \mathcal{TC}_{\kappa,2^i}} |V(T)| \ \leq \ \Lambda \cdot n \cdot \mathtt{Overlap}(\mathcal{TC}_{\kappa,2^i}).$$

The result follows by the bound of the Tree Cover Theorem 15.5.2 on $\mathtt{Overlap}(\mathcal{TC}_{\kappa,2^i})$. $\square$

We conclude the following.

Corollary 17.2.3 *For every n-vertex weighted graph $G = (V, E, \omega)$ and for every $\kappa \geq 1$, Algorithm* WEIGHTED_SPAN *constructs an $O(\kappa)$-spanner with $O(\kappa n^{1+1/\kappa} \Lambda)$ edges.*

We next present an elegant (and more efficient) greedy algorithm for constructing spanners for arbitrary weighted graphs. This algorithm bounds both the number of edges in the spanner and its total weight.

17.2.2 A greedy sequential algorithm

Algorithm GREEDY_SPAN(G, κ) constructs a κ-spanner for the given graph G. The algorithm can be thought of as a generalization of Kruskal's algorithm for constructing an MST (discussed in Section 5.5.2). In fact, if we take κ to be infinite, then the algorithm becomes identical to Kruskal's algorithm. The algorithm first sorts the edges of the graph by nondecreasing weights. Then the edges are scanned one by one, taking into the spanner only those edges whose omission would violate the desired stretch bound. That is, an edge e is included only if its weight is smaller than $1/\kappa$ times the distance between its endpoints in the current spanner (composed of all the edges included so far).

A formal description of the algorithm is given in Figure 17.9.

---

1. Sort E by nondecreasing edge weight, obtaining $E = \{e_1, \ldots, e_m\}$.

2. Set $E' \leftarrow \emptyset$.

3. **For** $j = 1$ to m **do**:

    (a) Let $e_j \leftarrow (u, v)$.

    (b) Compute $\hat{\Upsilon}(u, v)$, the shortest path from u to v in $G' = (V, E')$.

    (c) **If** $\omega(\hat{\Upsilon}(u, v)) > \kappa \cdot \omega(e_j)$, **then** set $E' \leftarrow E' \cup \{e_j\}$.

    End-for

4. Output $G' = (V, E')$.

Figure 17.9: Algorithm GREEDY_SPAN(G, κ).

Lemma 17.2.4 *The output subgraph G' has stretch factor* $\mathtt{Stretch}(G') \leq \kappa$.

Proof: Consider any two vertices x, y of the graph G, and let $\hat{\Upsilon}_{x,y} = (e_{i_1}, \ldots, e_{i_q})$ denote a shortest path connecting x and y in G. Consider any edge $e_{i_j} = (u, v)$ along this path. If e_{i_j} is not included in G', then at the time it was examined by the algorithm, the set E' of edges already added to the spanner by that time contained a path $\hat{\Upsilon}_{i_j} = \hat{\Upsilon}(u, v)$ of length at most $\kappa \cdot \omega(e_{i_j})$ connecting u to v. Since the algorithm never eliminates edges from E', this path exists in the final G'. It follows that it is possible to mimic the path $\hat{\Upsilon}_{x,y}$ in the spanner G' by replacing each "missing" edge $e_{i_j} \notin G'$ by its substitute $\hat{\Upsilon}_{i_j}$ (see Figure 17.10). The resulting path is clearly of total length $\kappa \cdot \omega(\hat{\Upsilon}_{x,y})$ or less. $\square$

Lemma 17.2.5 *The girth of G' satisfies $Girth(G') > \kappa + 1$.*

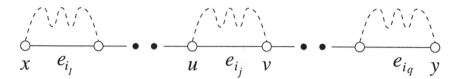

Figure 17.10: The path $\hat{\Upsilon}_{x,y}$ and the path replacing it in the spanner. The dashed path connecting u and v represents $\hat{\Upsilon}(u,v)$.

Proof: Consider an arbitrary cycle C in G'. Let $e_j = (u,v)$ be the last edge added to C. When the algorithm examined e_j, the set E' already contained all the other edges of C. Therefore the path $\hat{\Upsilon}(u,v)$ constructed by the algorithm satisfies $w(\hat{\Upsilon}(u,v)) \leq w(C - \{e_j\})$. Since e_j was added to E', $w(\hat{\Upsilon}(u,v)) > \kappa \cdot w(e_j)$. It follows that $w(C) > (\kappa + 1) \cdot w(e_j)$. But e_j is the heaviest edge in C, so $w(C) \leq |C| \cdot w(e_j)$. Hence $|C| > \kappa + 1$. The claim follows.   □

By the first claim of Lemma 15.1.2 we have the next corollary.

Corollary 17.2.6 $|E'| \leq n^{1+2/\kappa} + n$.

In fact, it can be shown that Algorithm GREEDY_SPAN also guarantees good bounds on the weight of the spanner constructed by it. Specifically, the following theorem holds.

Theorem 17.2.7 [Weighted spanner]: *For every integer $\kappa \geq 1$ and every n-vertex weighted graph $G = (V, E, \omega)$, Algorithm GREEDY_SPAN constructs a spanner $G' = (V, E')$ for G with* Stretch$(G') \leq 2\kappa + 1$, $|E'| = O(n^{1+1/\kappa})$ *and* $\omega(G') = \omega(MST(G)) \cdot O(n^{1/\kappa})$.

This result is near optimal w.r.t. all three measures. The lower bound serving as benchmark here is the following.

Theorem 17.2.8 *For every $\kappa \geq 3$, there exist (infinitely many) n-vertex graphs $G = (V, E, \omega)$ such that every spanner $G' = (V, E')$ for G with* Stretch$(G') \leq \kappa - 2$ *requires* $|E'| = \Omega(n^{1+1/\kappa})$ *and*

$$\omega(G') = \Omega(\omega(MST(G)) \cdot n^{1/\kappa}).$$

Proof: By Theorem 16.2.3, for every $\kappa \geq 3$, there exist (infinitely many) unweighted n-vertex graphs $G = (V, E)$ for which every $(\kappa - 2)$-spanner requires $\Omega(n^{1+1/\kappa})$ edges. Taking the weight of each edge in such a graph G to be 1, we get also the desired lower bound on the weight of the spanner.   □

An efficient spanner construction for planar graphs also exists, yielding the following result.

Theorem 17.2.9 *For every $\kappa \geq 1/2$ and every n-vertex weighted planar graph $G = (V, E, \omega)$ there is a polynomially constructible spanner $G' = (V, E')$ for G with* Stretch$(G') \leq 2\kappa + 1$, $|E'| < (n-1)(1 + 1/\kappa)$ *and* $\omega(G') < \omega(MST(G))(1 + 1/\kappa)$.

This construction is optimal in both measures.

17.2.3 Algorithm LIGHT_SPAN

Finally, we describe one more algorithm, named LIGHT_SPAN, for the construction of a low-stretch, sparse, light-weight spanner for an arbitrary weighted network G and integer κ. This algorithm again suffers from an extra factor of Λ in the size of the resulting edge set weight, but its main advantage is that it is amenable to an efficient distributed implementation, whereas the greedy algorithm GREEDY_SPAN is inherently sequential.

By combining several tree covers, Algorithm LIGHT_SPAN constructs the desired spanner as in Algorithm WEIGHTED_SPAN described earlier. The construction for tree covers follows the same general structure of Algorithm TREE_COVER. As in the SLT construction of the previous section, we approach the problem of reducing the total weight by constructing a sparse (but possibly heavy) tree cover, and an MST for the graph, and combining them in order to reduce the total weight.

The presented method falls short of achieving the additional goal of constructing light-weight, low-overlap tree covers along the way. However, as shown in the analysis, the constructed tree covers have a special structure which enables us to efficiently bound the costs of the spanner resulting from merging them together.

Let us first provide a brief outline of the algorithm LIGHT_SPAN(κ). At the outset of the algorithm, we construct an MST T_M for the entire graph G, and the corresponding tour L (with an arbitrary root vertex), using Procedure TOUR_MST of the previous section. This path is kept for further use throughout the rest of the algorithm (i.e., it is combined with each of the spanning trees of the clusters during the algorithm).

Next, for every $1 \leq i \leq \Lambda$, we construct a 2^i-tree-cover $\mathcal{TC}_i$ for G using Procedure LIGHT_TC to be described below. Finally, we take the union of all edges in the trees of these covers to form the spanner G'.

Algorithm LIGHT_SPAN is described formally in Figure 17.11.

---

1. $(T_M, L) \leftarrow$ TOUR_MST(r_0).

2. **For** $i = 1$ to Λ **do:**

    $\mathcal{TC}_i \leftarrow$ LIGHT_TC$(L, \kappa, 2^i, \theta)$.

    End-for

3. $E' \leftarrow \bigcup_i \bigcup_{T \in \mathcal{TC}_i} E(T)$.

4. **Output** $G' = (V, E')$.

Figure 17.11: Algorithm LIGHT_SPAN(κ).

Let us now describe the main procedure, LIGHT_TC$(L, \kappa, \rho, \theta)$, for constructing a ρ-tree-cover. For uniformity with the previous section and ease of presentation, we describe this algorithm too as using a parameter $\theta > 0$ for controlling the resulting trade-off. However, it is convenient to think of this parameter as set to $\theta = 1$.

First, set the separation parameter s to be $s = \rho$ and construct a cover $\mathcal{T}$ coarsening $\hat{\Gamma}_\rho(V)$ with an s-separated partial partition for each "layer" of the cover, as in Theorem 12.4.4. Note that this cover is composed of up to $2\kappa \cdot n^{1/\kappa}$ individual s-separated partial partitions, $\mathcal{S}_i$, and that the radius of each cluster in these partitions is bounded from above by $(3\kappa - 1)\rho$.

As in the construction of Algorithm TREE_COVER in Section 15.5, we construct a spanning tree for each cluster of each partial partition. Hence each partial partition contributes a collection of trees to the tree cover and the final tree cover is composed of the union

of these collections. One aspect in which the current construction differs from Algorithm
TREE_COVER is that here, the trees constructed in a single partial partition are not necessarily disjoint.

In what follows, we consider one partial partition S from the cover at hand and describe
the collection of trees contributed by S to the constructed tree cover.

For each cluster S in this partial partition, we construct a spanning tree $T(S)$ as follows.
We first identify the segment of L relevant to the cluster S. Let r_0 denote the "entry point"
of the path into the cluster S, namely, the first vertex of L that belongs to S. Analogously,
let r_E denote the "exit" point, namely, the last vertex of L that belongs to S. Then the
relevant segment of L, henceforth denoted $L(S)$, is its segment path from r_0 to r_E. This
segment is taken as the basis for our tree $T(S)$. Note that the path $L(S)$ may enter and
exit S several times and may even visit other clusters of the same decomposition in the
meantime. Hence our tree $T(S)$ may span other vertices besides those of S.

We next construct an SPT, $T_S(S)$, for the cluster S, rooted at r_0. We then construct
"break-points" B_i on $L(S)$ by scanning it from left to right, beginning at r_0, according to
the following rules. Break-point B_1 is vertex r_0 on the path L. From then on, break-point
B_{i+1} is the first point *in the cluster* S to the right of B_i such that

$$dist_L(B_i, B_{i+1}) \; > \; \theta \cdot dist_{T_S(S)}(r_0, \nu(B_{i+1})).$$

This process of selecting break-points is continued until reaching the point where the path
exits the cluster S for the last time. Note that although the path $L(S)$ may exit S, we only
select break-points among the vertices belonging to the cluster S.

Once all break-points are selected, we create a subgraph $G'(S)$ by taking the path segment $L(S)$ and adding $\hat{\Upsilon}(r_0, \nu(B_i), T_S(S))$ for all break-points B_i, $i > 1$. Finally, we
construct a shortest path tree $T(S)$ rooted at r_0 in the resulting graph G'. (Note that this
tree spans the entire cluster S, but is not confined to it, and may contain external vertices.)
The output tree cover $\mathcal{TC}$ is taken to consist of the union of all these trees $T(S)$.

Procedure LIGHT_TC is described formally in Figure 17.12. Figure 17.13 depicts the
break-points B_i selected for the path L in a cluster S within a 2^i-separated partial partition $\mathcal{S}$.

It may be helpful to pause and explain why we take the entire path segment $L(S)$ into
the subgraph $G'(S)$, rather than, say, just the segments of L totally contained within S.
This question is valid, especially since, as we shall see later, this choice of ours is the main
cause for the fact that the resulting tree cover fails to enjoy good bounds on its total weight
and overlap!

The difficulty that prevents us from taking only the intersection of L and S is that if we
do restrict ourselves to these segments of L, it may happen that the resulting graph $G'(S)$
is disconnected and, moreover, it may happen that certain vertices of S do not occur in G'
at all. To see how this might happen, consider a cluster S with only two vertices, v_1 and v_2,
and suppose that the tour of the path inside this cluster has the following behavior. The
path L enters S at $v_1 = r_0(S)$, immediately exits to a neighboring vertex w (s.t. $w \notin S$),
returns to visit v_2, and exits again, never to return. Suppose further that the segment
(v_1, w, v_2) of L is cheaper than the edge (v_1, v_2) that constitutes $T_S(S)$. In this case, G' is
empty.

Hence it is necessary at this stage to complete G' so that it is connected and spans
the entire set S. The simplest way for doing so is by taking the entire relevant segment
of L. (Let us comment that in fact, the way we bound the root-stretch of $r_0(S)$ in $G'(S)$
necessitates the addition of the entire relevant path segment even if $G'(S)$ is connected and
does span all of S.)

1. Set $s \leftarrow \rho$.

2. Construct a cover $\mathcal{T}$ coarsening $\hat{\Gamma}_\rho(V)$ with an s-separated partial partition for each "layer" of the cover.

3. $\mathcal{TC} \leftarrow \emptyset$.

4. **For** each cluster S in each partial partition $\mathcal{S}_i \in \mathcal{T}$ **do:**

   (a) /* Mark the segment of the path relevant to the cluster S */
   Let $0 \le I_0(S) \le 2(n-1)$ be the first vertex of L such that $\nu(I_0(S))$ belongs to S.

   /* The "entry point" of L into S */

   (b) Let $r_0(S) \leftarrow \nu(I_0(S))$.

   (c) Let $0 \le I_E(S) \le 2(n-1)$ be the last vertex of L such that $\nu(I_E(S))$ belongs to S.

   /* The "exit point" of L from S */

   (d) Let $r_E(S) \leftarrow \nu(I_0(S))$.

   (e) Construct an SPT, $T_S(S)$, for the cluster S, rooted at r_0.

   (f) Set E' to be the segment of L consisting of all the edges from $I_0(S)$ to $I_E(S)$.

   (g) $X \leftarrow I_0(S)$.   /* First break-point, B_1 */

   (h) $Y \leftarrow I_0(S)$.

   (i) /* Scan for break-points */
   Repeat

       i. **Repeat** $Y \leftarrow Y + 1$ **until** $\nu(Y) \in S$ and $dist_L(X,Y) > \theta \cdot dist_{T_S}(r_0, \nu(Y))$.

             /* Y is the next break-point, B_{i+1} */

       ii. $E' \leftarrow E' \bigcup \hat{\Upsilon}(r_0, \nu(Y), T_S)$.

       iii. $X \leftarrow Y$.

       until $Y = I_E(S)$.

   (j) Construct a shortest path tree $T(S)$ rooted at $r_0(S)$ in the resulting graph G''.

   (k) $\mathcal{TC} \leftarrow \mathcal{TC} \cup \{T(S)\}$.

   End-for

5. **Output** ($\mathcal{TC}$).

Figure 17.12: Procedure LIGHT_TC(L, κ, ρ, θ).

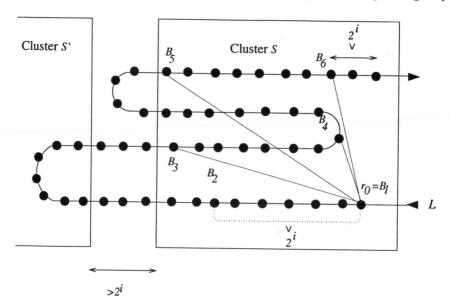

Figure 17.13: The path L and the break-points B_i selected for it in a cluster S within a 2^i-separated partial partition $\mathcal{S}$.

Analysis

Let us first establish the fact that the subgraph G' constructed by Algorithm LIGHT_SPAN(κ) is indeed an $O(\kappa)$-spanner.

Lemma 17.2.10 *The collection of trees $\mathcal{TC}$ constructed by Procedure* LIGHT_TC *is a ρ-tree cover with* $Depth(\mathcal{TC}) \leq (2\theta + 1)(6\kappa - 2)\rho$.

Proof: The fact that $\mathcal{TC}$ is a ρ-tree-cover follows just as in the proof for Algorithm TREE_COVER (the Tree Cover Theorem 15.5.2), once noting that for each cluster S, the constructed tree $T_S(S)$ is indeed a spanning tree for the induced subgraph $G(S)$.

It remains to prove the bound on $Depth(\mathcal{TC})$. Consider some cluster S in a certain partial partition $\mathcal{S}$. We need to bound the depth of the spanning tree $T(S)$ constructed for this cluster by our algorithm. Let r_0 be the root vertex selected for $T_S(S)$ in the construction. Since $T(S)$ is a shortest-paths tree with respect to r_0 in the spanning subgraph G' constructed for the cluster S, and the initial setting of E' is to the segment of L spanning the entirety of S, it follows just as in Lemma 17.1.3 that for an arbitrary vertex $x \in S$,

$$dist_{G'}(r_0, x) \leq (2\theta + 1)dist_{T_S(S)}(r_0, x) \leq (2\theta + 1)Diam(S)$$
$$\leq (2\theta + 1) \cdot 2 \cdot (3\kappa - 1)\rho$$

as required.   □

Lemma 17.2.11 *The constructed spanner G' satisfies* Stretch(G') $\leq 12(3\kappa - 1)$.

Proof: Consider an arbitrary pair of vertices $x, y \in V$. Suppose that

$$2^{i-1} < dist_G(x, y) \leq 2^i.$$

By definition, the ith level tree-cover $\mathcal{TC}_{\kappa, 2^i}$ constructed by us contains a tree $T(S)$ such that $\Gamma_{2^i}(x) \subseteq S$. Hence both $x, y \in S$. We will argue that the spanning tree $T(S)$ constructed by our algorithm for the cluster S (and added to the spanner) provides a path of the desired length to the spanner. Indeed, by the previous lemma, the depth of this tree satisfies $Depth(T(S)) \le 6(3\kappa - 1)2^i$. Hence we get that

$$
\begin{aligned}
dist_{G'}(x,y) &\le dist_{G'}(r_0,x) + dist_{G'}(r_0,y) \le 2 \cdot 6(3\kappa - 1)2^i \\
&\le 12(3\kappa - 1) \cdot dist_G(x,y)
\end{aligned}
$$

as required. □

Next, we would like to bound the sparsity and the weight of the spanner G' constructed by the algorithm. In order to do that, it is useful to separate the edges of the spanner into two classes by noting that for each cluster S, the tree $T(S)$ constructed for it (and later merged into the spanner) is composed of a segment $L(S)$ of the path L and certain shortcuts taken from $T_S(S)$. As all trees use the same path L, it is convenient to bound the contributions of the segments $L(S)$ to the spanner separately. Specifically, the number of edges contributed by all of these segments is at most the number of edges in T_M, namely, $n - 1$, and the total weight added to the spanner due to these segments is at most $\omega(MST)$.

Thus in what follows, we focus only on the costs entailed by the shortcuts. For that purpose, let us denote the tree composed of the edges of the shortcuts added to the tree $T(S)$ of the cluster S by $F(S)$, and let us denote the collection of trees constructed for a single partial partition $\mathcal{S}$ by $\mathcal{F}(\mathcal{S})$ and the collection of trees constructed for the tree cover TC_i by $\mathcal{F}(TC_i)$.

Lemma 17.2.12 *In the constructed spanner G', $|E(G')| = O(\Lambda \cdot \kappa \cdot n^{1+1/\kappa})$.*

Proof: Note first that since the shortcuts constructed in a cluster S are segments of the shortest-paths tree $T_S(S)$, the edges of the tree $F(S)$ are internal to S. Consequently, for a single partial partition $\mathcal{S}$, since the clusters in $\mathcal{S}$ are disjoint, the collection of trees $\mathcal{F}(\mathcal{S})$ contains less than $n - 1$ edges altogether. Since each cover TC_i is composed of at most $2\kappa \cdot n^{1/\kappa}$ partial partitions, it follows that the collection $\mathcal{F}(TC_i)$ contains $O(\kappa \cdot n^{1+1/\kappa})$ edges. Finally, the claim follows since the spanner consists of edges from the tree covers TC_i constructed on each of the Λ levels. □

Lemma 17.2.13 *The collection of trees $\mathcal{F}(TC)$ constructed by Procedure LIGHT_TC satisfies $\omega(\mathcal{F}(TC)) \le 4 \cdot \max\{\kappa, \frac{1}{\theta}\} \cdot \kappa \cdot n^{1/\kappa} \cdot \omega(T_M)$.*

Proof: Let us first look at the collection of trees $F(\mathcal{S})$ constructed by Procedure LIGHT_TC for one partial partition $\mathcal{S}$. Consider such a partial partition $\mathcal{S}$ and one cluster S in it. The tree $F(S)$ satisfies

$$
\omega(F(S)) \le \sum_{i>1} \omega(\hat{\Upsilon}(r_0, \nu(B_i), T_S(S))).
$$

We would now like to charge each shortcut to a segment of T_M. Specifically, let $L(S, B_{i-1}, B_i)$ denote the segment of L between break-points B_{i-1} and B_i computed for S, and let $L_{in}(S, B_{i-1}, B_i)$ denote the parts of this segment that are in the $\rho/2$ vicinity of S. Formally, let $\mathcal{N}(S) = \bigcup \Gamma_{\rho/2}(S)$. Then

$$
L_{in}(S, B_{i-1}, B_i) = L(S, B_{i-1}, B_i) \cap \mathcal{N}(S).
$$

For the purpose of this accounting operation, if an edge e of the path L has one endpoint inside $\mathcal{N}(S)$ and the other outside it, then we introduce an imaginary vertex at some point along this edge, thus splitting e into e_{in} and e_{out}, and break the weight $\omega(e)$ between these edges so that the imaginary vertex is placed precisely on the border of $\mathcal{N}(S)$. Note that while considering one partial partition $\mathcal{S}$, an edge may connect one endpoint in $\mathcal{N}(S)$ with another endpoint in $\mathcal{N}(S')$, in which case it may be broken twice in this way (in case the distance between S and S' strictly exceeds the separation parameter s).

By choice of the break-points B_i,

$$\omega(\hat{\Upsilon}(r_0, \nu(B_i), T_S(S))) \;=\; dist_{T_S(S)}(r_0, \nu(B_i)) \;<\; \frac{1}{\theta} \cdot \omega(L(S, B_{i-1}, B_i)). \qquad (17.4)$$

We claim that this implies that

$$\omega(\hat{\Upsilon}(r_0, \nu(B_i), T_S(S))) \;<\; \psi \cdot \omega(L_{in}(S, B_{i-1}, B_i)), \qquad (17.5)$$

where $\psi = \max\{\kappa, \frac{1}{\theta}\}$. To see this, consider two cases. In the first, the path segment leading from B_{i-1} to B_i never leaves the $\rho/2$-neighborhood of S. But then $L_{in}(S, B_{i-1}, B_i) = L(S, B_{i-1}, B_i)$, hence their weights are equal, and Equation (17.5) follows from Equation (17.4). In the second case, the path segment $L(S, B_{i-1}, B_i)$ leaves the $\rho/2$-neighborhood of S. But then it also returns to S and its segments from S until it reaches the external border and from the border back to S are each of weight at least $\rho/2$, hence the total weight of the internal path segment satisfies $\omega(L_{in}(S, B_{i-1}, B_i)) \geq \rho$. On the other hand, $\omega(\hat{\Upsilon}(r_0, \nu(B_i), T_S(S)))$ is bounded above by $\kappa\rho$, and again Equation (17.5) follows.

It follows from Equation (17.5) that the total weight of the shortcuts added to the cluster S is bounded as

$$\omega(F(S)) \;=\; \sum_{i>1} \omega(\hat{\Upsilon}(r_0, \nu(B_i), T_S)) \;<\; \psi \cdot \sum_{i>1} \omega(L_{in}(S, B_{i-1}, B_i)).$$

We now sum up the weights of all the trees $F(S)$ constructed for all the clusters S in the partial partition $\mathcal{S}$. For doing this, observe that the segments L_{in} charged against in our separate bounds for each cluster are all disjoint, since our clusters in the given partial partition $\mathcal{S}$ are separated to distance ρ, and the segments L_{in} are confined to $\rho/2$-neighborhoods of these clusters. It follows that the total sum of the shortcuts added is bounded by

$$\omega(\mathcal{F}(\mathcal{S})) \;=\; \sum_{S \in \mathcal{S}} \omega(F(S)) \;\leq\; \psi \cdot \omega(L) \;\leq\; 2\psi \cdot \omega(T_M).$$

The lemma now follows from the fact that there are at most $2\kappa \cdot n^{1/\kappa}$ partial partitions participating in $T\mathcal{C}_i$. $\square$

Lemma 17.2.14 *The constructed spanner G' satisfies*

$$\omega(G') = O(\Lambda \cdot \kappa^2 \cdot n^{1/\kappa})\omega(MST).$$

Proof: Taking $\theta = 1$, the weight of the edges added to the spanner on behalf of each of the Λ tree collections $\mathcal{F}(T\mathcal{C}_i)$ is bounded, by the previous lemma, by $4 \cdot \kappa^2 \cdot n^{1/\kappa} \cdot \omega(MST)$. The MST component, L, adds at most $\omega(T_M)$ overall. The claim follows. $\square$

We have shown the following result.

Theorem 17.2.15 *For every integer $\kappa \geq 1$ and every n-vertex weighted graph $G = (V, E, \omega)$, Algorithm* LIGHT_SPAN *constructs a spanner G' for G with* Stretch$(G') = O(\kappa)$, $|E(G')| = O(\kappa \cdot \Lambda \cdot n^{1+1/\kappa})$ *and* $\omega(G') = O(\kappa^2 \cdot \Lambda \cdot n^{1/\kappa} \cdot \omega(MST))$.

Hence by the above lower bound, as long as the weights associated with the links of the network are polynomial in n, the construction for a spanner with stretch $O(\kappa)$ is within a polylogarithmic factor away from optimality for both sparsity and total weight.

Bibliographical notes

The problem of constructing a spanning tree optimizing weight and stretch simultaneously was introduced in [BKJ83, Jaf85]. In particular, the examples of Figures 17.1 and 17.2 and Exercise 1 are taken from [BKJ83]. Both of these papers and [ABP90] used somewhat different definitions for stretch that are weaker than the one used here. Specifically, instead of bounding the root-stretch, $\texttt{Stretch}(T, r_0)$, [BKJ83] bounds the ratios of the sum of all distances, $(\sum_{v \in V} dist_T(r_0, v))/(\sum_{v \in V} dist_G(r_0, v))$, proving roughly an $O(\sqrt{n})$ upper bound on this ratio in an n-vertex graph.

In contrast, the variant of SLTs presented in [ABP90] is based on measuring the diameter ratio, namely, $Diam(T)/Diam(G)$, instead of the root stretch. In [ABP90] it is shown how to construct asymptotically optimal SLTs of this type, i.e., with (small) constant upper bounds on the total weight and diameter ratio overheads. These SLTs are used in [ABP90] for designing efficient algorithms for various data gathering and dissemination problems in the weighted complexity model of distributed networks developed therein. Additional usages for trees of similar types are discussed in [AHH+95].

The SLTs presented in Section 17.1, and the construction of Algorithm SLT, are due to [ABP91]. Other related types of "good" trees were studied extensively, cf. [RSM+94].

Algorithm GREEDY_SPAN and the upper and lower bounds of the Weighted Spanner Theorem 17.2.7, Theorem 17.2.8 and Theorem 17.2.9 are from [ADDJ90, ADD+93], except for the weight bound in Theorem 17.2.7, which was proved in [CDNS92]. The constructions described in the rest of the chapter are based on [ABP91].

The existence of sparse spanners has been studied also for the more restricted Euclidean case [Che86, DFS87, ADDJ90]. In this setting, G is a complete graph whose vertices are points in the plane and $dist(u, v)$ is the distance from the point u to the point v in some L_p metric. In [Che86, DFS87] it is shown that in this setting it is possible to construct linearly sized spanners. More specifically, the Delaunay triangulation (see [PS85] for a definition) in the same metric chosen for the distances is a natural candidate to be a spanner since it has $O(n)$ edges and tends to contain edges between points that are close together. In order for the triangulation to be well defined, it is traditional to assume that no four points are cocircular. In [Che86] it is shown that if distances are measured in the L_1 metric, then the L_1 Delaunay triangulation is a $\sqrt{10}$-spanner. In [DFS87] it is shown that if the distances are measured in the Euclidean (L_2) metric, then the corresponding Delaunay triangulation is a $\phi\pi$-spanner, where ϕ is the golden ratio. Fault-tolerant geometric spanners are studied in [LNS98].

The *total weight* of the spanner has also been considered in this context. Tight bounds were established on the total weight of the spanner, compared to the weight of the minimum spanning tree [DJ89, LL92, ADD+93, CDNS92]. In particular, it was established that for any κ, there exist spanners G' for the complete graph on the plane with stretch factor $\texttt{Stretch}(G') = O(\kappa)$ and weight within a multiple of $O(1 + 1/\kappa)$ of the weight of the minimum spanning tree $\omega(G') = O((1 + 1/\kappa)\omega(MST))$. Using low-degree spanners in the Euclidean case is the subject of [Soa94].

A mixed type of weighted spanners, where the cost of the spanner is taken to be its weight but stretch is measured in the unweighted sense, was studied in [Kor98]. The paper provides an $O(\log n)$ ratio approximation algorithm for the 2-spanner problem and establishes hardness results for this problem, as well as for the problem of approximating the more general minimum-weight κ-spanner problem for $\kappa \geq 3$ by a factor of $O(2^{\log^{1-\epsilon} n})$ for any fixed $\epsilon > 0$. These results were generalized and strengthened in [EP00a, EP00b].

Exercises

1. Prove that the examples of Figures 17.1 and 17.2 are asymptotically the worst possible in the sense that for every graph G and root r, $\omega(T_S) \leq (n - 1) \cdot \omega(MST)$ and $Diam(T_M) \leq (n - 1)Diam(G)$.

2. Give an SLT for each of the graphs of Figures 17.1 and 17.2.

3. (a) Give an example for a graph in which both the MST and the SPT are bad choices for simultaneously approximating the minimum weight and depth.

   (b) Give an SLT for the graph you have shown in part (a).

4. For the weighted ring, are the MST and the SPT always identical?

5. Analyze the time and message complexities of Algorithm SLT, assuming efficient procedures for MST and SPT construction.

Chapter 18

Spanners with low average stretch

So far, our evaluation for the quality of spanners relied on the worst-case measure of maximum stretch. This chapter examines a different quality measure for spanners, namely, their average stretch.

18.1 Basic properties of average stretch spanners

Let us first define the notion of the average stretch of a spanning subgraph. For our future purposes it is useful to give this definition in a slightly more general framework, where G is a multigraph.

Definition 18.1.1 [Average stretch]: *Let $G = (V, E, \omega)$ be a weighted multigraph and H a spanning subgraph of G. Assume that the edge weights $\omega(e)$ are normalized so that the lightest edge has weight 1. For every subset of edges E', denote*

$$\mathsf{Cost}(E', H, G) \; = \; \sum_{e=(u,v)\in E'} \frac{dist_H(u,v)}{\omega(e)}$$

and let

$$\texttt{Av\_Stretch}(G, H) \; = \; \frac{\mathsf{Cost}(E, H, G)}{|E|} \; .$$

(We write simply `Av_Stretch`(H) *when G is clear from the context.)*

Let us first consider the question of finding a spanning subgraph H with low average stretch. The Weighted Spanner Theorem 17.2.7 trivially gives us the following as a corollary.

Corollary 18.1.2 *For every weighted n-vertex graph $G = (V, E, \omega)$ and for every $k \geq 1$, there exists a (polynomial-time constructible) spanning subgraph $H = (V, E')$ such that $|E'| < n\lceil n^{1/k}\rceil$ and* `Av_Stretch`$(H) \leq 2k + 1$. $\quad\square$

Setting $k = \log n$ we get, in particular, the next corollary.

Corollary 18.1.3 *For every weighted n-vertex graph $G = (V, E, \omega)$, there exists a spanning subgraph $H = (V, E')$ such that $|E'| = O(n)$ and* `Av_Stretch`$(H) = O(\log n)$. $\quad\square$

On the other hand, we give some lower bounds for the problem.

Lemma 18.1.4 *For every $k \geq 1$ and constant $0 < c < 1$, there exist a constant $d > 0$ and (infinitely many) n-vertex graphs $G = (V, E)$ such that for every spanning subgraph H of G, if* Av_Stretch$(H) < ck$, *then H has at least $dn^{1+1/k}$ edges.*

Proof: By the second claim of Lemma 15.1.2, there exist (infinitely many) n-vertex graphs $G = (V, E)$ with girth k or higher and at least $\frac{1}{4}n^{1+1/k}$ edges. Fix $d = (1-c)/4$. Consider such a graph G, and suppose that H is a spanning subgraph of G with fewer than $dn^{1+1/k}$ edges. Then the number of edges of G that were not taken into H is at least $\frac{c}{4}n^{1+1/k}$. The high girth of G implies that for each of these edges, the shortest path connecting its endpoints in H is of length k or more. Therefore each of these edges contributes at least k to the summation in the expression for Av_Stretch(H). The edges of H contribute 1 each. Hence

$$\text{Av\_Stretch}(H) \; \geq \; \frac{1}{|E|}(dn^{1+1/k} \cdot 1 + \frac{c}{4}n^{1+1/k} \cdot k) \; = \; (1-c) + ck \; \geq \; ck. \qquad \square$$

And again for $k = \log n$ we get the following corollary.

Corollary 18.1.5 *For every constant $0 < c < 1$, there exist a constant $d > 0$ and n-vertex graphs $G = (V, E)$ such that for every spanning subgraph H of G, if H has fewer than dn edges, then* Av_Stretch$(H) \geq c \log n$. $\square$

Hence for general spanners, considering average stretch has no significant benefits over considering maximum stretch in the sense that sparsifying the spanner to a certain level reduces both the worst stretch and the average stretch to the same value (at least asymptotically in the worst case).

18.2   Low average stretch trees

As discussed earlier in Section 15.4, the obvious drawback of a shortest path tree rooted at a vertex v is that while it provides optimal routes from v to any other vertex, the quality of the routes provided by the tree between *other* pairs of vertices may be poor. This has motivated our interest in general (nontree) spanners.

However, in some applications (including, for instance, certain control tasks for communication networks), it may be infeasible or undesirable to use a non-tree spanner, and the use of a (single) *tree* as our spanning structure is preferred due to its practical advantages (in terms of simplicity of the routing and control processes, the cost of channels, and so on). A natural question one may ask therefore is whether there exists a spanning tree with better overall spanning properties than the shortest-path tree.

It follows from our discussion in Section 15.4 that no spanning tree can perform as well (or nearly as well) as a nontree spanner with respect to its maximum stretch bound. In particular, there are graphs G (e.g., the unweighted ring) for which any spanning tree incurs a maximum stretch of $\Omega(Diam(G))$ for some pairs of vertices.

It may therefore be useful to look for trees that attempt to minimize the *average* stretch factor over all graph edges or even over all pairs of vertices in the graph. This may in some cases provide an attractive alternative to the standard shortest-path tree.

Definition 18.2.1 [Minimum average stretch]: *Letting T range over all spanning trees of G, define*

$$S_{opt}(G) = \min_{T}\{\text{Av\_Stretch}(G, T)\} \;.$$

In the following sections, we describe a method for constructing spanning trees approximating $S_{opt}(G)$ for a given graph G.

18.2.1   Examples

Let us now consider several example graphs.

Example 1:   *The complete graph.*
   Let K_n be the unweighted n-vertex complete graph. For an n-vertex star T,

$$\texttt{Av\_Stretch}(T) \;=\; \frac{1}{\binom{n}{2}} \left((n-1) \cdot 1 + \binom{n-1}{2} \cdot 2 \right) \;=\; 2 - \frac{2}{n},$$

which is the best possible. Hence $S_{opt}(K_n) \le 2 - 2/n$. $\square$
   With arbitrary weights, the complete graph becomes rather complex. Therefore let us consider simpler graphs and introduce weights.

Example 2:   *Rings and multirings.*
   Let C_n denote the n-vertex ring, and let T be the tree omitting the largest weight edge e. Then we have

$$\texttt{Av\_Stretch}(T) \;=\; \frac{1}{n} \left((n-1) \cdot 1 + 1 \cdot \frac{\omega(C_n)}{\omega(e)} \right)$$

$$\le \; \frac{1}{n} \left((n-1) \cdot 1 + 1 \cdot (n-1) \right) \;=\; 2 - \frac{2}{n},$$

which is the best possible. Hence $S_{opt}(C_n) \le 2 - 2/n$ as well. $\square$

Example 3:   *Rings with diagonals.*
   Given n even, let W_n be the *wheel* graph consisting of an n-vertex ring C_n together with the chords joining antipodal points on the ring (see Figure 18.1(a)). Consider the following spanning trees for W_n. Let T_1 be a tree consisting of all the edges of the ring save one. Then

$$\texttt{Av\_Stretch}(T_1) \;=\; \frac{1}{3n/2} \left((n-1) \cdot 1 + 1 \cdot (n-1) + \frac{n}{2} \cdot \frac{n}{2} \right) \le \frac{n}{6}.$$

A better choice would be the tree T_2 consisting of a path of $\frac{n}{2}$ edges on C_n and the $\frac{n}{2} - 1$ diagonals having one endpoint in the path (see Figure 18.1(b)). Here we have

$$\texttt{Av\_Stretch}(T_2) \;=\; \frac{1}{3n/2} \left((n-1) \cdot 1 + 1 \cdot \frac{n}{2} + \left(\frac{n}{2} - 2 \right) \cdot 3 + 2 \cdot \frac{n}{2} \right) \;=\; \frac{8}{3} - \frac{14}{3n}.$$

Hence $S_{opt}(W_n) \le 8/3 - 14/(3n)$. $\square$

Example 4:   *Two-dimensional grids.*
   Lower bounding the value of $S_{opt}(G_n)$ for the 2-dimensional $\sqrt{n} \times \sqrt{n}$ grid G_n is difficult, and we only illustrate the construction by example: the tree T illustrated in Figure 18.2 has $\texttt{Av\_Stretch}(T) = O(\log n)$. Note that other choices of a spanning tree for the grid, such as the tree of Figure 18.3, might be far worse (see Exercise 3). $\square$

18.2.2   A lower bound on average stretch trees

All of our examples in the previous subsection had average stretch bounded by constants. However, it is relatively easy to construct example graphs G for which $\texttt{Av\_Stretch}(T) = \Omega(\log n)$ for every spanning tree T, establishing the following lower bound on $S_{opt}(G)$.

Theorem 18.2.2 *There exists a positive constant c such that, for n sufficiently large, there exists an unweighted n-vertex graph G such that $S_{opt}(G) \ge c \ln n$.*

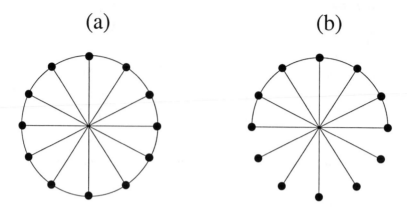

Figure 18.1: (a) The wheel graph. (b) The spanning tree T_2.

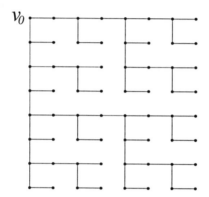

Figure 18.2: A spanning tree T with low average stretch for the 2-dimensional $\sqrt{n} \times \sqrt{n}$ grid G_n.

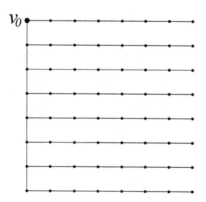

Figure 18.3: A spanning tree T with high average stretch for the grid G_n.

Proof: The second claim of Lemma 15.1.2 implies, by an appropriate choice of parameters, that there exists a positive constant a such that, for n sufficiently large, there exists an n-vertex graph G with $2n$ edges such that every cycle in G is of length at least $a \ln n$. (In particular, there are 4-regular graphs of girth $a \ln n$ constructed by growing a tree to depth approximately $\log_4 n$ and appropriately linking the leaves.) Let T be any spanning tree in G. Then $dist_T(u, v)/\omega(e) \geq a \ln n - 1$ for any nontree edge $e = (u, v)$. Since more than half the edges are nontree edges, it follows that, for every T,

$$\texttt{Av\_Stretch}(T) = \text{Cost}(E, T, G)/|E| \geq \frac{1}{2}(a \ln n - 1).$$

Thus, $S_{opt}(G) \geq \frac{1}{2}(a \ln n - 1)$. $\quad\square$

It is also known that the n-vertex grid necessitates average stretch $\Theta(\log n)$, and this result can also be generalized to multidimensional grids.

18.3 Constructing average stretch trees on unweighted graphs

Before deriving an upper bound for $S_{opt}(G)$ on weighted graphs, it is instructive to discuss the problem in the simpler setting of an unweighted graph.

18.3.1 Restricting attention to sparse multigraphs

Let us start with a preliminary result showing that for bounding $S_{opt}(G)$ from above, it is sufficient to consider multigraphs with at most $n(n+1)$ edges (counting multiplicities).

Lemma 18.3.1 *For every n-vertex weighted multigraph $G = (V, E, \omega)$, there exists a multigraph $G' = (V, E', \omega')$ with at most $n(n+1)$ edges such that $S_{opt}(G) \leq 2 \cdot S_{opt}(G')$.*

Proof: Let E^{set} be the set of all distinct edges in E, the edge multiset of $G = (V, E, \omega)$ (that is, E^{set} contains a single representative edge (u, v) for every pair of vertices u and v that are adjacent in G). For each edge $e \in E^{set}$, let $d(e)$ be the number of copies of e in E and $\omega'(e)$ be the lowest weight of a copy of e in G. Then the cardinality of E (i.e., the total number of edges in G counting repetitions) is

$$|E| = \sum_{e \in E^{set}} d(e).$$

Consider a new multigraph $G' = (V, E', \omega')$ with the same set of distinct edges, but with each edge e occurring $r(e)$ times instead of $d(e)$ times, where

$$r(e) = 1 + \left\lfloor \frac{d(e)|E^{set}|}{|E|} \right\rfloor. \tag{18.1}$$

Then the cardinality of the edge multiset E' of G' satisfies

$$|E'| = \sum_{e \in E^{set}} r(e) \leq |E^{set}| + \frac{|E^{set}|}{|E|} \sum_{e \in E^{set}} d(e) = 2|E^{set}|. \tag{18.2}$$

Since E^{set} contains at most one edge per pair of endpoints, including self-loops, it follows that G' has at most $n(n+1)$ edges, as required.

It remains to bound $S_{opt}(G')$. Combining Equations (18.1) and (18.2) we get

$$r(e) \geq \frac{d(e)|E^{set}|}{|E|} \geq \frac{d(e)|E'|}{2|E|} . \tag{18.3}$$

The multigraph G' has a spanning tree T such that

$$S_{opt}(G') = \frac{1}{|E'|} \sum_{e=(u,v)\in E^{set}} r(e) \cdot \frac{dist_T(u,v)}{\omega'(e)} . \tag{18.4}$$

Using Equations (18.3) and (18.4) and the choice of ω', we find that

$$S_{opt}(G') \geq \frac{1}{2|E|} \sum_{e=(u,v)\in E^{set}} d(e) \frac{dist_T(u,v)}{\omega(e)} .$$

But since T is a spanning tree of G as well as G', this last expression is at least $S_{opt}(G)/2$, so

$$S_{opt}(G) \leq 2S_{opt}(G') . \quad \square$$

18.3.2   Overview of the construction

Our starting point is the basic spanner construction algorithm for unweighted graphs described in Section 16.1. Recall that the spanner there is constructed by first applying the partition algorithm BASIC_PART of Section 11.5 and constructing a coarsening partition $\mathcal{T}$ as in the Partition Theorem 11.5.1. The spanner is now built on the basis of this partition by constructing an SPT for every cluster in $\mathcal{T}$ and connecting the clusters by selecting graph edges representing the intercluster edges, one for each pair of neighboring clusters.

Note that since the partition is composed of disjoint clusters, the spanning trees constructed in these clusters form a forest in the graph. The only possible cycles come from the addition of intercluster edges. Therefore a spanning tree can be built on the basis of such a partition as follows. First, construct an SPT T_C for every cluster C in the partition. Now, connect the forest into a single tree by selecting a suitable tree of intercluster edges.

This suggests the following iterative approach for constructing a spanning tree with low average stretch for a given graph $G = (V, E, \omega)$. In each iteration $j \geq 1$, the procedure handles a multigraph G_j (where G_1 is the original graph G). Each iteration j starts as in the above spanner construction algorithm, computing the partition $\mathcal{T}$ for G_j and constructing a spanning tree T_C inside each cluster C. This takes care of some of the edges, which are now "covered." (An edge is *covered* if it is internal to some cluster C that we have already constructed, namely, both its endpoints are contained in C, so it is spanned by the tree T_C.)

Now, instead of adding the intercluster edges, create an auxiliary multigraph $G_{j+1} = \tilde{G}(\mathcal{T})$ similar to the graph defined in Section 11.4.2 by collapsing each cluster into a single vertex and including a distinct edge between two such vertices for *each* original edge connecting these clusters. (This is why it is useful to handle multigraphs in this algorithm rather than simple graphs.) Next, apply the next iteration to G_{j+1}. The final tree will be composed of the union of the edges of the trees T_C constructed for each cluster C throughout the iterations.

The crucial point to observe is that among the edges of the set E, those edges "covered" by a cluster in an early iteration will typically enjoy a lower stretch than those left for later iterations. To see why this happens, consider first an edge $e = (u, u')$ covered by a cluster C in the first iteration. Then the path connecting u and u' in the final tree T is the path connecting them on the tree T_C, which is rather short, as the partitioning algorithm guarantees that C has a low radius.

In contrast, consider an edge $e = (u, u')$ which became an intercluster edge at the end of the first iteration with $u \in C$ and $u' \in C'$. Suppose that the vertices v_C and $v_{C'}$ of $G_2 = \tilde{G}(T)$ corresponding to C and C' were merged into the same cluster $\hat{C}$ in the second iteration. The path connecting v_C and $v_{C'}$ in the tree $T(\hat{C})$ spanning $\hat{C}$ is also guaranteed by the partitioning algorithm to be short, as $\hat{C}$ has low radius. However, the corresponding path connecting u and u' in T is potentially much longer, as it is "expanded" when retracting from G_2 to G by replacing each vertex v_{C_i} on it with an appropriate path segment on the internal tree T_{C_i}. (See Figure 18.4.)

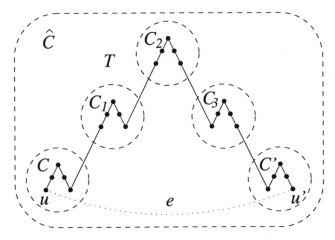

Figure 18.4: The path connecting u and u' in the spanning tree T.

Hence to compensate for this heavier cost for such intercluster edges, it is necessary to tune the parameters of the partitioning algorithm so that the number of edges that remain for later iterations is only a fraction of the edges handled in the current iteration, and therefore their contribution to the average stretch is controllable.

Consequently, instead of using algorithm BASIC_PART of Section 11.5 for constructing the partition, we need to use the modified partitioning algorithm of Section 13.3. This algorithm involves a parameter $x = x(n)$ and its output is a partition of the given graph into clusters with low radii (specifically, $O(x(n) \ln n)$), with the additional property that "most" of the graph edges are internal to clusters and only a fraction of $1/x(n)$ of the edges connect endpoints in different clusters. (See Theorem 13.3.1.)

Specifically, one can analyze the radii of the clusters constructed at each iteration $j \geq 1$ (henceforth called "j-clusters"). The partitioning procedure creates the clusters sequentially. Each cluster is "grown" by starting at a single vertex and successively merging it with (up to $O(y(n))$) layers of neighboring vertices. Hence as mentioned earlier, each j-cluster has radius $O(y(n))$ *in the current graph* G_j. However, in the original graph G, such clusters have radius $r_j = O(y^j(n))$. This can be easily argued inductively, noting that when a j-cluster is constructed, each merged layer increases the radius by up to

$$1 + 2r_{j-1},\tag{18.5}$$

where the 1 is contributed by the added edge and the $2r_{j-1}$ by the diameter of the $(j-1)$-cluster corresponding to the endpoint of that edge in G_j. The bound on r_j follows inductively since at most $O(y(n))$ layers are merged.

18.3.3   The construction algorithm

Let us now provide a more precise description of the algorithm for constructing a low average stretch spanning tree of G. By Lemma 18.3.1, it suffices to deal with an n-vertex multigraph having at most $n(n+1)$ edges in its edge multiset. Let E_j denote the set of edges from E that are still uncovered at the beginning of iteration j. The construction involves a parameter x depending on n, to be fixed later. The idea of the construction at iteration j is to partition the vertex set of G_j into disjoint clusters such that, defining $y = 9x \ln n$,

- each cluster has radius at most y^{j+1}, and

- the fraction of intercluster edges is at most $1/x$, i.e., $|E_{j+1}| \le |E_j|/x$.

This is achieved by invoking Algorithm $\text{Av\_Part}_e(G_j)$, used for forming the partition of the current graph $G_j = (V, E_j)$ in each iteration j.

The spanning tree T in an n-vertex multigraph G is constructed by algorithm Av_Str_Tree, presented in Figure 18.5.

---

1. Set $j \leftarrow 1$ and $G_j \leftarrow G$.

2. Set $x \leftarrow x(n)$ as defined above.

3. While $E_j \ne \emptyset$ do:

   (a) Invoke $S \leftarrow \text{Av\_Part}_e(G_j)$ to partition G_j into clusters.

   (b) Construct an SPT T_C for each cluster $C \in S$.

   (c) For each edge e of each of the constructed trees, add the corresponding edge of the original graph G to the output tree T.

   (d) Construct the next multigraph G_{j+1} by contracting each cluster of S into a single vertex, discarding covered edges (connecting endpoints in the same cluster) from E_j and replacing each intercluster edge by a new edge connecting the corresponding contracted vertices.

   (e) Set $j = j + 1$.

Figure 18.5: Algorithm Av_Str_Tree.

18.3.4   Analysis

By Property (2) of Theorem 13.3.1, we immediately get the following.

Lemma 18.3.2 $|E_j| \le |E|/x^j$ for every $j \ge 1$.

Combined with the fact that initially $|E| \le n(n+1)$, the lemma implies the following bound on the number of iterations.

Corollary 18.3.3 Algorithm Av_Str_Tree terminates after at most $\left\lceil \frac{3 \ln n}{\ln x} \right\rceil$ iterations. $\square$

The lemma enables us to also bound the radius of clusters generated during the execution.

Lemma 18.3.4 In iteration j, the radius of each cluster is bounded above by y^{j+1}.

Proof: We prove the bound on the radius of a cluster by induction on j. In order to analyze all iterations together (including iteration 1), hypothesize iteration 0 as the one that yielded the initial graph G, with each vertex representing a cluster of radius 1 (thus trivially satisfying the inductive claim). Now for $j \geq 1$, suppose the claim holds up to $j - 1$ and consider the jth iteration. At the beginning of the iteration, every vertex of the multigraph represents a cluster of radii up to y^j by the inductive hypothesis. Hence in constructing a cluster, each additional layer contributes up to $2y^j + 1$ to the radius. By Property (1) of Theorem 13.3.1, and as $|E| \leq n(n+1)$, the final radius of a cluster is at most $(2y^j + 1) \cdot x \ln |E| \leq 3y^j \cdot y/3 = y^{j+1}$, as required.   □

Using the above result we can bound the costs incurred by the edges, obtaining the following.

Lemma 18.3.5 $\text{Cost}(E, T, G) \leq 4x(9 \ln n)^{\lceil \frac{3 \ln n}{\ln x} \rceil} |E|$.

Proof: Let $\breve{E}_j$ denote the set of edges that were covered during iteration j, i.e., $\breve{E}_j = E_j \setminus E_{j+1}$. We first note that for every edge $e = (u, v) \in \breve{E}_j$, since e is covered during iteration j, $dist_T(u, v) \leq 2y^{j+1}$ by the previous lemma. Combined with the fact that $|\breve{E}_j| \leq |E_j| \leq |E|/x^j$ by Lemma 18.3.2, we have

$$\text{Cost}(\breve{E}_j, T, G) \leq 2x(9 \ln n)^{j+1} |E|.$$

Summing these costs over j and relying on Corollary 18.3.3, the lemma follows.   □

Lemma 18.3.6 $\text{Av\_Stretch}(G, T) = \exp(O(\sqrt{\ln n \ln \ln n}))$.

Proof: By the previous lemma,

$$\text{Av\_Stretch}(G, T) \leq 4x(9 \ln n)^{\lceil \frac{3 \ln n}{\ln x} \rceil}.$$

Selecting $x = \exp(c\sqrt{\ln n \ln \ln n})$ for an appropriate constant c optimizes this bound as stated in the lemma.   □

This completes the proof of the following theorem.

Theorem 18.3.7 [Average stretch-unweighted]: *There exists a constant c such that, for n sufficiently large, every n-vertex unweighted multigraph G satisfies $S_{opt}(G) \leq \exp(c\sqrt{\ln n \ln \ln n})$.*   □

18.4 Constructing average stretch trees on weighted graphs

18.4.1 Overview

Let us next outline the modifications needed for handling the weighted case. The main problem that needs to be overcome is that in the weighted case, all edges cannot be treated alike since when growing a cluster, a single layer merging step will increase the radius of the resulting cluster by the weight of the heaviest merged edge rather than by just one, thus the radii of constructed clusters cannot be controlled.

For describing the modified algorithm, it is convenient to think of the main clustering procedure of the above algorithm as a "machine" to whom the graph is "fed" for a number of iterations. The main modification is that in the weighted version, it is necessary to break the set of edges E into classes E^i, $i \geq 1$, according to weights, with E^i containing all edges whose weight is in the range $[y^{i-1}, y^i)$ for an appropriately chosen parameter $y = y(n, x)$ (with x a parameter to be determined in the same spirit as in the unweighted case). Intuitively, we would like to handle the lighter edges first.

We now feed the classes E^i to the "machine" in a pipelined fashion with overlaps. Namely, in iteration 1 only the edges of E^1 are considered, in the next iteration E^2 is added, and so on. In general, the class E^i is taken into consideration for the first time in the ith iteration and is processed for the next $\theta = O(\ln n / \ln x)$ iterations, each reducing the number of unsatisfied edges in it by a factor of x, until the entire of E^i is exhausted.

A crucial point that must be explained at this point is the role of the parameter y in the construction. In the weighted case, this parameter has two different functions. The first is similar to the one it had in the unweighted case, i.e., it is (more or less) the radius increase bound for constructed clusters. This means that clusters constructed for the graph G_j in the jth iteration will have radius at most $y/3$ in G_j. The second function of the parameter y is governing the weight range of the edge classes.

The combination of these two functions implies that in the construction of new clusters during a given iteration j, there is a balance between the contributions to the radius made by previously constructed clusters and by new edges. This is what guarantees that cluster radii are properly bounded *in the original graph G* as well. Specifically, the radius of a j-cluster (constructed in iteration j) is bounded by $r_j \leq y^{j+1}$. Formally, this can again be deduced inductively, noting that when a j-cluster is constructed each merged layer increases the radius by up to

$$y^j + 2r_{j-1} \leq 3y^j, \tag{18.6}$$

where, in analogy with (18.5), the y^j is contributed by the added edge and the $2r_{j-1}$ by the diameter of the $(j-1)$-cluster corresponding to the endpoint of that edge in G_j. This, combined with the fact that at most $y/3$ layers are added, yields the desired bound on r_j by induction.

18.4.2   The construction algorithm

Let us now provide a more precise description of the construction algorithm for the weighted case. Again, it suffices to deal with an n-vertex multigraph with at most $n(n+1)$ edges. Define the following parameters:

$$\begin{aligned} \theta &= \left\lceil \frac{3 \ln n}{\ln x} \right\rceil, \\ \psi &= 9\theta \ln n, \\ y &= x\psi. \end{aligned}$$

Break the set of edges E into classes E^i for $i \geq 1$ according to weights, defining

$$E^i = \{e \mid \omega(e) \in [y^{i-1}, y^i)\}.$$

(Recall that the edge weights are normalized to be greater than or equal to 1.)

As before, the algorithm proceeds in iterations, where each iteration constructs a partition of the graph and then contracts the clusters into single vertices for the next iteration. Let E^i_j denote the set of edges from E^i that are still uncovered at the beginning of iteration j. The radius property required of the partition remains the same as in the unweighted case, but the shrinkage requirement now becomes the following:

- in every nonempty edge class E^i, $1 \leq i \leq j$, the fraction of intercluster edges is at most $1/x$, i.e., $|E^i_{j+1}| \leq |E^i_j|/x$.

Note that this requirement implies that iteration j handles only edges from the edge multisets E^i for $i \leq j$, i.e., edges of weight less than y^j. Avoiding heavier edges is crucial for guaranteeing the radius bound in the first requirement, as discussed earlier.

The algorithm used for forming the partition of the current graph $G_j = (V, E_j)$ in each iteration j, named $\text{Av\_Part}_w(G_j)$, is a slightly modified version of Algorithm Av_Part_e of Section 13.3 used in the unweighted case. Algorithm $\text{Av\_Part}_w(G_j)$ builds the partition in an incremental fashion, constructing one cluster at a time. When constructing a new cluster around a vertex u in the subgraph $\hat{G} = (\hat{V}, \hat{E})$ of G_j induced by the vertices not yet selected, we stratify the vertices and edges of $\hat{G}$ into layers according to their *unweighted* distance from u as follows. For each integer $\rho \geq 0$, let $V(\rho) = \Gamma_\rho^{un}(v) \setminus \Gamma_{\rho-1}^{un}(v)$ be the set of vertices at unweighted distance exactly ρ from u in $\hat{G}$. Also, let $\hat{E}_j^i(\rho)$ denote the set of edges of $\hat{E}_j^i$ that join a vertex in $V(\rho)$ with a vertex in $V(\rho) \cup V(\rho - 1)$.

Procedure Av_Part_w is presented in Figure 18.6.

$S \leftarrow \emptyset$.
While $\hat{G} \neq \emptyset$ **do:**

1. Choose arbitrarily a center vertex u in $\hat{G}$.

2. Let ρ^* be the least ρ such that for all $1 \leq i \leq j$,

$$|\hat{E}_j^i(\rho + 1)| \;\leq\; \frac{1}{x} |\hat{E}_j^i(1) \cup \hat{E}_j^i(2) \cup \cdots \cup \hat{E}_j^i(\rho)|.$$

3. If no such ρ exists, then $C \leftarrow \hat{V}$;
   Else $C \leftarrow \Gamma_{\rho^*}(v) = \bigcup_{i=1}^{\rho^*} V(i)$.

4. Set $S \leftarrow S \cup C$ and remove the vertices of C from $\hat{V}$.

Figure 18.6: Procedure $\text{Av\_Part}_w(\hat{G})$.

Algorithm Av_Str_Tree remains essentially the same as in the unweighted case, except that the parameter y is defined differently and the sets E^i need to be set explicitly.

18.4.3 Analysis

For the weighted case, bounding the number of layers added to a cluster during the partitioning process in some iteration j relies on showing that in iteration j, the only sets E_j^i considered by the algorithm (i.e., the only nonempty ones) are those satisfying $j - \theta \leq i \leq j$. This allows us to prove a sequence of lemmas rather similar to the unweighted case.

Lemma 18.4.1 $|E_j^i| \leq |E^i|/x^{j-i}$ *for every* $1 \leq i \leq j$.

Lemma 18.4.2 *In iteration j, the radius of each cluster is bounded above by y^{j+1}.*

Lemma 18.4.3 $\text{Cost}(E, T, G) \leq 4x^2 \psi^{\theta+1} |E|$.

Theorem 18.4.4 [Average stretch]: *There exists a constant c such that for n sufficiently large, every n-vertex weighted multigraph G satisfies $S_{opt}(G) \leq \exp(c\sqrt{\ln n \ln \ln n})$.* □

18.5   Light trees with low average stretch

Finally, we also consider one more related problem, namely, that of constructing low average stretch spanning trees which are also light weight (as in Chapter 17). For this problem, it is again natural to ask whether it is possible to construct a tree T with simultaneously low $\mathtt{Av\_Stretch}(T)$ and $\omega(T)$. In this section we build on the Average Stretch Theorem 18.4.4 plus the weight reduction technique used in Chapter 17 for spanners and approach the problem as follows.

Given a weighted graph $G = (V, E, \omega)$, we construct a light-weight spanning tree T with low average stretch as follows. First, construct a light, sparse, low stretch spanner $G' = (V, E')$ for G as in the previous section, using $\kappa = \log n$. This yields $\mathtt{Stretch}(G') = O(\log n)$, $|E(G')| = O(n\Lambda \cdot \log n)$. $\omega(G') = O(\Lambda \cdot \log n \cdot \omega(MST))$.

Next, compute an arbitrary shortest path $\hat{\Upsilon}(e)$ in G' for every edge $e \in E$. For every edge $e' \in E'$, let the *support* set of e' in G be the set of edges whose path goes through e',

$$Supp(e') \;=\; \{e \in E \mid e' \in \hat{\Upsilon}(e)\}.$$

Define

$$g(e') \;=\; \left\lceil \sum_{e \in Supp(e')} \frac{\omega(e')}{\omega(e)} \right\rceil.$$

Now construct a weighted multigraph $G''(V, E'', \omega'')$ by taking each edge e' of G' with multiplicity $g(e')$. Finally, construct a tree T for G'' as in Section 18.4.

We claim that this tree has the desired properties. The weight analysis follows directly from the fact that T is no heavier than G', whose weight is guaranteed to be at most $O(\Lambda \cdot \log n)$ times heavier than $\omega(MST)$. It therefore remains only to analyze the average stretch of the tree T.

Lemma 18.5.1 *The average stretch of the tree T satisfies*

$$\mathtt{Av\_Stretch}(G, T) \;\leq\; c' \log n \cdot \exp(c\sqrt{\log n \log \log n})$$

for some constants c, c'.

Proof: For an edge $e = (u, w)$ in a graph H, denote $dist_H(e) = dist_H(u, w)$. Let us first observe that

$$|E''| \;=\; \sum_{e' \in E'} g(e') \leq \sum_{e' \in E'} \left(1 + \sum_{e \in Supp(e')} \frac{\omega(e')}{\omega(e)}\right) = |E'| + \sum_{e \in E} \sum_{e' \in \hat{\Upsilon}(e)} \frac{\omega(e')}{\omega(e)}$$

$$=\; |E'| + \sum_{e \in E} \frac{dist_{G'}(e)}{\omega(e)} = |E'| + \mathsf{Cost}(E', G', G).$$

Since G' guarantees a stretch factor of $\mathtt{Av\_Stretch}(G') \leq \mathtt{Stretch}(G') = O(\log n)$, it follows that there exists a constant c such that

$$|E''| \;\leq\; c|E| \cdot \log n. \tag{18.7}$$

Next, let us observe that for every edge $e \in E$,

$$dist_T(e) \;\leq\; \sum_{e' \in \hat{\Upsilon}(e)} dist_T(e').$$

Therefore

$$
\begin{aligned}
\mathsf{Cost}(E,T,G) &= \sum_{e\in E}\frac{dist_T(e)}{\omega(e)} \leq \sum_{e\in E}\frac{1}{\omega(e)}\sum_{e'\in\hat{\Upsilon}(e)}dist_T(e')\\
&= \sum_{e\in E}\sum_{e'\in\hat{\Upsilon}(e)}\frac{dist_T(e')}{\omega(e)} = \sum_{e'\in E'}\sum_{e\in Supp(e')}\frac{dist_T(e')}{\omega(e)}\\
&= \sum_{e'\in E'}\frac{dist_T(e')}{\omega(e')}\cdot\sum_{e\in Supp(e')}\frac{\omega(e')}{\omega(e)} \qquad\qquad (18.8)\\
&\leq \sum_{e'\in E'}\frac{dist_T(e')}{\omega(e')}\cdot g(e') = \sum_{e''\in E''}\frac{dist_T(e'')}{\omega(e'')} = \mathsf{Cost}(E'',T,G'').
\end{aligned}
$$

Combining Equations (18.7) and (18.8) yields

$$
\begin{aligned}
\mathtt{Av\_Stretch}(G,T) &= \frac{1}{|E|}\cdot\mathsf{Cost}(E,T)\\
&\leq \frac{c\log n}{|E''|}\cdot\mathsf{Cost}(E'',T) = \frac{c\log n}{|E''|}\cdot\mathtt{Av\_Stretch}(G'',T)\,,
\end{aligned}
$$

and when we apply the Average Stretch Theorem 18.4.4 we get the desired result. $\qquad\square$
This establishes the following.

Theorem 18.5.2 *There exist constants c, c', c'' such that, given an n-vertex weighted graph $G = (V, E, \omega)$, there is a polynomially constructible spanning tree T such that $\mathtt{Av\_Stretch}(T) \leq c'\log n\cdot\exp(c\sqrt{\log n\log\log n})$ and $\omega(T) \leq c''\Lambda\cdot\log n\cdot\omega(MST)$.*

Bibliographical notes

The problem of constructing a spanning tree with low average stretch has been studied in [AKPW95] in the context of devising a randomized competitive online algorithm for the k-server problem and the results brought here are taken from that paper. The results of Section 18.5 are from [ABP91]. Low average stretch spanning trees turn out to help in improving the complexity of certain distributed directories [DH98, PR99a].

The closely related *minimum communication cost spanning tree (MCT)* problem, introduced in [Hu74], requires selecting a spanning tree of a network that minimizes the total cost of transmitting a given set of communication requirements between n sites over the tree edges. The relationships between the MCT problem and low average stretch spanning trees are investigated in [Pel97, PR98, PR99a]. The MCT problem has applications to the design of communication networks. In addition, it is strongly related to certain approximation algorithms based on probabilistic approximation of metric spaces [Bar96b, Bar98, CCGG98] and spreading metrics [ENRS95].

Low average stretch spanning trees and approximation algorithms for the MCT problem in the *Euclidean* and *metric* settings, as well as various other special cases, are studied in [Won80, WLB+00, CCG+98, PR98].

Exercises

1. Find a spanning tree for the wheel with better average stretch than the tree proposed in Example 3.

2. Suppose that the wheel is modified into a weighted graph by assigning a weight C to the edges of the ring and a weight D to the diagonals.

   (a) What will be the average stretch of the trees T_1 and T_2 given in Example 3? For which values of C and D would you prefer each of these trees?

   (b) Given specific values of C and D, construct a tree with constant ($O(1)$) average stretch. (Hint: Consider a tree obtained by taking $\frac{n}{2k}$ near-equally spaced diagonals and adding the necessary ring edges for an appropriately selected $k = k(C, D)$.)

3. (a) Define the spanning tree illustrated in Figure 18.2 for the 2-dimensional $m \times m$ grid for every $m \geq 2$.

   (b) Prove that the average stretch of this tree is $O(\log m)$.

   (c) Estimate the average stretch factor of the spanning tree depicted in Figure 18.3 for the grid.

4. Complete the analysis of Section 18.4.3 for the weighted case (i.e., prove Lemmas 18.4.1, 18.4.2 and 18.4.3).

5. ($*$) Prove that $S_{opt}(G) = O(\text{polylog}(n))$ for every n-vertex weighted multigraph G.

6. ($*$) Prove the claim of Exercise 5 for one of the following restricted graph classes: unweighted graphs, planar graphs or Euclidean graphs.

Chapter 19

Proximity-preserving labeling systems

So far, we have not discussed *actual* representations that can be used in order to maintain our structures, i.e., ways and means for storing these structures succinctly and deducing information about them efficiently. In this chapter, we address this issue by considering various useful labeling schemes for the vertices and edges of graphs.

19.1 Adjacency-preserving labelings

The cover-based or skeletal structures we focus on are geared towards capturing relatively *rough* information on the structure of the graph and its locality properties. This means that we are interested in maintaining properties such as the approximate distances and neighborhoods. Nevertheless, before considering efficient representations for structures of these types, it may be instructive to digress a bit and consider the more standard graphs representations, aiming at maintaining the *exact* structure of the graph, namely, the precise set of adjacencies among its vertices.

Most traditional approaches to the problem of graph representation are based on storing the adjacency information using some kind of a data structure, e.g., an adjacency matrix. Such representation enables one to decide, given the labels of two vertices, whether or not they are adjacent in the graph simply by looking at the appropriate entry in the table. However, note that this decision cannot be made in the absence of the table. That is, the labels themselves contain no useful information and they serve only as "place holders" or pointers to entries in the table.

In this section, we present and illustrate representations based on more "informative" labeling schemes, allowing us to infer adjacency *directly* from the labels in question without using any additional memory.

Obviously, labels of unrestricted size can be used to encode any desired information in them. Specifically, it is possible to encode the entire row i in the adjacency matrix of the graph in the label chosen for vertex i. It is clear, however, that a labeling scheme is most useful if it uses relatively *short* labels (say, of length polylogarithmic in n) and yet allows us to deduce adjacencies efficiently (say, within polylogarithmic time). This leads to the following definition.

Definition 19.1.1 [$l(n)$ adjacency-labeling scheme]: *A family $\mathcal{F}$ of graphs has an $l(n)$ adjacency-labeling scheme if there is a function Label labeling the vertices of each n-vertex graph in $\mathcal{F}$ with distinct labels of up to $l(n)$ bits and there exists a polynomial time algorithm that given two labels of vertices in a graph from $\mathcal{F}$, decides the adjacency of these vertices.*

The family $\mathcal{F}$ is said to be adjacency-labelable *if it has a $k \log n$ adjacency-labeling scheme for some fixed k.*

It should be clear that our restriction on the size of the labels implies that the class of all graphs is not adjacency-labelable. Specifically, for a class of graphs to be adjacency-labelable, each graph must be labeled using only $O(n \log n)$ bits. Therefore at most $2^{O(n \log n)}$ graphs can be represented. This implies the following.

Lemma 19.1.2 *A family $\mathcal{F}$ of graphs that contains more than $2^{O(n \log n)}$ graphs of n vertices is not adjacency-labelable. In particular, the families of bipartite graphs and chordal graphs are not adjacency-labelable.*

Let us next consider some cases of adjacency-labelable graph families, beginning with the family of trees.

19.1.1   Adjacency labeling for trees

The vertices of a given n-vertex tree T can be labeled by Algorithm NEIG_LABEL, described in Figure 19.1.

Label assignment

1. Arbitrarily root the tree.

2. Arbitrarily prelabel each vertex v of T with a distinct integer $I(v)$ from $[1, n]$.

3. Label the root of the tree with its prelabel.

4. **For** each nonroot vertex v with parent w in the tree **do:**
   Label v with $Label(v) \leftarrow (I(v), I(w))$.

Deciding adjacency

Two vertices v, u are adjacent iff the first entry in $Label(v)$ is identical to the second entry in $Label(u)$ or vice versa.

Figure 19.1: Algorithm NEIG_LABEL.

Lemma 19.1.3 *In an n-vertex tree, the adjacency labels contain at most $\lceil 2 \log n \rceil$ bits each.*

Figure 19.2 depicts a tree T, its prelabeling and the corresponding adjacency labels attached to the vertices.

Incidentally, this representation allows us to decide the "parent" and "sibling" relations as well. It is also straightforward to extend this labeling scheme into one enabling us to decide neighborhood to distance k for fixed $k \geq 1$; simply label each vertex by the prelabels of itself plus its ancestors up to height $k - 1$.

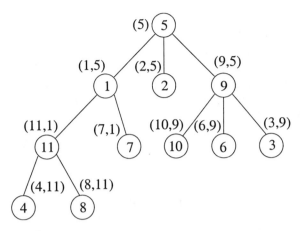

Figure 19.2: A tree T and its adjacency labeling.

19.1.2 Graphs with bounded arboricity

The *arboricity* (sometimes called also *density*) of a graph G is defined as

$$\max_{\emptyset \subset W \subseteq V} \left\{ \frac{|E(G(W))|}{|W| - 1} \right\}$$

(recall that $G(W)$ is the subgraph of G induced by W). It is known that the edges of a graph G with arboricity k can be decomposed into k disjoint forests and, furthermore, that this decomposition can be computed polynomially.

Thus using the same idea employed for trees, it is possible to construct a $(k+1) \log n$ adjacency-labeling scheme for G as follows. Given G and its decomposition into k forests, arbitrarily prelabel each vertex v of G with a distinct integer $I(v)$ from $[1, n]$ and arbitrarily root each tree in all k forests. Now, label each vertex v with $Label(v) = (I(v), I(w_1), \ldots, I(w_k))$, where w_i is v's parent in the ith forest. (If v is a root in this forest, then set the appropriate entry to 0.) The labels contain at most $\lceil (k+1) \log n \rceil$ bits each. Deciding the adjacency of two vertices v, u is done, as before, by checking whether one of them is the parent of the other in any of the forests.

Among the graph families falling into this category are graphs of bounded degree and graphs of bounded genus. For instance, the family of planar graphs (which have arboricity 3) is $4 \log n$ adjacency-labelable.

19.1.3 Universal graphs

Another interesting construct related to adjacency-labeling schemes is that of *universal graphs*.

Definition 19.1.4 [Universal graph]: *The (unweighted) graph $G = (V, E)$ is universal for the class of (unweighted) graphs S if for every graph $G' \in S$ there is a subset of vertices $W \in V$ such that the induced subgraph $G(W)$ is isomorphic to G'.*

A family $\mathcal{F}$ of graphs has universal graphs of size $g(n)$ if for every n, the set $\mathcal{F}_n$ of graphs in $\mathcal{F}$ with up to n vertices has a universal graph G_n with $g(n)$ or fewer vertices.

Theorem 19.1.5 *If a family $\mathcal{F}$ of unweighted graphs has a $k \log n$ adjacency-labeling scheme, then it has universal graphs of size n^k.*

Proof: Given n, form the universal graph G_n as follows. Label the n^k vertices of G_n by 1 through n^k. For every two labels i, j, apply the adjacency decision algorithm of the family $\mathcal{F}$ to i and j and connect the corresponding vertices by an edge iff the answer is positive.

Consider a graph $G \in \mathcal{F}$ with n or fewer vertices. The adjacency-labeling scheme of $\mathcal{F}$ labels the vertices of G using labels from 1 to n^k. Let W be the set of vertices of G_n whose labels are used for G. By the definition of the adjacency algorithm, the induced subgraph $G_n(W)$ is isomorphic to G.   □

Corollary 19.1.6 *The family of unweighted planar graphs has universal graphs of size n^4.*

19.2 Distance-preserving labelings

The ability to decide adjacency is only one of the basic properties a representation may be required to possess. From our point of view, it may be even more interesting to go one step further along this line of study and address the somewhat more general question of retrieving information about arbitrary (i.e., possibly nonadjacent) vertices. For example, one nice property we may require a labeling scheme to possess is the ability to determine the *distance* between two given vertices efficiently (say, within polylogarithmic time).

Definition 19.2.1 *[$l(n)$ distance labeling scheme]: A family $\mathcal{F}$ of weighted graphs has an $l(n)$ distance labeling scheme if there is a function Label labeling the vertices of each n-vertex graph in $\mathcal{F}$ with distinct labels of up to $l(n)$ bits and there exists a polynomial time algorithm that given two labels of vertices u, v in a graph G from $\mathcal{F}$, computes the distance between these vertices in the graph.*

It is clear that distance labeling schemes with short labels are available for highly regular graph classes, such as rings, grids, tori, hypercubes and the like. For larger classes of graphs, it seems harder to capture precise distance information using short labels. Nevertheless, note that for *very* large graph classes the problem becomes easy again: for a family of n-vertex graphs with $\Omega(\exp(n^{1+\epsilon}))$ nonisomorphic graphs, any labeling scheme must use labels whose total combined length is $\Omega(n^{1+\epsilon})$, hence at least one label must be of $\Omega(n^\epsilon)$ bits.

We now describe a distance labeling scheme for the family of trees. The construction makes use of the following notion.

Definition 19.2.2 *[Tree separator]: Given a tree T, a separator is a vertex v_0 whose removal breaks T into disconnected subtrees of at most $n/2$ vertices each.*

We rely on the following well-known fact regarding tree separators.

Lemma 19.2.3 *Every n-vertex tree T, $n \geq 2$, has a separator (which can be found in linear time).*

The labeling system

The vertices of a given n-vertex tree T are labeled by Algorithm TREE_LABEL, given in Figure 19.3. Figure 19.5 describes a recursive procedure DIST_CALC for computing the distance between two vertices u, v in T.

Figure 19.4 depicts a tree T and its recursive partitioning and distance labeling.

Lemma 19.2.4 *The labeling algorithm TREE_LABEL uses $O(\log^2 n)$ bit labels.*

Label assignment

1. **Preprocessing:** Arbitrarily prelabel each vertex v of T with a distinct integer $I(v)$ from $[1, n]$.

2. Invoke recursive labeling procedure SUB_TREE_LABEL(T).

Recursive labeling procedure SUB_TREE_LABEL(T')

1. If T' contains a single vertex v_0, then label it by $Label(v_0) \leftarrow (I(v_0)\,,\,0\,,\,0)$ and return.

2. Find a separator v_0 for T'.   /* The removal of v_0 breaks T' into disconnected subtrees $T_1, \ldots, T_k$, each with at most $n/2$ vertices. */

3. Recursively apply procedure SUB_TREE_LABEL(T_i) to label each vertex v in each subtree T_i by $Label_i(v)$.

4. **For** each vertex $v \in T_i$ **do:**

   (a) Let $\mathcal{J}(v) \leftarrow (I(v_0)\,,\,dist(v, v_0, T)\,,\,i)$.
   (b) Label v by $Label(v) \leftarrow \mathcal{J}(v) \circ Label_i(v)$.

5. Label v_0 by $Label(v_0) \leftarrow (I(v_0)\,,\,0\,,\,0)$.

Figure 19.3: Algorithm TREE_LABEL(T).

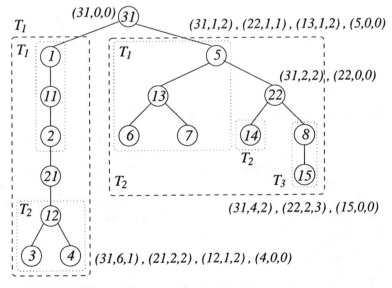

Fields: *(center , distance , tree #)*

Figure 19.4: A tree T and its recursive partitioning and distance labeling.

Deciding the distance

Input: Two labels

$$Label(u) \;=\; \mathcal{J}_1(u) \circ \cdots \circ \mathcal{J}_q(u) \quad \text{and} \quad Label(v) \;=\; \mathcal{J}_1(v) \circ \cdots \circ \mathcal{J}_p(v)$$

(of vertices u, v in T).

1. **If** $p = 1$, then return the second field in $\mathcal{J}_1(u)$.

2. **If** $q = 1$, then return the second field in $\mathcal{J}_1(v)$.

3. **If** $p, q > 1$, then **do:**

   (a) Let $\mathcal{J}_1(u) \leftarrow (I(w) \, , \; dist(u, w, T) \, , \; i)$
       and $\mathcal{J}_1(v) \leftarrow (I(w) \, , \; dist(v, w, T) \, , \; j)$
       for some i, j.

   (b) **If** $i \neq j$, then return the sum of the second fields in $\mathcal{J}_1(u)$ and $\mathcal{J}_1(v)$.

   (c) **Else** $(i = j)$ **do:**

       i. Peel off the first triple $\mathcal{J}_1(u)$ from $Label(u)$ and the triple $\mathcal{J}_1(v)$ from
          $Label(v)$, remaining with $Label_i(u) = \mathcal{J}_2(u) \circ \cdots \circ \mathcal{J}_q(u)$ and $Label_i(v) =$
          $\mathcal{J}_2(v) \circ \cdots \circ \mathcal{J}_p(v)$;

       ii. Recursively invoke procedure DIST_CALC($Label_i(u), Label_i(v)$) to com-
           pute $dist(u, v, T_i)$;

       iii. Return $dist(u, v, T_i)$.

Figure 19.5: Procedure DIST_CALC($Label(u), Label(v)$).

Proof: On each level of the recursion, the sublabel $\mathcal{J}(v)$ contains at most $\lceil 3 \log n \rceil$ bits. As the maximum tree size is halved in each application of the recursive labeling procedure, there are at most $\log n$ levels, hence the lemma follows. $\square$

Lemma 19.2.5 *For every weighted tree T and vertices u, v, the output of Procedure* DIST_CALC *is* $dist(u, v, T)$.

Proof: Consider an arbitrary pair of vertices $u, v \in V$ in T with labels

$$Label(u) = \mathcal{J}_1(u) \circ \cdots \circ \mathcal{J}_q(u) \quad \text{and} \quad Label(v) = \mathcal{J}_1(v) \circ \cdots \circ \mathcal{J}_p(v),$$

respectively. Let us examine the cases considered by the procedure one by one. If $p = 1$, then v is the chosen separator of T, hence $Label(v) = (I(v) \, , \; 0 \, , \; 0)$ and $\mathcal{J}_1(u) = (I(v) \, , \; dist(u, v, T) \, , \; i)$ for some i. Consequently, the second field in $\mathcal{J}_1(u)$ indeed gives the required distance. The case $q = 1$ is symmetric to the previous case.

Now suppose both $p, q > 1$ with

$$\mathcal{J}_1(v) \;=\; (I(w) \, , \; dist(v, w, T) \, , \; i) \quad \text{and} \quad \mathcal{J}_1(u) \;=\; (I(w) \, , \; dist(u, w, T) \, , \; j)$$

for some i, j. The first subcase considered by the procedure is where $i \neq j$. In this case, the unique path connecting v to u in T goes through w, and therefore $dist(v, u, T) = dist(v, w, T) + dist(u, w, T)$.

The second and final subcase is when $i = j$. In this case, both v and u belong to the same subtree T_i in the partition induced by the separator w and hence the path connecting them in

T (and determining their distance) is contained in its entirety in T_i. Therefore $dist(u, v, T)$ is equal to $dist(v, u, T_i)$, which is the value computed by the recursive invocation of the procedure.   □

We conclude the following.

Theorem 19.2.6 *There exists an $O(\log^2 n)$ distance labeling scheme for the class of n-vertex weighted trees.*   □

19.3 Distance-approximating labelings

Instead of insisting on labeling schemes capturing precise distance information, we may settle for labeling schemes that efficiently provide a decent *estimate* on the distance between any two given vertices.

Definition 19.3.1 [$(l(n), R)$ approximate-distance labeling scheme]: *A family $\mathcal{F}$ of weighted graphs has an $(l(n), R)$ approximate-distance labeling scheme (for some fixed $R > 1$) if there is a function Label labeling the vertices of each n-vertex graph in $\mathcal{F}$ with distinct labels of up to $l(n)$ bits, and there exists a polynomial time algorithm that given two labels of vertices u, v in a graph G from $\mathcal{F}$ provides an estimate $\tilde{D}(u, v)$ for the distance between these vertices in the graph such that*

$$\frac{1}{R} \cdot \tilde{D}(u, v) \ \leq \ dist(u, v, G) \ \leq \ R \cdot \tilde{D}(u, v).$$

We next describe an approximate-distance labeling scheme for arbitrary weighted graphs based on the tree covers of Section 15.5. The scheme is constructed in a way similar to Algorithm WEIGHTED_SPAN for the construction of a spanner for weighted graphs, from Section 17.2. The vertices of a given n-vertex graph G are labeled by Procedure GRAPH_LABEL, given in Figure 19.6. Figure 19.7 describes Procedure DIST_ESTIMATE for estimating the distance between two vertices u, v in T.

Label assignment

1. **Preprocessing:** For every $1 \leq i \leq \Lambda$, construct a 2^i-tree-cover $\mathcal{TC}_i = \mathcal{TC}_{\kappa, 2^i}$ for G as in Algorithm TREE_COVER (the Tree Cover Theorem 15.5.2).

2. Separately in each tree cover $\mathcal{TC}_i$, assign a distinct tag (from 1 to n) to each of the trees in $\mathcal{TC}_i$.

3. Assign each vertex v a label composed of the concatenation of Λ tuples,

   $Label(v) \leftarrow (T_1(v), \ldots, T_\Lambda(v))$, where the tuple $T_i(v)$ consists of the tags of all the trees in $\mathcal{TC}_i$ containing v.

Figure 19.6: Procedure GRAPH_LABEL(G, κ).

Lemma 19.3.2 *The labeling procedure GRAPH_LABEL uses $O(\Lambda \cdot \log n \cdot \kappa \cdot n^{1/\kappa})$ bit labels.*

Proof: Note that the tags attached to the trees in the tree covers require at most $O(\log n)$ bits each since there are at most $\lceil 2\kappa \cdot n^{1/\kappa} \rceil \cdot n$ trees in each tree cover. Each vertex v occurs on at most $\texttt{Overlap}(\mathcal{TC}_i)$ different trees in $\mathcal{TC}_i$, hence its ith tuple $T_i(v)$ contains at most this many tags. The result now follows by the bound of the Tree Cover Theorem 15.5.2 on $\texttt{Overlap}(\mathcal{TC}_{\kappa, 2^i})$.   □

Estimating the distance

Input: Two labels

$$Label(u) \; = \; (T_1(u), \ldots, T_\Lambda(u)) \quad \text{and} \quad Label(v) \; = \; (T_1(v), \ldots, T_\Lambda(v))$$

(of vertices u, v in G).

1. Compare corresponding tuples in the labels one by one (starting with $T_1(v)$ and $T_1(u)$ and going upwards) until reaching the first level j such that $T_j(v)$ and $T_j(v)$ contain a common tag.

2. Set $\tilde{D}(u, v) \leftarrow \sqrt{2\kappa} \cdot 2^j$.

3. Return $\tilde{D}(u, v)$ as the estimate for $dist_G(u, v)$.

Figure 19.7: Procedure DIST_ESTIMATE($Label(u), Label(v), \kappa$).

Lemma 19.3.3 *For every weighted graph* $G = (V, E, \omega)$ *and vertices* u, v, *the estimate returned by Algorithm* DIST_ESTIMATE *satisfies*

$$\frac{1}{R} \cdot \tilde{D}(u, v) \; \leq \; dist_G(u, v) \; \leq \; R \cdot \tilde{D}(u, v)$$

for $R = \sqrt{8\kappa}$.

Proof: Consider an arbitrary pair of vertices $u, v \in V$. Suppose that

$$2^{i-1} \; < \; dist_G(u, v) \; \leq \; 2^i.$$

Also suppose that the algorithm returned $\tilde{D}(u, v) = \sqrt{2\kappa} \cdot 2^j$ as the estimate for this distance. That is, j was the first level on which u and v shared a common tree in $\mathcal{TC}_j$.

By definition, the tree cover $\mathcal{TC}_i = \mathcal{TC}_{\kappa, 2^i}$ constructed for the graph contains a tree T such that $\Gamma_{2^i}(u) \subseteq V(T)$. Hence both $u, v \in V(T)$. Therefore necessarily $j \leq i$ and hence

$$dist_G(u, v) \; \geq \; 2^{i-1} \geq 2^{j-1} \; = \; \frac{1}{\sqrt{8\kappa}} \cdot (\sqrt{2\kappa} \cdot 2^j) \; = \; \frac{1}{R} \cdot \tilde{D}(u, v).$$

For the other direction, let T' be the tree common to u and v in $\mathcal{TC}_j$. By the Tree Cover Theorem 15.5.2, $Depth(T') \leq (2\kappa - 1) \cdot 2^j$. Consequently, the tree T provides a path of length at most $2 \cdot (2\kappa - 1) \cdot 2^j$ connecting u and v, hence necessarily

$$dist_G(u, v) \; \leq \; 4\kappa \cdot 2^j \; = \; \sqrt{8\kappa} \cdot (\sqrt{2\kappa} \cdot 2^j) \; = \; R \cdot \tilde{D}(u, v). \qquad \square$$

Setting $\kappa = \log n$, we have the following theorem.

Theorem 19.3.4 *There exists an* $(O(\Lambda \cdot \log^2 n), \sqrt{8 \log n})$ *distance-labeling scheme for the class of* n-*vertex weighted graphs.* $\qquad \square$

19.4   Interval-tree labeling

A generalization of the adjacency-labeling approach for the class of trees, which will prove very useful to us later on, involves finding a labeling representation encoding the *ancestor-hood* relation of the tree rather than just its *parenthood* relation. In this section we discuss a technique called *interval tree labeling*, aimed at providing such a representation.

The idea is to attach a label in the form of an interval of integers $Int(v)$ to each vertex v of the tree T, such that the labels satisfy the following property.

Inclusion property: For every two vertices u and v of the tree T, $Int(v) \subseteq Int(u)$ iff v is a descendent of u in T.

This scheme is based on constructing a *depth-first* numbering of the tree and is given in Algorithm INTER_LABEL, described in Figure 19.8. Figure 19.9 depicts a tree T, its *DFS* numbering and the corresponding interval labels attached to the vertices.

Lemma 19.4.1 *The intervals attached to the vertices of the tree T by Algorithm* INTER_LABEL *are of size $O(\log n)$ bits and they obey the inclusion property.*   □

Let us remark that the interval labeling enjoys one more useful property, namely, the intervals associated with sibling vertices in the tree are ordered according to the order of the depth-first tour that created the labeling. This property will come in handy in our later applications.

Bibliographical notes

Labeling systems of general graphs based on Hamming distances were studied in [Bre66, BF67]. An (m, T)-labeling system is based on labeling each vertex of the graph with an m-bit label, such that two vertices are adjacent iff their labels are at Hamming distance T or less of each other. In [BF67] it is shown that every n-vertex graph has a $(2n\Delta^C, 4\Delta^C - 4)$-labeling.

Label assignment

1. Perform a depth-first search tour of the tree T, starting at the root, and assign the vertices $u \in T$ a depth-first numbering $DFS(u)$.

2. Label a vertex u by the interval $[DFS(u), DFS(w)]$, where w is the last descendent of u visited by the DFS tour.

Figure 19.8: Algorithm INTER_LABEL.

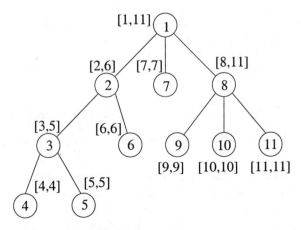

Figure 19.9: A tree T, its DFS numbering and its interval labels.

The results on restricted graph classes with short labels (Lemma 19.1.2), the relationships with universal graphs, the examples of Section 19.1 and Exercise 1 are due to [KNR88]. Several other graph classes are given adjacency-labeling schemes in [KNR88], including various intersection-based graphs such as interval graphs and c-decomposable graphs (see [FJ90]).

The characterization of bounded-arboricity graphs in terms of their decomposition into spanning trees is due to [NW61], and the polynomial decomposition algorithm is due to [PQ82].

The results on distance-preserving and distance-approximating labeling schemes are from [Pel00a]. The tightness of the labeling scheme for trees follows from a matching lower bound proven in [GPPR00], establishing that $\Omega(\log^2 n)$ bit labels are necessary for the class of all trees. The labeling scheme for trees has been extended into $O(\log^2 n)$ distance labeling schemes for the classes of interval graphs and permutation graphs in [KKP00].

It is also shown in [GPPR00] that general n-vertex graphs can be labeled with labels of size $O(n)$ bits. On the other hand, there are bounded degree n-vertex graphs that require labels of size $\Omega(n)$. Graph families with a k-separator support a distance labeling with labels of size $O(k \log n + \log^2 n)$. This implies, for instance, an upper bound of $O(\sqrt{n} \log n)$ for planar graphs and of $O(\log^2 n)$ for graphs of bounded treewidth. In contrast, for planar there exists a lower bound of $\Omega(n^{1/3})$ on the label size required for distance labeling [GPPR00].

An alternative approach for constructing proximity-preserving labeling schemes can be based on low-distortion embeddings of general metrics in low-dimensional Euclidean spaces [Bou85, LLR95]. See [Pel00a] for further discussion of this direction.

The *interval tree labeling* technique discussed in Section 19.4 is introduced in [SK85]. Other types of informative labeling schemes are studied in [Pel00b].

Exercises

1. Describe a universal graph of size $O(n^2)$ for the set of n-vertex trees.

2. Describe a universal graph of size $O(n^4)$ for the set of n-vertex planar graphs.

3. Give a distance preserving labeling scheme with $O(\log n)$-bit labels for n-vertex paths, rings, grids and hypercubes.

4. Prove Lemma 19.2.3.

5. A *constant* approximate-distance labeling scheme is a scheme whose distance estimation algorithm returns the same estimate $\tilde{D}(u,v) = k$ (for some fixed integer $k \geq 1$) for every two distinct labels. Characterize the class of graphs which enjoy a legal $(\log n, R)$ approximate-distance labeling scheme of this type (for some fixed integer $R \geq 1$).

6. Consider the family $\mathcal{SP}_n$ of n-vertex split graphs (defined in Section 16.3.2).

    (a) Show that any $l(n)$-distance labeling scheme for $\mathcal{SP}_n$ must have $l(n) = \Omega(n)$ size labels.

    (b) Show that $\mathcal{SP}_n$ has a labeling scheme using $(\log n + O(1))$-bit labels which provides approximate distances with an additive error of at most one (i.e., $\tilde{D}(u,v) \leq dist(u,v,G) \leq \tilde{D}(u,v) + 1$).

Part III

Distributed constructions and applications of LP-representations

Chapter 20

A basic algorithm for constructing network partitions

In the previous parts we have introduced the two basic components underlying the locality-sensitive approach to distributed computing, namely, distributed network algorithms and LP-representations. We are now ready to approach the issue of integrating these two ingredients together, which is the topic of the final part of the book.

In the next three chapters we focus on the preliminary aspect of how useful LP structures for a given network can be efficiently constructed by distributed algorithms.

In particular, in this chapter we describe a simple distributed implementation for Algorithm BASIC_PART presented in Section 11.5 for constructing a sparse partition of a given unweighted graph $G = (V, E)$. This will serve both as an illustration for the basic distributed techniques discussed so far and as an introduction to the topic of efficient distributed construction methods for covers, partitions and decomposition, which will be discussed in the following two chapters.

We then turn to illustrating the potential applicability of locality-preserving graph representations in the area of distributed network algorithms. This is done by revisiting some of the distributed tasks and applications introduced in the first part and examining the impact of using suitably chosen LP structures for their implementation.

20.1   Overall structure of the algorithm

The implementation we present, named Algorithm DIST_PART, follows the general structure of the Algorithm BASIC_PART. Thus it is in essence based on a single "thread" of computation in which at any given moment there is a single vertex serving as the "locus of activity" and running the execution. In fact, this statement is valid only concerning the high-level flow of the algorithm; at a lower level, various components of the construction are performed in a truly distributed fashion. Still, it is accurate to say that at any given moment in the execution, all vertices actively participating at that moment are within distance $2\kappa + 2$ of each other, where κ is the parameter governing the cluster growth rate in the algorithm and, more specifically, within or bordering with a single cluster.

Most distributed applications of sparse partitions require having, in addition to the partition itself, an explicitly marked intercluster edge between any two adjacent clusters. Consequently, the implementation described in this chapter will also select such representative intercluster edges. This selection is in fact done in a truly parallel fashion.

Hence in designing the distributed Algorithm DIST_PART, we need to take care of three components of the operation:

- a procedure CLUSTER_CONS for constructing a cluster around a chosen center v,

- a procedure NEXT_CTR for selecting the next center v around which to grow a cluster, and

- a procedure REP_EDGE for selecting a representative intercluster edge between any two adjacent clusters.

We next discuss each of these components separately.

20.2   The cluster construction procedure CLUSTER_CONS

Invoked at the center v, our procedure simultaneously constructs both the cluster and a BFS tree rooted at v spanning it. To do that, we employ a variant of Algorithm DIST_DIJK, described in Section 5.2. This algorithm is based on "growing" the cluster and the tree iteratively, adding a new layer in each iteration.

There are two main changes that need to be introduced to that algorithm. First, in the global BFS algorithm the exploration messages are sent by each vertex to all its neighbors save those known to belong to the tree. In contrast, in the variant used for Procedure CLUSTER_CONS, there are additional vertices to be ignored, namely, all those known to belong to previously constructed clusters.

The second change is that here, the BFS tree is grown only to a limited depth. This is the result of growing the new layers tentatively, based on the condition specified in the procedure. More specifically, each phase is modified as follows. Before we decide to expand the tree by adding the new layer (namely, the one just discovered by the exploration messages), we first perform a count of the number of new vertices in that layer. This is done by a convergecast process, invoking Procedure CONVERGE($\sum, Z,$ Leaves), where each leaf w sets Z_w to the number of new children attached to it in the new layer, and these numbers are added up and passed on by intermediate tree vertices.

The root v can then compare the final count Z_v with the total number of vertices already in the tree (known to it from the previous phase) and compute the ratio of these two numbers. If the ratio is greater than $n^{1/\kappa}$, then v broadcasts the next *Pulse* message, which (in particular) confirms the addition of the new layer and starts the next phase. Otherwise, the root broadcasts a message *Reject*, indicating the rejection of the new layer and the completion of the current cluster.

The final broadcast step can also be used to mark the cluster by a unique name, say, the identifier of its center, $ID(v)$, and inform all vertices of that name. This information is used in order to define the borders of the cluster. In particular, once the construction of the cluster is completed, each vertex in it informs all of its neighbors of its new residence. This way, vertices of the cluster under construction know which of their neighbors already belong to existing clusters.

20.3   The next center selection procedure NEXT_CTR

Since the "center of activity" of the algorithm is always located at the currently constructed cluster, a natural idea would be to select as the center for the next cluster a vertex adjacent to the cluster, namely, one of the vertices in the rejected layer. The choice can be made through a convergecast process, invoking Procedure CONVERGE($Arb, Y,$ Leaves), in which each leaf w sets Y_w to an arbitrary neighbor from the rejected layer and Arb is a function selecting one of its arguments arbitrarily. (Alternatively, the min function can be used, causing the selection of the minimum-identifier neighbor.)

One problem with this approach is that it does not specify what to do if the next layer turns out to be *empty*. Such an event does not necessarily signify the completion of the entire process, as it may be that some yet unclustered vertices still exist elsewhere in the graph (see Exercise 1).

This potential problem makes it clear that in order to ensure the completion of the process, it is necessary to search throughout the graph and verify that there are no forgotten unclustered vertices. Thus the cluster construction procedure of the previous section must be used within a global search procedure. For that purpose we use the depth-first search process and, more specifically, Algorithm DIST_DFS of Section 5.4. The DFS process progresses on the tree of constructed cluster. It starts at some originator vertex r_0 and employs the cluster construction procedure CLUSTER_CONS to construct the first cluster. Whenever the rejected layer of a constructed cluster is not empty, it chooses one of the vertices in that layer as the center for the next cluster. Each center of a new cluster remembers the previous cluster (namely, the one from which it was selected) as its parent in the cluster DFS tree. Once the search cannot progress forward from some cluster (due to an empty "next layer"), the DFS process backtracks from the current cluster to the previous one and tries to find an available center among its neighboring vertices. If no neighbors are available, the process continues to backtrack in the usual DFS fashion on the cluster DFS tree. The process terminates once it backs up all the way to the originating vertex r_0 and can no longer continue to new (unclustered) vertices.

It is important to note that the DFS process may visit some cluster C a number of times, and whenever the DFS process backtracks into C, the search for a potential new center must be conducted again. That is, even if a number of potential candidates were found by C in a previous search, and their identities are still stored at the cluster's center, we may not rely on that "stock" of candidates, but rather must perform a new convergecast process over C. (See Exercise 2).

20.4 The intercluster edge selection procedure REP_EDGE

The final stage of the entire construction algorithm DIST_PART is to select one representative intercluster edge between every two adjacent clusters. Consider two such clusters C and C'. Let $E(C, C')$ denote the set of edges connecting C and C'. These edges are known to their endpoints in C as such, since the vertices of C know the cluster-residence of each of their neighbors. Therefore the representative edge can be selected from among all the edges of $E(C, C')$ by a convergecast process. Of course, it is necessary to ensure that the same edge is selected by both C and C'. This can be imposed by defining a unique ordering on the edges and then picking the minimum edge in that ordering. Define the *ID-weight* of an edge $e = (v, w)$, where $ID(v) < ID(w)$, as the pair $\langle ID(v), ID(w) \rangle$, and order edges lexicographically by their *ID*-weights. This ensures distinct weights (assuming distinct vertex identifiers) and allows consistent selection of intercluster edges. Note that given this rule, different clusters are allowed to proceed with their selection process *in parallel*.

One problem that remains to be overcome is that the selection process as just described must be carried out at cluster C for *every* adjacent cluster C' individually. One way of doing this is to pipeline the individual processes in the way described in Section 3.4.3. The only remaining difficulty is that pipelining these processes as described therein requires each vertex of C to know the identities of all clusters adjacent to C. This information can be disseminated throughout the cluster C using the combined convergecast and broadcast dissemination process described in Section 4.3.2.

20.5 Analysis

Finally, we analyze the time and message complexities of the resulting Algorithm DIST_PART. Let us discuss each of the three components of the algorithm separately.

Denote the sequence of clusters constructed by the algorithm by $(C_1, C_2, \ldots, C_p)$. For each cluster C_i, let E_i denote the set of edges with at least one endpoint in C_i. Denote the cardinalities of these sets by $n_i = |C_i|$ and $m_i = |E_i|$. Denote the radius of C_i by $r_i = Rad(C_i)$.

The depth-bounded variant of the distributed Algorithm DIST_DIJK for constructing the cluster C_i (and its BFS spanning tree) requires $O(r_i^2)$ time and $O(n_i r_i + m_i)$ messages. Therefore we get $\text{Time}(\text{CLUSTER\_CONS}) = \sum_i O(r_i^2)$ and $\text{Message}(\text{CLUSTER\_CONS}) = \sum_i O(n_i r_i + m_i)$. A straightforward argument shows that $\text{Time}(\text{CLUSTER\_CONS}) = O(n\kappa)$, relying on the fact that $r_i \leq \kappa$ and $r_i \leq n_i$ and that $\sum_i n_i = n$. A slightly more careful analysis (see Exercise 3) reveals that in fact, in the relevant range of $\kappa \leq \log n$ (after which already $n^{1/\kappa} = O(1)$),

$$\text{Time}(\text{CLUSTER\_CONS}) = O(n).$$

As for the communication involved, note that an edge may occur in at most two distinct sets E_i, hence

$$\text{Message}(\text{CLUSTER\_CONS}) = O(n\kappa + |E|).$$

Let us now turn to the second component of the algorithm, NEXT_CTR. Note that the DFS process on the cluster tree is more expensive than the plain depth-first search procedure DIST_DFS. This is because in performing a DFS process on a graph, each visit of the process at a vertex requires $O(1)$ time (and no communication). In contrast, whenever the process of procedure NEXT_CTR visits a cluster C_i, deciding on the next step requires time and messages proportional to r_i and n_i, respectively. Fortunately, the message complexity does not depend on m_i, as the relevant information is assumed to have been gathered and stored at the leaves of the cluster by Procedure CLUSTER_CONS. Thus the entire DFS process (not counting the interludes of performing Procedure CLUSTER_CONS whenever visiting a new vertex) requires

$$\text{Time}(\text{NEXT\_CTR}) = O(p\kappa) = O(n\kappa)$$

and

$$\text{Message}(\text{NEXT\_CTR}) = O(pn) = O(n^2).$$

Finally, let us consider REP_EDGE. Denote the number of neighboring clusters surrounding cluster C_i by s_i. Then the stage of disseminating the identifiers of neighboring clusters throughout the cluster requires $O(s_i + r_i)$ time and at most $O(s_i n_i)$ messages, and the stage of (pipelined) intercluster edge selection has similar costs. In total, relying on the fact that $s_i \leq n$, we get

$$\text{Time}(\text{REP\_EDGE}) = \max_i \{O(s_i + r_i)\} = O(n)$$

and

$$\text{Message}(\text{REP\_EDGE}) = \sum_i O(s_i n_i) = O(n^2).$$

Theorem 20.5.1 *Given an n-vertex unweighted graph* $G = (V, E)$ *and an integer* $\kappa \geq 1$, *the distributed Algorithm* DIST_PART *requires* Time(DIST_PART) $= O(n\kappa)$ *and* Message(DIST_PART) $= O(n^2)$.   □

20.6   Improvements

Let us next describe some modifications to the construction method of Algorithm DIST_PART that result in considerably reducing its complexities. First, let us consider procedure NEXT_CTR again. In order to reduce its complexities, it is possible to modify it as follows. Let us start the entire algorithm by computing a spanning tree T for the network. This can be done by flooding, with complexities Time $= O(n)$ and Message $= O(|E|)$. Next, the DFS procedure for searching a new center for the next cluster can be executed on T rather than on the formed cluster graph. The process starts from the root of T, v_1, which is selected as the first center. In general, whenever a vertex v_i is chosen as the new center, the DFS process is halted until the cluster construction around v_i (by Procedure CLUSTER_CONS) is completed. At that point, the DFS process is resumed from v_i, searching T until finding a vertex v_{i+1} that does not belong to any of the clusters already constructed. The process is iterated until the entire tree T is traversed. The cost of Procedure NEXT_CTR is thus reduced to Time(NEXT_CTR) $=$ Message(NEXT_CTR) $= O(n)$.

The other expensive procedure is REP_EDGE, selecting the intercluster edges. It turns out that a small modification in our requirements allows us to discard this procedure altogether. The modification is to allow more than a single intercluster edge for two adjacent clusters. Under this relaxation, instead of using Procedure REP_EDGE, intercluster edges can be picked during the cluster construction stage by Procedure CLUSTER_CONS. Specifically, whenever Procedure CLUSTER_CONS completes the construction of a cluster C, each vertex v in the rejected layer selects the edge connecting it to C (namely, the edge on which it was contacted in the exploration stage) and marks it as an intercluster edge. (If v has received a number of exploration messages, then it selects one of the connecting edges arbitrarily.) Notice that this rule entails no extra cost in time or communication. One major difference from the previous implementation is that now two clusters might be connected by more than one intercluster edge. In other words, the outcome of the algorithm is a cluster multigraph rather than a cluster graph. However, the analysis carried out earlier proves that the total number of intercluster edges in the resulting cluster multigraph is still bounded by $O(n^{1+1/\kappa})$ (see Exercise 6). It turns out that the behavior and correctness of a number of applications of such partitions (and most significantly, synchronizer γ discussed later on in Chapter 25) are unaffected by this change.

Theorem 20.6.1 *Given an n-vertex unweighted graph* $G = (V, E)$ *and an integer* $\kappa \geq 1$, *the modified implementation of the distributed Algorithm* DIST_PART *requires* Time $= O(n)$ *and* Message $= O(E + n\kappa)$.   □

(In fact, let us remark that the message complexity of Procedure CLUSTER_CONS can be reduced further to $O(|E|)$, thus reducing the total message complexity of the algorithm to $O(|E|)$.)

Given the connection between basic spanners and partitions captured in Section 16.1, we get the following.

Corollary 20.6.2 *Given an n-vertex unweighted graph* $G = (V, E)$ *and an integer* $\kappa \geq 1$, *there exists a distributed algorithm for constructing a κ-spanner for G with* $O(n^{1+1/\kappa})$ *edges in* Time $= O(n)$ *and* Message $= O(E)$.   □

Bibliographical notes

Both Algorithm BASIC_PART and its distributed implementation, Algorithm DIST_PART, were given in [Awe85a], although the analysis of REP_EDGE therein, and hence the final bounds, are slightly looser. The improvements of Section 20.6 are due to [MS00].

Exercises

1. Describe a scenario in which in some constructed cluster the next layer is empty, and yet some unclustered vertices still exist in the graph.

2. Explain (by a counter-scenario) why whenever the DFS process backtracks into a cluster C it is necessary to perform a new search for a potential center among the adjacent vertices.

3. Prove that $\text{Time}(\text{CLUSTER\_CONS}) = O(n)$.

4. Improve the bounds on $\text{Time}(\text{NEXT\_CTR})$ and $\text{Message}(\text{NEXT\_CTR})$ or provide an example proving their tightness.

5. Provide an example proving the tightness of the bounds on $\text{Time}(\text{REP\_EDGE})$ and $\text{Message}(\text{REP\_EDGE})$.

6. Prove that in the modified procedure of Section 20.6, the total number of intercluster edges is still bounded by $O(n^{1+1/\kappa})$.

7. Prove the complexity bounds of Theorem 20.6.1.

8. Given an MST and an SPT on the graph G, describe an efficient distributed implementation for Algorithm SLT on G and analyze the resulting time and message complexities.

9. Give the most efficient distributed implementation possible for Algorithm GREEDY_SPAN.

Chapter 21

Efficient algorithms for constructing covers

One problem with the partitioning algorithm of the last chapter, as well as those of Chapters 11, 12 and 13, is that they are inherently sequential and hence do not support efficient preprocessing. Since sparse covers are used in a variety of dynamically changing distributed applications, it is highly desirable to be able to construct them using an efficient distributed algorithm. As usual, efficiency can be measured by either time or message complexity. In this chapter, we discuss efficient distributed asynchronous algorithms for constructing sparse graph covers.

21.1 Fast synchronous distributed algorithms

So far, we do not have a *fast* deterministic distributed algorithm for any of our cover construction problems (where by "fast algorithm" we mean an algorithm of time complexity polylogarithmic in n). Turning to randomized algorithms, the situation is slightly better. Although general constructions such as Algorithm MAX_COVER are not available to us, there is a fast randomized distributed algorithm for constructing a coarsening cover for *neighborhood* covers in unweighted graphs. The complexity of the algorithm depends on the neighborhood radius. In fact, the algorithms presented next construct a low (average or maximum) degree cover of the network in the sense of Section 14.2. The main procedure of these algorithms is a randomized variant of Procedure SEP_PART from Section 12.3.3 restricted to the 0-neighborhood cover $\hat{\Gamma}_0(V)$ and to separation $s = 2$ (i.e., clusters are required to be nonadjacent). However, these algorithms guarantee bounds only on the weak diameter of the resulting clusters.

Let us describe this randomized procedure, named Procedure RAND_PART. We assume the $\mathcal{LOCAL}$ model (i.e., congestion-free synchronous communication with all vertices starting to execute the algorithm at the same time). As before, it is assumed that each processor v has a unique integer identifier, $ID(v)$. The algorithm can easily be modified to work without this assumption by starting the solution on an anonymous network with a preprocessing stage in which processors choose identifiers at random from some sufficiently large domain.

Before we start describing the procedure, let us clarify what is meant by a distributed algorithm for constructing a partial partition. At the end of the procedure's execution, each vertex is supposed to know whether or not it belongs to a cluster of the constructed partial partition and, if it does, to which cluster (clusters are identified, say, by the identifier of

1. Set
$$B \leftarrow \left\lfloor \frac{2 \log n}{\log(1/p)} \right\rfloor.$$

2. Select an integer radius r_v at random, according to a truncated geometric distribution,
$$\mathbb{P}(r_v = j) \;=\; \begin{cases} p^j(1-p), & j = 0, \ldots, B-1, \\ p^B, & j = B. \end{cases}$$

3. Broadcast the pair $(ID(v), r_v)$ to all the vertices in your r_v-neighborhood, $\Gamma_{r_v}(v)$. This is done by a standard broadcast protocol using a counter for keeping track of the distance.

4. Select the pair $(ID(w), r_w)$ with the largest identifier, $ID(w)$, among all the messages received (including your own identifier $ID(v)$), and set $H(v) = w$.

5. If $dist(w, v) < r_w$, then join the cluster C_w rooted at w.
   /* If $dist(w, v) = r_w$, then remain without a home cluster. */

Figure 21.1: Procedure RAND_PART(p) (code for vertex v).

their center vertex).

Procedure RAND_PART uses a probability parameter $0 < p < 1$ and operates in three simple stages, described in Figure 21.1.

Note that it is possible for a cluster C_v constructed by the procedure to be disconnected and, moreover, it is possible that v itself has elected to join a different cluster than its own, as depicted in the following example.

Example: *Disconnected clusters on the ring.*

Consider a network whose underlying topology is a ring of 100 processors, $V = \{0, \ldots, 99\}$, with $ID(v) = v$. Suppose that vertices 98 and 99 have drawn the radii $r_{98} = 5$ and $r_{99} = 2$. This results in $C_{99} = \{98, 99, 0\}$ (with $\{1, 97\}$ remaining homeless due to their positioning on the border of cluster C_{99}) and $C_{98} = \{2, 94, 95, 96\}$ (with $\{3, 93\}$ remaining homeless due to its positioning on the border of cluster C_{98}), as depicted in Figure 21.2. Hence C_{98} is disconnected and does not contain 98 itself. □

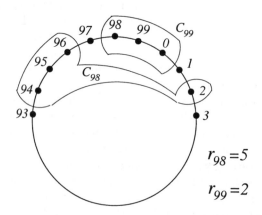

Figure 21.2: Clusters C_{98} and C_{99} in the example.

Let us next analyze the properties of Procedure RAND_PART. Consider some execution of the procedure. Let the clusters constructed by the procedure be denoted $\mathcal{S} = \{C_{v_1}, \ldots, C_{v_m}\}$, and denote the set of all vertices that were assigned a home cluster during the execution by $R = \bigcup_{i=1}^{m} C_{v_i}$.

Lemma 21.1.1 *With probability at least $1 - 1/n$, every vertex v chooses a radius $r_v < B$.*

Proof: The probability of the desired event can be written as

$$\mathbb{P}\left(\bigcap_{v \in V} r_v < B\right) = \prod_{v \in V} (1 - \mathbb{P}(r_v = B)) = (1 - p^B)^n.$$

By choice of B,

$$p^B \leq \left(2^{\log p}\right)^{\frac{-2 \log n}{\log p}} = n^{-2},$$

and therefore

$$(1 - p^B)^n \geq (1 - n^{-2})^n \geq e^{-1/n} \geq 1 - \frac{1}{n}. \qquad \square$$

Lemma 21.1.2 *The partition $\mathcal{S}$ constructed by Procedure RAND_PART on a given n-vertex unweighted graph $G = (V, E)$ enjoys the following properties.*

1. *The partition $\mathcal{S}$ is a 2-separated partial partition,*

2. *$W\,Rad(\mathcal{S}) \leq \frac{2 \log n}{\log(1/p)}$,*

3. *$\mathbb{P}(v \in R) \geq p(1 - 1/n)$ for each vertex v in G.*

Proof: The first property is proved by contradiction. Suppose $\mathcal{S}$ is not 2-separated. Since the clusters are clearly disjoint, there must be two adjacent vertices in G belonging to different clusters in $\mathcal{S}$, $w_1 \in C_{v_1}$ and $w_2 \in C_{v_2}$. Without loss of generality, suppose $ID(v_1) > ID(v_2)$. By the construction rule of the clusters (step 3 of the procedure), $ID(v_2)$ is the largest identifier seen by w_2 during the execution. Turning to w_1, again by step 3 of the procedure, $dist(v_1, w_1) < r_{v_1}$. Consequently, since w_1 and w_2 are neighbors in G, we have that $dist(v_1, w_2) \leq r_{v_1}$. Therefore w_2 should have received the broadcast message of v_1 containing the identifier $ID(v_1)$, namely, a larger identifier than $ID(v_2)$; this is a contradiction.

The second property follows directly from the definition of the distribution by which step 1 of the procedure is performed as the (weak) radius of a cluster can never exceed $B - 1$.

It remains to prove the third property. Let us fix a vertex w and estimate the probability that it gets to select a home cluster, i.e., that $w \in R$. A necessary condition for a vertex v to be chosen as $H(w)$ is that $dist(w, v) \leq B$ and that $ID(v) \geq ID(w)$. Hence the set of candidates to become $H(w)$ is

$$Q = \{v \mid dist(w, v) \leq B \text{ and } ID(v) \geq ID(w)\}.$$

Arrange these candidates by decreasing order of their identifiers, setting

$$Q = \{v_1, \ldots, v_l\},$$

where $ID(v_i) > ID(v_{i+1})$. Note that $v_l = w$.

However, if $dist(H(w), w) = B$, then w will not join a home cluster. Thus w may join R only if $H(w)$ belongs to the following set:

$$Q^* = \{v \in Q \mid dist(w, v) < B\}.$$

Let us define the following basic events. The event whose probability we need to compute is

$$\mathcal{R} = \text{``}w \in R\text{''}.$$

Denoting

$$\mathcal{H}_i = \text{``}H(w) = v_i\text{''},$$

the event $\mathcal{R}$ can be partitioned into disjoint subevents as follows.

$$\mathbb{P}(\mathcal{R}) = \sum_{v_i \in Q^*} \mathbb{P}(\mathcal{R} \cap \mathcal{H}_i) = \sum_{v_i \in Q^*} \frac{\mathbb{P}(\mathcal{R} \cap \mathcal{H}_i)}{\mathbb{P}(\mathcal{H}_i)} \cdot \mathbb{P}(\mathcal{H}_i). \tag{21.1}$$

In order to estimate these probabilities, let us break $\mathcal{R}$ and $\mathcal{H}_i$ further into subevents, defining the event

$$\mathcal{E}_i^{(<)} = \text{``}r_{v_i} < dist(v_i, w)\text{''}$$

and defining the events $\mathcal{E}_i^{(=)}$, $\mathcal{E}_i^{(>)}$ and $\mathcal{E}_i^{(\geq)}$ analogously and, finally, defining

$$\mathcal{F}_j = \bigcap_{i=1}^{j-1} \mathcal{E}_i^{(<)}.$$

The events $\mathcal{R}$ and $\mathcal{H}_i$ are precisely captured as

$$\mathcal{H}_i = \mathcal{F}_i \cap \mathcal{E}_i^{(\geq)}$$

and

$$\mathcal{R} \cap \mathcal{H}_i = \mathcal{F}_i \cap \mathcal{E}_i^{(>)}.$$

Since the event $\mathcal{F}_i$ is independent of the events $\mathcal{E}_i^{(>)}$ or $\mathcal{E}_i^{(\geq)}$, we have

$$\mathbb{P}(\mathcal{H}_i) = \mathbb{P}(\mathcal{F}_i) \cdot \mathbb{P}(\mathcal{E}_i^{(\geq)}), \tag{21.2}$$

$$\mathbb{P}(\mathcal{R} \cap \mathcal{H}_i) = \mathbb{P}(\mathcal{F}_i) \cdot \mathbb{P}(\mathcal{E}_i^{(>)}). \tag{21.3}$$

Let us now estimate these probabilities for some fixed $v_i \in Q^*$. Denote $d = dist(w, v_i)$. By the choice of probability distribution on r_{v_i} it can be easily verified that for every $v_i \in Q^*$, and since $d < B$,

$$\mathbb{P}(\mathcal{E}_i^{(>)}) = \sum_{j=d+1}^{B} \mathbb{P}(r_{v_i} = j) = (1-p) \sum_{j=d+1}^{B-1} p^j + p^B$$

$$= p^{d+1} \cdot (1-p) \sum_{j=0}^{B-d-2} p^j + p^B = p^{d+1}(1 - p^{B-d-1}) + p^B$$

$$= p^{d+1}, \tag{21.4}$$

and $\mathbb{P}(\mathcal{E}_i^{(=)}) = \mathbb{P}(r_{v_i} = d) = (1-p)p^d$, hence

$$\mathbb{P}(\mathcal{E}_i^{(\geq)}) = p^{d+1} + (1-p)p^d = p^d. \tag{21.5}$$

It follows from Equations (21.2), (21.3), (21.4) and (21.5) that for $v_i \in Q^*$,

$$\frac{\mathbb{P}(\mathcal{R} \cap \mathcal{H}_i)}{\mathbb{P}(\mathcal{H}_i)} = \frac{\mathbb{P}(\mathcal{F}_i) \cdot \mathbb{P}(\mathcal{E}_i^{(>)})}{\mathbb{P}(\mathcal{F}_i) \cdot \mathbb{P}(\mathcal{E}_i^{(\geq)})} = \frac{p^{d+1}}{p^d} = p, \tag{21.6}$$

hence by Equation (21.1)

$$\mathbb{P}(\mathcal{R}) = \sum_{v_i \in Q^*} p \cdot \mathbb{P}(\mathcal{H}_i) = p \cdot \mathbb{P}(H(w) \in Q^*)$$

$$\geq p \cdot \mathbb{P}(dist(H(w), w) < B) p \cdot \mathbb{P}(r_{H(w)} < B) \geq p \cdot \mathbb{P}\left(\bigcap_{v \in V} r_v < B\right)$$

and by Lemma 21.1.1

$$\mathbb{P}(\mathcal{R}) \geq p\left(1 - \frac{1}{n}\right)$$

as required. $\qquad \square$

Lemma 21.1.3 *With high probability,* $\frac{3 \log n}{p}$ *applications of Procedure* RAND_PART(p) *suffice to construct a 2-separated cover for* $\hat{\Gamma}_0(V)$.

Proof: Let $q = p(1 - 1/n)$. By Part 3 of Lemma 21.1.2, the probability that a vertex v is still uncovered after i applications of Procedure RAND_PART(p) is bounded by $(1 - q)^i$. Hence with probability at least $1 - n(1 - q)^i$, all vertices are covered after i applications. For $i = -2 \log n / \log(1 - q)$, this probability is at least $1 - 1/n$. As $-\ln(1 - q) \geq q$, it follows that $i = \frac{3 \log n}{p} \geq \frac{2 \log n}{q}$ applications suffice. $\qquad \square$

Picking $p = n^{-1/\kappa}$, we get by Lemmas 21.1.2 and 21.1.3 a cover $\mathcal{S}$ that subsumes $\hat{\Gamma}_0(V)$ with high probability, such that

$$WRad(\mathcal{S}) \leq 2 \log n / \log n^{1/\kappa} \leq 2\kappa$$

and

$$\Delta^C(\mathcal{S}) \leq 3 \log n \cdot n^{1/\kappa}.$$

The algorithm can be modified in a natural way to yield a (synchronous) coarsening algorithm for ρ-neighborhoods.

21.2 Low communication synchronous algorithms

The construction algorithm introduced in Chapter 20, and similar constructions for covers (based on the methods of Chapters 12 and 13), yield distributed implementations of high message complexity, namely, $\Theta(n^2)$. In this section we are concerned with communication-efficient distributed coarsening algorithms in the $\mathcal{CONGEST}$ model for constructing two particular types of sparse graph covers. The constructions are applicable to edge-weighted graphs.

In particular, the first (synchronous) algorithm we present, SYNC_AV_COVER, yields an average-degree coarsening (with parameter κ) of a ρ-neighborhood cover $\hat{\Gamma}_\rho(V)$ and has message complexity Message(SYNC_AV_COVER) $= O(E + n^{1+1/\kappa} \cdot \log n)$, and the second (synchronous) algorithm, SYNC_MAX_COVER, yields a maximum-degree coarsening (with parameter κ) of a ρ-neighborhood cover $\hat{\Gamma}_\rho(V)$ with message complexity Message(SYNC_MAX_COVER) $= O(E + n^{1+1/\kappa} \cdot \kappa^2)$.

For the purpose of our algorithms, we define a weight function $\xi : V \to R^+$ on the *vertices* of the graph. We also denote, for a subset of vertices $X \subseteq V$, $\xi(X) = \sum_{v \in X} \xi(v)$. Throughout the derivation of the algorithm we leave the exact values of the function ξ unspecified, but require that

- $\xi(v) > 0$ for every $v \in V$, and

- $\xi(V) \le n^2$.

For the complexity analysis of the distributed implementation, we fix the value of $\xi(v)$ in several different ways, obeying these constraints.

21.2.1   Basic procedures

The previous approach

Before going into a detailed description of the new algorithms, it may be useful to first reexamine the algorithms AV_COVER and MAX_COVER introduced previously and explain why a naive distributed implementation of these algorithms might result in high costs, even when the network is synchronous and the original cover to be coarsened consists of simple neighborhoods, i.e., is $\hat{\Gamma}_\rho(v)$.

The algorithms AV_COVER and MAX_COVER are based on "growing" the coarsening clusters iteratively. In each iteration, we merge into the *kernel* at hand an additional layer consisting of all input clusters that intersect that kernel and are not yet subsumed by other output clusters. We would like the number of messages required by this process to be proportional to the size (i.e., the number of vertices) of the constructed cluster. Therefore preconstructing all the ρ-neighborhoods of the input cover, or "marking" them (i.e., identifying, for each vertex, the neighborhoods in which it participates), may be too expensive, since the total size of clusters in the original cover may be as high as $\Omega(n^2)$.

The natural approach for constructing a cluster according to the above strategy is therefore by performing a breadth first search process (and growing a BFS tree) from the kernel outwards for depth 2ρ. However, it may happen that the BFS process has traversed a large territory in vain and failed to discover any new (input) clusters to merge. In such a case, the cost of this BFS expedition may be unaccounted for.

A possible way to overcome such unjustified expenditures is to avoid entering a territory unless knowing in advance that it contains some as yet unmerged input cluster. This requires us to know whether the vertices at the *border* of the unexplored territory belong to such a cluster. Thus the problem can again be overcome if we assume that the input cover is "marked" and we know for every vertex which clusters it belongs to. Unfortunately, as discussed earlier, this assumption is generally too costly to guarantee by a special preprocessing stage.

Let us remark that even if we manage to ensure that searches do not enter territories unnecessarily, this in itself still does not guarantee the desired bound on message complexity; it is also necessary to ensure that the searches are done efficiently. In this context, a search resulting in the construction of a cluster Z is efficient if its cost is $O(|Z|)$ and is inefficient if its cost is proportional to (or higher than) $|E(Z)|$, the number of edges in Z.

Procedure CLUSTER

The algorithms described in this section share a common structure to some extent, and therefore it is convenient to describe them using a joint procedure, named Procedure SYNC_PART.

In the remainder of this subsection we describe this procedure, as well as the procedure CLUSTER invoked by it, and analyze some of their properties.

Let us begin with the subprocedure CLUSTER. This procedure, invoked at a vertex v, constructs two different output clusters, $Z \in \mathcal{Z}$ and $Y \in \mathcal{Y}$, centered at v. It also identifies two sets of vertices, denoted $\Psi(Z)$ and $\Psi(Y)$. The vertices in $\Psi(Z)$ are those whose ρ-neighborhood is fully subsumed by Z, while the vertices in $\Psi(Y)$ are those whose ρ-neighborhood is fully subsumed by Y. Moreover, the four sets of vertices should be thought of as forming an "internal kernel" $\Psi(Y)$ plus three additional "layers" of width ρ each around the vertex v (see Figure 21.3), i.e.,

$$v \in \Psi(Y) \subseteq Y \subseteq \Psi(Z) \subseteq Z.]$$

The clusters are constructed by merging together some neighborhoods of vertices from U. The construction begins by designating the vertex v itself as the initial cluster Y. The cluster is then repeatedly merged with intersecting neighborhoods of vertices from U. This is done in a layered fashion, adding two layers of width ρ at a time. The layers are added by performing a BFS process similar to Procedure CLUSTER_CONS of Section 21.1, from Y, to depth 2ρ. The original cluster Y plus the new inner layer now constitute the collection $\Psi(Z)$, while $\Psi(Z)$ plus the outer layer form the resulting cluster Z.

The BFS process is performed only on vertices that have not yet been added to any pre- ·
viously constructed Y cluster. Essentially, this prevents the search from entering territories that were already covered and helps to guarantee the desired time bound.

If there is a need to perform another iteration, then $\Psi(Y)$ and Y are expanded to contain $\Psi(Z)$ and Z, respectively, and the new iteration is performed with respect to this new Y. The merging process is carried out repeatedly until reaching a certain sparsity condition. Specifically, the sparsity condition has to ensure that the next iteration increases the number of vertices in both Y and $\Psi(Y)$, and the weight $\xi(Y)$ of the vertices in Y, by more than some appropriate factor. The procedure then returns the four sets constructed by it.

Procedure CLUSTER is formally described in Figure 21.4.

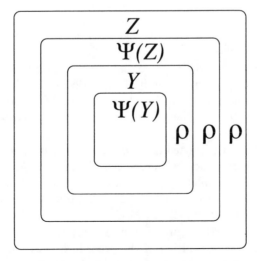

Figure 21.3: The structure of a cluster Z.

---

1. $\Psi(Z) \leftarrow \{v\}$.

2. $Z \leftarrow \{\Gamma_\rho(v)\}$.

3. **Repeat**   /* build cluster around v */

   (a) $\Psi(Y) \leftarrow \Psi(Z)$.

   (b) $Y \leftarrow Z$.

   (c) Perform a multiorigin BFS process w.r.t. Y in $G(V \setminus \bigcup \mathcal{Y})$ to depth 2ρ.

   (d) Add all vertices encountered to Z.

   (e) $\Psi(Z) \leftarrow \{v \mid v \in U \cap Z, \ dist(v, Y) \leq m\}$.

   until $|Z| \leq n^{1/\kappa} \cdot |Y|$ **and** $\xi(Z) \leq n^{1/\kappa} \cdot \xi(Y)$
   and $|\Psi(Z)| \leq |R|^{1/\kappa} \cdot |\Psi(Y)|$.

4. **Return** $(\Psi(Y), Y, \Psi(Z), Z)$.

Figure 21.4: Procedure CLUSTER(R, U, v).

Procedure SYNC_PART

The role of this procedure is to construct a partial cover for the neighborhoods of the vertices in the set R. Throughout, the procedure maintains the set of "remaining" vertices U. This set is a subset of R, containing those vertices from R whose neighborhoods have not yet been subsumed by the constructed cover. Initially $U = R$ and the procedure returns once $U = \emptyset$.

The procedure SYNC_PART is designed to be used in both of the main algorithms presented later on. Its output consists of three components. The first two of these are relevant for Algorithm SYNC_MAX_COVER, and the last is relevant for Algorithm SYNC_AV_COVER.

The general structure of Procedure SYNC_PART(R) is as follows. It starts by setting U, the collection of *unprocessed* vertices, to R. The procedure operates in iterations, each iteration calling on procedure CLUSTER(R, U, v) with some vertex $v \in R$ as a parameter and getting back the sets $\Psi(Y), Y, \Psi(Z), Z$. It then adds the resulting cluster Z to a collection $\mathcal{Z}$ and the cluster Y to a collection $\mathcal{Y}$.

The procedure generates two different partial covers. The first is the collection $\mathcal{Z}$, which is a cover subsuming all the ρ-neighborhoods of all vertices in R. The second is the collection $\mathcal{Y}$, which subsumes the ρ-neighborhoods of all vertices in $\Psi(R)$. An important property of the procedure SYNC_PART is that the partial cover $\mathcal{Y}$ constructed by it consists of *disjoint* clusters.

Throughout the process, the procedure also keeps the "unmerged" collections $\mathcal{Y}, \mathcal{Z}$ containing the original R neighborhoods merged into Y and Z. At the end of the iterative process, when Y and Z are completed, every vertex in the collection $\Psi(Z)$ is removed from U. Then a new iteration is started. These iterations proceed until U is exhausted. The procedure then outputs the sets $\Psi(R)$, $\mathcal{Y}$ and $\mathcal{Z}$.

Note that for each of the vertices in $\Psi(R)$, its ρ-neighborhood is covered by some cluster $Y \in \mathcal{Y}$ constructed during the execution of the procedure. Also, for each of the vertices in R, its ρ-neighborhood is covered by some cluster $Z \in \mathcal{Z}$ constructed during the execution of the procedure. However, for some original R vertices, their neighborhoods are not subsumed by any cluster in $\mathcal{Y}$; these are precisely the clusters merged into some external layer $\mathcal{Z} \setminus \mathcal{Y}$.

---

1. $U \leftarrow R$.

2. $\Psi(R) \leftarrow \emptyset$.

3. $\mathcal{Y}, \mathcal{Z} \leftarrow \emptyset$.

4. **While** $U \neq \emptyset$ **do:**

    (a) Select an arbitrary vertex $v \in U$.

    (b) $(\Psi(Y), Y, \Psi(Z), Z) \leftarrow \text{CLUSTER}(R, U, v)$.

    (c) $\Psi(R) \leftarrow \Psi(R) \cup \Psi(Y)$.

    (d) $U \leftarrow U \setminus \Psi(Z)$.

    (e) $\mathcal{Y} \leftarrow \mathcal{Y} \cup \{Y\}$.

    (f) $\mathcal{Z} \leftarrow \mathcal{Z} \cup \{Z\}$.

    End-while

5. **Return** $(\Psi(R), \mathcal{Y}, \mathcal{Z})$.

Figure 21.5: Procedure SYNC_PART(R).

It is important to note that each newly formed cluster in $\mathcal{Y}$ consists of only the kernel Y and not the entire cluster Z, which contains an additional "external layer" of neighborhoods of R vertices. The role of this external layer is to act as a "protective barrier" shielding the generated cluster Y and providing the desired disjointness between the different clusters Y added to $\mathcal{Y}$.

Procedure SYNC_PART is formally described in Figure 21.5.

Properties of the procedures

We now analyze the properties of the two procedures described above. The properties of Procedure CLUSTER are summarized by the following lemma.

Lemma 21.2.1 *Given an n-vertex weighted graph $G = (V, E, \omega)$ and integers $\kappa, m \geq 1$, consider an invocation of Procedure CLUSTER(R, U, v) from Procedure SYNC_PART. The output of Procedure CLUSTER(R, U, v) satisfies the following properties:*

1. $Y \subseteq Z$.

2. $|Z| \leq n^{1/\kappa} \cdot |Y|$.

3. $\xi(Z) \leq n^{1/\kappa} \cdot \xi(Y)$.

4. $|\Psi(Z)| \leq |R|^{1/\kappa} \cdot |\Psi(Y)|$.

5. $\Psi(Y) \subseteq \Psi(Z)$.

6. $Y \cap Y' = \emptyset$ *for every* $Y' \in \mathcal{Y}$.

7. $Rad(Z) = O(\kappa \rho)$.

8. $Rad(Y) = O(\kappa \rho)$.

9. $dist(w, Y') > \rho$ for every $w \in U \setminus \Psi(Z)$ and $Y' \in \mathcal{Y} \cup \{Y\}$.

10. $\{Z\}$ coarsens $\hat{\Gamma}_\rho(\Psi(Z))$.

11. $\{Y\}$ coarsens $\hat{\Gamma}_\rho(\Psi(Y))$.

Proof: Claim (1) is immediate from the procedure, and the next three claims, (2), (3), (4), are immediate from the termination condition of the loop. Claim (5) follows from the fact that the set $\Psi(Z)$ grows in each iteration. The disjointedness of the newly formed kernel from all previous ones (Claim (6)) again follows directly from the construction.

Claim (8), giving the radius bound on Y, follows from Claim (7), since $Y \subseteq Z$. The bound on Z (Claim (7)) follows in a way similar to the proof in the centralized algorithms, noting that each iteration involves increasing either $|Y|$ by a factor of $n^{1/\kappa}$ or $\xi(Y)$ by a factor of $n^{1/\kappa}$ or $|\Psi(Y)|$ by a factor of $|R|^{1/\kappa}$ and, furthermore, that the first and third of these events cannot happen for more than κ times and the second cannot happen for more than 2κ times (since $\xi(V) \le n^2$). Therefore the number of iterations is at most 4κ and each of them increases the radius by at most 2ρ.

Claims (9) and (10) are proved by induction on the iterations of the main loop of Procedure SYNC_PART. The induction basis holds vacuously prior to the first iteration, as initially $\mathcal{Y} = \emptyset$. For the inductive step, assume Claim (9) holds after the $(i - 1)$st iteration of the loop and consider the ith iteration. We need to prove that Claims (9) and (10) hold upon completion of this invocation of Procedure CLUSTER.

Consider a vertex w such that $w \in U$ upon this invocation of Procedure CLUSTER and $dist(w, Y) \le \rho$ upon its completion. Consider the last iteration of the loop in Procedure CLUSTER that created the cluster Y. We argue that w, along with its entire $\Gamma_\rho(w)$ neighborhood, must have been covered by the BFS process spawned from the set Y in that iteration. To formalize this argument, note that upon completion of Procedure CLUSTER in the previous iteration, w belonged to $U \setminus \Psi(Z)$ (otherwise, it would not belong to U now). Therefore, by the inductive assumption, $dist(w, Y') > \rho$ for all $Y' \in \mathcal{Y}$ created prior to Y. Consequently, $\Gamma_\rho(w) \subseteq G(V \setminus \bigcup \mathcal{Y})$ before the creation of cluster Y. Also, since $dist(w, Y) \le \rho$, it follows that $Y \cap \Gamma_\rho(w) \ne \emptyset$, so $\Gamma_\rho(w)$ and Y are in the same connected component of $G(V \setminus \bigcup \mathcal{Y})$. It follows that the BFS process that proceeded from Y to distance 2ρ must have traversed the entire neighborhood $\Gamma_\rho(w)$. Hence w has been added to $\Psi(Z)$ and $\Gamma_\rho(w) \subseteq Z$. This proves Claims (9) and (10) for the ith invocation of Procedure CLUSTER.

Finally, Claim (11) follows from the fact that the sets Y and $\Psi(Y)$ of one iteration are Z and $\Psi(Z)$ of the previous one, respectively. $\square$

The properties of Procedure SYNC_PART are summarized by the following lemma.

Lemma 21.2.2 *Given an n-vertex weighted graph $G = (V, E, \omega)$, a set of vertices R and integers $\kappa, m \ge 1$, the collections $\mathcal{Z} = \{Z_i \mid 1 \le i \le l\}$ and $\mathcal{Y} = \{Y_i \mid 1 \le i \le l\}$ and the set of vertices $\Psi(R)$ constructed by Procedure SYNC_PART(R) satisfy the following properties:*

1. $\bigcup \mathcal{Y} \subseteq \bigcup \mathcal{Z}$.

2. $\Delta^C(\mathcal{Y}) = 1$.

3. $Rad(\mathcal{Z}) = O(\kappa\rho)$.

4. $Rad(\mathcal{Y}) = O(\kappa\rho)$.

5. $\bar{\Delta}(\mathcal{Z}) \le n^{1/\kappa}$.

6. $\sum_{Z \in \mathcal{Z}} \xi(Z) \leq \xi(V) \cdot n^{1/\kappa}$.

7. $\mathcal{Z}$ coarsens $\hat{\Gamma}_\rho(R)$.

8. $\mathcal{Y}$ coarsens $\hat{\Gamma}_\rho(\Psi(R))$.

9. $|\Psi(R)| \geq |R|^{1-1/\kappa}$.

Proof: Claims (1), (2), (3) and (4) follow directly from Claims (1), (6), (7) and (8) of the previous Lemma 21.2.1, respectively.

Claims (5) and (6) are derived from Claims (2), (3) and (6) of the previous lemma as in the proof of the centralized algorithm (Lemma 12.3.1 or the Average Cover Theorem 12.2.1).

Claims (7) and (8) follow from Claims (10) and (11) of the previous lemma, Lemma 21.2.1, respectively.

Claim (9) is derived as follows. Note that the sets $\Psi(Z)$ generated in each application of Procedure CLUSTER are disjoint and $R = \bigcup \Psi(Z)$. Likewise, the sets $\Psi(Y)$ are disjoint and $\Psi(R) = \bigcup \Psi(Y)$. It now follows from Claim (4) that $|R| \leq |R|^{1/\kappa} |\Psi(R)|$, hence the claim follows. $\square$

21.2.2 Average-degree coarsening

In this section we describe Algorithm SYNC_AV_COVER, whose task is to construct coarsening covers with low *average* degree. The input to the algorithm is an n-vertex graph $G = (V, E, \omega)$ and integers $\rho, \kappa \geq 1$. The algorithm consists of a single application of Procedure SYNC_PART to the vertex set V, i.e., the algorithm executes

$$(\Psi(R), \mathcal{Y}, \mathcal{Z}) \leftarrow \text{SYNC\_PART}(V),$$

taking the cluster collection $\mathcal{Z}$ returned by the procedure as its output.

Theorem 21.2.3 *Given an n-vertex weighted graph $G = (V, E, \omega)$ and integers $\kappa, m \geq 1$, the algorithm SYNC_AV_COVER constructs a coarsening cover $\mathcal{Z}$ that satisfies the following properties:*

1. *$\mathcal{Z}$ coarsens $\hat{\Gamma}_\rho(V)$,*

2. *$Rad(\mathcal{Z}) = O(\kappa\rho)$, and*

3. *$\bar{\Delta}(\mathcal{Z}) \leq n^{1/\kappa}$.*

Proof: The three properties stated in the lemma follow from Claims (7), (3) and (5) of Lemma 21.2.2, respectively. $\square$

21.2.3 Maximum-degree coarsening

This section describes Algorithm SYNC_MAX_COVER, presented formally in Figure 21.6, whose task it is to construct a sparse coarsening cover with low maximum degree.

The input to the algorithm is an n-vertex graph $G = (V, E, \omega)$ and integers $\rho, \kappa \geq 1$. The output collection of cover clusters, $\mathcal{X}$, is initially empty. The algorithm maintains the set of "remaining" vertices R. These are the vertices whose neighborhoods are not yet subsumed by the constructed cover. Initially $R = V$, and the algorithm terminates once $R = \emptyset$.

The algorithm operates in at most $\kappa \cdot n^{1/\kappa}$ phases. Each phase consists of the activation of the procedure SYNC_PART(R), which adds a subcollection of output clusters $\mathcal{Y}$ to $\mathcal{X}$ and removes the set of subsumed vertices $\Psi(R)$ from R. Here we make use of one of the properties of procedure SYNC_PART, namely, that the partial covers $\mathcal{Y}$ constructed by it consist of *disjoint* clusters. This guarantees that each phase of the algorithm contributes at most one to the degree of each vertex in the output cover $\mathcal{X}$.

Note that for each of the vertices in $\Psi(R)$, its ρ-neighborhood is covered by some cluster $Y \in \mathcal{Y}$ constructed during the execution of the procedure. However, for some original R vertices, their neighborhoods are not subsumed by any cluster in $\mathcal{Y}$; these are precisely the clusters merged into some external layer $\mathcal{Z} - \mathcal{Y}$. Therefore there may be clusters left in R after the main algorithm removes the elements of $\Psi(R)$. This is why a single application of Procedure SYNC_PART is not enough and many phases are necessary.

---

1. $R \leftarrow V$.   /* R is the collection of remaining (unsubsumed) balls */

2. $\mathcal{X} \leftarrow \emptyset$.   /* $\mathcal{X}$ is the output cover */

3. **Repeat**

   (a) $(\Psi(R), \mathcal{Y}, \mathcal{Z}) \leftarrow$ SYNC_PART(R).   /* invoke procedure SYNC_PART */

   (b) $\mathcal{X} \leftarrow \mathcal{X} \cup \mathcal{Y}$.

   (c) $R \leftarrow R \setminus \Psi(R)$.

   until $R = \emptyset$

4. **Return** ($\mathcal{X}$).

Figure 21.6: Algorithm SYNC_MAX_COVER.

Theorem 21.2.4 *Given an n-vertex weighted graph $G = (V, E, \omega)$, a cover $\hat{\Gamma}_\rho(V)$ and integers $\kappa, m \geq 1$, Algorithm SYNC_MAX_COVER constructs a coarsening cover $\mathcal{X}$ that satisfies the following properties:*

1. *$\mathcal{X}$ coarsens $\hat{\Gamma}_\rho(V)$,*

2. *$Rad(\mathcal{X}) = O(\kappa\rho)$,*

3. *Procedure SYNC_PART is invoked $O(\kappa n^{1/\kappa})$ times,*

4. *$\Delta^C(\mathcal{X}) = O(\kappa n^{1/\kappa})$.*

Proof: Claims (1) and (2) follow directly from Claims (8) and (4) of the previous lemma, respectively.

Claim (3) is proved by Property (9) of Lemma 21.2.2, as in the proof of the centralized algorithm (the Maximum Cover Theorem 12.4.1).

Claim (4) follows from this bound as well, combining it with Claim (2) of the previous lemma. This completes the proof of Theorem 21.2.4. $\square$

21.2.4 Synchronous distributed implementations

In this section we discuss the synchronous distributed implementation of the algorithms presented in the last two sections.

Performing a BFS process in the graph $G(V \setminus \bigcup \mathcal{Y})$ raises two related issues. The first is how to avoid going into vertices of $\bigcup \mathcal{Y}$. This can be achieved by requiring that whenever a vertex is added to some set Y, it informs all its neighbors of that fact. Since the clusters $Y \in \mathcal{Y}$ are disjoint, the total message cost of these messages throughout the algorithm is $O(|E|)$.

The second issue we face is bounding the complexity of the BFS process. A straight-forward implementation will traverse all edges and therefore result in a cost of $O(|E(Z)|)$ messages for exploring a cluster Z, where $E(Z)$ is the set of edges of the cluster Z. We also need to account for the other computational ingredients of the algorithms. However, these seem to be rather efficient. In particular, counting the cardinalities of various sets is done at most $O(\kappa)$ times in the cluster, over the tree itself, adding $O(\kappa)$ messages per vertex per cluster. This leaves us with a total message complexity of $O(\kappa|Z| + |E(Z)|)$ for Procedure CLUSTER constructing a cluster Z. Also, the selection of vertex $v \in U$ from which CLUSTER(R, U, v) is called can be done by traversing the vertices of the clusters in a DFS fashion, which results in $O(1)$ messages per edge per cluster, which is dominated by the complexity of the BFS process. Thus, the total message complexity of Procedure SYNC_PART is

$$\text{Message}(\text{SYNC\_PART}) = O\left(\sum_{Z \in \mathcal{Z}} \kappa|Z| + |E(Z)|\right). \tag{21.7}$$

This complexity can be quite high, and therefore our remaining task is to bound it more efficiently.

There are two approaches to handling this problem. The first is based on bounding the total number of edges in the clusters of the cover $\mathcal{Z}$ generated by Procedure SYNC_PART. This can be done by setting the vertex weights to be $\xi(v) = deg_G(v)$. Then $|E(Z)| \leq \xi(Z) \leq 2|E(Z)|$, and $\xi(V)$ becomes $2|E|$, and hence by Claim (6) of Lemma 21.2.2 and Equation (21.7), the message complexity of Procedure SYNC_PART becomes $\text{Message}(\text{SYNC\_PART}) = O((\kappa n + |E|)n^{1/\kappa})$. Consequently, the message complexity of SYNC_AV_COVER is $\text{Message}(\text{SYNC\_AV\_COVER}) = O((\kappa n + |E|)n^{1/\kappa})$, too, and the complexity of SYNC_MAX_COVER becomes $\text{Message}(\text{SYNC\_MAX\_COVER}) = O((\kappa n + |E|)\kappa n^{2/\kappa})$. Note that in fact we can always normalize the constant in the exponent into 1 by substituting 2κ for κ in this expression. This is done by invoking the procedures with parameter $\kappa' = 2\kappa$ given an input parameter κ to the algorithm. Since all other occurrences of κ in the analysis are significant only up to a constant factor (namely, are within the "Big Oh" notation), there are no changes except that the resulting message complexity becomes $\text{Message}(\text{SYNC\_MAX\_COVER}) = O((\kappa n + |E|)\kappa n^{1/\kappa})$.

This approach immediately leads to solutions with message complexity $O(|E| \cdot \text{polylog}(n))$ for applications requiring $\kappa = \log n$.

However, a better solution can be based on combining the above approach with the alternative approach of performing the construction within the clusters of $\mathcal{Z}$ at a cost proportional to a function of n and $|Z|$ but *independent* of the number of edges in Z. The idea is to avoid scanning all the edges of the cluster. In particular, one would like to scan only edges that are to be eventually added to the BFS tree and avoid scanning nontree edges. This can be done as follows.

We are given an input graph G plus parameters ρ, κ and have to compute an (either average or maximum degree) coarsening. First, we construct an average degree coarsening cover $\mathcal{S}$ for the lowest level neighborhood cover, $\hat{\Gamma}_1(V)$, on the graph G, using algorithm SYNC_AV_COVER with parameters $\kappa' = \log n$ and $\rho' = 1$. Observe that this can be done efficiently using our first technique and the message complexity of constructing $\mathcal{S}$ is $O(|E| + n \log n)$.

We now use the resulting cover $\mathcal{S}$ as a *communication mechanism*, as follows. Identify with each vertex v a *home-cluster* $S_v \in \mathcal{S}$, such that $\Gamma_1(v) \subseteq S_v$. Fix a *center* vertex in each cluster $S \in \mathcal{S}$. Finally, run the desired algorithm (SYNC_AV_COVER or SYNC_MAX_COVER) on the input parameters, but for the following changes. First, perform all communication required for the algorithm through the centers. Specifically, each vertex w joining a cluster Z is required to report this fact to its center r_w. Also, whenever a vertex v wants to explore another layer of the BFS tree (and thus increase its cluster Z), it asks its center r_v which of its neighbors are still listed as not belonging to the cluster Z. The center r_v maintains a status list for all vertices in its cluster and can therefore supply the information to v. In case it doesn't know, it can get the information from w's center, r_w. Second, set the vertex weights to be $\xi(v) = deg_{\mathcal{S}}(v)$. Then $\xi(V)$ becomes $O(n)$.

In order to analyze the cost of this method, observe that each vertex occurs in at most $\xi(v)$ clusters of $\mathcal{S}$ and therefore for every vertex w about to join the cluster Z, its center r_w will be queried at most $O(\xi(v))$ times. Also, the cost of each of these queries is $O(\log n)$. Counting the cardinalities of various sets again adds $O(\kappa)$ messages per vertex per cluster. Hence we get a total message complexity of

$$\text{Message(SYNC\_PART)} = O\left(\sum_{Z \in \mathcal{Z}} \xi(Z) \log n + \kappa |Z| \right) \qquad (21.8)$$

for Procedure SYNC_PART(R). By Claim (6) we get

$$\text{Message(SYNC\_PART)} \;=\; O(\xi(V) \cdot n^{1/\kappa} \cdot \log n) \;=\; O(n^{1+1/\kappa} \cdot \log n).$$

In estimating the total communication requirements of the algorithm, we should now also take into account the cost of constructing $\mathcal{S}$. Summarizing, we get the following theorem.

Theorem 21.2.5 *Given an n-vertex weighted graph $G = (V, E, \omega)$ and a parameter $\kappa, m \geq 1$, the complexities of Algorithm SYNC_AV_COVER are*

$$\begin{aligned} \text{Message(SYNC\_AV\_COVER)} \;&=\; O(E + n^{1+1/\kappa} \cdot \log n), \\ \text{Time(SYNC\_AV\_COVER)} \;&=\; O(n^{1+1/\kappa} \cdot \log n). \end{aligned}$$

Theorem 21.2.6 *Given an n-vertex weighted graph $G = (V, E, \omega)$ and a parameter $\kappa, m \geq 1$, the complexities of Algorithm SYNC_MAX_COVER are*

$$\begin{aligned} \text{Message(SYNC\_MAX\_COVER)} \;&=\; O(E + n^{1+1/\kappa} \cdot \kappa^2), \\ \text{Time(SYNC\_MAX\_COVER)} \;&=\; O(n^{1+1/\kappa} \cdot \kappa^2). \end{aligned}$$

Let us comment that it is actually possible to replace the $\log n$ factor appearing in the expressions for the message complexity of algorithm SYNC_MAX_COVER by κ. This is done as follows. After constructing the cover $\mathcal{S}$, we use it for constructing *another* average degree cover $\mathcal{S}'$, only this time with parameters $\kappa' = \kappa$ and $\rho' = 1$. This is done as just described, incurring a total cost of $O(|E| + n^{1+1/\kappa} \cdot \log n)$. We then use the new cover $\mathcal{S}'$ as a communication mechanism. This changes $\xi(V)$ into $O(n^{1+1/\kappa})$ and reduces the cost of querying the centers from $O(\log n)$ to $O(\kappa)$, thus changing the total message complexity of Algorithm SYNC_AV_COVER to

$$\text{Message(SYNC\_MAX\_COVER)} \;=\; O(|E| + \kappa^2 \cdot n^{1+1/\kappa}).$$

As an example, constructing a regional matching system, based on a hierarchy of $\log n$ maximum degree covers with parameters $\kappa = \log n$ and $\rho = 2^i$ for $1 \leq i \leq \log n$, requires a total message complexity of $O(|E| + n \log^3 n)$.

Bibliographical notes

The randomized algorithm of Section 21.1 is due to [LS91c]. This algorithm was originally described as an algorithm for constructing a network decomposition (as in Section 14.2).

The communication efficient synchronous algorithms of Section 21.2 are due to [AP90a, ABCP93], and similar ideas have also been developed in [Coh93] for the efficient construction of sparse spanners. The synchronous algorithms are turned into asynchronous ones as well in [ABCP93] via a powerful bootstrapping technique referred to as "bootstrap resynchronization." The resulting asynchronous algorithm, ASYN_MAX_COVER, yields a maximum-degree coarsening (with parameter κ) of a ρ-neighborhood cover $\hat{\Gamma}_\rho(V)$ with complexities

$$\text{Message}(\text{ASYN\_MAX\_COVER}) = O(E + n^{1+1/\kappa} \cdot \kappa^3 \cdot \log n) \text{ and}$$

$$\text{Time}(\text{ASYN\_MAX\_COVER}) = O(n^{1+1/\kappa} \cdot \kappa^3 \cdot \log n).$$

By combining the ideas of [ABCP93] with those of [AR92] and [AP90b], a near-optimal synchronizer has been developed, yielding in turn a near-optimal algorithm for constructing a BFS tree from scratch with $O(|E| + n \cdot \log^4 n)$ messages and time.

Chapter 22

Efficient algorithms for constructing network decompositions

This chapter concerns fast distributed algorithms for constructing a network decomposition. The centralized algorithm presented in Section 14.2 is inherently sequential and its distributed implementation will require at least $\Omega(n)$ time. Here we present a faster (deterministic) distributed algorithm for the problem on unweighted graphs in the synchronous, congestion-free $\mathcal{LOCAL}$ model, based on a different approach.

22.1 Constructing s-separated, r-ruling sets

Let us first define the following notion.

Definition 22.1.1 [s-separated, r-ruling set]: *An s-separated, r-ruling set (or simply an (s,r)-set) in a graph G is a set of vertices $W = \{w_1, \ldots, w_m\}$ with the following two properties.*

1. *$dist(w_i, w_j) \geq s$ for every $1 \leq i < j \leq m$, and*

2. *for every $v \notin W$ there exists some $1 \leq i \leq m$ such that $dist(w_i, v) \leq r$.*

We would like to associate with an (s,r)-set W for G a partition of the vertices of G into connected clusters, $\mathcal{S}(W) = \{S_1, \ldots, S_m\}$, such that $w_i \in S_i$ and $Rad(w_i, G(S_i)) \leq r$ for every $1 \leq i \leq m$. We refer to this partition, illustrated in Figure 22.1, as the (s,r)-*partition* associated with W.

The simple rule of placing each vertex $v \notin W$ in the cluster built around the closest element of W (i.e., placing v in some cluster S_i such that $dist(w_i, v) \leq dist(w_j, v)$ for every $j \neq i$) can cause the formation of disconnected clusters (see Exercise 1). However, this problem can be corrected by using a modified rule based on breaking ties in a consistent manner (say, preferring the element w_i with the smallest ID from among those closest to v).

Consequently, we construct the (s,r)-partition $\mathcal{S}(W)$ associated with W using Procedure SEP_RULE_PART given in Figure 22.2.

Lemma 22.1.2 *The clusters of the collection $\mathcal{S}(W)$ defined by Procedure SEP_RULE_PART are guaranteed to be connected.* $\square$

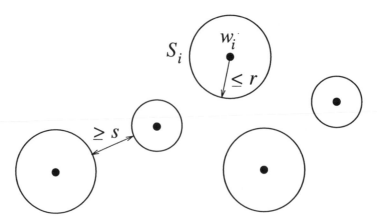

Figure 22.1: An (s, r)-partition – schematic description.

---

1. **For** every vertex $v \in V$ **do:**

    (a) Define the *v-weight* of any vertex $w_i \in W$ as the pair $\langle dist(w_i, v), ID(w_i) \rangle$.

    (b) Order the vertices of W lexicographically by their v-weights.

    (c) Set *leader(v)* to be the vertex $w_i \in W$ of minimum v-weight.
      /* i.e., satisfying for every $j \neq i$, **either** $dist(w_i, v) < dist(w_j, v)$
      or $dist(w_i, v) = dist(w_j, v)$ and $ID(w_i) < ID(w_j)$. */

2. For every $1 \leq i \leq m$, set $S_i = \{v \mid leader(v) = w_i\}$.

Figure 22.2: Procedure SEP_RULE_PART.

Note also that given W, the construction of $S(W)$ can be performed in a distributed manner (in our synchronous, congestion-free model) by constructing a BFS tree from each vertex $w \in W$ (in parallel), truncating each tree upon colliding with contending trees started at the other vertices of W and resolving ties by the rule of Procedure SEP_RULE_PART. This construction requires time $O(r)$, using an appropriate variant of Algorithm FLOOD of Chapter 3 (see Exercise 3).

Let us now restrict ourselves to unweighted graphs. Consider a set of vertices U with distinct K-bit identifiers for $K = O(\log n)$. Let us next describe a recursive procedure named SR(U) for constructing a $(3, 2K)$-set $W(U)$ for U (or more precisely, for the induced graph $G(U)$). Each vertex $v \in U$ maintains a bit variable $\hat{b}_v$ set to 1 if v joins $W(U)$ and 0 otherwise.

Let us first give a global outline of the procedure. If $|U| = 1$, then it returns the single vertex $v \in U$ as the required set. Otherwise, it separates the set U into two sets, U_0 and U_1, according to the last bit in the vertex identifiers and recursively computes a $(3, 2K - 2)$-set W_i for each set U_i by invoking SR(U_0) and SR(U_1). The resulting set $W = W_1 \cup W_2$ is clearly $(2K - 2)$-ruling, but it might no longer be 3-separated. To restore the desired separation, the procedure then erases from W_1 every vertex that is "too close" to some vertex of W_0 (which may in turn increase the ruling distance by 2).

To describe the algorithm from the point of view of a single vertex, we feed the recursive procedure SR with a parameter x which is a binary string of $\ell = |x| \leq K$ bits. Let $U_x \subseteq U$ denote the collection of (up to $2^{K-\ell}$) vertices whose ID ends with the suffix x. The procedure is applied to a set U_x and returns with a $(3, 2(K - \ell))$-set for the vertices of U_x.

---

1. Let $ID(v) = a_1 a_2 \ldots a_K$.

2. Set $\ell \leftarrow |x|$.

3. If $\ell = K$, then set $\hat{b}_v \leftarrow 1$ and **Return**.   /* singleton $U_x = \{v\}$ */

4. Set $b \leftarrow a_{K-\ell}$.

5. $\hat{b}_v \leftarrow \mathrm{SR}(bx)$.

6. **If** $b = 1$ and there exists a vertex $u \in U_{0x}$ such that $dist(u,v) \leq 2$ and $\hat{b}_u = 1$,
   then $\hat{b}_v \leftarrow 0$.

Figure 22.3: Procedure SR(x) (code for vertex v).

Procedure SR is described in Figure 22.3.

Letting λ denote the empty word, we make the following claim.

Lemma 22.1.3 *Procedure* SR(λ) *produces a* $(3, 2K)$-*set for the network* G, *and* Time(SR(λ)) $= O(\log n)$.

Proof: To establish the correctness of the construction, we prove by induction on ℓ the length of the string x handed to the procedure as parameter (starting with $\ell = K$) that SR(x) produces a $(3, 2(K - \ell))$-set for the vertices of $G(U_x)$, the subgraph induced by U_x. The base case is immediate, and the general case is proved as follows. Consider the execution of SR(x). First note that the set W_b (for $b = 0, 1$) is a $(3, 2(K - (\ell+1)))$-set for U_{bx} (by the inductive assumption). The 3-separation might be violated by taking $W = W_0 \cup W_1$, but it is restored by the algorithm by eliminating from W every vertex $w \in W_1$ that is too close to some vertex of W_0. It remains to prove that the ruling distance is not increased too much. For a vertex $v \in U_{0x} \setminus W_0$, the vertex ruling it in W_0 still rules it in W. The same applies to vertices $v \in U_{1x} \setminus W_1$ whose ruling vertex in W_1 was not eliminated. The only problem is with vertices $v \in U_{1x} \setminus W_1$ whose ruling vertex $w \in W_1$ was eliminated due to the existence of some $w' \in W_0$ such that $dist(w, w') \leq 2$. But then, by the inductive hypothesis,

$$dist(v, w') \leq dist(v, w) + dist(w, w') \leq 2(K - (\ell+1)) + 2 = 2(K - \ell),$$

as required.

As for the time bound, it follows from the fact that each level of the recursion requires $O(1)$ time units, and there are $K = O(\log n)$ levels.   □

Corollary 22.1.4 *Algorithm* SR(V) *produces a* $(3, 2 \log n)$-*set on the given unweighted n-vertex graph* $G = (V, E)$ *and requires* $O(\log n)$ *time.*   □

22.2 Decomposition construction

We now describe a recursive procedure DIST_DECOMP(U) producing a (d, c)-decomposition $\mathcal{T}$ for the graph $G(U)$ induced by U. The procedure uses an integer parameter θ, to be determined later. The procedure will color only clusters with degree θ or less and will therefore produce a decomposition with $c \leq \theta$ colors. (Henceforth we use the term *colored decomposition* to refer to a decomposition along with an appropriate coloring for it.) A high-level description of the procedure (yielding a colored decomposition) is given in Figure 22.4.

1. Split the vertices of U into two sets according to their degrees, setting

$$H \quad \leftarrow \quad \{v \in U \mid deg(v) \geq \theta\},$$
$$L \quad \leftarrow \quad U \setminus H.$$

2. Invoke Procedure RECURSECOLOR(L), coloring L in colors φ from 1 through θ.

3. Construct a $(3, 2 \log n)$-set W for $G(H)$ and a corresponding $(3, 2 \log n)$-partition $\mathcal{S}(W)$.

4. Construct the (logical) cluster graph $\tilde{G}(\mathcal{S})$ obtained by contracting each cluster $S_i \in \mathcal{S}$ into a single vertex s_i (in actuality represented by the leader w_i). Let $U(\mathcal{S}) \leftarrow \{s_i \mid S_i \in \mathcal{S}\}$.

5. Invoke Procedure DIST_DECOMP($U(\mathcal{S})$) recursively and obtain a colored decomposition T' for $U(\mathcal{S})$ (with coloring φ).

6. **For** round $i = 1$ through θ **do:**

   For every vertex $v \in L$ with $\varphi_v = i$ (in parallel) **do:**

   $\varphi_v \leftarrow$ FIRST_FREE($\Gamma(v), \mathcal{P}_\theta$), where $\Gamma(v)$ consists of v's neighboring vertices in $L \cup U(\mathcal{S})$.

   Inform neighbors in L of new color.

7. Return $T' \cup L$ (with coloring φ).

Figure 22.4: Procedure DIST_DECOMP(U) (global description).

One element of this algorithm that needs to be explained in more detail is how to execute an algorithm on the (logical) cluster graph $\tilde{G}(\mathcal{S})$ obtained by contracting clusters into single vertices. As mentioned in the algorithm, this logical graph is simulated by representing each super-vertex s_i (corresponding to a cluster S_i) by the leader w_i of the cluster. Communication of s_i with a neighboring s_j must therefore be carried out by message exchanges between the respective leaders w_i and w_j. The implication on complexity is immediate.

Analysis

Lemma 22.2.1 $|W| \leq n/(\theta + 1)$.

Proof: Note that since W is 3-separated, the 1-neighborhoods $\Gamma(w_i)$ are all disjoint and since each w_i has degree θ or higher in U, each such neighborhood contains at least $\theta + 1$ vertices of U (although it might contain fewer vertices in $G(H)$). □

Lemma 22.2.2 $Rad(w_i, S_i) \leq 2 \log n$. □

It follows that if T' is a (d', c)-decomposition for $U(\mathcal{S})$, then in the original graph G it is an $(c_1 \log n \cdot d', c)$-decomposition for H for some constant $c_1 > 0$.

Also, letting $T(n)$ denote the running time of Procedure DIST_DECOMP(U) on U, we have

$$T(n) \leq \log n + \theta \log n + c_1 \log n \cdot T\left(\frac{n}{\theta}\right).$$

The first term is the cost of constructing the $(3, 2\log n)$-set W, the second is the cost of coloring the set L (twice) and the last term is the cost of the recursive step, magnified by the slowdown due to the need to simulate the execution on $U(\mathcal{S})$ by the cluster leaders.

Letting ℓ denote the number of levels of the recursion needed until $H = \emptyset$, we have that $\ell = \log n / \log \theta$ and therefore

$$T(n) \leq \theta \log n \cdot (c_1 \log n)^{\ell+1}.$$

Setting $\theta = (c_1 \log n)^{\ell+1}$ gives a bound of $2^{c_0 \sqrt{\log n \log \log n}}$ on θ, c, d and $T(n)$ for some constant $c_0 > 0$.

Theorem 22.2.3 *There exists a deterministic distributed algorithm for constructing a $(2^\epsilon, 2^\epsilon)$-decomposition for a given unweighted n-vertex graph in time $O(2^\epsilon)$, for $\epsilon = \sqrt{c_0 \log n \log \log n}$ for some constant $c_0 > 0$.* $\square$

Bibliographical notes

The concept of network decomposition and the first fast algorithm for that problem were introduced in [AGLP89]. The deterministic distributed algorithm of [AGLP89] yielded a $(2^\epsilon, 2^\epsilon)$-decomposition of an arbitrary network in time $O(2^\epsilon)$ for $\epsilon = c_0 \sqrt{\log n \log \log n}$ for some constant $c_0 > 0$. This was later improved to $\epsilon = c_0 \sqrt{\log n}$ in [PS92b], which is currently the fastest known distributed algorithm for this problem.

In [ABCP92a] it is shown how to improve the resulting decomposition (though not the running time) and get an $(O(\log n), O(\log n))$-decomposition. Efficient *parallel* computation of decompositions was studied in [ABCP92b]. Faster sequential construction (linear in $|E|$) was given in [Cow94].

Exercises

1. Prove that if we form a collection of clusters $\mathcal{S}$ for a given (s, r)-set W by placing each vertex $v \notin W$ arbitrarily in some cluster S_i such that $dist(w_i, v) \leq dist(w_j, v)$ for every $j \neq i$, then $\mathcal{S}$ might contain disconnected clusters.

2. Prove Lemma 22.1.2.

3. Describe and prove the variant of Algorithm FLOOD of Chapter 3 needed to construct $\mathcal{S}$ for a given (s, r)-set W. (See Lemma 3.3.2.)

4. Let G^k denote the kth power of the graph $G = (V, E)$, namely, the graph $G' = (V, E')$ defined by $E' = \{(v, w) \mid dist_G(v, w) \leq k\}$. Prove that the set W is an MIS in G^k iff it is a $(k+1, k)$-set in G.

5. More generally, prove that the set W is an (s, r)-set in G^k iff it is an $((s-1)k+1, rk)$-set in G.

Chapter 23

Exploiting topological knowledge: Broadcast revisited

We now turn to illustrating the applicability of LP-representations in the area of distributed network algorithms via revisiting some distributed tasks introduced in Part I. In particular, this chapter deals with the fundamental paradigm of broadcast.

23.1 Restricted flooding using preconstructed structures

23.1.1 Quality measure

In this section we take a fresh look at the broadcast operation, not as an internal control operation of the system but as a service provided to the end-users of the network. As such, it may be appropriate to evaluate the efficiency of a broadcast protocol using quality measures similar to those applied to routing protocols in Section 9.3. In particular, let us define a quality measure analogous to the Dilation measure defined for routing schemes, based on the communication cost measure Comm, i.e., where the "actual delivery time" of a message is measured by the weighted length of the route traversed by the message. This measure concerns the worst-case delay in the delivery time of the message incurred for each of the recipients individually.

Given a broadcast protocol Π and a weighted network $G = (V, E, \omega)$, let $\mathsf{Comm}(\Pi, v)$ denote the communication cost (representing the actual delivery time) of routing a message from the broadcast source vertex r_0 to the destination v using the protocol Π. The cheapest possible cost (or lowest possible time) for delivering a message from the broadcast source to the destination v is $dist(r_0, v)$.

Definition 23.1.1 [Broadcast dilation]: *Given a broadcast protocol Π and a weighted network $G = (V, E, \omega)$, the* dilation factor *for a particular destination v is the ratio between the communication cost $\mathsf{Comm}(\Pi, v)$ and the optimal cost required for this task, $dist(r_0, v)$,*

$$\mathsf{Dilation}(\Pi, v) \; = \; \frac{\mathsf{Comm}(\Pi, v)}{dist(r_0, v)} \; .$$

Define the maximum dilation factor *of the broadcast protocol Π on the network G to be*

$$\mathsf{Dilation}(\Pi, G) \; = \; \max_{v \in V} \{\mathsf{Dilation}(\Pi, v)\}.$$

Let us reconsider Algorithms FLOOD and TCAST of Chapter 3 and this time look also at the delay-related cost measures Comm and Dilation. We have the following bounds.

Lemma 23.1.2

1. *Using a tree T,*

$$\mathsf{Comm}(\textsc{Tcast}) = \omega(T) \quad and \quad \mathsf{Dilation}(\textsc{Tcast}) = \mathtt{Stretch}(T, G).$$

2. *On a network G,*

$$\mathsf{Comm}(\textsc{Flood}) = \omega(G) \quad and \quad \mathsf{Dilation}(\textsc{Flood}) = \mathtt{Stretch}(G).$$

These bounds apply to both the synchronous and asynchronous models.   □

23.1.2   Flooding on a subgraph

The observation motivating the algorithm presented next is that the generic Algorithm FLOOD can be applied in a more controlled manner, avoiding the flooding of all edges. Let us denote by $\textsc{Flood}(G')$ the variant of FLOOD in which message flooding is restricted to the edges of the (spanning) subgraph G'. Namely, a vertex receiving the message for the first time forwards it only on those of its adjacent edges that belong to G'. The tree broadcast algorithm of Section 3.2 can actually be thought of as applying $\textsc{Flood}(T)$ on a spanning tree T.

An obvious prerequisite to the use of Algorithm $\textsc{Flood}(G')$ is that the subgraph G' is preconstructed and stored in the network. In particular, each vertex must know which of its adjacent edges belong to G'. Thus using this algorithm requires a preprocessing stage in which the subgraph is constructed and stored.

There is a natural relationship between the properties of the subgraph G' and the complexity measures of the resulting broadcast algorithm $\textsc{Flood}(G')$. Specifically, we have the following obvious connections.

Lemma 23.1.3 *The algorithm $\textsc{Flood}(G')$ for broadcasting on a subgraph G' has message complexity $\mathsf{Message}(\textsc{Flood}(G')) = |E(G')|$, communication cost $\mathsf{Comm}(\textsc{Flood}(G')) = \omega(G')$ and dilation factor $\mathsf{Dilation}(\textsc{Flood}(G')) = \mathtt{Stretch}(G').$*

23.1.3   Selecting an appropriate subgraph

Let us now consider the question of selecting an appropriate subgraph for performing restricted flooding. Lemma 23.1.3 indicates that in order for this approach to be effective with respect to our complexity measures, the selected subgraph G' should be both sparse (in terms of number of edges) and light-weight and should also have low stretch factor.

Tree broadcast revisited

As discussed earlier, the tree broadcast algorithm of Section 3.2 consists of executing $\textsc{Flood}(T)$ on a spanning tree T rooted at the source of the broadcast.

For a general spanning tree T, the relationships expressed in Lemma 23.1.3 yield $\mathsf{Message}(\textsc{Flood}(T)) = n - 1$ and $\mathsf{Comm}(\textsc{Flood}(T)) = \omega(T)$. Also, restricting ourselves to broadcasting from a vertex r_0 on a spanning tree T yields $\mathsf{Dilation}(\textsc{Flood}(T)) = \mathtt{Stretch}(T, r_0)$.

Clearly, the message complexity of this algorithm is optimal. The need to optimize the other two complexity measures brings us back to a question dealt with earlier (in Section

17.1), namely, bringing down $\omega(T)$ and $\texttt{Stretch}(T, r_0)$ simultaneously. Indeed, concentrating on the first of those measures has led researchers to propose that broadcast be performed on an MST, while concentrating on the second measure naturally leads to proposing the use of an SPT rooted at the source of the broadcast.

Using a light, low-stretch tree as constructed by Algorithm SLT in Section 17.1, we get the following by the SLT Theorem 17.1.4.

Theorem 23.1.4 *For every n-vertex weighted graph G and for every source v, there exists a spanning tree SLT_v providing a broadcast algorithm* $\text{FLOOD}(SLT_v)$ *with*

$$\begin{aligned}
\text{Message}(\text{FLOOD}(SLT_v)) &= n - 1, \\
\text{Comm}(\text{FLOOD}(SLT_v)) &= O(\omega(MST)) \\
\textit{and } \text{Dilation}(\text{FLOOD}(SLT_v)) &= O(1).
\end{aligned}$$

The main disadvantage of this tree-based approach for broadcast is that a tree that is efficient for one root may perform poorly for a different root with respect to the Dilation measure. Hence using this method requires us to maintain a *separate tree* for every possible broadcast source in the network. This requirement may lead to heavy memory requirements and update costs and complicate the control process at the vertices of the network.

Broadcasting on a light spanner

An alternative broadcast method, aimed at overcoming this difficulty, is based on the approach of performing $\text{FLOOD}(G')$ on a nontree spanner G' of G with the desired properties indicated by Lemma 23.1.3. Specifically, using a light, sparse, low-stretch spanner as constructed by Algorithm LIGHT_SPAN in Section 17.2, we get the following corollary by Theorem 17.2.15.

Corollary 23.1.5 *For every n-vertex weighted graph G and integer $\kappa \geq 1$, there exists a spanner G' providing every source v with a broadcast algorithm Π_v with* $\text{Message}(\Pi_v) = O(\kappa \cdot \Lambda \cdot n^{1+1/\kappa})$, $\text{Comm}(\Pi_v) = O(\kappa \cdot \Lambda \cdot n^{1/\kappa} \cdot \omega(MST))$ *and* $\text{Dilation}(\Pi_v) = O(\kappa)$. $\square$

Setting $\kappa = \log n$ we get a broadcast algorithm $\text{FLOOD}(G')$ whose complexities are optimal up to a polylogarithmic factor in all three measures.

Theorem 23.1.6 *For every n-vertex weighted graph G, there exists a spanner LWS such that Algorithm $\text{FLOOD}(LWS)$ has complexities*

$$\begin{aligned}
\text{Message}(\text{FLOOD}(LWS)) &= O(n \cdot \log n \cdot \Lambda), \\
\text{Comm}(\text{FLOOD}(LWS)) &= O(\log n \cdot \Lambda \cdot \omega(MST)) \\
\textit{and } \text{Dilation}(\text{FLOOD}(LWS)) &= O(\log n). \qquad \square
\end{aligned}$$

Figure 23.1 summarizes the above discussion by comparing the complexities of the various options presented.

23.2 Topological knowledge and broadcast

So far we have assumed that some preconstructed structure exists in the network and can be used for performing the broadcast operation. Let us now focus on the case where no preconstructed structures exist in the network (i.e., the broadcast operation has to be performed "from scratch") and study the inherent complexity of the broadcast problem in such a case. We will focus mainly on the message complexity of the problem.

Algorithm	Message	Comm	Dilation	Time	Mem
FLOOD	$\|E\|$	$\omega(G)$	1	$Diam(G)$	0
FLOOD(MST)	n	$\omega(MST)$	n	n	Δ^C
FLOOD(SPT)	n	$n \cdot \omega(MST)$	$Diam(G)$	$Diam(G)$	Δ^C
FLOOD(SLT)	n	$\omega(MST)$	$Diam(G)$	$Diam(G)$	Δ^C
n SLT trees	n	$\omega(MST)$	1	$Diam(G)$	$n\Delta^C$
FLOOD(LWS)	$n\Lambda$ $\cdot \log n$	$\Lambda \cdot \omega(MST)$ $\cdot \log n$	$\log n$	$Diam(G)$ $\cdot \log n$	Λ $\cdot \log n$

Figure 23.1: Comparison of various broadcast algorithms. (In all of the tree constructions, Δ^C can be made $O(n^{1/\kappa})$ at the cost of increasing Dilation and Time by a factor of κ.)

23.2.1   Three models of topological knowledge

When discussing the applicability of various broadcast algorithms to a communication network, a central issue is the amount of knowledge available at the vertices regarding the topology of the network. The model assumed so far allows the use of preconstructed structures. Turning to the case where no preconstructed structures exist in the network, there are three commonly studied models, representing two possible extreme situations of knowledge.

In the first model (which we denote KT_∞ for reasons which will become clear later), one assumes that every vertex has full knowledge of the network topology. In this model, broadcast can be performed with the minimal number of messages, i.e., the message complexity of the problem is Message $= \Theta(n)$. This is because each vertex can use its knowledge in order to locally construct the (same) spanning tree T without sending any message. Then the tree broadcast Algorithm FLOOD(T) of Section 23.1 can be applied.

At the other extreme are two models, which we denote KT_0 and KT_1. The model KT_0, earlier referred to as the *clean network* model, is based on the assumption that a vertex knows nothing on the topology, not even the identities of its neighbors. (This model is not to be confused with the anonymous model, in which no identifiers are available at all.) The model KT_1 assumes only a little more knowledge than KT_0. That is, initially each processor knows only its own identity and the identity of its neighbors, but nothing else.

23.2.2   Topological knowledge and message complexity of broadcast

For the model KT_0, it is known that flooding is the best that can be done as far as message complexity is considered. That is, $\Theta(|E|)$ is a tight bound for the message complexity of the broadcast problem. This lower bound is based on the intuition that every edge must be traversed at least once.

Lemma 23.2.1 *Every algorithm for broadcast under the model KT_0 must send at least one message over every edge of the network.*

Proof: Suppose that there exists a broadcast algorithm Π disobeying this claim, and consider a graph G and an edge $e = (u, w)$ in it such that Π has an execution η which completes broadcast on G without sending any message over e. Then G can be replaced by a graph G' whose topology is identical to G except that G' contains two new vertices u' and w' and the edge e is replaced by two edges $e_1 = (u, w')$ and $e_2 = (u', w)$. (See Figure 23.2.)

Since the network is clean, u and w cannot distinguish between the two topologies. Clearly, no other vertex can distinguish between these topologies either. It follows that

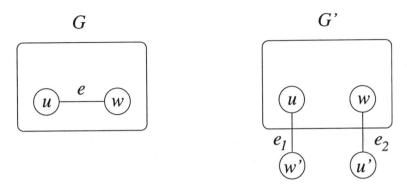

Figure 23.2: The graphs G and G'.

algorithm Π can be executed over G' in exactly the same way. More formally, we argue that algorithm Π has an execution η' over G' such that η and η' are *identical* in the sense that in each round, each processor is in the same local state and it sends and receives the same messages throughout both executions. (Note that in the synchronous model, both η and η' are unique.)

It follows that in execution η' of Π over G', u and w will fail to forward the message to u' and w'. So these two vertices will not get the message, contradicting the assumption that Π is a (correct) broadcast algorithm. $\square$

Theorem 23.2.2 *Every broadcast protocol Π for the model KT_0 has message complexity* Message(Π) $= \Omega(|E|)$. $\square$

23.3 The message complexity of broadcast in KT_1

Although the models KT_0 and KT_1 are close to each other, there are important differences between them as far as broadcast is concerned. An interesting observation that illustrates this is that in the KT_1 model, the intuition behind Lemma 23.2.1 fails. This is implied by the following algorithm for performing broadcast in the model KT_1.

23.3.1 The traveler algorithm

Consider a "traveler" (or a "token" message, representing the algorithm's center of activity) that performs a DFS traversal on the communication graph. The traveler carries with it the list L of the vertices it has visited so far. Whenever the traveler is at a vertex v and needs to pick the next neighbor to be visited, it compares the list L with the list of v's neighbors and makes its next choice only from among those neighbors that are not yet in L. If all neighbors of v have already been visited, the traveler backtracks on the edge from which it originally arrived at v.

Note that the use of the list L enables the traveler to restrict its "forward" steps to a *tree* spanning the network (specifically, a *DFS tree*) and avoid traversing nontree edges (or "backward" edges). Thus the traveler will not traverse every graph edge, but only the $n-1$ tree edges, each being traversed exactly twice.

While this broadcast algorithm, named Algorithm TRAVELER, indicates that there is no need to traverse every graph edge, it does not disprove the $\Omega(|E|)$ lower bound. Indeed, observe that the total number of *basic* ($O(\log n)$ bit) messages sent by this algorithm is not $2n$, but rather $\Theta(n^2)$, as the lists carried by the traveler may contain up to $\Omega(n)$ vertex identifiers; thus the traversal of an edge may require up to $\Omega(n)$ basic messages. This behavior is no coincidence, as we shall see later on.

23.3.2   The lower bound proof

The lower bound can be proven even if we restrict ourselves to the synchronous communication model in which communication takes place in "rounds", with processors transmitting only in the very beginning of a round and all messages received by the end of the round. Clearly, any lower bound proven for the synchronous model will hold also for asynchronous networks. On the other hand, the proof as sketched next is only applicable to deterministic algorithms. (Nevertheless, the lower bound holds also for randomized algorithms.)

Let us now sketch the essential idea behind the proof of the $\Omega(|E|)$ lower bound on the message complexity of broadcast algorithms in the model KT_1. Intuitively, we would like to follow the logic of the proof of Lemma 23.2.1. Unfortunately, the basic premise of the lemma's proof, namely, that "every edge must be traversed," fails for the model KT_1, as demonstrated by Algorithm TRAVELER. However, a closer inspection of this algorithm reveals that it can only escape traversing a particular edge e by letting one endpoint of e know that the other has already got the message. This, in turn, can only be done by sending *some* message to this endpoint, which is at least as expensive as traversing the edge e itself. Hence intuitively we may say that in such a scenario the edge e has been "utilized," just as if a message has actually crossed it. It is this observation that our proof should capture formally by appropriately defining the notion of "edge utilization" and by proving that one way or another, all edges must be utilized.

Recall that initially, each vertex v in the graph G is assigned a unique identifier $ID(v)$, taken from an ordered set of integers $S = \{s_1 < s_2 < \cdots\}$, so that the system configuration consists of a pair (G, ID), where $ID : V \mapsto S$ is the ID-assignment. Also recall that we assume that each s_i is represented by a string of $c \log n$ bits for constant c, hence an identifier can be included in a single basic message. More specifically, let us require that a basic message may contain up to B vertex identifiers for some constant B.

Definition 23.3.1 [Edge utilization]: *We say that an edge $e = (u, v) \in E$ is* utilized *during an execution of the protocol Π on the graph (G, ID) if at least one of the following three events takes place:*

1. *A message is sent on e.*

2. *Processor u either sends or receives a message containing $ID(v)$.*

3. *Processor v either sends or receives a message containing $ID(u)$.*

We now claim that the number of messages sent during a given execution and the number of edges utilized during that execution are closely related.

Lemma 23.3.2 *Let m denote the number of utilized edges in an execution of protocol Π on the network (G, ID), and let M denote the number of (basic) messages sent during the execution. Then $M = \Omega(m)$.*

Proof: Consider a message transmitted over the edge $e = (u, v)$. This message contains the identifiers of at most B vertices, say, $z_1, \ldots, z_B$. Each of these vertices z_i may cause at most two edges to become utilized, namely, (u, z_i) and (v, z_i) (if they exist). In addition, the edge e itself becomes utilized. It follows that the number of edges that may get utilized by a single message is at most $2B + 1$ and therefore $m \leq (2B + 1)M$. Recalling that B is a constant, the lemma follows. $\quad\square$

It follows that in order to prove our lower bound, it is sufficient to provide a lower bound on the number of edges utilized by the algorithm on our networks. The lower bound proof is centered around the following lemma.

Lemma 23.3.3 *Every deterministic algorithm for broadcast under the model KT_1 must utilize every edge of the network.*

Proof Sketch: Suppose that there exists a broadcast algorithm Π disobeying this claim, and consider a graph G and an edge $e = (u, w)$ in it such that Π completes broadcast on G without utilizing e. As in Lemma 23.2.1, our proof revolves on showing that in this case, algorithm Π must fail to broadcast on the modified network G' of Figure 23.2.

We would like to argue that u and w must "hear" of one another during any execution of a broadcast protocol on G. The intuition behind the proof is that in case e is not utilized, no processor in the network can distinguish the case in which it takes part in the execution η on G from the case in which it takes part in the execution η' on G'. The only potential difference between these executions lies in whether u and v are neighbors or not where $e = (u, v)$. But this neighborhood relation cannot be tested if no messages bearing the identifier of one processor are communicated from/to the other.

There are two main difficulties in making this intuition more precise. The first is that the protocol Π may in general use the topological knowledge of vertices in arbitrary ways. This forces us to take into account the possibility that the protocol may have some way of taking advantage of the fact that u stores a different identifier of its neighbor over e in G and G'.

For simplicity, we shall bypass this difficulty in this proof sketch by restricting the power of the protocol and limiting the kinds of operations that it may apply to the vertex identifiers. Specifically, we shall confine ourselves to the model of *comparison* protocols by limiting the allowed local computations involving processor identifiers to comparing two identifiers.

In the comparison model, it is possible to select ID-assignments ID and ID' such that the configuration (G', ID') essentially "preserves" the execution of Π over the configuration (G, ID). Specifically, we would like ID' to look like ID for all the original vertices of G, and in addition, we would like w' to look like w to u, and u' to look like u to w. Since only comparisons are allowed, this requires only that the identifiers $ID'(u)$ and $ID'(u')$ behave identically with respect to comparisons with any other identifier in the network and similarly for the identifiers $ID'(w)$ and $ID'(w')$. This can be achieved, e.g., by making the assignments ID and ID' select the even integers in the range 2 through $2n$ for the vertices of G and taking $ID'(u) = ID(u) + 1$ and $ID'(w) = ID(w) + 1$.

The second difficulty in formalizing the intuition outlined earlier is that unlike the proof of Lemma 23.2.1, here it is *not* true that the executions η and η' are identical. Recall that an execution η is an alternating sequence of configurations and events,

$$\eta = (C_0, \phi_1, C_1, \phi_2, C_2, \cdots).$$

Note that the local states of the processors u and w are different in the executions η and η' since they contain different neighbor identifiers. Moreover, the local states of the processors u' and w' exist *only* in η'. Hence the configurations occurring in η and η' are inherently different.

The crucial point is that given these two ID-assignments, the executions of Π on (G, ID) and (G', ID'), henceforth denoted η and η', are "externally similar." By this we mean that the subsequences consisting of the *message events* which take place in the two executions are identical.

In fact, proving this property involves implicitly proving a stronger resemblance between the executions, including identical local states at all vertices other than u, w, u' and w' and an order-preserving correspondence among the ID-variables stored at u, w, u' and w' in the two executions. More specifically, suppose that u has k ID-variables $X_1, \ldots, X_k$. (There are no other inputs in our setting.) For every $t \geq 1$, let $X_i[t]$ and $X_i'[t]$ denote the values of the variable X_i after step t of the executions η and η', respectively. Then for every $t \geq 1$ and $1 \leq i < j \leq k$, we have $X_i[t] > X_j[t]$ iff $X_i'[t] > X_j'[t]$ and $X_i[t] < X_j[t]$ iff $X_i'[t] < X_j'[t]$. The same holds for w, u' and w'.

Definition 23.3.4 [Externally similar executions]: *The executions η and η' are externally similar if the messages sent by each processor over each edge of the network in each round of these two executions are identical.*

In particular, the definition implies that no messages were sent over edges of G' that do not exist in G.

Lemma 23.3.5 *The executions η and η' are externally similar.*

Proof Sketch: Let us suppose, to the contrary, that the two executions η and η' deviate and examine the first round t in which this happens. Let us consider the processor z that is the first to deviate (i.e., send different messages in the two executions).

Note that any vertex other than u or w maintains identical local views in η and η' at any time up to round t, since in both executions it starts with identical input and topological knowledge and receives the same messages. Consequently, since the algorithm Π is deterministic, such a vertex will behave the same at round t as well. Hence z must be either u or w.

It remains to argue that u or w cannot deviate either, leading to a contradiction. For this, we rely on the observation that, since only comparisons are allowed on vertex identifiers, the set of identifiers locally known to a vertex can be thought of as ordered and the only information that can be used on these identifiers involves their relative location in this ordering.

Note that the information received by u up to round t does not contain the identifier of w (since the edge e is not utilized in the execution of Π over (G, ID)). Consequently, at the beginning of round t, the information u possesses locally (restricted to comparisons) is identical in η and η'. That is, it knows exactly the same number of identifiers in both executions, with $ID(w)$ and $ID'(w')$ occurring in the same relative location on the list of known identifiers in η and η', respectively. (This would be different had u received a message containing $ID(w)$, since then the number of distinct identifiers u knows in η' is larger by one than in η.)

Hence every comparison made by u would yield the same result in the two executions and the outcome of u's local computation at round t must be the same in both executions. Since the messages sent by u in round t of η do not contain $ID(w)$ (again, since e is assumed not to have been utilized in η), its messages in η' do not contain $ID'(w')$ either and hence the messages sent by it in the two executions must be identical. Hence u cannot be the one to deviate. A similar argument applies to w, leading to the desired contradiction.   □

This enables us to complete the proof of the lemma by noting that the fact that η and η' must be externally similar implies that in G', no messages are sent over the edges leading to u' and w', implying that algorithm Π fails to perform broadcast on (G', ID') and thus contradicting the fact that Π is a broadcast protocol.   □

Theorem 23.3.6 *Every deterministic broadcast protocol* Π *for the model* KT_1 *has message complexity* Message(Π) $= \Omega(|E|)$. $\square$

The lower bound is shown for synchronous networks, but it clearly holds also if communication is asynchronous. It can be made to work even when the vertices know the size of the network (by working with graphs G, G' of the same size). The proof can be modified to apply to randomized protocols as well. Finally, using a Ramsey Theory argument, the theorem can be shown to hold also for deterministic protocols in an unrestricted model of computation in which vertices are allowed to perform arbitrary operations on vertex identifiers.

Another interesting observation is that the theorem no longer holds if, in addition to arbitrary computations, we allow protocols with time unbounded in terms of the network topology. This is because once such behavior is allowed, one may encode an unbounded number of identifiers by the choice of transmission round and hence implement, say, Algorithm TRAVELER. (This clearly relates only to the synchronous communication model. In the asynchronous model such encoding is impossible!)

An interesting corollary to Theorem 23.3.6 is that constructing a spanning tree in a network whose topology is *unknown* is harder than constructing a spanning tree in a network whose topology is *known*.

23.4 Partial topological knowledge

23.4.1 A hierarchy of topological knowledge models

Once we establish this gap between the extreme models KT_∞ and KT_1 (or KT_0), it becomes interesting to look at intermediate points in which processors are allowed only partial knowledge of the topology and investigate the implications of such knowledge with regard to the message complexity of the broadcast operation. These intermediate points attempt to capture common situations in which vertices know more about their nearby vicinity than about other regions of the network.

We formalize such situations by introducing a hierarchy of models KT_κ on unweighted graphs $G = (V, E)$ (for every integer $\kappa \geq 0$) in which, loosely speaking, every vertex knows the structure of its κ-neighborhood, or more precisely, the topology of a subgraph of radius κ around it, $G(\Gamma_\kappa(v))$. Hence the models KT_0 and KT_1 described earlier correspond to the lowest two levels of this hierarchy, while KT_∞ corresponds to the highest levels, i.e., the models KT_κ with κ being the diameter of the network or larger.

In fact, this intuitive definition is slightly incompatible with our previous definition for KT_1. According to our original definition of KT_1, a vertex v should know only its adjacent edges. In contrast, according to the new neighborhood-based definition, in KT_1 a vertex v knows also which pairs of its neighbors are connected by edges.

To ensure the compatibility between the two definitions, it is possible to modify our general definition of KT_κ as follows. For every $v \in V$ and $e = (u, w) \in E$ denote

$$dist(v, e) \; = \; \min\{dist(v, u), dist(v, w)\}.$$

In the model KT_κ, each vertex v knows all (and only) the edges e such that $dist(v, e) < \kappa$.

According to this definition (which conforms with our earlier definitions of KT_0, KT_1 and KT_∞), for general $\kappa \geq 1$, v knows almost all the induced subgraph $G(\Gamma_\kappa(v))$; the only "unknowns" are the (possible) edges connecting two vertices at distance exactly κ from v. (We comment that the results shown next for general κ hold with only small changes under both definitions.)

23.4.2   The information-communication trade-off

For the hierarchy of models KT_κ, a general trade-off result holds. For every fixed $\kappa \geq 1$, the number of basic messages required for broadcast in the model KT_κ is $\Theta(\min\{|E|, n^{1+\frac{\Theta(1)}{\kappa}}\})$.

The lower bound is proved by mimicking the proof sketched earlier for the case of the model KT_1, only restricting our attention to graphs G of $Girth(G) \geq 2\kappa + 1$. Defining a *short cycle* as one of length 2κ or less, such graphs contain no short cycles.

Given a graph G, the modified graph G' is constructed as follows. First, eliminate the edge $e = (u, v)$ from G, obtaining a graph H. Next, construct copies of the $(k-1)$-neighborhoods of u and w in H, marking the copy of each vertex z by z'. (Note that given our assumption on the girth of G, the subgraphs induced by these neighborhoods must be trees.) Finally, attach these copies to H by adding the edges $e_1 = (u, w')$ and $e_2 = (w, u')$. (See Figure 23.3.)

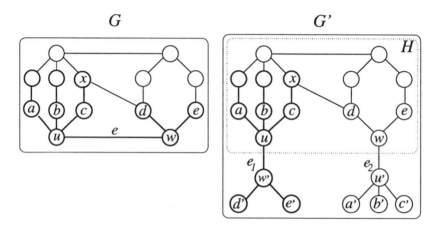

Figure 23.3: An example of a graph G and the corresponding G' for $\kappa = 2$. Here G has girth 5. Bold edges and vertices are those visible from u. (Note that the edge (x, d) is not visible from u.)

Intuitively, in a graph G of girth $2\kappa+1$ or higher, the extra topological knowledge (which, pictorially, provides vertices with "vision to distance κ") cannot be used for "cross-checking" since the picture seen from any vertex u in G and G' is indistinguishable up to this distance. (In contrast, if the girth of the graph G is 2κ or smaller, then a vertex z residing opposite u on a "short" cycle (of length $\leq 2\kappa$) with u and w is "seen twice" by u in G, whereas in G', u sees two different vertices z and z' with distinct identifiers, hence the two settings are distinguishable.)

However, since graphs with such girth have a relatively low number of edges (by Lemma 15.1.2), we can only prove the following lemma.

Lemma 23.4.1 *There exists a constant $c' > 0$ such that for every two integers $\kappa, n \geq 1$ there exists an n-vertex unweighted graph $G = (V, E)$ with $Girth(G) \geq 2\kappa$, where $|E| = \Omega(n^{1+\frac{c'}{\kappa}})$, such that any protocol for broadcast in the model KT_κ must utilize at least $\Omega(|E|/\kappa)$ edges of G.* $\square$

Theorem 23.4.2 *There exists a constant $c > 0$ such that for every integer $\kappa \geq 1$ and n-vertex unweighted graph $G = (V, E)$, every broadcast protocol Π for the model KT_κ has message complexity $\mathsf{Message}(\Pi) = \Omega(\min\{|E|, n^{1+\frac{c}{\kappa}}\})$.* $\square$

Again, this lower bound holds even if the network is synchronous, all the vertices start the protocol at the same round and the size of the network is known to each vertex.

This lower bound, and the corresponding upper bound described next, suggests that there exists an inherent trade-off between the information that the vertices have about the communication graph and the number of messages needed to perform the broadcast. The more knowledgeable vertices are about the network, the cheaper it is to perform broadcast.

23.4.3 The $\kappa - $ FLOOD algorithm

In this section we match the above lower bound for KT_κ by showing that for any integer $\kappa \geq 1$ and for any connected graph $G = (V, E)$ in the model KT_κ, broadcast can be performed with at most $O(\min\{|E|, n^{1+\frac{c}{\kappa}}\})$ messages for some constant $c > 0$.

The key observation behind the algorithm is that if a vertex knows all the edges at distance κ or less from it, then it can detect all short cycles (i.e., of length 2κ or less) going through it. This enables us to disconnect all short cycles locally by deleting one edge in each such cycle.

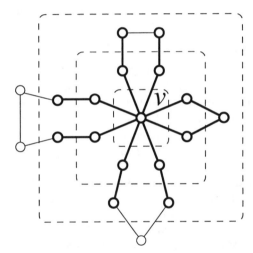

Figure 23.4: An example of cycles detectable in KT_κ for $\kappa = 2$. Bold edges and vertices are those visible from u.

Algorithm $\kappa - $ FLOOD

Assume some (locally computable) assignment of distinct weights to the edges. For example, label each edge $e = (u, w)$ by the pair $(ID(u), ID(w))$ of its endpoint identifiers and interpret these labels as weights by comparing them lexicographically.

Define a subgraph $\bar{G} = (V, \bar{E})$ of G by marking the heaviest edge in every short cycle "unusable" and including precisely all unmarked edges in $\bar{E}$.

Note that only the vertices incident to an edge e are required to know whether or not e is usable. Therefore, given the partial topological knowledge of the vertices, such edge deletions can be performed locally by the vertices incident to each edge without sending a single message.

Now perform broadcast by applying Algorithm FLOOD($\bar{G}$) on the remaining graph $\bar{G}$. That is, whenever a vertex receives the message for the first time, it sends it over all the usable edges $e \in \bar{E}$ incident to it.

Lemma 23.4.3 *If G is connected, then $\bar{G}$ is connected as well.*   □

An immediate consequence of the marking process used to define $\bar{G}$ is that all short cycles are disconnected and hence we have the following lemma.

Lemma 23.4.4 *The girth of $\bar{G}$ satisfies $Girth(\bar{G}) \geq 2\kappa + 1$.*   □

From Lemma 23.4.4 and Part (1) of Lemma 15.1.2 we conclude the following.

Corollary 23.4.5 $|\bar{E}| = O(n^{1+\frac{c}{\kappa}})$ *for a constant $c > 0$.*

Consequently, Algorithm $\kappa -$ FLOOD requires $O(|\bar{E}|) = O(n^{1+\frac{c}{\kappa}})$ messages. This completes the proof of the following theorem.

Theorem 23.4.6 *There exists a constant $c > 0$ such that for every integer $\kappa \geq 1$ and for every n-vertex unweighted graph $G = (V, E)$, Algorithm $\kappa -$ FLOOD performs broadcast in the model KT_κ and the number of messages it uses is* $\mathsf{Message}(\kappa -$ FLOOD$) = O(\min\{|E|, n^{1+\frac{c}{\kappa}}\})$.   □

Note that this upper bound holds even if the network is asynchronous.

Bibliographical notes

The results of Section 23.1 are due to [ABP91].

The results concerning the knowledge-communication trade-off exhibited by distributed broadcast protocols are taken from [AGPV90]. (The proof therein covers also the extended cases of randomized protocols and unrestricted computational power.) Essentially the same lower bound for the KT_1 case has been independently obtained by [RK87] (except the lower bound of [RK87] does not hold if the size of the network is known).

Most previously known lower bounds on the leader election problem, as well as lower bounds on various related problems, were proved in the KT_∞ model, i.e., for networks whose topology is *known* to all vertices and in particular, networks with a very *regular* structure. Among others, network topologies considered in lower bounds proofs include rings [AAHK86, ASW85, Bur80, Fre83, FL87, GS86, MW86, MZ86, PKR82], complete graphs [AG85a, Fre83, KMZ84, KMZ85], grids [Fre83], binary trees [Fre83] and others. Other results, e.g., [KMZ84], are obtained in the other extreme model, KT_0, and strongly rely on the assumption that processors do not a priori know the identities of their neighbors.

Exercises

1. Prove Lemma 23.4.3.

2. Given a weighted graph $G = (V, E, \omega)$, consider the following two spanners for G. Let $S_g = (V, E_g)$ be the spanner constructed for G by Algorithm GREEDY_SPAN of Section 17.2 with parameter $\kappa = 2t$ (for some integer $t \geq 1$), and let $S_b = (V, E_b)$ be the spanner constructed for G by Algorithm $\kappa' -$ FLOOD described above for $\kappa' = t$.

    (a) What can you say about the relationship between the two spanners? (That is, is $E_g = E_b$? Or does one of the two contain the other? Or none of the above?)

    (b) How would your answer change if the graph G were unweighted (i.e., if $\omega(e) = 1$ for every edge $e \in E$)?

3. Prove or disprove: Assuming synchronous communication, the time complexity of Algorithm $\kappa -$ FLOOD in model KT_κ is at most $O(\kappa Diam(G))$.

Chapter 24

How local are global tasks? MST revisited

24.1 Existential versus universal optimality

Certain distributed network problems have the property that for every $n \geq 1$ there exist n-vertex graphs for which the running time of any distributed algorithm for the problem is $\Omega(n)$. For such problems, the task of optimizing the running time is sometimes claimed successful once an $O(n)$ time algorithm is obtained, as this bound is "the best possible." This type of optimality may be thought of as "existential" optimality. Namely, there are points in the class of input instances under consideration for which the algorithm is optimal. A stronger type of optimality, which we may analogously call "universal" optimality, is when the proposed algorithm solves the problem optimally on *every* instance.

An interesting "fringe-benefit" of universal optimality is that a universally-optimal algorithm precisely identifies the parameters of the problem that are inherently responsible for its complexity. For example, it may be argued that an $O(n)$ time algorithm for broadcast is time-optimal since broadcast cannot be performed any faster on the n-vertex path. Yet a more careful look reveals that the inherent parameter dictating the complexity of the broadcast task is the network's diameter $Diam$, and indeed, there exists an $O(Diam)$-time distributed broadcast algorithm (in the synchronous model), as discussed in Chapter 3.

The interesting general question is therefore to identify the inherent graph parameters associated with the distributed complexity of various fundamental network problems and develop universally-optimal algorithms for them.

This question is closely related to our discussion on the role of *locality* in distributed computing. Various problems (such as the MIS and coloring problems discussed earlier) are known to be essentially local and hence amenable to a localized algorithm with very fast (e.g., polylogarithmic) running times. In contrast, one may consider problems that are essentially *global*, i.e., ones that do not admit localized solutions, but rather always require the algorithm to "traverse" the network. Problems of this type still raise the interesting (if more modest) questions of deciding whether $\Omega(n)$ time is essential or if the network's *diameter* is the inherent parameter. In the latter case, it would be desirable to devise algorithms for these network problems that have a better complexity for the case of graphs with low diameter.

In this chapter, we reconsider the problem of a distributed algorithm for constructing an MST. This problem has been discussed earlier in Chapter 5 and has been shown to have a communication-efficient algorithm with time $O(n \log n)$. As with other problems, it is natural to ask whether $O(n)$ time is universally optimal or can be improved. The MST problem proves to be an interesting candidate for this type of study. Recall that for a fragment F of the graph, $Diam^{un}(F)$ denotes the unweighted diameter of F, i.e., the maximum unweighted distance between any two vertices of G. In other tree constructions, such as the BFS tree, it is intuitively clear that the true time bound should be related to the network's diameter $Diam^{un}$ since the depth of the constructed tree is proportional to $Diam^{un}$. In contrast, the MST of a given network may be considerably deeper than $Diam^{un}$ and, in fact, may be as high as $\Omega(n)$. Hence construction methods based on communication on the tree structure itself are doomed to require $\Omega(n)$ time, and the problem of devising a time-efficient distributed MST algorithm, breaking the $\Omega(n)$ barrier, seems intrinsically harder.

In order to be able to concentrate on the central issue of time complexity, we shall ignore the message complexity of our algorithm, i.e., the number of messages it uses, and focus on the synchronous model. Note, however, that the latter restriction is not essential, since our decision to ignore message complexity allows us to freely use a synchronizer of our choice; for example, recall that synchronizer α (presented in Chapter 6) enables an asynchronous network to run any protocol that was designed for synchronous networks, with the same time complexity, at the cost of increasing the message complexity.

Let us first consider the extreme $\mathcal{LOCAL}$ model in which messages of arbitrary size are allowed to be transmitted in a single time unit. In that model, the refined distinctions we focus on here disappear as clearly, if unbounded-size messages are allowed, then the MST problem can be trivially solved in time $O(Diam^{un}(G))$ by collecting the entire graph's topology and edge weight assignment into a central vertex, computing an MST locally and broadcasting the result throughout the network. In case the MST construction operation is initiated by a single vertex r_0, $\Omega(Diam^{un}(G))$ is also a lower bound on the required time since r_0 must first wake up all the other vertices and this cannot be done in less than $Rad(G)$ time units in the worst case.

Lemma 24.1.1 *In the $\mathcal{LOCAL}$ model, distributed MST construction with a single initiator requires time $\Theta(Diam(G))$.*

Interestingly, in case all the vertices wake up simultaneously, it is no longer obvious that the parameter deciding the time complexity of the problem is the diameter of the network. Rather, another parameter becomes relevant, namely, the *cycle-radius* of the graph, defined next.

Definition 24.1.2 [Cycle radius]: *The* external radius *of the cycle C in the graph $G = (V, E)$ is*

$$ExRad(C) = \min_{v \in V} \{\max_{w \in C} \{dist_G(v, w)\}\}.$$

The vertex v attaining the minimum is called the external-center *of C. The cycle-radius of the graph $G = (V, E)$ is $CycRad(G) = \max_{C \in G} \{ExRad(C)\}$.*

Lemma 24.1.3 *For every graph $G = (V, E)$, $CycRad(G) \leq Rad(G)$.*

The following is a universal lower bound for the distributed MST construction problem.

Lemma 24.1.4 *For every graph $G = (V, E)$, distributed MST construction in the $\mathcal{LOCAL}$ model requires time $\Omega(CycRad(G))$, even assuming simultaneous wakeup.*

Assuming the vertices of the network know the entire topology in advance, and the only uncertainty concerns the edge weights, the above lower bound can be met by a straightforward algorithm.

Lemma 24.1.5 *In the $\mathcal{LOCAL}$ model, assuming simultaneous wakeup and complete topological knowledge at all vertices, distributed MST construction can be achieved in time $O(CycRad(G))$.*

Consequently, throughout the remainder of the chapter we assume the $\mathcal{CONGEST}$ model, in which messages have size $O(\log n)$, and a vertex may send at most one message on each edge at each time unit. We also make the assumption that the edge weights are polynomial in n, so an edge weight can be sent in a single message. In this model, determining the time complexity of distributed MST construction becomes more interesting since congestion may affect the performance of the algorithm.

In the next section we present a distributed MST algorithm whose time complexity is sublinear in n and linear in $Diam^{un}$ (specifically, $O(Diam^{un}(G) + n^{\epsilon} \cdot \log^* n)$ for $\epsilon = \frac{\ln 3}{\ln 6} = 0.6131..$). In fact, the constant can be reduced and made arbitrarily close to $1/2$. Then, in Section 24.3 we present a $\Omega(\sqrt{n}/\log n)$ lower bound on the time complexity of distributed MST construction in some low diameter graphs.

24.2 A fast MST algorithm

24.2.1 Overview of the algorithm

The fast MST algorithm, named Algorithm FAST-MST, is based on a careful combination of the two distinct approaches presented earlier (in Sections 5.5 and 5.6) for the distributed construction of an MST. Thus before explaining our algorithm, it is instrumental to review the two approaches and try to understand their shortcomings when used individually.

The first approach is the *distributed growth*, which is at the basis of Algorithm GHS of Section 5.5. Recall that this algorithm does not utilize a central controller vertex, or "center of activity," but rather allows a number of processes to proceed simultaneously and independently in the network and gradually grow the MST fragments from scratch in a distributed manner. In each iteration of the algorithm, the vertices of each fragment explore the immediate neighborhood of the fragment and collectively decide on a neighboring fragment to merge with (by adding the connecting edge to the tree), thus creating a larger fragment of the final MST, relying on a distributed version of the "blue" rule for MST construction.

It is crucial to understand why algorithms based on this approach cannot guarantee a time complexity proportional to $Diam^{un}(G)$. The inherent difficulty lies in the fact that the communication necessary for making the merging decisions for each fragment is done *on the fragment itself*. This is a problem since the MST is not guaranteed to have depth proportional to $Diam^{un}(G)$, and neither are any of its fragments. In fact, it is easy to come up with examples for n-vertex graphs with diameter 1 whose MST has depth $n - 1$ (see Exercise 4). Thus any approach based on communicating over the MST itself will have time complexity proportional to n in the worst case on some graphs.

Note, however, that in the initial stages of Algorithm GHS, the fragments are still small and therefore communication on them is not as expensive. The idea on which the fast MST algorithm is based is thus to start by running Algorithm GHS up to an appropriately chosen point, and then switch to a different algorithm. In order for this idea to work, it is essential to have a version of Algorithm GHS that controls the rate of growth of the different fragments, preventing some fragments from growing too large while other fragments are still very small. (Algorithm GHS as described earlier does allow uncontrolled growth of fragments.)

The second approach to the distributed construction of an MST, called *coordinated elimination*, is based on synchronous, coordinated, centralized operation. One naive example for an algorithm operating in this way is the centralized MST construction algorithm for the $\mathcal{LOCAL}$ model mentioned in Section 24.1, in which the entire graph's topology is collected into a central vertex, which then computes an MST locally and broadcasts the result throughout the network. In the $\mathcal{CONGEST}$ model, this algorithm is slowed down considerably by the heavy communication bottlenecks that are bound to be created along the paths leading to the center vertex.

A more sophisticated attempt to utilize the second approach is based on the idea that some of this communication burden can be reduced by delegating the work of the central controller vertex to other vertices along the paths leading to the center. This can be achieved if instead of attempting to *build* the MST, we concentrate on *eliminating candidate edges* using the "red rule" for MST construction. This idea is implemented in Section 5.6 using Procedure PIPELINE, relying on the fact that the MST problem is a matroid problem.

As shown earlier (Lemmas 5.5.8 and 5.6.9), the time complexity of both MST construction algorithms, namely, the "distributed growth" Algorithm GHS and the "coordinated elimination" MST algorithm based on Procedure PIPELINE, is at least as high as $\Omega(n)$. However, a closer inspection reveals that Algorithm GHS proceeds fast in its initial stage and then gradually slows down, whereas Procedure PIPELINE is slow due to handling many edges in the earlier stages of the problem. Consequently, Algorithm FAST-MST presented next is based on *combining* the two approaches, starting with Algorithm GHS and then switching to Procedure PIPELINE.

The algorithm thus consists of two stages. The first stage involves running a modified version of Algorithm GHS named CONTROLLED-GHS. The purpose of the modification is to produce a balanced outcome in terms of number and diameter of the resulting fragments. This is achieved by computing in each phase a small dominating set on the fragment forest and merging fragments accordingly. The small dominating set is computed by invoking the distributed Procedure SMALL_DOM_SET of Section 8.3.

At the end of the first stage of the algorithm, the vertices are organized into a "small" number $N \ll n$ of fragments, all of which have a "small" diameter $d \ll n$. Edges internal to clusters are "decided" in the sense that for each edge internal to a cluster, it is known whether or not it belongs to the MST. The only remaining candidates to join the MST are the outgoing (or inter-fragment) edges. (In fact, for any two fragments F_i and F_j, at most one relevant candidate edge exists among the possibly many edges connecting them, namely, the minimum-weight one.) More importantly, the solution contains only $N - 1$ edges, hence the remaining problem is a matroid problem of rank $N - 1$.

This problem can therefore be solved in Stage II as follows. First, build a BFS tree B. Then, use Procedure PIPELINE over the tree B to eliminate most of the remaining edges, upcasting to the root $r_0(B)$ only $N - 1$ edges forming a tree connecting the fragments. These edges, combined with the internal trees spanning each fragment, yield the final MST. This is done in time $O(Diam^{un}(G) + N)$. Finally, $r_0(B)$ broadcasts the identities of the remaining $N - 1$ edges.

The details of the two stages are given in the remainder of the section, followed by the analysis of the total complexity.

24.2.2   Stage I: Controlled-GHS

In this section, we provide the modified version of Algorithm GHS for MST, named Algorithm CONTROLLED-GHS, which achieves the following. For two parameters $N, d \ll n$ to be specified later,

1. upon termination, the number of fragments is bounded from above by N, and

2. throughout the execution, the diameter of every fragment F satisfies $Diam^{un}(F) \leq d$.

CONTROLLED-GHS

Algorithm CONTROLLED-GHS starts with singleton fragments, just like Algorithm GHS (see Section 5.5.2), and executes a total of I phases. Each phase outputs a collection of MST fragments that serve as the input for the next phase. Each phase of CONTROLLED-GHS consists of the following two subphases.

Subphase 1: Execute a phase of Algorithm GHS up to the point where each input fragment F has chosen its minimum-weight outgoing edge, i.e., has decided which other fragment in the current fragment collection it wants to merge with.

This decision induces a fragment forest structure $\hat{G} = (\hat{F}, \hat{E})$ on the initial fragment collection. As described in Lemma 5.5.7, the connected components of this fragment forest are nearly trees of fragments, possibly with length-2 loops at the tree roots, as in Figure 5.10.

Subphase 2: Break the resulting tree-like connected components into "small" ($O(1)$ depth) trees, and merge only these small trees.

This process is depicted in Figure 24.1. To accomplish Subphase 2, the algorithm first computes a dominating set $M(\tilde{T})$ on each tree $\tilde{T}$ of the fragment forest $\hat{G}$. Note that the vertices of this tree are input fragments of the current phase of the algorithm. Let $M(\hat{G})$ be the union over the trees $\tilde{T}$ (of the $\hat{G}$ forest) of $M(\tilde{T})$. The algorithm then lets each fragment $F \notin M(\hat{G})$ pick one neighboring fragment $F' \in M(\hat{G})$ and merge with it. This causes the actual merges performed in a phase of CONTROLLED-GHS to have the form of "stars" in the fragment forest $\hat{G}$ and prevents merges along long chains, hence bounding the diameter of the resulting fragments.

The dominating sets are computed using the distributed Procedure SMALL_DOM_SET of Section 8.3, applied separately to each tree $\tilde{T}$ in the fragment forest $\hat{G}$. Note that although Procedure SMALL_DOM_SET is applied to the trees of the fragment forest $\hat{G}$, it is actually executed on the original network itself. Hence the procedure needs to be adapted by simulating each fragment by a single representative, say, its root.

Analysis of CONTROLLED-GHS

The bounds on the number and diameter of fragments are established by the next lemma. Given a fragment forest $\hat{G}$, let $Diam^{un}(\hat{G}) = \max_{F \in \hat{F}}\{Diam^{un}(F)\}$. Let $\hat{G}_i = (\hat{F}_i, \hat{E}^i)$ denote the fragment forest produced by Algorithm CONTROLLED-GHS at the end of the ith phase. ($\hat{G}_0$ is the initial set of vertices.)

Lemma 24.2.1 *In each phase i of CONTROLLED-GHS,*

1. *the number of fragments at least halves, i.e., $|\hat{F}_i| \leq |\hat{F}_{i-1}|/2$, and*

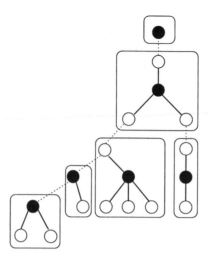

Figure 24.1: A Phase of CONTROLLED-GHS: viewing the tree T of Figure 8.8(b) as a connected component of the fragment forest $\hat{G}$, T is broken into "small" trees (represented by the solid edges) around the vertices of the dominating set $M(\hat{G})$ (denoted by the black circles).

2. *the maximum diameter of a fragment increases by a factor of at most 3 (possibly plus 2), i.e., $Diam^{un}(\hat{G}_i) \leq 3Diam^{un}(\hat{G}_{i-1}) + 2$.*

Proof: The number of new fragments in each tree-like connected component $\tilde{T}$ of the fragment forest $\hat{G}$ at the end of a phase is equal to $|M(\tilde{T})|$. By Lemma 8.3.3, $|M(\tilde{T})| \leq |V(\tilde{T})|/2$. Hence the same holds for the entire fragment forest, and Claim 1 of the lemma follows. Claim 2 is readily satisfied since the merges are star-shaped.   □

Corollary 24.2.2 *After running* CONTROLLED-GHS *for I phases,*

1. *the number of fragments in $\hat{G}_I$ is at most $N(I) = \frac{n}{2^I}$, and*

2. *$Diam^{un}(\hat{G}_I) \leq d(I) = 3^I - 1$.*   □

Let us now turn to analyzing the time complexity of CONTROLLED-GHS. We first examine the performance of Procedure SMALL_DOM_SET.

Lemma 24.2.3 *Procedure* SMALL_DOM_SET *takes time $O(\log^* n) \cdot Diam^{un}(\hat{G})$ when executed on a fragment forest $\hat{G}$.*

Proof: It is easy to see that if a fragment F is a leaf in some tree $\tilde{T}$ the fragment forest $\hat{G}$, then it identifies itself as such and subsequently marks itself $\check{L}_0$ in time $O(Diam^{un}(F))$. Similarly, fragments mark themselves $\check{L}_1$ and $\check{L}_2$ in time $O(Diam^{un}(F))$ as well. Another part that affects the time complexity is the MIS computation. By Lemma 8.3.4, the time complexity of Procedure SMALL_DOM_SET is $O(\log^* n)$. Note that since the procedure is executed on the original network itself, it is slowed down by a factor of $O(Diam^{un}(\hat{G}))$. Hence the implementation of Procedure SMALL_DOM_SET on the fragments of $\hat{G}$ is slowed down to $O(\log^* n) \cdot Diam^{un}(\hat{G})$ in our case.   □

The properties of the CONTROLLED-GHS algorithm are now summarized by the following *graph decomposition* lemma.

Lemma 24.2.4 *When Algorithm* CONTROLLED-GHS *is activated for I phases, it takes* $O(3^I \cdot \log^* n)$ *time and yields a fragment forest $\hat{G}_I$ of up to $N(I) = n/2^I$ fragments of diameter $Diam^{un}(\hat{G}_I) \leq d(I) = 3^I - 1$. Each fragment in the forest is a fragment of an MST of the graph G.*

Proof: By Lemma 24.2.3, each phase i, $1 \leq i \leq I$, of Algorithm CONTROLLED-GHS takes time at most $Diam^{un}(\hat{G}_{i-1}) \cdot O(\log^* n)$. By Corollary 24.2.2, this is at most $3^{i-1} \cdot O(\log^* n)$. Thus the total time is given by

$$\sum_{i \leq I} 3^{i-1} \cdot O(\log^* n) \ \leq \ 3^I \cdot O(\log^* n) \ .$$

The size and diameter properties of the resulting fragment forest follow directly from Corollary 24.2.2. □

24.2.3   Stage II: Edge elimination

The second stage of the algorithm starts at the point where we are given a fragment graph $\hat{G}_I = (\hat{F}_I, \hat{E}_I)$ such that $\hat{F}_I$ contains $N \leq N(I)$ MST fragments and $\hat{E}_I$ is the collection of interfragment edges, which are the remaining candidates for joining the MST. We need to reduce the total number of remaining interfragment edges (to the necessary $N - 1$). This is done using Procedure PIPELINE.

The first step in Stage II involves the construction of a BFS tree B rooted at some vertex $r_0(B)$. In the synchronous model, this can be accomplished in time $O(Diam^{un}(G))$.

Towards applying Procedure PIPELINE, we view the problem as a matroid problem. The elements of the universe consist of the candidate edges, i.e., the edge set $\hat{E}_I$. The set system (namely, the collection of independent sets) is characterized by defining a set of edges as independent if it is cycle-free. In other words, for a set of edges Q and a cycle-free subset $U \subseteq Q$, the set Dep identified by Procedure PIPELINE contains all edges $e \in Q \setminus U$ such that $U \cup \{e\}$ contains a cycle.

Note that there could be many parallel interfragment edges connecting any two fragments, hence the total number of interfragment edges could be considerably larger than N^2. However, the parameter determining the complexity of Procedure PIPELINE is the rank of the problem, which is $N - 1$ in our case.

By the analysis of Procedure PIPELINE, the edges reported by each intermediate vertex to its parent in the tree form a forest, active vertices are never idle until they terminate and each vertex v upcasts edges in nondecreasing weight order. Subsequently, by Lemma 5.6.8 we have the following.

Lemma 24.2.5 *When Stage II is activated on a fragment forest $\hat{G}_I$ of $N \leq N(I) = n/2^I$ fragments, it requires $O(N + Diam^{un}(G))$ time and its output is an MST for G.*

24.2.4   The complexity of the combined algorithm

Combining the two stages, we get the distributed Algorithm FAST-MST for MST construction, presented in Figure 24.2.

Summarizing the results of the last two sections, we get the following.

Theorem 24.2.6 *For every graph n-vertex G, Algorithm* FAST-MST *has time complexity* $O(Diam^{un}(G) + n^\epsilon \cdot \log^* n)$ *for $\epsilon = \frac{\ln 3}{\ln 6} = 0.6131$.*

1. Perform Algorithm CONTROLLED-GHS for I phases.

2. Construct a BFS tree.

3. Perform edge elimination using Procedure PIPELINE.

Figure 24.2: Algorithm FAST-MST.

Proof: The complexities of the two stages of our algorithm are as follows. For the given parameter I specified for the first stage, that stage requires $3^I \cdot O(\log^* n)$ time, while the second stage takes time $Diam^{un}(G) + \frac{n}{2^I}$. The total time complexity is thus optimized when choosing I such that $3^I = \frac{n}{2^I}$, namely, $I = \frac{\ln n}{\ln 6}$. For this choice of I, we get $3^I = \frac{n}{2^I} = n^\epsilon$ for $\epsilon = \frac{\ln 3}{\ln 6}$, which yields a total time complexity of $O(Diam^{un}(G) + n^\epsilon \cdot \log^* n)$.   □

A limitation of Algorithm FAST-MST, compared to Algorithm GHS, is that the tree it constructs is unrooted and undirected. Nevertheless, it is possible to modify the algorithm so that it constructs a rooted tree, with each vertex knowing its parent and children, at the same time complexity (see Exercise 5).

24.3   A lower bound

In this section we establish the (asymptotic) existential near-optimality of Algorithm FAST-MST by showing that $\Omega(\sqrt{n}/\log n)$ is a lower bound as well, even on low diameter networks. Specifically, for any integer $m \geq 2$, we construct a family of $O(m^4)$-vertex networks of diameter $Diam^{un} = O(m)$ for which $\Omega(m^2/\log n)$ time is required for constructing a minimum spanning tree in the $\mathcal{CONGEST}$ model.

In fact, a stronger result can be shown. For every integer $n \geq 1$, there exists a family of n-vertex networks of diameter $\Theta(\log n)$ for which MST construction requires $\Omega(\sqrt{n}/\log^2 n)$ time. While it is not clear that the $\Omega(\log n)$ limitation on the diameters for which the lower bound holds is essential, *some* limitation must apparently exist. This follows from the observation that the n-vertex complete graph ($Diam^{un} = 1$) admits a simple $O(\log n)$ time distributed MST construction algorithm. (See Exercise 1.)

Towards proving the lower bound on distributed MST construction, we first establish a lower bound on the time complexity of a problem referred to as the *mailing problem*, which can be informally stated as follows. Given a particular type of graph named F_m for integer $m \geq 2$ with two vertices s and r in it, it is required to deliver an m^2-bit string $\mathcal{X}$ generated in s to r. The graph F_m has $n = O(m^4)$ vertices and diameter $O(m)$, yet we show that the time required for mailing from s to r on F_m is $\Omega(m^2/\log n) = \Omega(\sqrt{n}/\log n)$.

The lower bound applies in a rather general setting. In particular, vertices are allowed to have unique identifiers. The vertices do not know the assignment of edge weights in the entire network, but they may know the entire topology and of course the weights of their own edges. That is, for every edge $e = (u, v) \in E$, the weight $\omega(e)$ is known to the adjacent vertices, u and v. Communication may be synchronous. (Clearly, the lower bounds hold for asynchronous networks as well.)

24.3.1   A lower bound for the mailing problem on F_m

Let us now introduce the mailing problem formally, define the graphs F_m and establish a lower bound on time complexity of the mailing problem for m^2-bit strings on F_m.

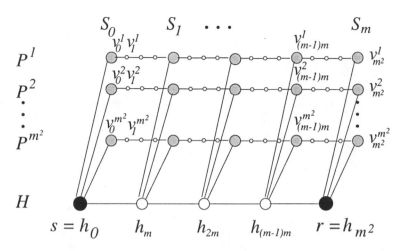

Figure 24.3: The graph F_m.

The mailing problem

Consider some graph G with two distinguished vertices denoted s and r, referred to as the *sender* and the *receiver*, respectively. Both the sender s and the receiver r store b boolean variables each, $X_1^s, \ldots, X_b^s$ and $X_1^r, \ldots, X_b^r$, respectively, for some integer $b \geq 1$. An input of the problem consists of an initial assignment $\mathcal{X} = \{x_i \mid 1 \leq i \leq b\}$, where $x_i \in \{0,1\}$, to the variables of s, such that $X_i^s = x_i$. Given such an instance, the mailing problem requires s to deliver the string $\mathcal{X}$ to r, i.e., upon termination, the variables of r should contain the output $X_i^r = x_i$ for every $1 \leq i \leq b$. Henceforth, we refer to this problem as $\mathtt{Mail}(G, s, r, b)$. Throughout the remainder of this section we consider this problem on graphs F_m with $b = m^2$ for some integer $m \geq 2$.

The graphs F_m

Let us now define the collection of graphs denoted F_m for $m \geq 2$. The graph F_m is constructed from m^2 paths $\mathcal{P}^1, \ldots, \mathcal{P}^{m^2}$ with each path $\mathcal{P}^j$ consisting of $m^2 + 1$ vertices $\{v_0^j, \ldots, v_{m^2}^j\}$ and an additional special path $\mathcal{H}$ on $m+1$ vertices $\{h_{im} \mid 0 \leq i \leq m\}$, referred to as the *highway*. Each highway vertex h_{im} is connected to the corresponding path vertices v_{im}^j by a *spoke* edge (h_{im}, v_{im}^j). These spoke edges can be grouped into $m + 1$ *stars* S_i, $0 \leq i \leq m$, with each star S_i consisting of the highway vertex h_{im} and the m^2 vertices $v_{im}^1, \ldots, v_{im}^{m^2}$, i.e., $E(S_i) = \{(v_{im}^j, h_{im}) \mid 1 \leq j \leq m^2\}$. See Figure 24.3.

Note that the graph F_m consists of $n = \Theta(m^4)$ vertices and its diameter is $O(m)$. Finally, we set the intended sender and receiver to be $s = h_0$ and $r = h_{m^2}$.

The lower bound

We would now like to prove that solving the mailing problem on the graph F_m with a $b = m^2$-bit string $\mathcal{X}$ requires $\Omega(m^2/\log n)$ time. Intuitively, this happens because routing the string $\mathcal{X}$ from s to r along ordinary paths would be too slow, hence our only hope is to route the string along the highway, or at least use interleaved paths, mixing highway segments with segments of ordinary paths. However, F_m does not have sufficient capacity for routing all m^2 bits from s to r along such short (or "relatively short") paths.

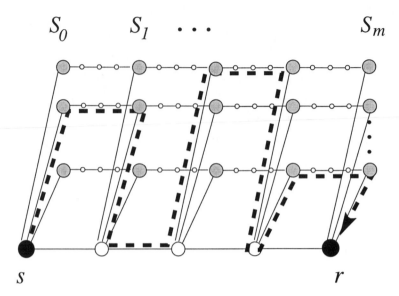

Figure 24.4: The path p_i.

This intuition yields a rather simple proof of the claim if we limit ourselves to a restricted class of algorithms, referred to as *explicit delivery* algorithms. These are algorithms in which the input bits are required to be delivered in an explicit way, namely, each bit x_i must be shipped from s to r along some path p_i (naturally, the paths of different bits may be identical or partly overlap).

Lemma 24.3.1 *For every $m \geq 1$, at least $m^2/(2 \log n)$ time is required for solving the mailing problem* $\mathtt{Mail}(F_m, h_0, h_m^2, m^2)$ *by an explicit delivery algorithm.*

Proof: Let p_i denote the path of the bit $x_i \in \mathcal{X}$ leading from $s = h_0$ to $r = h_{m^2}$. Any such path in F_m must go through each and every one of the $m + 1$ stars S_j. The message can travel from any star S_j to the following star S_{j+1} either through the highway edge $(h_{jm}, h_{(j+1)m})$ or through the corresponding segment of one of the ordinary paths $\mathcal{P}^k$. (See Figure 24.4.) (Of course, the message is free to follow a longer path, visiting some of the stars more than once; this will only worsen the situation.)

Let ℓ_i denote the number of occurrences of highway edges in the path p_i. The total length of p_i satisfies $|p_i| \geq (m - \ell_i) \cdot m + \ell_i$ since whenever the path has not used the highway edge between stars S_j and S_{j+1}, the length of the alternative segment over some ordinary path is at least m. The time required for a message to traverse a path is at least its length. Therefore, if $\ell_i < \lfloor m/2 \rfloor$ for some $1 \leq i \leq m^2$, then $|p_i| \geq m^2/2$ and the claim follows. So suppose that $\ell_i \geq \lfloor m/2 \rfloor$ for all i. Summing over all m^2 paths p_i, one obtains that the total number of occurrences of highway edges in the paths p_i is

$$\sum_{i=1}^{m^2} \ell_i \geq \frac{m^3}{2} .$$

As the highway $\mathcal{H}$ contains m edges, at least one of the edges must be traversed by at least $m^2/2$ messages, which requires at least $m^2/(2 \log n)$ time. $\square$

The lower bound can be extended to apply also to *arbitrary* algorithms, in which the information can be conveyed from s to r in arbitrary ways. This may include applying arbitrary functions to the bits at s and sending the resulting values, possibly modifying and "recombining" these values in intermediate vertices along the way, in a way that will allow r to extract the original bits from the messages it receives. For handling such a general class of algorithms, the proof must be formalized in a more careful way.

Let us next outline the proof for the general case. Consider the set of possible states a vertex v may be in at any given stage t of the execution of a mailing algorithm on some m^2-bit input $\mathcal{X}$. (The state of a vertex consists of all its local data, hence it is affected by its input, topological knowledge and history, namely, all incoming messages.) As the computation progresses, the tree of possible executions diverges, and thus the set of possible states of v becomes larger. In particular, when the execution starts at round 0, each of the vertices is in one specific initial local state, except for the sender s, which may be in any one of 2^{m^2} states, determined by the value of the input string $\mathcal{X}$. Upon termination, the string $\mathcal{X}$ should be known to the receiver r, meaning that r should be in one of 2^{m^2} states. The proof argument is based on analyzing the growth process of the sets of possible states and showing that this process is slow, forcing the algorithm to spend at least $\Omega(m^2/B)$ time until the set of possible states of r is of size 2^{m^2}.

Lemma 24.3.2 *Solving the mailing problem* $\mathtt{Mail}(F_m, h_0, h_{m^2}, m^2)$ *requires* $\Omega(m^2/\log n)$ *time for every* $m \geq 1$.

24.3.2 A lower bound for the MST problem on F_m

We now use the lower bound obtained for the mailing problem in order to show that the distributed MST problem cannot be solved faster than $\Omega(m^2/\log n)$ on weighted versions of the graphs F_m.

According to our convention, the output of the MST problem at each vertex v is an assignment to the (Boolean) output variables Y_e^v for every edge e, assigning $Y_e^v = 1$ if $e \in MST(G)$ and $Y_e^v = 0$ otherwise.

To prove the lower bound on the MST problem, we define a family of weighted graphs $\mathcal{J}_m$, based on F_m but differing in their weight assignments, and then show that any algorithm solving the MST problem on the graphs of $\mathcal{J}_m$ can also be used to solve the mailing problem on F_m with the same time complexity. Subsequently, the lower bound for the distributed MST problem follows from the lower bound given in the previous section for the mailing problem in F_m.

The graph family $\mathcal{J}_m$

For every graph F_m, we define a family of weighted graphs

$$\mathcal{J}_m = \{J_{m,\theta} = (F_m, \omega_\theta) \mid 1 \leq \theta \leq 2^{m^2}\},$$

where ω_θ is an edge weight function fixed as follows. Recall that in the graph F_m there are three types of edges, namely, highway edges, edges of paths $\mathcal{P}^j$ and star spokes. In all the weight functions ω_θ, all the edges of the highway $\mathcal{H}$ and the paths $\mathcal{P}^j$ are assigned the weight 0. The spokes of all stars except S_0 and S_m are assigned an infinite weight. The spokes of the star S_m are assigned the weight 2.

The only differences between different weight functions ω_θ occur on the m^2 spokes of the star S_0. Specifically, each of these m^2 spokes is assigned a weight of either 1 or 3; there are thus 2^{m^2} possible combinations of weight assignments. (See Figure 24.5.)

Since discarding any combination of infinite weight edges from the graph $J_{m,\theta}$ leaves it connected, and since any tree containing an infinite weight edge has infinite weight, the following is clear.

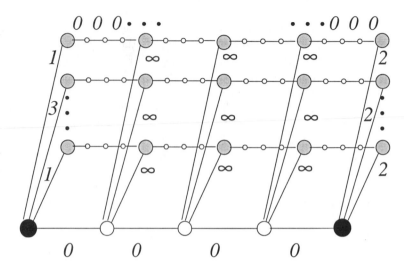

Figure 24.5: The weight assignment for the graphs of $\mathcal{J}_m$.

Lemma 24.3.3 *No infinite weight spoke edge belongs to the MST of $J_{m,\theta}$, for every $1 \leq \theta \leq 2^{m^2}$.*

Also, since the zero-weight edges of $\mathcal{H}$ and $\mathcal{P}^j$ are cycle-free, and all other edges have nonzero weight, we also have the following.

Lemma 24.3.4 *For every $m \geq 2$ and $1 \leq \theta \leq 2^{m^2}$, all the edges of the highway $\mathcal{H}$ and the paths $\mathcal{P}^j$ for $1 \leq j \leq m^2$ belong to the MST of $J_{m,\theta}$.*

Lemma 24.3.5 *For every $1 \leq \theta \leq 2^{m^2}$ and $1 \leq j \leq m^2$, exactly one of the two spokes (s, v_0^j) and $(r, v_{m^2}^j)$ belongs to the MST of $J_{m,\theta}$, namely, the lighter one.*

Proof Sketch: Since the MST must be connected, at least one of the spokes (s, v_0^j) and $(r, v_{m^2}^j)$ must belong to it, as otherwise the path $\mathcal{P}^j$ is completely disconnected from the rest of the graph, by Lemma 24.3.3. The proof is completed upon noting that the MST cannot contain both of those edges since that would close a cycle with the (zero-weight) edges of $\mathcal{H}$ and $\mathcal{P}^j$.   □

The situation is thus summarized in Figure 24.6.

A lower bound on MST in $\mathcal{J}_m$

Recall that the weight of each edge is known only to the vertices adjacent to that edge; no vertex knows the topology of the network, and each vertex knows only its immediate surroundings.

Lemma 24.3.6 *Any distributed algorithm for constructing an MST on the graphs of the class $\mathcal{J}_m$ can be used to solve the $\mathtt{Mail}(F_m, h_0, h_{m^2}, m^2)$ problem on F_m with the same time complexity.*

Proof: Consider an algorithm Π_{mst} for the MST problem, and suppose that we are given an instance of the $\mathtt{Mail}(F_m, h_0, h_{m^2}, m^2)$ problem with input string $\mathcal{X}$. We use the algorithm Π_{mst} to solve this instance of the mailing problem as follows. The sender $s = h_0$ initiates

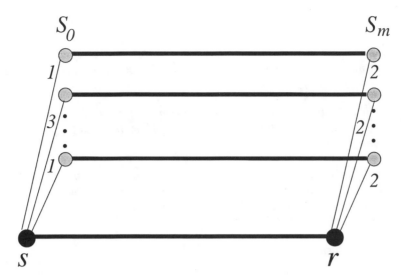

Figure 24.6: Bold edges belong to the MST. Membership of S_0 and S_m spokes in the MST depends on the weight assignment.

the construction of an instance of the MST by turning F_m into a weighted graph from $\mathcal{J}_m$, setting the edge weights as follows: for each $x_i \in X$, $1 \le i \le m^2$, it sets the weight $\omega(e_i)$ corresponding to the spoke edge $e_i \in E(S_0)$ to be

$$\omega(e_i) = \begin{cases} 3 & \text{if } x_i = 1; \\ 1 & \text{otherwise.} \end{cases}$$

The rest of the graph edges are assigned fixed weights as specified above. Note that the weights for all the vertices except s and its immediate neighbors in S_0 do not depend on the particular input instance at hand, hence a single round of communication between s and its S_0 neighbors suffices for performing this assignment. Every vertex v in the network, upon receiving the first message of algorithm Π_{mst}, adopts the weight values defined by the edge weight function. From this point on, v may proceed with executing algorithm Π_{mst} for the MST problem.

Once algorithm Π_{mst} terminates, the receiver vertex r determines its output for the mailing problem by setting $X_i^r \leftarrow Y_{e_i}^r$ for $1 \le i \le m^2$.

By Lemma 24.3.5, the lighter of the two edges (s, v_0^i) and $(r, v_{m^2}^i)$ for $1 \le i \le m^2$ belongs to the MST; thus in the set of variables $Y_{e_1}^r, \ldots, Y_{e_{m^2}}^r$ obtained by the vertex r as a result of solving the MST problem, $Y_{e_i}^r = 1$ corresponds to the assignment of $\omega(h_0, v_0^i) = 3$ to the ith edge of S_0, while $Y_{e_i}^r = 0$ corresponds to the assignment of 1 to that edge. Hence the resulting algorithm has correctly solved the given instance of the mailing problem. □

Theorem 24.3.7 *For every $m \ge 1$, any distributed algorithm for constructing an MST on the graphs of the family $\mathcal{J}_m$ requires $\Omega(m^2/\log n)$ time.* □

Corollary 24.3.8 *Any distributed algorithm for the MST construction problem requires $\Omega(\sqrt{n}/\log n)$ time on some n-vertex graphs of diameter $O(n^{1/4})$.*

This result can be generalized to graphs of lower diameter. In particular, it is possible to prove the following (see Exercise 8).

Corollary 24.3.9

1. *For every $K \geq 2$, there exists a family of n-vertex graphs of diameter $O(Kn^{1/2K})$ such that any distributed algorithm for the MST problem requires $\Omega(\sqrt{n}/\log n)$ time on some of those graphs.*

2. *For every $n \geq 2$, there exists a family of n-vertex graphs of diameter $O(\log n)$ such that any distributed algorithm for the MST problem requires $\Omega(\sqrt{n}/\log^2 n)$ time on some of those graphs.*

Taking $K = 3$, for instance, the graph F_m^3 used for proving the above result for diameter $O(n^{1/6})$ is based on m^3 copies of a basic $(m^3 + 1)$-vertex path $\mathcal{P}$ connected to two different highways, denoted $\mathcal{H}^1, \mathcal{H}^2$ and consisting of $m + 1$ and $m^2 + 1$ vertices, respectively. See Figure 24.7, showing the graph F_3^3.

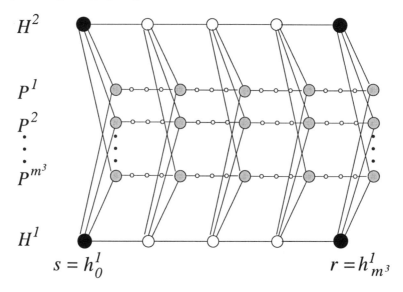

Figure 24.7: The graph F_3^3.

Bibliographical notes

Algorithm FAST-MST of Section 24.2 was introduced in [GKP98], and its time complexity was later improved to $O(\sqrt{n}\log^* n + Diam^{un}(G))$ in [KP98b]. A variant of Algorithm FAST-MST based on carrying interfragment communication on a global BFS tree, with time complexity $O(\sqrt{n}\log^* n + Diam^{un}(G)\log n)$, is presented in [Rub99b] (see Exercise 3). Exercise 5 is due to [Rub99a]. The lower bound presented in Section 24.3 was established in [PR99b]. Exercise 9 can be solved using Yao's method [Yao77], cf. [Pel99a].

Exercises

1. Give a $O(\log n)$ time distributed MST construction algorithm for the n-vertex complete graph (with $Diam^{un}(G) = 1$).

2. Prove Lemmas 24.1.3, 24.1.4 and 24.1.5.

3. (a) Describe a version of Algorithm GHS in which the internal communication of each fragment (namely, the broadcast and convergecast operations) is carried out on a global BFS tree rather than internally on the fragment itself.

   (b) Analyze the resulting time complexity in the synchronous $\mathcal{CONGEST}$ model.

   (c) Describe a version of Algorithm FAST-MST based on the same idea, and analyze its time complexity.

4. Show an n-vertex graph of radius 1 whose MST has depth $n - 1$ (in fact, a drawing of such a graph appears in one of the earlier chapters!).

5. Modify Algorithm FAST-MST so that it constructs a rooted tree and each vertex knows its parent and children, with the same time complexity.

6. Prove Lemma 24.3.2, establishing formally the lower bound on the mailing problem.

7. Formulate and prove a lemma analogous to Lemma 24.3.1 for the graph F_m^3.

8. Prove Corollary 24.3.9 for the case of $K = 3$.

9. (∗) Extend the lower bound of Lemma 24.3.2 on the mailing problem into a lower bound on the expected time complexity of any *randomized* (Las Vegas) distributed algorithm for the mailing problem.

Chapter 25

Local coordination: Synchronizers and MIS revisited

25.1 Locality-based synchronizers

Synchronizers constitute one of the most versatile and powerful applications yet found for the locality-sensitive method. Synchronizers γ and δ, described next, exemplify the gains possible from employing partitions and spanners, respectively, in the $\mathcal{ASYNC}$ model.

The synchronizers α and β described in Chapter 6 exhibit a trade-off between their time and message overheads. Synchronizers γ and δ presented next are based on a combination of the two previous ones, which achieves some reasonable middle points on the time-messages trade-off scale. In particular, it is possible to achieve $\mathsf{Message}_{pulse}(\gamma) = O(\kappa n)$ and $\mathsf{Time}_{pulse}(\gamma) = O(\log_\kappa n)$, where κ is a parameter taken from the range $2 \leq \kappa < n$, and a similar trade-off is possible for δ.

25.1.1 Synchronizer γ

For setting up synchronizer γ, we assume that we are given a low-degree partition $\mathcal{S}$ as described in Chapter 11. The existence of an efficient partition is guaranteed by the Partition Theorem 11.5.1. For each cluster S in the partition $\mathcal{S}$, we define a rooted spanning tree T_S of depth $Rad(S)$. In addition, between any two neighboring clusters there is one designated *synchronization link* serving for communication between them. This is illustrated in Figure 25.1.

The safety information is handled in Phase B of synchronizer γ in three stages. In the first stage, each cluster S separately applies the two phases of synchronizer β on the tree T_S. By the end of this stage, every processor knows that its cluster is safe (i.e., every processor in the cluster is safe). In the second stage, every processor incident to a synchronization link sends a message to the other cluster, saying that its cluster is safe. Finally, the third stage is a repetition of the first one, except the convergecast performed in each cluster S carries different information: whenever a processor learns that all the clusters neighboring it or any of its descendants are safe, it reports this fact to its parent. Again, when the root learns that all the neighboring clusters are safe, it broadcasts this fact along the tree T_S, letting the processors of the cluster S start a new pulse. Figure 25.2 illustrates the resulting five-phase process.

We need to prove that the above procedure properly implements Phase B and imposes

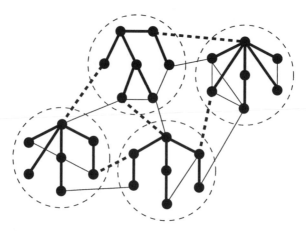

Figure 25.1: Underlying structure for synchronizer γ.

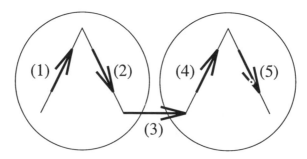

Figure 25.2: The phases of synchronizer γ in each cluster:
(1) CONVERGE($\bigwedge$, $Safe(v,p)$),
(2) TCAST($Cluster\_safe(p)$),
(3) send $Cluster\_safe(p)$ messages to adjacent clusters,
(4) CONVERGE($\bigwedge$, $Adj\_cluster\_safe(v,p)$),
(5) TCAST($All\_safe(p)$).

the readiness rule. It is easy to verify that after phase (2), all the neighbors of a vertex v that reside in the same cluster are safe, as are all other vertices in v's cluster, and that after phase (5), v learns that every vertex in every cluster bordering its own is safe, including in particular all its neighbors.

Combined with the delay rule, we get by Corollary 6.1.5 the following lemma.

Lemma 25.1.1 *Synchronizer γ is correct.*   □

Let us now turn to discuss the complexities of synchronizer γ. To set up synchronizer γ, it is necessary to construct a partition $\mathcal{S}$ in the network. A basic distributed algorithm for achieving this is discussed in Chapters 20 and 21, and the initialization costs $\mathsf{Time}_{init}(\gamma)$ and $\mathsf{Message}_{init}(\gamma)$ are dictated by the particular implementation used. As for the time and message overheads of synchronizer γ, we have the following.

Lemma 25.1.2

  1. $\mathsf{Message}_{pulse}(\gamma) = O(n^{1+1/\kappa})$,

  2. $\mathsf{Time}_{pulse}(\gamma) = O(\kappa)$.

Proof: The overhead complexities follow from the procedure and the properties of the partition $\mathcal{S}$ guaranteed by the Partition Theorem 11.5.1. Specifically, the time required to implement a single pulse is bounded by two broadcast/convergecast rounds in each cluster (plus one step of exchanging messages among border vertices in neighboring clusters), hence $\mathsf{Time}_{pulse}(\gamma) \leq 4Rad(\mathcal{S}) + 1 = O(\kappa)$.

As for the message complexity, the broadcast/convergecast rounds carried separately in each cluster cost $O(n)$ messages overall, since the clusters are disjoint. The single communication step among neighboring clusters, however, requires $n \cdot \bar{\Delta}_c(\mathcal{S}) = O(n^{1+1/\kappa})$ messages, hence the bound on $\mathsf{Message}_{pulse}(\gamma)$. $\quad\square$

25.1.2 Synchronizer δ

The γ synchronizer was based on a partition of the network. In the remainder of this section, we discuss the relationships between synchronizers and *spanners*. We show two complementary relationships between κ-spanners and synchronizers. On the one hand, the nonexistence of a κ-spanner of a certain size implies a lower bound on the complexities of any synchronizer for the network. On the other hand, the existence of a κ-spanner can be used for constructing a synchronizer of a new type, named synchronizer δ.

Let us first describe the construction of the δ synchronizer, given a κ-spanner for the network. Assume that the network $G = (V, E)$ has a κ-spanner $G' = (V, E')$ of m edges. The synchronizer δ for G is constructed as follows. The safety information is transmitted over the spanner in rounds, which may be viewed as "subpulses." When a processor v learns that it is safe, it sets a counter c to 0 and sends the message "safe" to all its neighbors *in the spanner*. Then it waits to hear a similar message from all these neighbors. Upon receiving a "safe" message from all neighbors (again, in the spanner), it increases its counter and repeats the process (i.e., it sends the message "safe" again and then waits for similar messages and so on). This is done for κ rounds. When $c = \kappa$, the processor v may generate its next pulse.

Lemma 25.1.3 *When v holds $c = i$, every processor u at distance i or less from v in G' is safe.*

Proof: The proof is by induction on i. For $i = 0$ the claim is immediate, as v reaches this stage of the synchronizer only after it is safe itself. Now consider the time when v increases c to $i+1$. This is done after v receives $i+1$ "safe" messages from every neighbor in G'. These neighbors each send the $(i + 1)$st message only after having $c = i$. Thus, by the inductive hypothesis, for every such neighbor u, every processor w at distance i or less from u in G' is safe. Thus every processor w at distance $i + 1$ or less from v in G' is safe, too. $\quad\square$

Corollary 25.1.4 *When v holds $c = \kappa$, every neighbor of v in G is safe.*

Proof: By the lemma, when v holds $c = \kappa$, every processor u at distance κ from v in G' is safe. By the definition of κ-spanners, every neighbor of v in G is at distance κ or less from v in G'. Thus every such neighbor is safe. $\quad\square$

Based on this construction we get the following.

Lemma 25.1.5 *If the network G has a κ-spanner with m edges, then it has a synchronizer δ with $\mathsf{Time}_{pulse}(\delta) = O(\kappa)$ and $\mathsf{Message}_{pulse}(\delta) = O(\kappa m)$.* $\quad\square$

It is interesting to note that the underlying structure of the synchronizers presented earlier can also be related to the notion of spanners. Clearly, the information flow in synchronizer γ is performed over the κ-spanner defined by the trees spanning the clusters plus the intercluster edges. Also, synchronizer α is based essentially on the fact that every graph is its own 1-spanner, and synchronizer β can be thought of as performed over a minimal-size $Diam(G)$-spanner of the network. (Note, though, that in synchronizers β and γ, the *order* in which the information flows over the underlying structure is inherently different from synchronizer δ.)

As an illustration for a network in which synchronizer δ is preferable to the previous synchronizers, consider the hypercube. It is possible to construct synchronizers of type α, β or γ for the hypercube using the above constructions, but the resulting complexities are not optimal. In contrast, we can rely on the existence of a construction for a 3-spanner with a linear ($O(2^d)$) number of edges for the hypercube of dimension d (Theorem 16.3.5) presented in Section 16.3. This yields an optimal δ synchronizer (i.e., with overheads $\mathsf{Time}_{pulse} = O(1)$ and $\mathsf{Message}_{pulse} = O(n)$) for the hypercube.

Theorem 25.1.6 *For every $d \geq 0$, the d-cube has a synchronizer of type δ with optimal time and message complexities $\mathsf{Time}_{pulse}(\delta) = O(1)$ and $\mathsf{Message}_{pulse}(\delta) = O(2^d)$.* $\square$

25.1.3   A lower bound for spanner-based synchronizers

The lower bound presented next complements the construction of the previous subsection and establishes close relationships between the quality of spanners for a given undirected graph (in terms of the stretch factor, κ, and the number of spanner edges, $|E'|$) and the time and message complexities of synchronizers for the network based on this spanner.

Lemma 25.1.7 *If the network G has no κ-spanner with at most m edges, then every synchronizer ν for G requires either $\mathsf{Time}_{pulse}(\nu) \geq \kappa + 1$ or $\mathsf{Message}_{pulse}(\nu) \geq m + 1$.*

Proof: Let us assume that the network $G = (V, E)$ has no κ-spanner of m edges and yet has a synchronizer ν with $\mathsf{Message}_{pulse}(\nu) \leq m$, i.e., using m or fewer messages per pulse. The requirement from the synchronizer is to ensure that a processor does not produce a new pulse before it gets all the messages sent to it in the previous pulse. Thus between every two consecutive pulses there must be some transfer of information between each pair of neighbors in the network. Otherwise, the completely asynchronous nature of the network will force these neighbors to wait forever for a message that may still be on its way. Consider the set E' of edges through which the messages of the synchronizer were sent. The information flow between every pair of neighbors in G has to go through the edges of E'. Since only m or fewer messages were sent, the number of these edges is at most m. Therefore by hypothesis, the subgraph $G' = (V, E')$ is not a κ-spanner. This implies that there is an edge $(u, v) \in E$ such that the distance between u and v in G' is at least $\kappa + 1$. Thus the information flow between u and v may require $\kappa + 1$ time units, so the time complexity of the synchronizer ν is at least $\kappa + 1$. $\square$

25.2   Deterministic decomposition-based MIS algorithm

Perhaps the most significant application of the concept of network decomposition, introduced in Section 14.2, is in derandomizing various existing polylog(n) randomized distributed algorithms for $(\Delta + 1)$-coloring and MIS and obtaining deterministic algorithms with improved time complexity in the $\mathcal{LOCAL}$ model.

Let us first assume that we are given a (d, c)-decomposition for the given graph G and, furthermore, that we know the coloring of the clusters in $\tilde{G}$, the cluster graph associated with the decomposition (i.e., we are given the colored decomposition).

$\hat{b} \leftarrow -1$

For phase $i = 1$ through c **do:**   /* Each phase consists of $O(d \log^2 n)$ rounds */

- **If** v's cluster is colored i, **then do:**

    1. **If** v has not decided yet ($\hat{b} = -1$), **then** participate in an MIS computation on the cluster using Algorithm PRAM_MIS.

    2. **If** v has joined the MIS ($\hat{b} = 1$), then inform all neighbors.

- **Else if** v is informed of a neighbor that joined the MIS, **then** decide $\hat{b} \leftarrow 0$.

Figure 25.3: Algorithm DECOMP2MIS(d, c) (code for vertex v).

An MIS for the graph can now be computed by Algorithm DECOMP2MIS, which operates as follows. The algorithm proceeds in $\chi(\tilde{G}) = c$ phases. In each phase i, it computes an MIS among the vertices belonging to the clusters colored i. Note that since these clusters are not adjacent, it is possible to compute an MIS for each of them independently in parallel. This can be done using the distributed deterministic Algorithm PRAM_MIS of Section 8.5, in complexity proportional to the clusters' diameter, i.e., $O(d \cdot \log^2 n)$. Note that a vertex joining the MIS must mark *all* its neighbors as excluded off the MIS, including those belonging to other colors. Hence the vertices that participate in phase i are not all the occupants of the clusters colored i, but only those that were not excluded in earlier phases.

The resulting Algorithm DECOMP2MIS is presented in Figure 25.3.

Since the number of phases is $\chi(\tilde{G}) = c$, the entire process requires time $O(c \cdot d \cdot \log^2 n)$, so we have the following.

Lemma 25.2.1 *Given a colored (d, c)-decomposition for G, the deterministic distributed Algorithm DECOMP2MIS computes an MIS for G in time $O(dc \log^2 n)$.*   □

By the decomposition Theorem 14.2.2, every graph G has an $(O(\kappa), O(\kappa n^{1/\kappa}))$-decomposition for any parameter $\kappa \geq 1$. Hence taking $\kappa = \log n$, we get an $O(\text{polylog}(n))$ time distributed algorithm for MIS.

Corollary 25.2.2 *Given a colored $(O(\log n), O(\log n))$-decomposition for G, there exists a deterministic distributed MIS algorithm with time complexity $O(\text{polylog}(n))$.*   □

Of course, the assumption that an appropriate decomposition is known in advance may not necessarily hold, and it may be necessary to compute such a decomposition from scratch. The fastest deterministic algorithm for doing that (see bibliographical notes of Chapter 22) requires time $O(2^\epsilon)$ for $\epsilon = c\sqrt{\log n}$ for constant $c > 0$. Using it as a preprocessing step yields an MIS algorithm with a similar complexity. (Note that $2^{\sqrt{c \log n}}$ is asymptotically larger than any polylogarithmic function in n, but smaller than n^ϵ for any $\epsilon > 0$.)

Corollary 25.2.3 *There exists a deterministic distributed MIS algorithm with time complexity $O(2^{\sqrt{c \log n}})$.*   □

Bibliographical notes

Synchronizer γ was introduced in [Awe85a]. Synchronizer δ and the connection to spanners were presented in [PU89b]. Later, a memoryless synchronizer with near optimal overheads was given in [AP90b]. This synchronizer can be used to significantly improve the asynchronous distributed solutions of classical network problems. Indeed, the synchronizer of

[AP90b] can be used to yield, in particular, a near optimal asynchronous BFS algorithm [AP90b, AR92].

Specifically, given this type of synchronizer in the network, it is possible to simulate the standard BFS tree construction algorithm Π_S based on FLOOD, whose complexities in the synchronous model are $\mathsf{Message}(\Pi_S) = O(|E|)$ and $\mathsf{Time}(\Pi_S) = O(Diam(G))$, directly under the synchronizer of [AP90b, AR92], to obtain an asynchronous BFS algorithm Π_A with message and time complexities $\mathsf{Message}(\Pi_A) = O(|E| + n\log^3 n)$ and $\mathsf{Time}(\Pi_A) = O(Diam(G) \cdot \log^3 n)$. For performing BFS in a network in which no synchronizer was established, one can set up such a synchronizer using the efficient preprocessing algorithms of [AP90a, ABCP93] discussed in Chapter 21, yielding essentially the same overall message complexity (specifically, $\mathsf{Message}(\Pi_A) = O(|E| + n\log^4 n)$). This provided a near-optimal solution to a long standing and extensively studied problem [Gal82, Fre85, Awe85a, AG85b, AG87, Awe89].

The synchronizer methodology was later extended to handling dynamic networks in [APSPS92].

The idea of using network decomposition for achieving fast deterministic distributed MIS algorithms is due to [AGLP89]. This approach was studied further in [PS92b, PS95]. Unfortunately, network decomposition still eludes a polylogarithmic time deterministic algorithm, so the results of Corollary 25.2.3 seem to be hard to improve upon. In fact, achieving polylogarithmic deterministic solutions for MIS and coloring is one of the main challenging open problems remaining in the field, and network decompositions are likely to play an important role in future solutions.

The close relationships between different coloring problems and the locality properties of graphs were intensively studied, and various aspects of these relationships are discussed in [MNS95, NS95, Lin93, SV93].

Exercises

1. Consider again the setting of Exercise 4 in Chapter 6. Suppose that the synchronizer used is γ and the partition into clusters, the spanning tree of each cluster, the inter-cluster edges and the location of v and v' are as shown in Figure 25.4. What is the range of possible pulse numbers at v'?

2. (∗) Devise a polylogarithmic time deterministic distributed algorithm for MIS and $(\Delta + 1)$-coloring.

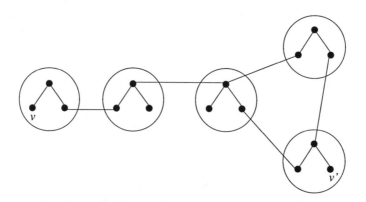

Figure 25.4: The setting of synchronizer γ in Exercise 1.

Chapter 26

Hierarchical cluster-based routing

The problem of efficient (low-dilation) message routing with succinct (low-memory) routing tables is one of the most natural candidate problems for clustered hierarchical treatment (and indeed, the first problem for which such an approach was considered). In this chapter, we explore the extent to which the performance of routing schemes can be optimized.

It turns out that there exists an almost tight trade-off between the dilation factor and the space requirement of any routing scheme for general networks. Specifically, it can be shown that any routing scheme for general n-vertex networks that achieves a dilation factor $\kappa \geq 1$ must use a total of $\Omega(n^{1+1/(2\kappa+4)})$ bits of routing information in some network. This lower bound holds for unweighted networks as well and concerns the total memory requirements of the scheme (and therefore extends directly also to the maximum requirements per vertex). For $\kappa < 2$, the lower bound becomes $\Omega(n^2)$.

We now complement this lower bound by presenting a family of hierarchical routing schemes RS_κ (for every fixed integer $\kappa \geq 1$) for arbitrary weighted networks, which guarantee a dilation factor of $\mathsf{Dilation}(RS_\kappa) = O(\kappa^2)$ and require using $\mathsf{Max\_Mem}(RS_\kappa) = O(n^{1/\kappa}\Lambda \cdot \log n)$ memory bits of routing information per vertex in the network. This trade-off is thus analogous to the one between cluster radius and overlap in sparse covers, although its proof is more subtle due to the more general setting.

Implicit in the algorithmic technique presented for this problem is the use of a sparse subgraph for routing purposes. Specifically, the construction method essentially defines a sparse subnetwork (specifically, an $O(\kappa^2)$-spanner) of only $O(n^{1+1/\kappa}\Lambda \cdot \log n)$ edges and uses precisely these edges for the routing.

26.1 Interval tree routing

In this section we discuss a basic routing scheme for networks whose topology is a tree. This scheme is called *interval tree routing* or *ITR*.

26.1.1 The scheme

The scheme is based on assigning the vertices of T an interval labeling, as in Section 19.4, and using it for the routing decisions. Hence for every $u \in V$, $Label(u) = Int(u)$ as defined in Section 19.4. The scheme is constructed as follows.

Data structures: A vertex u stores its own label $Int(u)$ and the labels of each of its children in the tree.

Forwarding protocol: Routing a message from a sender u to a destination v is based directly on the interval labels. In particular, consider any intermediate vertex w along the route. Upon receiving the message, the processor compares $Int(v)$, the interval label of the destination, with its own label $Int(w)$. Four possibilities exist.

1. $Int(w) = Int(v)$: then w is v and it accepts the message.

2. $Int(w) \subset Int(v)$: then w is a descendent of v, hence w forwards the message upwards to its parent in the tree.

3. The two labels represent disjoint intervals: then v and w belong to different subtrees and again w forwards the message upwards to its parent.

4. $Int(v) \subset Int(w)$: then v is a descendent of w in the tree and, in that case, w examines the interval labels of its children, looking for the unique child w' whose interval label satisfies $Int(v) \subseteq Int(w')$ (meaning that v is a descendent of w'), and forwards the message to w'. This can be done efficiently, say, by binary search on the children's labels.

26.1.2   Analysis

Note that the ITR scheme guarantees the delivery of a message sent from v to u along the (unique) shortest path between them (of length $dist_T(u,v)$) and the only communication required for routing messages using this scheme involves forwarding the message along this route. Consequently, the communication cost of the scheme is optimal, and the ITR routing scheme has the following properties.

Lemma 26.1.1 *For every weighted tree $T = (V, E, \omega)$, the ITR scheme has dilation* Dilation$(ITR, G) = 1$ *and requires using $O(\Delta(T) \log n)$ bits of routing information per vertex and a total of $O(n \log n)$ bits throughout the network.* $\square$

26.1.3   *ITR* for general networks

ITR can be used as a routing scheme for an arbitrary (nontree) network G. In order to do so, it is necessary to start by constructing an appropriate (shortest path) spanning tree T for G and then apply ITR to this tree. This will yield a routing scheme with total memory requirements of $O(n \log n)$ bits throughout the network, but the maximum memory requirements per vertex depend on the maximum degree of the selected tree, and the dilation of the scheme may be as high as $Rad(G)$.

   The problem of high maximum degree can be alleviated to some extent by applying the Degree Bounding Theorem 15.2.2 and embedding in T a virtual tree T' whose maximum degree is $\Delta(T') \leq 2m$, satisfying that $Depth_{T'}(v) \leq (2 \log_m n - 1)Depth_T(v)$ for every vertex v, where m is a tuning parameter. In particular, selecting $m = n^{1/\kappa}$ for some integer $\kappa \geq 1$, we get a tree T' with maximum degree $\Delta(T') \leq 2n^{1/\kappa}$ and $Depth(T') \leq (2\kappa - 1)Rad(G)$.

   One more comment is in order at this point on the implementation of this routing scheme. Recall that the tree T' is a *virtual* tree with a special embedding in the graph itself. Thus implementing the routing scheme in the actual physical graph requires that we implement the embedding as well. At first look, it may seem that this implementation may force us to use an amount of memory proportional to the real degrees of vertices in the "real" spanning tree T. However, it turns out that the embedding can be implemented using memory only at the vertices corresponding to endpoints of the *virtual* edges, and thus the required amount of memory is proportional to the degrees of vertices in T'.

In order to do this, we need to rely on property (2) of the Degree Bounding Theorem 15.2.2. By this property, each edge $e = (u, w)$ of T' corresponds to a path of length at most 2 in the original tree T, i.e., possibly going through an intermediate vertex v_e. Therefore it is possible to store the information on the embedding of the virtual edge e (necessary for routing messages that need to "traverse" e by following its corresponding path in the graph) *without* having to store any routing information at v_e. That is, in order to traverse e, the message header supplied at u, the first end-vertex of e, should contain the port selection information for *both* steps (from u to v_e and from v_e to w) in the actual graph G.

Lemma 26.1.2 *For every weighted graph $G = (V, E, \omega)$ and parameter κ, using the ITR scheme on an appropriately chosen tree T' guarantees the delivery of messages between vertices in G with communication $O(\kappa Rad(G))$ and requires using $O(n^{1/\kappa} \log n)$ bits of routing information per vertex and a total of $O(n \log n)$ bits overall.* $\square$

26.2   The routing scheme

In this section we describe our hierarchical cluster-based routing strategy and the structures it uses in the network.

26.2.1   Partial routing schemes

The routing schemes presented in this section are structured in a complex manner and are typically composed of a number of *partial* routing schemes. A partial routing scheme is one that is guaranteed to perform its task only for a restricted subset of sender-destination pairs and is allowed to "fail" for certain other pairs. The use of such schemes gives rise to some special difficulties, but at the same time allows additional flexibility.

The main complication arising from the use of a partial routing scheme involves the need to handle "unknown destination" failures. The failure of a routing attempt due to failing to reach the destination is in fact a frequently occurring event in communication networks. Such failure can result from a variety of reasons, such as an erroneous specification by the sender or a disconnected link along the way. But in our case it may also occur due to attempting to use a partial routing scheme in order to route a message from a given sender to a given destination outside its scope. It is therefore desirable that the routing scheme be able to handle such events efficiently. In fact, the demands from the partial routing scheme in such a case are rather modest, and in particular, it is expected to return the message to the sender with an appropriate notification. Furthermore, it is desirable to exclude the possibility that a failed routing attempt will consume a large portion of the network's resources before identifying failure and terminating.

On the positive side, partial routing schemes allow us to employ flexible and dynamic "Trial and Error" routing strategies. To this end we also make use of the special structure of the header functions in our definition of a routing scheme. Let us recall that the header functions H_v used to compute the next header depend on the *current* header attached to the message; the port functions also depend on the header. Hence, a processor w may try to forward a message employing a specific partial routing scheme by using a certain header h and exit port i; then if the attempt fails and the message returns to w, it can detect this fact and try an alternative partial routing scheme with a different header h' and port i' and so on. (In contrast, basing the port function on the label of the destination alone would yield a rigid scheme in which all routes are simple, i.e., cycle-free, since a cycle is doomed to be repeated forever.)

The basic component we use as a partial routing scheme is the ITR scheme. In the previous section we described the ITR scheme for routing over trees. In this section we utilize ITR as a partial routing scheme by defining it on a partial tree spanning only a subnetwork G' of the network G.

Very few changes are needed in the scheme in order to make it a partial scheme. In particular, the forwarding protocol has to allow for the possibility that at a certain point during the routing, none of the four possibilities tested for by the forwarding protocol of Section 26.1 apply. In this case, a "routing failure" is detected and an appropriate message is returned to the sender using essentially the same mechanism. (Note that the need to inform the sender of routing failures implies that the label of the sender must be included in the message header.)

The modified scheme has the following property: in case the destination label is illegal (i.e., in case the destination is not found in G), a "failure" message is returned with total message complexity $O(\kappa Rad(G'))$.

26.2.2   Overview of the hierarchical scheme

The hierarchical approach is based on constructing a *hierarchy* of tree covers in the network and using this hierarchy for routing. In each level of the hierarchy, each tree of the cover has its own internal ITR routing mechanism, constructed as earlier, enabling routing to and from the root. Messages are *always* transferred to their destinations using the internal ITR mechanism of *some* tree along a route going through the root. It is clear that this approach reduces the memory requirements of the routing schemes, since one has to define routing paths only for trees of the cover, but increases the communication cost, since messages need not be moving along shortest paths. Through an appropriate choice of the tree cover we guarantee that both overheads are low.

26.2.3   Regional routing schemes

The ITR scheme described earlier is used as a routing component within a more general scheme in order to route messages in a subgraph G' of the given network, as described in Section 26.1. Basic ITR components are integrated into our routing scheme using tree covers. Each level of the hierarchy constitutes a *regional (C, ρ)-routing scheme*, defined as follows.

Definition 26.2.1 [Regional (C, ρ)-routing scheme]: *A regional (C, ρ)-routing scheme is a scheme with the following properties.*

1. *For every two processors u, v, if $dist(u, v) \leq \rho$, then the scheme succeeds in delivering messages from u to v. Otherwise, the routing might end in failure, in which case the message is returned to u.*

2. *In either case, the communication cost of the entire process is at most C.*

In this subsection we describe how given a ρ-tree cover $\mathcal{TC}$, one can construct a regional (C, ρ)-routing scheme $RS_{\mathcal{TC}}$ with $C = O(Depth(\mathcal{TC}))$ using $O(\mathtt{Overlap}(\mathcal{TC}) \cdot \Delta^{\mathcal{TC}}(\mathcal{TC}) \cdot \log n)$ memory bits per vertex for any integer $\rho \geq 1$. Using the Balanced Tree Cover Theorem 15.5.3, this yields an $(O(\kappa^2 \rho), \rho)$-routing scheme using $O(\kappa \cdot n^{1/\kappa} \cdot \log n)$ memory bits per vertex for any integers $\kappa, \rho \geq 1$.

Data structures: Consider the given ρ-tree cover $\mathcal{TC}$. Assign each tree T in this tree cover a distinct label, $Label(T)$. Next, set up an ITR component $ITR(T)$ on each tree $T \in \mathcal{TC}$.

These routing components are integrated into a routing scheme as follows. First, recall that every vertex v has a home tree $T = home(v)$ in the tree cover $\mathcal{TC}$ containing its entire ρ-neighborhood. The routing label selected for v will be the pair $Label(v) = (Label(T), Int_T(v))$ composed of the identifier of v's home tree, $Label(T)$, and v's routing label in $ITR(T)$, $Int_T(v)$.

Since a vertex v may occur in more than one tree of the tree cover, it has to store routing information for each $ITR(T')$ component it participates in and not only for its home tree. The routing tables stored in a vertex v are kept sorted by tree identifiers, so when v participates in forwarding a message in one tree, it can determine the next step in logarithmic time. Of course, this requires message headers to include also a field identifying the tree used in the current routing operation.

Forwarding protocol: A processor u routes a message to a destination v with label $Label(v) = (Label(T), Int_T(v))$ as follows. First, u examines whether it belongs to the tree T. If not, then it can immediately detect an "unknown destination" failure and terminate the routing procedure. If u does belong to T, then it sends the message to v using the $ITR(T)$ component. Since both v and u belong to T, the message will arrive v.

Analysis

The correctness and complexity of the constructed regional scheme are dealt with in the following lemma relying on the properties of the tree routing mechanism and the constructed cover.

Lemma 26.2.2 *For every n-vertex weighted graph $G = (V, E, \omega)$ and ρ-tree-cover $\mathcal{TC}$ for G, the scheme $RS_{\mathcal{TC}}$ described above is a regional (C, ρ)-routing scheme with $C = O(Depth(\mathcal{TC}))$ and can be implemented using $O(\mathtt{Overlap}(\mathcal{TC}) \cdot \Delta^{TC}(\mathcal{TC}) \cdot \log n)$ memory bits per vertex.*

Proof: Let us first determine the dilation guarantees of the scheme $RS_{\mathcal{TC}}$. Suppose that $dist(u, v) \leq \rho$ for some processors u, v. By definition, $v \in \Gamma_\rho(u)$. Let T be the home tree of u. Then $\Gamma_\rho(u) \subseteq V(T)$, so $v \in T$. Hence by Lemma 26.1.1, the tree routing on T will succeed in passing the message from v to u. Furthermore, the routing proceeds along a path of length at most $O(Depth(\mathcal{TC}))$ (and in case of failure, no communication is required at all).

Implementing the routing scheme $RS_{\mathcal{TC}}$ involves the following space requirements. By Lemma 26.1.1, each vertex v needs to store up to $deg_T(v) \log n$ bits for every tree $T \in \mathcal{TC}$ to which it belongs. As a vertex v belongs to no more than $\mathtt{Overlap}(\mathcal{TC})$ trees in $\mathcal{TC}$, and its degree in each of those trees is no more than $\Delta^{TC}(\mathcal{TC})$, we get a total of $O(\mathtt{Overlap}(\mathcal{TC}) \cdot \Delta^{TC}(\mathcal{TC}) \cdot \log n)$ bits per vertex. $\square$

Corollary 26.2.3 *For every graph G and integers $\kappa, \rho \geq 1$, there exists a regional $(O(\kappa^2 \rho), \rho)$-routing scheme $RS_{\kappa, \rho}$ which can be implemented using $O(\kappa \cdot n^{1/\kappa} \cdot \log n)$ memory bits per vertex.*

Proof: Applying the Balanced Tree Cover Theorem 15.5.3 to construct a tree cover $\mathcal{TC}_{\kappa, \rho}$ with $Depth(\mathcal{TC}) = O(\kappa^2 \rho)$, $\Delta^{TC}(\mathcal{TC}) = O(n^{1/\kappa})$ and $\mathtt{Overlap}(\mathcal{TC}) = O(\kappa \cdot n^{1/\kappa})$, we get a regional $(O(\kappa^2 \rho), \rho)$-routing scheme $RS_{\kappa, \rho}$ using $O(\kappa \cdot n^{2/\kappa} \cdot \log n)$ bits per vertex. Finally, note that substituting 2κ for κ in the construction modifies the memory bound into $O(\kappa \cdot n^{1/\kappa} \cdot \log n)$, while multiplying the dilation bound by 4. $\square$

26.2.4   The hierarchical routing scheme

Finally, we present our family of *hierarchical routing schemes*. We rely on the existence of a special hierarchy of tree covers, as follows.

Definition 26.2.4 [Tree cover hierarchy]: *A hierarchical D_R-family of tree covers is a family of ρ_i-tree covers $\mathcal{TC}_i$, where $\rho_i = 2^i$ for $1 \leq i \leq \Lambda$, with the property that there exists a bound D_R such that $\text{Depth}(\mathcal{TC}_i) = O(D_R \cdot \rho_i)$.*

Given such a D_R-family of tree covers, construct the hierarchical scheme RS as follows.

Data structures: For every $1 \leq i \leq \Lambda$ construct a regional $(O(D_R \cdot \rho_i), \rho_i)$-routing scheme $R_i = RS_{\mathcal{TC}_i}$ as in the last subsection. Each processor v participates in all Λ regional routing schemes R_i. In particular, v has a home tree $home_i(v)$ in each R_i, it has a routing label $Label_i(v)$ in each level i and it stores all the information it is required to store for each of these schemes. The complete routing label of v is the concatenation of all Λ regional labels, $Label(v) = (Label_1(v), \ldots, Label_\Lambda(v))$.

Forwarding protocol: The routing procedure operates as follows. Suppose a vertex u wishes to send a message to a vertex v. Then u first needs to identify the lowest-level regional scheme R_i that can be used for this routing operation. That is, u first checks to see whether it belongs to the tree $home_1(v)$. If it doesn't, then it checks the second level and so on. Once u identifies the first level i on which it belongs to $home_i(v)$, it forwards the message to v on the $ITR(home_i(v))$ component of the regional scheme R_i.

Analysis

Lemma 26.2.5 *The hierarchical routing scheme RS has $\text{Dilation}(RS) = O(D_R)$.*

Proof: Suppose that a processor u needs to send a message to some other processor v. Let $d = dist(u,v)$ and $j = \lceil \log d \rceil$ (i.e., $2^{j-1} < d \leq 2^j$). The sender u looks for the lowest level i on which it belongs to v's home tree. By Lemma 26.2.2, u must belong to $home_j(v)$ and therefore the regional scheme R_j is necessarily applicable if no previous level was. (Note that the highest-level scheme, R_Λ, has $\rho_\Lambda = 2^\Lambda \geq Diam(G) \geq d$ and therefore will always succeed.)

By Lemma 26.2.2,

$$\textsf{Comm}(RS, u, v) \ \leq \ |\Upsilon(RS, u, v)| \ \leq \ O(D_R \cdot 2^j) \ \leq \ O(D_R) \cdot dist(u, v). \qquad \square$$

Theorem 26.2.6 *For every n-vertex weighted graph $G = (V, E, \omega)$ with a hierarchical D_R-family of tree covers $\mathcal{TC}_i$, it is possible to construct (in polynomial time) a hierarchical routing scheme RS with $\text{Dilation}(RS) = O(D_R)$ using $\textsf{Mem}(RS) = O(\sum_{i=1}^{\Lambda} \textsf{Overlap}(\mathcal{TC}_i) \cdot \Delta^{TC}(\mathcal{TC}_i) \cdot \log n)$ memory bits per vertex.*

Proof: Construct the Λ regional schemes R_i as in the previous subsection. The memory requirements of the hierarchical scheme are thus composed of Λ terms, each bounded as in Lemma 26.2.2. $\square$

Corollary 26.2.7 *For every n-vertex weighted graph $G = (V, E, \omega)$ and fixed integer $\kappa \geq 1$, it is possible to construct (in polynomial time) a hierarchical routing scheme RS_κ with $\text{Dilation}(RS_\kappa) = O(\kappa^2)$ using*

$$\textsf{Mem}(RS_\kappa) = O(\kappa \cdot n^{1/\kappa} \cdot \log n \cdot \Lambda)$$

memory bits per vertex.

Proof: Construct the routing scheme relying on Corollary 26.2.3 for obtaining the Λ tree covers. Those tree covers have $D_R = O(\kappa^2)$ and their memory requirements are $O(\kappa \cdot n^{1/\kappa} \cdot \log n)$ each. The total memory requirements are thus Λ times larger. $\qquad\square$

26.3 Low dilation, low buffer deadlock-free routing

The final version of the routing problem we address involves the problem of deadlock-free routing and, specifically, the two basic characteristics of deadlock prevention policies, namely, their buffer requirements and the quality of the allowed routes. The two extreme methods described in Sections 9.4.3 and 26.3.1 exhibit either very high dilation or very high buffer requirements. It therefore seems plausible that some trade-off exists between these two approaches, allowing buffer-economical solutions with low dilation for deadlock-free routing.

Indeed, it turns out that using it is possible to devise intermediate solutions based on LP-representations. In particular, routing schemes similar in spirit to those described earlier in this chapter can provide considerable savings in buffer requirements by making relatively modest compromises in the lengths of the routes.

26.3.1 *ITR* buffer-routing

Let us first consider the *ITR* routing scheme, based on a spanning tree T for the network, and modify it into a deadlock-free buffer-routing scheme. It turns out that this is doable using only two buffers per vertex. Specifically, at each vertex v we allocate two buffers, called the *inbound* and *outbound* buffers and denoted by $B_I(v)$ and $B_O(v)$, respectively. The first buffer is dedicated to message traffic towards the root of T and the other to message traffic going away from the root.

For every two vertices u, v in the network, the route connecting them in T is composed of two segments: an *inbound segment* going from u towards the root of T, until reaching $L = L(u, v)$, the lowest common ancestor of u and v, and an *outbound segment* going from L towards v. A message traveling from u to v on this route uses the inbound buffers $B_I(w)$ at the vertices w that it passes in the inbound segment. At L, it switches from the inbound buffer $B_I(L)$ to the outbound buffers $B_O(L)$. Finally, in the outbound segment, the message uses the outbound buffers $B_O(w)$. Figures 26.1(a) and 26.1(b) depict a tree T and its associated buffer graph $\mathcal{B}$, respectively.

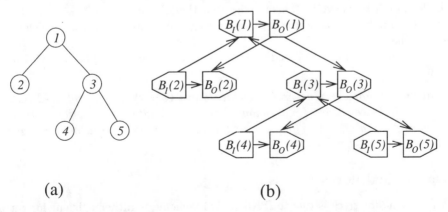

(a)   (b)

Figure 26.1: (a) The tree T. (b) The associated buffer graph $\mathcal{B}$.

We make the following observation.

Lemma 26.3.1 *The resulting buffer graph $\mathcal{B}$ is acyclic.*   □

Corollary 26.3.2 *The ITR buffer-routing scheme is deadlock-free.*   □

While the ITR buffer-routing scheme is very efficient w.r.t. its buffer utilization, it has potentially high dilation, as discussed earlier. We comment that the individual buffer-routing scheme described in Section 9.4.2 can be thought of as a variant of the ITR scheme based on using n separate SPTs T_v, one rooted at each $v \in V$, and routing the messages directed at each destination v over the tree T_v.

26.3.2   Tree-cover routing

We now present a deadlock-free routing strategy named RS^B_{TC} and analyze its behavior. The construction of the Tree Cover Theorem 15.5.2 is used in order to set up our routing scheme as follows. Given a parameter κ, we first construct the tree covers $\mathcal{TC}_{\kappa,\rho_i}$ for $\rho_i = 2^i$, $1 \leq i \leq \Lambda$, as in Theorem 15.5.2, and let

$$\mathcal{TC}_\kappa = \bigcup_{i=1}^{\Lambda} \mathcal{TC}_{\kappa,\rho_i}.$$

For every tree $T \in \mathcal{TC}_\kappa$, we construct an ITR buffer-routing scheme as in Section 26.3.1. These partial schemes are now combined in the natural way: for every two vertices u, v in the network, we select the route connecting them in the tree T mutual to both of them, whose existence is asserted in the Balanced Tree Cover Theorem 15.5.3. (In case there are several such trees, choose the one yielding the shortest route.)

The resulting buffer-routing scheme RS^B_{TC} satisfies the following.

Lemma 26.3.3 *The scheme RS^B_{TC} is deadlock-free.*

Proof: Consider the buffer graph $\mathcal{B} = (V_\mathcal{B}, E_\mathcal{B})$ induced by the construction. Note that $\mathcal{B}$ is partitioned into connected components induced by the collection of trees. Namely, for each tree T in the collection $\mathcal{TC}_\kappa$, the buffers

$$\{B_I(w, T), B_O(w, T) \mid w \in T\}$$

form a connected component $\mathcal{B}_T$ of $\mathcal{B}$ with no directed edges between any two components $\mathcal{B}_T$ and $\mathcal{B}_{T'}$. Moreover, by Lemma 26.3.1, the component $\mathcal{B}_T$ is acyclic. It follows that the entire buffer graph $\mathcal{B}$ is acyclic. This implies that the scheme is deadlock-free. The first-in, first-out (FIFO) policy for handling arriving messages guarantees progress, which completes the proof of the lemma.   □

The above construction, combined with the Balanced Tree Cover Theorem 15.5.3, implies the following.

Theorem 26.3.4 *For every n-vertex weighted graph $G = (V, E, \omega)$ and fixed integer $\kappa \geq 1$, it is possible to construct (in polynomial time) a deadlock-free buffer-routing scheme which requires $2\kappa \cdot \lceil n^{1/\kappa} \cdot \Lambda \rceil$ buffers per vertex, and the routes are at most 8κ longer than optimal.*   □

Bibliographical notes

The ITR scheme for trees is due to [SK85]. This scheme is rather efficient for certain restricted graph families and was also the basis for the concept of *interval routing*, developed later for a wider variety of networks (cf. [vLT87, Fre93, FGS96, FG98]). When considering

ITR schemes for classes of graphs other than trees, a natural question is to identify which graphs admit interval routing along shortest paths [EMZ97, NS96]. Another natural extension is to allow using more than one interval on each edge, raising the questions of how many intervals are necessary to ensure shortest path routing and how such a scheme can be implemented [GP99, GG98, GP98]. For surveys of the many recent developments in this area see [vLT94, Gav97].

The problem of efficiency-memory trade-offs for routing schemes was first raised in [KK77], which proposed a general approach for hierarchically clustering a network into κ levels and using the resulting structure for routing. The total memory used by the scheme is $O(n^{1+1/\kappa} \log n)$. In order to apply the method of [KK77], one needs to make some fairly strong assumptions regarding the existence of a certain partition of the network. Several variations and/or improvements were studied later; cf. [KK80, Per85, Sun82].

Most subsequent work on the problem has focused on solutions for special classes of network topologies. Optimal (dilation factor 1) routing schemes with memory requirement $O(n \log n)$ were designed for simple topologies like trees [SK85], unit-cost rings, complete networks and grids [vLT86, vLT87] and networks at the lower end of a hierarchy (beginning with the outerplanar networks) identified in [FJ88]. The problem of designing memory-efficient near-optimal routing schemes was cast in a theoretical formulation in [FJ88, FJ89], where it was also given precise solutions for various graph classes up to and including planar graphs. Near-optimal routing schemes were constructed in [FJ89, FJ90] for c-decomposable networks, for constant c and for planar networks. The schemes for c-decomposable networks guarantee a dilation factor ranging between 2 and 3 (specifically, $1 + 2/a$ where $a > 1$ is the positive root of the equation $a^{\lceil (c+1)/2 \rceil} - a - 2 = 0$) and have a memory requirement of $O(c^2 \log c \cdot n \log^2 n)$. The schemes for planar networks guarantee a dilation factor of 7 and have a memory requirement of $O(\frac{1}{\epsilon} n^{1+\epsilon} \log n)$ bits for any $0 < \epsilon < \frac{1}{3}$. A crucial step in constructing these routing schemes is assigning names to the vertices as part of the routing scheme. The above optimal schemes use $O(\log n)$-bit labels. The schemes of [FJ90] for c-decomposable networks use $O(c \log c \log n)$-bit names, and the schemes of [FJ89, FJ90] for planar networks use $O(\frac{1}{\epsilon} \log n)$-bit names. As another example, the construction of 3-spanners for the family of chordal graphs described earlier (in Section 16.3) can be used to construct routing schemes for these graphs with dilation ≤ 3 and $O(n \log^2 n)$ bits of memory.

Work on compact routing schemes for arbitrary networks began with [PU89a], where the problem is dealt with for general unweighted networks. Lower bounds for the space-efficiency trade-off of routing schemes were studied in [PU89a, FG95, GP95, GP96, FG96, BHV96, KK96]. The two lower bounds mentioned earlier are due to [PU89a] and [GP95], respectively. The solution of [PU89a] was later generalized in a number of ways, and various qualities of the resulting schemes were improved in [PU87, ABLP89, ABLP90, Pel93, AP92]. For instance, the schemes were extended to weighted graphs, they were modified to work in a setting where vertices can freely select their own labels, they were provided with efficient preprocessing procedures and so on. The scheme presented in Section 26.2 is based on a variant of the scheme of [AP92]. In fact, the trade-off obtained in the schemes of Section 26.2 is still not optimal, and it is conceivably possible to reduce the dilation factor of the routing schemes from $O(\kappa^2)$ to $O(\kappa)$. Recent developments concerning compact routing schemes with low dilation are presented in [KKU95, FG97, GG97, NO99, Cow99, CW00].

The case of dynamic networks is dealt with in [AGR89] in the limited setting of networks whose topology is a tree and the topological changes are restricted to growing (i.e., new edges and vertices are occasionally added to the network).

Recently, the routing problem was dealt with in the context of the new generation of ATM and optical networks [GZ94, CGZ94, DKKP99].

The deadlock-free routing solution described here is taken from [AKP91, AKP94]. It follows the hierarchical paradigm advocated in [BC89, Sch91]. In fact, the notion of distinguishing routing within a tree from routing between trees is already present in [MS80]. Deadlock-free routing was studied extensively in many contexts, including interval routing (cf. [Fla97]).

Exercises

1. Design a hierarchical routing scheme for 2-dimensional Euclidean graphs and analyze its complexities using Theorem 26.2.6 and Exercise 4 of Chapter 15.

2. Prove Lemmas 9.4.2, 9.4.4 and 26.3.1.

Chapter 27

Regional directories: Resource finding revisited

A number of strategies for answering local queries and local resource allocation were discussed in Chapter 10 from a worst-case point of view. The purpose of this chapter is to present a design for regional and hierarchical distributed directories based on clustered representations. Such directories relate the cost of the search to the actual distance of the searching client from the searched item and thus guarantee efficient performance for each request instance, depending on its specific characteristics, rather than just a global complexity bound.

27.1   Answering local queries using regional directories

Consider the repeated ρ-local query problem discussed in Section 10.1.1. Let us restrict the problem by adding the following two assumptions.

- Queries are restricted to a single range value ρ, and

- Each vertex of the network knows the entire topology.

The restricted problem admits a more efficient solution using the concept ρ-regional matchings from Section 14.3. We next present an algorithm LQ that given a ρ-local query QUERY(f, v) issued by a vertex v, returns to v the value of $f(\mathcal{X}_\rho(u))$. Algorithm LQ makes use of a specific type of a distributed data structure, called a ρ-regional directory, which is constructed using the ρ-regional matching $\mathcal{RW}$ of Corollary 14.3.4. Note that the read set of each vertex v, Read(v), consists of a single vertex.

Data structures: Given a ρ-regional matching $\mathcal{RW}$ as in Corollary 14.3.4, the data items are organized in the ρ-regional directory $\mathcal{RD}$ as follows:

> For every vertex v, each vertex u in the write set Write(v) stores the data value X_v.

Query protocol: A vertex v that issues a query QUERY(f, v) sends the query to the unique vertex z in its read set Read(v). The vertex u computes the value of $f(\mathcal{X}_\rho(z))$ locally. It then returns the result to v.

Update protocol: Whenever the value X_v changes, v informs each vertex u in the write set Write(v).

The correctness of the above solution for the ρ-local query problem (based on the proposed implementation for a ρ-regional directory) can be verified in a straightforward manner from the properties of ρ-regional matchings.

Lemma 27.1.1 *If $\mathcal{RW}$ is a ρ-regional matching, then the query protocol of Algorithm* LQ *correctly answers the ρ-local query* QUERY(f, v).

Proof: We first need to argue that u stores all the values of $\mathcal{X}_\rho(v) = \{X_w \mid w \in \Gamma_\rho(v)\}$. To see why this is true, consider some vertex $w \in \Gamma_\rho(v)$. This w satisfies $dist(w, v) \leq \rho$ and hence by definition of $\mathcal{RW}$, Write$(w) \cap$ Read$(v) \neq \emptyset$. As Read$(v) = \{u\}$, this necessarily means that $u \in$ Write(w), which in turn implies that u stores X_w in the regional directory $\mathcal{RD}$.

Moreover, as u knows the entire topology, it knows which of the vertices whose data it stores belong to $\Gamma_\rho(v)$. Hence u can identify the set $\mathcal{X}_\rho(v)$ precisely and apply the function f to it.   □

We now show that the complexities of queries and update operations in a regional directory depend on the parameters of the regional matching used for constructing it.

Lemma 27.1.2 *The query protocol of Algorithm* LQ *answers ρ-local queries with message complexity* Message$($QUERY$(f, v)) \leq 2\rho \log n$. *Updates of the data value X_v by a vertex v cost $O(\rho \cdot \log^2 n)$ messages. Also, assuming the data items X_v require at most B bits each, the total memory requirements of the ρ-regional directory are* Mem$($QUERY$(f, v)) = O(n \log n \cdot B)$.   □

Proof: Observe that each query is answered by sending a message and getting a reply along a path of length at most $\rho \cdot \mathrm{Str}_{read}(\mathcal{RW}) \cdot \Delta_{read}(\mathcal{RW}) \leq \rho \cdot \log n$. Likewise, updates require a total of at most $\rho \cdot \mathrm{Str}_{write}(\mathcal{RW}) \cdot \Delta_{write}(\mathcal{RW}) \leq \rho \cdot \log^2 n$ messages. Finally, the bound on the total memory requirements of the ρ-regional directory follows from the fact that each data item is stored in at most $\Delta_{write}(\mathcal{RW}) \leq \log n$ copies.   □

27.2   Local resource finding using regional directories

Let us now turn to the local resource finding problem discussed in Section 10.2 and describe a solution to the problem based on regional directories.

27.2.1   The hierarchical directory controller

The basic component in the resource controller described next is the ρ-regional directory $\mathcal{RD}$, which is essentially the one described in the previous section, setting the variable X_v stored at each vertex v to be the pair

$$X_v = \langle ID(v), \mathrm{F}(v) \rangle .$$

In other words, each vertex v stores and constantly updates the status of its free bit $\mathrm{F}(v)$ at all vertices in its write set Write(v).

The queries applied to this directory are specialized to the FIND operation. That is, while looking for a resource unit, the searching client u issues a query to the unique vertex in its read set, $z \in$ Read(u), asking whether there exists a free resource unit at some vertex among those storing their free bit at z, namely, querying the existence of a pair $\langle ID(v), \mathrm{F}(v) \rangle$ stored at z such that $\mathrm{F}(v) = 1$. In case no such pair exists, the operation is said to end in failure. Note that by definition of a ρ-regional matching, this might happen only if $dist(u, z) > \rho$.

This basic component is utilized within our main, global directory structure. The *hierarchical directory controller* HDC is defined as follows.

Data structures: Given a hierarchy of 2^i-regional matchings for $1 \le i \le \Lambda$, as in Corollary 14.3.4 of the Regional Matching Theorem, construct a hierarchy of 2^i-regional directories $\mathcal{RD}_i$ for every $1 \le i \le \Lambda$.

Each processor v participates in each of the 2^i-regional directories $\mathcal{RD}_i$ for $1 \le i \le \Lambda$. In particular, each vertex v has sets $\text{Write}_i(v)$ and $\text{Read}_i(v)$ in each $\mathcal{RD}_i$.

Query protocol: A FIND(HDC, v) instruction is performed as follows. The querying client v attempts to locate the nearest free resource unit by successively querying the regional directories $\mathcal{RD}_i$ one by one, starting at the lowest level $i = 1$ and going successively farther until reaching the first level i on which it succeeds. (There must be such a level, since the highest level always succeeds.)

Update protocol: Whenever a vertex v changes the status of its free bit $F(v)$ to b, it should invoke the UPDATE(v, b) operation and update its record X_v in the regional directory $\mathcal{RD}_i$ on all levels $1 \le i \le \Lambda$.

Lemma 27.2.1 *In response to a request by processor v, the hierarchical directory controller HDC always locates a resource unit at distance $O((\text{Str}_{write} + \text{Str}_{read}) \cdot D_{server}(v))$. Furthermore, the message complexity of this search is $\text{Message}(\text{FIND}(v)) = O(\Delta_{read} \cdot \text{Str}_{read} \cdot D_{server}(v))$.*

Proof: Suppose that a processor v issues an instruction FIND(HDC, v). Suppose that the resource unit nearest to v is stored at vertex u, i.e., $D_{server}(v) = dist(u, v)$, and suppose that $2^{i-1} < D_{server}(v) \le 2^i$. By definition, there exists some vertex w in $\text{Read}_i(v) \cap \text{Write}_i(v)$. The requesting vertex v successively tries using its level j read sets for $j = 1, 2, \ldots$ until succeeding in locating a free resource unit. As w stores the free bit $F(u) = 1$, the search will necessarily succeed in finding some resource unit in RD_i and allocating it to v (if no lower level directory did). The claim now follows from the fact that

$$dist(u, v) \le dist(u, w) + dist(w, v) \le \text{Str}_{write}(RD_i) \cdot 2^{i+1} + \text{Str}_{read}(RD_i) \cdot 2^{i+1}$$

and $2^{i+1} < 4 \cdot D_{server}(v)$.

As for the message complexity of the entire process, we note that the communication between v and its read set $\text{Read}_i(v)$ costs at most $\text{Str}_{read}(RD_i) \cdot \Delta_{read}(RD_i) \cdot 2^i$ messages, and the entire search sums up to

$$
\begin{aligned}
\text{Message}(\text{FIND}(v)) &= \sum_{j=1}^{i} O(2^{j+1} \cdot \text{Str}_{read}(RD_i) \cdot \Delta_{read}(RD_i)) \\
&= O(2^{i+1} \cdot \text{Str}_{read}(RD_i) \cdot \Delta_{read}(RD_i)) \\
&= O(\text{Str}_{read}(RD_i) \cdot \Delta_{read}(RD_i) \cdot D_{server}(v)) . \qquad \square
\end{aligned}
$$

Lemma 27.2.2 *The message complexity of an update operation of the hierarchical directory controller HDC involving a vertex v is $\text{Message}(\text{UPDATE}(v, b)) = O(\text{Str}_{write}(RD_i) \cdot \Delta_{write}(RD_i) \cdot \text{Diam}(G))$.*

Proof: The update algorithm requires v to update its level j write set $\text{Write}_j(v)$ on all levels. Updating the vertices of $\text{Write}_i(v)$ requires at most $\text{Str}_{write}(RD_i) \cdot \Delta_{write}(RD_i) \cdot 2^i$

messages, and the entire search sums up to

$$\sum_{j=1}^{\Lambda} O(2^{j+1} \cdot \text{Str}_{write}(RD_i) \cdot \Delta_{write}(RD_i))$$

$$= O(Diam(G) \cdot \text{Str}_{write}(RD_i) \cdot \Delta_{write}(RD_i)). \quad \square$$

Lemma 27.2.3 *The hierarchical directory controller* HDC *can be implemented using a total of* $O(n \cdot \Delta_{write} \cdot \Lambda + n \cdot \Delta_{read} \cdot \Lambda \cdot \log n)$ *memory bits throughout the network.*

Proof: The regional directory implementation requires each vertex v to post its free bit $F(v)$ at the vertices of $\text{Write}_i(v)$. Summing over n vertices and Λ levels, this gives a total memory of $O(n \cdot \Delta_{write} \cdot \Lambda)$. In addition, each processor v needs to know the identity of the vertices in $\text{Read}(v)$. This requires a total additional amount of $O(\Delta_{read} \cdot n \cdot \Lambda \cdot \log n)$ bits. $\square$

Summarizing the above three lemmas, we get Lemma 27.2.4.

Lemma 27.2.4 *Given an appropriate family of regional matchings, the hierarchical directory controller* HDC *is an* $O(\text{Str}_{write} + \text{Str}_{read})$-*dilated resource controller, it has message complexities*

$$\text{Message}(\text{FIND}(v)) = O(\Delta_{read} \cdot \text{Str}_{read} \cdot D_{server}(v)) \quad and$$
$$\text{Message}(\text{UPDATE}(v)) = O(\text{Str}_{write}(RD_i) \cdot \Delta_{write}(RD_i) \cdot Diam(G))$$

and requires a total of $O(n \cdot \Delta_{write} \cdot \Lambda + n \cdot \Delta_{read} \cdot \Lambda \cdot \log n)$ *memory bits throughout the network.* $\square$

Applying the regional matching of Corollary 14.3.4, we get the following result.

Theorem 27.2.5 *It is possible to construct an* $O(\log n)$-*dilated resource controller with message complexities* $\text{Message}(\text{UPDATE}(v)) = O(\log^2 n \cdot Diam(G))$ *and* $\text{Message}(\text{FIND}(v)) = O(\log n \cdot D_{server}(v))$ *and with memory requirements of* $O(n \cdot \log n \cdot \Lambda)$ $\square$

27.2.2   Achieving a 1-dilated resource controller

There are a number of reasons why the resource controller HDC described in the previous section is not 1-dilated. One obvious reason is that when a vertex $z \in \text{Read}(v)$ is approached by v during a $\text{FIND}(v)$ operation, it does not attempt to select the resource unit closest to v when several different units are available. Part of the difficulty is that z is perhaps incapable of telling which resource unit is closer to v, since it does not know the exact location of v or of the resource units it points at. This difficulty is alleviated in a setting where vertices are assumed to have complete knowledge of the topology. In such a setting, we may assume that whenever z is asked by v for a resource unit, it will direct v to the one closest to it.

Unfortunately, this does not completely solve the problem. For example, consider the following scenario. Suppose that the resource unit closest to v is stored at a vertex w such that $D_{server}(v) = dist(v, w) = 2^i + 1$. Suppose further that the first resource unit is discovered by v while using the level i regional directory and, specifically, as a response to querying some vertex $z \in \text{Read}_i(v)$. It is possible that the reply provided by z concerned a resource unit stored at a vertex w' whose distance from v is $dist(v, w') = 2^i \cdot \log n$. In fact, z may know of w' but not of w. This may happen even in the specific HDC controller

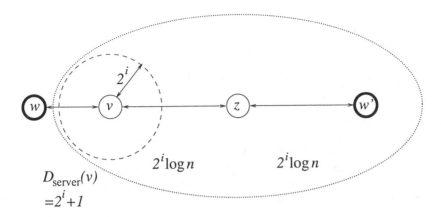

Figure 27.1: A bad scenario for resource allocation. Server locations are marked by bold circles. The dashed circle encloses v's 2^i-neighborhood, and the dotted ellipse marks all vertices v using z in their read-set, i.e., such that $z \in \text{Read}(v)$.

used above, in which z knows of v's entire 2^i-neighborhood since w is not contained in that neighborhood. (See Figure 27.1.)

However, the problem can be solved by a minor modification to the scheme at the price of increasing the message complexity of the FIND operation by a factor of $O(\log n)$ (see Exercise 2). Hence applying this modification to the $O(\log n)$-dilated resource controller of Theorem 27.2.5, we get the following result.

Theorem 27.2.6 *It is possible to construct a 1-dilated resource controller with message complexities*

$$\text{Message}(\text{UPDATE}(v)) = O(\log^2 n \cdot Diam(G)) \text{ and}$$
$$\text{Message}(\text{FIND}(v)) = O(\log^2 n \cdot D_{server}(v))$$

and with memory requirements of $O(n \cdot \log n \cdot \Lambda)$.   □

27.3   A lower bound for regional resource finding

27.3.1   A yardstick for updates

The update costs of the last solution given for the resource finding problem are still bounded by a "global" parameter. We would like both the update and the search complexities to be as low as possible. This requires us to first establish the natural limits of the problem.

Suppose a vertex v is currently looking for a resource unit. Then $D_{server}(v)$ places an obvious lower bound on the message complexity of $\text{FIND}(v)$ since the requesting vertex needs either to get hold of the resource or to transfer some task to it.

Analogously, we need a measure for estimating the *usefulness* of a vertex to *other* vertices.

Definition 27.3.1 [J-usable server]: *Given a κ-dilated resource controller and a configuration $\bar{F}$ in which $F(v) = 1$, we say that the server v is J-usable if there exists a potential client at distance J from v, namely, a vertex w that may wish to use resource units from v (if available).*

The maximum distance J to which v is J-usable is defined as

$$D_{client}(v) \;=\; \max\{J \mid v \text{ is } J-usable\}.$$

The next lemma follows immediately from the definitions.

Lemma 27.3.2 *A necessary condition for the server v to be J-usable is that there exists some $w \in V$ such that $J \le \kappa \cdot D_{server}(w)$.*

Suppose a vertex v has changed its status with respect to the resource. For example, suppose the vertex v just consumed its last unit. Intuitively, it seems that v's neighborhood in radius $D_{\mathrm{client}}(v)$ should be informed of the change. This is not a lower bound on the message complexity of an update, as indicated by the existence of the local policy discussed earlier, but we argue that if one wishes to maintain a close to optimal search complexity, then a message complexity of updates is $\Omega(D_{\mathrm{client}})$. This intuition is formalized in the following lower bound.

27.3.2   The lower bound

While an inherent lower bound of $\Omega(D_{\mathrm{server}}(v))$ holds for the FIND(v) operation, there is no analogous bound for the UPDATE operation. For example, the update-free policy discussed in Section 10.2.4 requires no update activities at all. A processor in need for a resource unit must perform an exhaustive search.

However, there is a certain trade-off between the message complexities of the FIND and UPDATE operations. This trade-off states that if one insists on low complexity for searches, i.e., $\kappa \cdot D_{\mathrm{server}}$ for some constant κ, then the message complexity of updates is essentially $\Omega(D_{\mathrm{client}})$.

In fact, the trade-off does not hold for all graphs. For example, on a ring or a path, the update-free policy fares well for both searches and updates (see Exercise 3). The trade-off holds, though, for other graph families and we demonstrate it for the family of square grid graphs. The bound is formalized as follows.

Theorem 27.3.3 *For every integer $\kappa \ge 1$ and $q > 100\kappa^2$, and for any κ-dilated resource controller, there is an infinite class of graphs on which if the complexity of updates satisfies* Message(UPDATE(v)) $\le D_{client}(v)/q$ *for every vertex v and every configuration, then the complexity of searches satisfies* Message(FIND(v)) $= \Omega(D_{server}(v) \cdot q/\kappa^3)$. $\Box$

Proof: The graphs we consider are $n \times n$ grids. Consider a given κ-dilated resource controller and an integer $q > 100\kappa^2$ such that the premise of the theorem is satisfied. Consider a given configuration. Let v be the vertex farthest away from any resource, and let $d = D_{\mathrm{server}}(v)$. By the assumption of the theorem,

$$\text{Message}(\text{UPDATE}(w)) \le \frac{D_{\mathrm{client}}(w)}{q}$$

for any vertex w.

Lemma 27.3.4 *For every processor w, $D_{client}(w) \le \kappa d$.*

Proof: Consider some processor w, and let $J = D_{\mathrm{client}}(w)$. By definition of D_{client}, w is J-usable. Hence, there exists some vertex z at distance J from w such that $J \le \kappa \cdot D_{\mathrm{server}}(z) \le \kappa d$. $\Box$

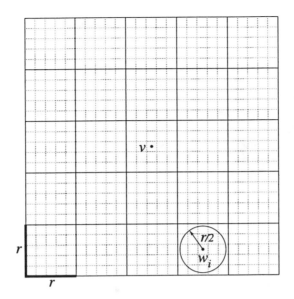

Figure 27.2: The subgrid $\hat{G}$.

Hence, denoting

$$r = \frac{2\kappa d}{q},$$

we have that $\mathsf{Message}(\mathrm{UPDATE}(w)) \leq r/2$ for any vertex w.

Consider the $\frac{d}{\kappa} \times \frac{d}{\kappa}$ subgrid of G centered at v. This subgrid may extend beyond the legal boundaries of the original grid in case v is closer to these boundaries than d/κ. In this case, restrict the subgrid to its "real" segment, which is at least a $\frac{d}{2\kappa} \times \frac{d}{2\kappa}$ subgrid of G containing v. Restrict it further to the largest subgrid $\hat{G}$ whose dimensions are divisible by $3r$. This subgrid is necessarily empty of resources. Break $\hat{G}$ into $r \times r$ squares. There are at least $\frac{q}{4\kappa^2}$ such squares in each row and column of $\hat{G}$ (which is at least some constant > 1 by the assumption on q), and overall the number of squares, denoted m, satisfies

$$m = \Omega\left(\frac{q^2}{\kappa^4}\right).$$

Let $w_1, \ldots, w_m$ denote the center vertices of these squares (without loss of generality assuming r is odd). See Figure 27.2.

We consider $m+1$ different scenarios, denoted $S_0, S_1, \ldots, S_m$. In scenario S_i for $1 \leq i \leq m$, w_i gets a released resource unit and issues an $\mathrm{UPDATE}(w_i, 1)$ instruction, then v needs a resource unit and issues a $\mathrm{FIND}(v)$ instruction. In scenario S_0, v asks for a resource immediately. Note that by assumption, the execution subgraph of any $\mathrm{UPDATE}(w_i, 1)$ instruction is restricted to the $r \times r$ square surrounding w_i. Also note that in scenario S_i, $1 \leq i \leq m$, v must be given the added resource unit at w_i, since the only other possible alternatives are at distance d away, while after the update, $D_{\mathrm{server}}(v) = dist(v, w_i) \leq d/\kappa$. In contrast, in scenario S_0, v's request must be satisfied with a resource unit from outside $\hat{G}$.

It follows that in scenario S_0, before v is allowed to search outside the subgrid $\hat{G}$, it must verify that none of the other scenarios is in fact taking place. This requires that there is some information transfer between v and all m squares.

Lemma 27.3.5 *Any algorithm involving information transfer between v and all m squares requires $\Omega(mr)$ messages.*

Proof: The claim can be verified by the following argument. Partition the arrangement of squares into larger super-squares, each composed of 3×3 original squares. Charge the algorithm only for the steps required for getting from the boundary of the super-square to the middle square in each super-square. This charge is at least r. There are $m/9$ super-squares, hence the claim follows.   □

Substituting the values of m and r, we get that the message complexity of the FIND operation is

$$\text{Message}(\text{FIND}(v)) = \Omega(mr) = \Omega\left(\frac{q^2}{\kappa^4} \cdot \frac{\kappa d}{q}\right) = \Omega\left(\frac{q}{\kappa^3} \cdot D_{\text{server}}(v)\right).   □$$

27.4   A controller based on a refinement hierarchy

Using regional directories based on regional matchings as discussed in Section 27.2 goes halfway towards a satisfactory solution of the problem in the sense that it can guarantee close to optimal FIND operations, as well as reasonable memory requirements. However, these directories are geared for static data, and the cost of updates is still higher than $Diam(G)$. Essentially, updates are expensive since, despite the fact that the directories are organized in a hierarchical fashion, an UPDATE operation is forced to update all levels in the hierarchy and higher levels require communication with centers farther away.

The solution proposed in this section makes use of the refinement hierarchies of Section 14.1 and manages to control the complexity of UPDATE operations as well. More specifically, we describe a method for constructing an $O(\log^2 n)$-dilated resource controller whose complexities for both searches and updates are only polylogarithmically greater than the optimum implied by the lower bound of the previous section. We present the protocols of the controller and the structures it uses in the network, prove its correctness and analyze its complexity.

The controller is based on a hierarchy of sparse covers. The main problem that prevents us from using a plain hierarchy of covers as done for routing in Chapter 26 is that the hierarchy is composed of a collection of independent, unrelated covers with no structural relations between them. This kind of "loose" hierarchy is inadequate when the control task at hand requires also some "regional" knowledge, such as the number of available units in a given region of the network, or even just the existence of available units in a region. For maintaining such regional information, it is necessary to employ a *refinement hierarchy* of the type presented in Section 14.1. The strict containment relationship in the new construction enables smooth and efficient flow of control information between the levels.

Specifically, the controller is based on a hierarchy of *pivot vertices* in the network, corresponding to the refinement hierarchy, with higher level pivots controlling higher-level clusters (i.e., larger regions of the network). The construction is parameterized by a fixed integer $\kappa \geq 1$, and the resulting *refinement hierarchy controller*, denoted RHC_κ, is an $O(\kappa^2)$-dilated resource controller.

27.4.1   Control algorithms

We now describe the additional constructs needed for the resource controller and the search and update algorithms. Suppose a refinement hierarchy

$$\{(\mathcal{P}_i, \mathcal{T}_i) \mid 0 \leq i \leq \Lambda\}$$

is defined for the network as in Section 14.1. Each level i pivot $p \in \mathcal{P}_i$ maintains a free bit $F_i(p)$, set to 1 iff there are free resource units in some vertex of $T_i(p)$ and set to 0 otherwise, i.e.,

$$F_i(p) = \bigvee_{v \in T_i(p)} F(v).$$

Maintenance of the correct setting of this bit is based on the following simple fact, derived immediately from Property (H1) of the hierarchy.

Lemma 27.4.1 *For every i level pivot $p \in \mathcal{P}_i$,*

$$F_i(p) = \bigvee_{p' \in \mathsf{Sub}_{i-1}(p)} F_{i-1}(p'). \qquad \Box$$

We now associate with every vertex $v \in V$ a *level i server pivot*, $\mathsf{Server}_i(v)$, which is some pivot $p \in \mathcal{P}_i$ whose cluster $T_i(p)$ contains $\Gamma_{\vartheta^i}(v)$. We know that such a pivot exists by Property (H3) of the hierarchy. (In case there are several appropriate pivots, select one arbitrarily.)

Whenever a processor v needs a resource unit, it searches for one by applying to its level i server pivot, $\mathsf{Server}_i(v)$, for successively higher levels, $i = 1, 2, \ldots$, until reaching a level i such that the pivot $p = \mathsf{Server}_i(v)$ has available resources in the cluster $T_i(p)$ controlled by it (i.e., $F_i(p) = 1$). When that happens, the pivot directs the request downwards in the hierarchy until it reaches some vertex storing a free resource unit locally. This vertex then establishes direct contact with the requesting processor and supplies it with the resource unit.

Let us now describe how updates are performed. A level i pivot $p \in \mathcal{P}_i$ maintains its own free bit $F_i(p)$ and, in addition, the free bits $F_{i-1}(p')$ of every subordinate $p' \in \mathsf{Sub}_{i-1}(p)$. Thus the update process has to maintain the correct setting of the $F_i(p)$ bits at all levels, both at the pivot p itself and at the copies stored at its supervisors. This is done by direct updates, relying on Lemma 27.4.1. That is, whenever a level i pivot $p \in \mathcal{P}_i$ changes the status of its $F_i(p)$ bit, it informs each of its supervisors $p' \in \mathsf{Super}_{i+1}(p)$. These supervisors update their copies of the free bits and, if necessary, correct their own bit and propagate it further upwards.

In particular, suppose that the vertex v has acquired a newly released resource unit. If v had a unit prior to this release, then nothing changes and no update is necessary. However, if v had no free resources before, then it is necessary to update all its level 1 supervisors $p \in \mathsf{Super}_1(v)$. Those of them that had resources before require no further updates. However, if one or more of them were empty before, i.e., it currently flips its F_1 bit, then it needs to update its supervisors as well and so on. A dual operation occurs when a vertex v changes its status by consuming its last free resource unit.

27.4.2 Correctness and analysis

The following fact is immediate from the algorithm and Lemma 27.4.1.

Lemma 27.4.2 *The free bits F_i are always correct, namely, a pivot $p \in \mathcal{P}_i$ has $F_i(p) = 1$ iff there are free resource units in some vertex of $T_i(p)$.* $\qquad \Box$

Lemma 27.4.3 *In response to a request by processor v, the controller RHC always locates a resource unit at distance $O(\kappa^2 \cdot D_{server}(v))$. Furthermore, the message complexity of this search is $\mathsf{Message}(\mathrm{FIND}(v)) = O(\kappa^2 \cdot D_{server}(v))$.*

Proof: Suppose that the resource unit nearest to v is stored at vertex u, i.e., $D_{\text{server}}(v) = dist(u, v)$, and suppose $\vartheta^{i-1} < D_{\text{server}}(v) \le \vartheta^i$. By definition, $u \in \Gamma_{\vartheta^i}(v)$. The requesting vertex v successively tries using its level j pivots for $j = 1, 2, \ldots$ until succeeding in locating a free resource unit.

Let $p = \texttt{Server}_i(v)$. By definition, $\Gamma_{\vartheta^i}(v) \subseteq T_i(p)$, so $u \in T_i(p)$. Hence $\texttt{F}_i(p) = 1$ and therefore the pivot p will necessarily succeed in finding some resource unit in $T_i(p)$ and allocating it to v (if no lower level pivot did). The claim now follows from the fact that $Rad(T_i(p)) \le \vartheta^{i+1}$ by Property (H4) of the hierarchy and $\vartheta^{i+1} < \vartheta^2 \cdot D_{\text{server}}(v)$.

As for the message complexity of the entire process, we note that passing a message between a level j pivot p and a vertex v in its cluster $T_j(p)$ costs $O(\vartheta^{j+1})$ messages, and the entire search involves $O(1)$ such communications on each level up to i, summing up to

$$\sum_{j=1}^{i} O(\vartheta^{j+1}) = O(\vartheta^{i+1}) = O(\vartheta^2 \cdot D_{\text{server}}(v)). \qquad \square$$

Lemma 27.4.4 *The message complexity of an update operation of* RHC *involving a vertex v is* $\texttt{Message}(\text{UPDATE}(v)) = O(\kappa^2 \cdot n^{2/\kappa} \cdot D_{client}(v))$.

Proof: The update algorithm requires v to update its level j supervisors in all levels until no change occurs at some level. Suppose $\vartheta^{i-1} < D_{\text{client}}(v) \le \vartheta^i$. Then we claim that no further updates are necessary at levels higher than i. This completes the proof, since by Property (H5) of the hierarchy, in each update from level $j-1$ pivots to their supervisors at level j, both the number of participating updating pivots and the number of participating updated pivots are bounded by $O(\kappa \cdot n^{1/\kappa})$. Hence there are only $O(\kappa^2 \cdot n^{2/\kappa})$ update messages at each level and each of these messages costs at most $O(\vartheta^j)$.

In order to prove the claim, it is necessary to show that every level i ancestor p of v has $\texttt{F}_i(p) = 1$ both prior to and following the update operation. The proof is by contradiction. Consider such a pivot p. There are two cases to examine. First, suppose the update is due to v acquiring a (first) resource unit, yet $\texttt{F}_i(p) = 0$ prior to the update (so it now needs to be set to 1). By Property (H2) of the hierarchy, the cluster $T_i(p)$ contains $\Gamma_{\vartheta^i}(w)$ for some vertex w. It follows that $D_{\text{server}}(w) \ge \vartheta^i$ prior to the update. Since both v and w are in $T_i(p)$, by Property (H4) of the hierarchy,

$$dist(v, w) \le \vartheta^{i+1} \le \vartheta \cdot D_{\text{server}}(w),$$

hence v is ϑ^{i+1}-usable, contradicting the fact that $D_{\text{client}}(v) \le \vartheta^i$. The second case is when the update is due to v losing its last resource unit, and $\texttt{F}_i(p)$ needs to be reset to 0 as a result of this change. Then a similar contradiction applies to the state following the update. (Note that $D_{\text{client}}(v)$ does not change during an update operation involving v itself.) $\square$

Constructing a local resource controller RHC based on a refinement hierarchy as above while fixing $\kappa = \log n$, we get the desired result.

Theorem 27.4.5 *It is possible to construct an* $O(\log^2 n)$-*dilated resource controller with message complexities* $\texttt{Message}(\text{UPDATE}(v)) = O(\log^2 n \cdot D_{client}(v))$ *and* $\texttt{Message}(\text{FIND}(v)) = O(\log^2 n \cdot D_{server}(v))$. $\square$

27.4.3   Modification: Exact counting

A simple variant of the above construction can be used in order to enable each pivot to obtain an *exact count* of the number of free resource units at each subordinate cluster. Instead of maintaining just a Boolean flag, $\texttt{F}_i(v)$ has to be an integer counter. Whenever a vertex v acquires or loses a resource unit, it informs all of its ancestors in every level. Each ancestor then updates its own counter as well as the counters of each of its subordinates, based on its knowledge of the residents of these clusters. The update operation requires informing all levels of the hierarchy, hence its message complexity becomes dependent on $Diam(G)$, specifically $O(\kappa n^{1/\kappa} Diam(G))$. Searches can be performed as before, with the advantage that now multiple-unit requests can be handled at once (whereas in the flag-based system, each request has to be handled unit by unit).

In case it is desirable to avoid having to remember the cluster structure by each pivot, it is possible to rely on more detailed update messages. Specifically, the header of an update message issued by vertex v may include a list of all its ancestors at all levels, thus enabling proper updates of the relevant counters in all pivots. This increases the message complexity of updates to $O(\kappa^2 n^{2/\kappa} Diam(G))$.

In comparison, while the "exact count" method provides us with a more accurate picture of the resource distribution in the network, it is more expensive in its update costs, both due to the higher cost of a single operation and due to the fact that every change must be accounted for (in contrast, the Boolean system requires vertices to issue update messages only when changing from an "empty" to a "nonempty" state).

Bibliographical notes

A distance-dependent *name server* component was incorporated in the routing schemes of [ABLP89]. An explicit definition and treatment distance-dependent directories was given in [Pel93]. The construction presented in Section 27.2 is a somewhat improved and simplified variant of that in [Pel93]. This construction is considerably different than the directory component of [ABLP89], which uses volume-based covers rather than radius-based ones. The lower bound of Section 27.3 and the construction of Section 27.4 are due to [AKP92].

One of the major applications of clustered LP-representations to network control concerns the basic task of tracking *mobile* entities (such as mobile users, migrating processes, client-server connections, etc.) in a distributed system. The problem of designing efficient online tracking mechanisms for mobile entities was studied in [AP90c, AP91, AP95]. This problem can be interpreted in our current terminology as keeping track of a *fixed* set of resource units that can move about in the network. Thus the only allowable operation on a unit is a "move" operation and the mechanism keeps track of their current location. The scheme was also studied experimentally in [WWS98].

A lower bound on the trade-off between the communication costs of moves and searches in a tracking mechanism for mobile users on the hypercube is derived in [AKRS94], based on their lower bound on the trade-off between the radius and degree for ρ-regional matchings on hypercubes. The result applies also to the closely related problem of *distributed job scheduling*. Locality-sensitive algorithmic schemes for the problems of distributed job balancing and *distributed resource allocation* in general were developed in [AKP92, RB97, BFR95]. The problem of distributed job balancing arises in a setting where jobs arrive online at different sites and each job has to be executed on one of the processors. The goal is to balance the load on the processor without wasting too much of the network resources on communication. Locality-sensitive policies can be used in order to find a reasonable trade-off between those requirements. Another related application, also tackled using LP-representations, is that of distributed competitive online paging [ABF93]. The tracking problem has been studied extensively since then. Some related references include [Wir95, MGS95, CMM95, ELL+95, LMP+95].

Recently, the problem of tracking mobile users has received some attention in the models of wireless networks and cellular phone networks. In those models, the problem is complicated by the fact that in order to save costly wireless communication, mobile users do not always inform the network vertices about their exact location. Hence a host vertex might not be aware of a mobile user that is currently residing at it. This necessitates some additional tracking mechanisms in such systems. A number of recent papers studied efficient methods for manipulating information regarding the location of mobile users in wireless networks [BK93, BKS94, PRS97, PS96, JL95, AH95, HA95, MHS94, RY95, BC98]. See also [IB94] for a review of mobile wireless computing, and [AMH$^+$99] for a more recent overview.

Exercises

1. Consider modifying the directory of Section 27.1 for handling local queries by basing it on the variant of a regional matching proposed in Exercise 2.

    (a) Explain what problems arise in computing the answer to a query.

    (b) Describe a procedure for answering queries in which the function f is the *maximum* over $\mathcal{X}_\rho(v)$.

    (c) What are the space and message complexities of the resulting directory?

2. Describe a modification of the resource controller of Section 27.2 to make it 1-dilated, thus proving Theorem 27.2.6.

3. Describe how to modify the UPDATE$(v, 1)$ operation of the resource controller of Section 27.4 in order to reduce its complexity to $O(\kappa \cdot n^{1/\kappa} \cdot D_{\text{client}}(v))$, assuming each level i pivot has a precise picture of its cluster and the clusters of its level $i-1$ subordinates (i.e., it knows which vertices reside in each of these clusters).

4. Consider the following "mobile" variant of the resource allocation problem. There is a single "mobile" resource unit, which can move about the network. Whenever a vertex v needs the resource unit, it must find its current residence w and request it, upon which the unit relocates itself from w to v. After releasing the unit, it remains at v until it is requested at some other vertex.

    (a) Describe a solution to the mobile variant of the problem on a tree T, which guarantees that the message complexity of the search is at most $O(Depth(T))$, and no special update messages are necessary beyond the messages involved in the search and the relocation trip taken by the resource unit.

    (b) ($*$) Design an efficient solution for the problem on general graphs.

Chapter 28

Additional applications in other settings

The basic premise behind employing LP-representations is that using them (as a substitute for using the entire network) allows us to maintain smaller amounts of information (namely, remember fewer edges, know less about the structure of the graph and so on), thus reducing the computational and storage costs involved. The price to be paid is that using sparse, approximate representations incurs a certain loss of accuracy. Hence while our focus in this book was on applications in the area of distributed network algorithms, it is evident that these representations should in principle be useful in any situation where exact solutions are not essential or are too expensive to obtain.

In this final brief chapter, we review some additional applications of LP-representations in other settings beyond that of distributed network algorithms.

A promising recent direction concerns using LP-representations for developing *sequential* approximation algorithms for various network-related combinatorial optimization problems. Let us next discuss a number of those applications.

The low-stretch spanning tree problem has been studied in [AKPW95] in the context of devising a randomized *competitive online* algorithm for the *k-server* problem. Partition-based competitive algorithms for online problems were also studied in [AAB96].

It is well known that the problem of computing (all-pairs or single-source) *shortest paths* in a given graph enjoys a polynomial-time sequential solution. Consequently, it is perhaps not the most natural candidate problem for which one would consider developing an approximation algorithm. However, it was recently observed that if one is willing to consider "almost" shortest paths, then spanners, or techniques related to their construction, can be used to derive approximate shortest paths somewhat faster than the time required for obtaining the exact solution. This approach was examined in [KS92, ABCP93, Coh93, DHZ96].

Spanners seem to have natural applications in communication networks for the purpose of "sparsifying" a dense network in order to save in the set-up costs as well as in the communication costs for various maintenance tasks. Recently, approximations for a number of variants of the *network design* problems were developed using spanners and SLTs [MP94, SCRS97]. It is possible that more sophisticated use of spanners may lead to even better bounds, perhaps combining the approaches of [MP94, SCRS97] with some known heuristics for the problem.

In the geometric setting, spanners were used for deriving better approximation algorithms for problems such as the Euclidean Traveling Salesman problem and the Euclidean

Steiner Minimum Tree problem [RS98].

Finally, sparse covers were recently used for deriving approximate solutions to NP-hard variants of problems such as min-cut and multicommodity flow [KPR93, Alt94, Med94, PT95]. This approach has also led to better solutions to a number of variants of the network design problems.

Bibliography

[AAB96]   B. Awerbuch, Y. Azar, and Y. Bartal. On-line generalized Steiner problem. In *Proc. 7th ACM-SIAM Symp. on Discrete Algorithms*, pages 68–74, ACM, New York, 1996.

[AAHK86]   K. Abrahamson, A. Adler, L. Higham, and D. Kirkpatrick. Probabilistic solitude verification on a ring. In *Proc. 5th ACM Symp. on Principles of Distributed Computing*, pages 161–173, August 1986.

[AAPS96]   Y. Afek, B. Awerbuch, S.A. Plotkin, and M. Saks. Local management of a global resource in a communication network. *J. ACM*, 43:1–19, 1996.

[ABCP92a]   B. Awerbuch, B. Berger, L. Cowen, and D. Peleg. Fast network decomposition. In *Proc. 11th ACM Symp. on Principles of Distributed Computing*, pages 169–177, August 1992.

[ABCP92b]   B. Awerbuch, B. Berger, L. Cowen, and D. Peleg. Low diameter graph decomposition is in NC. In *Proc. 3rd Scandinavian Workshop on Algorithm Theory*, LNCS Vol. 621, Springer, New York, pages 83–93, 1992.

[ABCP93]   B. Awerbuch, B. Berger, L. Cowen, and D. Peleg. Near-linear cost sequential and distributed constructions of sparse neighborhood covers. In *Proc. 34th IEEE Symp. on Foundations of Computer Science*, pages 638–647, 1993.

[ABF93]   B. Awerbuch, Y. Bartal, and A. Fiat. Competitive distributed file allocation. In *Proc. 25th ACM Symp. on Theory of Computing*, pages 164–173, May 1993.

[ABLP89]   B. Awerbuch, A. Bar-Noy, N. Linial, and D. Peleg. Compact distributed data structures for adaptive network routing. In *Proc. 21st ACM Symp. on Theory of Computing*, pages 230–240, May 1989.

[ABLP90]   B. Awerbuch, A. Bar-Noy, N. Linial, and D. Peleg. Improved routing strategies with succinct tables. *J. Algorithms*, 11:307–341, 1990.

[ABP90]   B. Awerbuch, A. Baratz, and D. Peleg. Cost-sensitive analysis of communication protocols. In *Proc. 9th ACM Symp. on Principles of Distributed Computing*, pages 177–187, 1990.

[ABP91]   B. Awerbuch, A. Baratz, and D. Peleg. Efficient broadcast and light-weight spanners. Technical Report CS92-22, The Weizmann Institute of Science, Rehovot, Israel, 1992.

[ADD82]   G.R. Andrews, D.P. Dobkin, and P.J. Downey. Distributed allocation with
           pools of servers. In *Proc. 1st ACM Symp. on Principles of Distributed Com-
           puting*, pages 73–83, August 1982.

[ADD+93]   I. Althöfer, G. Das, D. Dobkin, D. Joseph, and J. Soares. On sparse spanners
           of weighted graphs. *Discrete Comput. Geom.*, 9:81–100, 1993.

[ADDJ90]   I. Althöfer, G. Das, D. Dobkin, and D. Joseph. Generating sparse spanners for
           weighted graphs. In *Proc. 2nd Scandinavian Workshop on Algorithm Theory*,
           LNCS Vol. 447, pages 26–37, July 1990.

[AG85a]   Y. Afek and E. Gafni. Time and message bounds for election in synchronous
           and asynchronous complete networks. In *Proc. 4th ACM Symp. on Principles
           of Distributed Computing*, pages 186–195, August 1985.

[AG85b]   B. Awerbuch and R.G. Gallager. Distributed BFS algorithms. In *Proc. 26th
           IEEE Symp. on Foundations of Computer Science*, 1985.

[AG87]   B. Awerbuch and R.G. Gallager. A new distributed algorithm to find breadth
           first search trees. *IEEE Trans. on Information Theory*, IT-33(3):315–322, 1987.

[AGLP89]   B. Awerbuch, A. Goldberg, M. Luby, and S. Plotkin. Network decomposition
           and locality in distributed computation. In *Proc. 30th IEEE Symp. on Foun-
           dations of Computer Science*, pages 364–369, May 1989.

[AGPV90]   B. Awerbuch, O. Goldreich, D. Peleg, and R. Vainish. A tradeoff between
           information and communication in broadcast protocols. *J. ACM*, 2:238–256,
           1990.

[AGR89]   Y. Afek, E. Gafni, and M. Ricklin. Upper and lower bounds for routing schemes
           in dynamic networks. In *Proc. 30th IEEE Symp. on Foundations of Computer
           Science*, pages 370–375, May 1989.

[AH95]   I.F. Akyildiz and J.S.M. Ho. Dynamic mobile user location update for wireless
           PCS networks. *Wireless Networks Journal*, 1:187–196, 1995.

[AHH+95]   C.J. Alpert, T.C. Hu, J.H. Huang, A.B. Kahng, and D. Karger. Prim-Dijkstra
           tradeoffs for improved performance driven routing tree design. *IEEE Trans. on
           Computer-Aided Design*, 14:890–896, 1995.

[AKP91]   B. Awerbuch, S. Kutten, and D. Peleg. On buffer-economical store-and-forward
           deadlock prevention. In *Proc. IEEE INFOCOM*, pages 410–414, 1991.

[AKP92]   B. Awerbuch, S. Kutten, and D. Peleg. Online load balancing in a distributed
           network. In *Proc. 24th ACM Symp. on Theory of Computing*, pages 571–580,
           1992.

[AKP94]   B. Awerbuch, S. Kutten, and D. Peleg. On buffer-economical store-and-forward
           deadlock prevention. *IEEE Trans. on Communication*, 42:2934–2937, 1994.

[AKPW95]   N. Alon, R.M. Karp, D. Peleg, and D. West. A graph-theoretic game and its
           application to the k-server problem. *SIAM J. Comput.*, 24:78–100, 1995.

[AKRS94]   N. Alon, G. Kalai, M. Ricklin, and L. Stockmeyer. Lower bounds on the com-
           petitive ratio for mobile user tracking and distributed job scheduling. *Theoret.
           Comput. Sci.*, 130:175–201, 1994.

[Alt94]   I. Althöfer. Small integral flows need only sparse networks. *Networks*, 24:263–266, 1994.

[AMH⁺99]   I.F. Akyildiz, J. McNair, J.S.M. Ho, H. Uzunalioglu, and W. Wang. Mobility management in next generation wireless systems. *IEEE Proc. Journal*, 87:1347–1385, 1999.

[AP90a]   B. Awerbuch and D. Peleg. Efficient distributed construction of sparse covers. Technical Report CS90-17, The Weizmann Institute of Science, Rehovot, Israel, July 1990.

[AP90b]   B. Awerbuch and D. Peleg. Network synchronization with polylogarithmic overhead. In *31st IEEE Symp. on Foundations of Computer Science*, pages 514–522, October 1990.

[AP90c]   B. Awerbuch and D. Peleg. Sparse partitions. In *31st IEEE Symp. on Foundations of Computer Science*, pages 503–513, October 1990.

[AP91]   B. Awerbuch and D. Peleg. Concurrent online tracking of mobile users. In *Proc. of the Annual ACM SIGCOMM Symp. on Communication Architectures and Protocols*, September 1991.

[AP92]   B. Awerbuch and D. Peleg. Routing with polynomial communication-space trade-off. *SIAM J. Discrete Math.*, 5:151–162, 1992.

[AP95]   B. Awerbuch and D. Peleg. Online tracking of mobile users. *J. ACM*, 42:1021–1058, 1995.

[APSPS92] B. Awerbuch, B. Patt-Shamir, D. Peleg, and M. Saks. Adapting to asynchronous dynamic networks with polylogarithmic overhead. In *Proc. 24th ACM Symp. on Theory of Computing*, pages 557–570, 1992.

[AR92]   Y. Afek and M. Ricklin. Sparser: A paradigm for running distributed algorithms. In *Proc. 6th Workshop on Distributed Algorithms*, LNCS Vol. 647, Springer, Berlin, pages 1–10, 1992.

[AS88]   B. Awerbuch and M. Sipser. Dynamic networks are as fast as static networks. In *Proc. 29th IEEE Symp. on Foundations of Computer Science*, pages 206–220, 1988.

[ASW85]   H. Attiya, M. Snir, and M. Warmuth. Computing on anonymous ring. In *Proc. 4th ACM Symp. on Principles of Distributed Computing*, pages 196–203, August 1985.

[AW98]   H. Attiya and J. Welch. *Distributed Computing: Fundamentals, Simulations and Advanced Topics*. McGraw–Hill, England, 1998.

[Awe85a]   B. Awerbuch. Complexity of network synchronization. *J. ACM*, 4:804–823, 1985.

[Awe85b]   B. Awerbuch. A new distributed depth-first-search algorithm. *Inform. Process. Lett.*, 20:147–150, 1985.

[Awe85c]   B. Awerbuch. Reducing complexities of the distributed max-flow and breadth-first-search algorithms by means of network synchronization. *Networks*, 15:425–437, 1985.

[Awe87]   B. Awerbuch. Optimal distributed algorithms for minimum weight spanning tree, counting, leader election and related problems. In *Proc. 19th ACM Symp. on Theory of Computing*, pages 230–240, May 1987.

[Awe89]   B. Awerbuch. Distributed shortest paths algorithms. In *Proc. 21st ACM Symp. on Theory of Computing*, pages 230–240, May 1989.

[Bar96a]   V.C. Barbosa. *An Introduction to Distributed Algorithms*. MIT Press, Cambridge, MA, 1996.

[Bar96b]   Y. Bartal. Probabilistic approximation of metric spaces and its algorithmic applications. In *Proc. 37th IEEE Symp. on Foundations of Computer Science*, pages 184–193, 1996.

[Bar98]   Y. Bartal. On approximating arbitrary metrics by tree metrics. In *Proc. 30th ACM Symp. on Theory of Computing*, pages 161–168, 1998.

[BC89]   B.J. Brachman and S.T. Chanson. A hierarchical solution for application level store-and-forward deadlock prevention. In *Proc. 1989 ACM SIGCOMM Symp. on Communication Architectures and Protocols*, pages 25–32, September 1989.

[BC98]   Y. Bejerano and I. Cidon. An efficient mobility management strategy for personal communication systems. In *Proc. MOBICOM '98, Fourth Annual ACM, IEEE Conference on Mobile Cpmputing and Networking*, pages 215–222, October 1998.

[BCLR86]   S. Bhatt, F. Chung, F.T. Leighton, and A. Rosenberg. Optimal simulations of tree machines. In *Proc. 27th IEEE Symp. on Foundations of Computer Science*, pages 274–282, 1986.

[BD86]   H.-J. Bandelt and A. Dress. Reconstructing the shape of a tree from observed dissimilarity data. *Adv. in Appl. Math.*, 7:309–343, 1986.

[BF67]   M.A. Breuer and J. Folkman. An unexpected result on coding the vertices of a graph. *J. Math. Anal. Appl.*, 20:583–600, 1967.

[BFR95]   Y. Bartal, A. Fiat, and Y. Rabani. Competitive algorithms for distributed data management. *J. Comput. Systems Sci.*, 5:341–358, 1995.

[BG92]   D. Bertsekas and R. Gallager. *Data Networks*. 2nd Edition. Prentice–Hall International, London, 1992.

[BH97]   U. Brandes and D. Handke. NP-completeness results for minimum planar graphs. In *Proc. 23rd Int. Workshop on Graph-Theoretic Concepts in Computer Science*, LNCS Vol. 1335, Springer, Berlin, pages 85–99, 1997.

[BHG86]   P. Bernstein, V. Hadzilacos, and N. Goodman. *Concurrency Control and Recovery in Database Systems*. Addison–Wesley, Reading, MA, 1986.

[BHV96]   H. Buhrman, J.-H. Hoepman, and P. Vitányi. Optimal routing tables. In *Proc. 15th ACM Symp. on Principles of Distributed Computing*, pages 134–142, May 1996.

[BK93]   J. Bar-Noy and I. Kessler. Tracking mobile users in wireless communication networks. In *Proc. IEEE INFOCOM*, pages 1232–1239, 1993.

[BKJ83]   K. Bharath-Kumar and J.M. Jaffe. Routing to multiple destinations in com-
           puter networks. *IEEE Trans. on Communication*, COM-31:343–351, 1983.

[BKP92]   J. Bar-Ilan, G. Kortsarz, and D. Peleg. How to allocate network centers. *J.
           Algorithms*, 15:385–415, 1992.

[BKS94]   J. Bar-Noy, I. Kessler, and M. Sidi. Mobile users: To update or not to update?
           In *Proc. IEEE INFOCOM*, pages 570–576, 1994.

[Bol78]   B. Bollobás. *Extremal Graph Theory*. Academic Press, New York, 1978.

[Bou85]   J. Bourgain. On Lipschitz embeddings of finite metric spaces in Hilbert spaces.
           Israel J. Math., 52:46–52, 1985.

[BP91]   J. Bar-Ilan and D. Peleg. Approximation algorithm for selecting network cen-
           ters. In *Proc. 2nd Workshop on Algorithms and Data Structures*, Springer,
           Berlin, pages 343–354, 1991.

[Bre66]   M.A. Breuer. Coding the vertexes of a graph. *IEEE Trans. Inform. Theory*,
           IT-12:148–153, 1966.

[Bur80]   J.E. Burns. A formal model for message passing systems. Technical Report
           TR91, Computer Science Department, Indiana University, Bloomington, IN,
           September 1980.

[Cai91]   L. Cai. Tree 2-spanners. Technical Report TR 91-4, Simon Fraser University,
           Burnaby, B.C., Canada, 1991.

[Cai94]   L. Cai. NP-completeness of minimum spanner problems. *Discrete Appl. Math.*,
           48:187–194, 1994.

[CC95a]   L. Cai and D. Corneil. Isomorphic tree spanner problems. *Algorithmica*, 14:138–
           153, 1995.

[CC95b]   L. Cai and D.G. Corneil. Tree spanners. *SIAM J. Discrete Math.*, 8:359–387,
           1995.

[CCG+98]   M. Charikar, C. Chekuri, A. Goel, S. Guha, and S. Plotkin. Approximating a
           finite metric by a small number of tree metrics. In *Proc. 39th IEEE Symp. on
           Foundations of Computer Science*, pages 379–388, 1998.

[CCGG98]   M. Charikar, C. Chekuri, A. Goel, and S. Guha. Rounding via trees: Determin-
           istic approximation algorithms for group steiner trees and k-median. In *Proc.
           30th ACM Symp. on Theory of Computing*, pages 114–123, 1998.

[CDNS92]   B. Chandra, G. Das, G. Narasimhan, and J. Soares. New sparseness results on
           graph spanners. In *Proc. 8th ACM Symposium on Computational Geometry*,
           Internat. J. Comput. Geom. Appl., 5:125–144, 1992.

[CGZ86]   C.T. Chou, I.S. Gopal, and S. Zaks. Synchronizing asynchronous bounded-delay
           networks. Research Report RC-12274, IBM, Yorktown Heights, NY, October
           1986.

[CGZ94]   I. Cidon, O. Gerstel, and S. Zaks. A scalable approach to routing in ATM
           networks. In *Proc. 8th Workshop on Distributed Algorithms*, LNCS Vol. 857,
           pages 209–222, Springer, Berlin, 1994.

[Cha79]   E.J.H. Chang. *Decentralized algorithms in distributed systems*. Ph.D. thesis, University of Toronto, Toronto, Canada, 1979.

[Che86]   L.P. Chew. There is a planar graph almost as good as the complete graph. In *2nd Symp. on Computational Geometry*, pages 169–177, 1986.

[Chv79]   V. Chvatal. A greedy heuristic for the set-covering problem. *Math. Oper. Res.*, 4:233–235, 1979.

[CK94]   L. Cai and M. Keil. Spanners in graphs of bounded degree. *Networks*, 24:233–249, 1994.

[CKMP90]   I. Cidon, S. Kutten, Y. Mansour, and D. Peleg. Greedy packet scheduling. In *Proc. 4th Workshop on Distributed Algorithms*, LNCS Vol. 486, pages 169–184, 1990.

[CL85]   K.M. Chandy and L. Lamport. Distributed snapshots: Determining global states of distributed systems. *ACM Trans. on Comput. Syst.*, 1:63–75, 1985.

[CLR90]   T.H. Cormen, C.E. Leiserson, and R.L. Rivest. *Introduction to Algorithms*. MIT Press/McGraw-Hill, Cambridge, MA, 1990.

[CMM95]   G.W. Cho, L.F. Marshall, and F. Marshall. An efficient location and routing scheme for mobile computing environments. *IEEE J. on Selected Areas in Communications*, 13:868–879, 1995.

[Coh93]   E. Cohen. Fast algorithms for constructing t-spanners and paths with stretch t. In *Proc. 34th IEEE Symp. on Foundations of Computer Science*, pages 648–658, 1993.

[Coo83]   S.A. Cook. The classification of problems which have fast parallel algorithms. Technical Report 164/83, Department of Computer Science, University of Toronto, Toronto, Canada, 1983.

[Cow94]   L. Cowen. A linear-time algorithm for network decomposition. Technical Report 94-56, DIMACS, Rutgers University, New Brunswick, NJ, December 1994.

[Cow99]   L.J. Cowen. Compact routing with minimum stretch. In *Proc. Tenth ACM-SIAM Symp. on Discrete Algorithms*, pages 255–260, SIAM, Philadelphia, 1999.

[CV86]   R. Cole and U. Vishkin. Deterministic coin tossing with applications to optimal parallel list ranking. *Inform. Comput.*, 70:32–56, 1986.

[CW00]   L. Cowen and C.G. Wagner. Compact roundtrip routing in directed networks. In *Proc. 19th ACM Symp. on Principles of Distributed Computing*, to appear.

[DFS87]   D.P. Dobkin, S.J. Friedman, and K.J. Supowit. Delaunay graphs are almost as good as complete graphs. In *Proc. 28th IEEE Symp. on Foundations of Computer Science*, pages 20–26, 1987.

[DH98]   M.J. Demmer and M.P. Herlihy. The arrow distributed directory protocol. In *Proc. 12th Symp. on Distributed Computing*, pages 119–133, Springer, Berlin, September 1998.

[DHZ96]   D. Dor, S. Halperin, and U. Zwick. All pairs almost shortest paths. In *Proc. 37th IEEE Symp. on Foundations of Computer Science*, pages 452–461, 1996.

[Dij74]   E.W. Dijkstra. Self stabilizing systems in spite of distributed control. *Comm. of the ACM*, 17:643–644, 1974.

[DJ89]   G. Das and D. Joseph. Which triangulations approximate the complete graph? In *Proc. Int. Symp. on Optimal Algorithms*, LNCS Vol. 401, Springer, New York, pages 168–192, 1989.

[DKKP99]   S. Dolev, E. Kranakis, D. Krizanc, and D. Peleg. Bubbles: Adaptive routing scheme for high-speed dynamic networks. *SIAM J. Comput.*, 29:804–833, 1999.

[DM78]   Y.K. Dalal and R.M. Metcalfe. Reverse path forwarding of broadcast packets. *Comm. of the ACM*, 12:1040–1048, 1978.

[DP95]   D. Dubhashi and A. Panconesi. Near-optimal distributed edge coloring. In *Algorithms—ESA '95*, LNSC Vol. 979, pages 448–459, Springer, Berlin, 1995.

[DZ99]   W. Duckworth and M. Zito. Sparse hypercube 3-spanners. *Discrete Appl. Math.* To appear.

[ELL+95]   C. Eynard, M. Lenti, A. Lombardo, O. Marengo, and S. Palazzo. A methodology for the performance evaluation of data query strategies in universal mobile telecommunication systems. *IEEE J. on Selected Areas in Communications*, 13:893–907, 1995.

[EMZ97]   T. Eilam, S. Moran, and S. Zaks. The complexity of the characterization of networks supporting shortest-path interval routing. In *4th International Colloquium on Structural Information & Communication Complexity (SIROCCO)*, Danny Krizanc and Peter Widmayer, editors, pages 99–111, Carleton University Press, Northfield, MN, 1997.

[ENRS95]   G. Even, J. Naor, S. Rao, and B. Schieber. Divide-and-conquer approximation algorithms via spreading metrics. In *Proc. 36th IEEE Symp. on Foundations of Computer Science*, pages 62–71, 1995.

[EP99]   M. Elkin and D. Peleg. The client-server 2-spanner problem and applications to network design. Technical Report MCS99-24, The Weizmann Institute, Rehovot, Israel, 1999.

[EP00b]   M. Elkin and D. Peleg. Strong inapproximability of the basic k-spanner problem. In *Proc. 27th Int. Colloq. on Automata, Languages and Programming*, to appear.

[EP00a]   M. Elkin and D. Peleg. The hardness of approximating spanner problems. In *Proc. 17th Symp. on Theoretical Aspects of Computer Science*, Springer, Berlin, 2000.

[ER88]   S. Even and S. Rajsbaum. Lack of global clock does not slow down the computation in distributed networks. Technical Report 522, The Technion, Haifa, Israel, October 1988.

[ER90]   S. Even and S. Rajsbaum. The use of a synchronizer yields maximum computation rate in distributed networks. In *Proc. 22nd ACM Symp. on Theory of Computing*, pages 95–105, 1990.

[ER95]   S. Even and S. Rajsbaum. Unison, cannon and sluggish clocks in networks controlled by a synchronizer. *Math. Systems Theory*, 28:421–435, 1995.

[Eve79]   S. Even. *Graph Algorithms.* Computer Science Press, Rockville, MD, 1979.

[FG95]   P. Fraigniaud and C. Gavoille. Memory requirement for universal routing schemes. In *Proc. 14th ACM Symp. on Principles of Distributed Computing*, pages 223–230, August 1995.

[FG96]   P. Fraigniaud and C. Gavoille. Local memory requirement of universal routing schemes. In *Proc. 8th ACM Symp. on Parallel Algorithms and Architecture*, pages 183–188, June 1996.

[FG97]   P. Fraigniaud and C. Gavoille. Universal routing schemes. *Journal of Distributed Computing*, 10:65–78, 1997.

[FG98]   P. Fraigniaud and C. Gavoille. Interval routing schemes. *Algorithmica*, 21:155–182, 1998.

[FGS96]   M. Flammini, G. Gambosi, and S. Salomone. Interval routing schemes. *Algorithmica*, 16:549–568, 1996.

[FJ88]   G.N. Frederickson and R. Janardan. Designing networks with compact routing tables. *Algorithmica*, 3:171–190, 1988.

[FJ89]   G.N. Frederickson and R. Janardan. Efficient message routing in planar networks. *SIAM J. Comput.*, 18:843–857, 1989.

[FJ90]   G.N. Frederickson and R. Janardan. Space-efficient message routing in c-decomposable networks. *SIAM J. Comput.*, 19:164–181, 1990.

[FL87]   G.N. Frederickson and N. Lynch. Electing a leader in a synchronous ring. *J. ACM*, 34:98–115, 1987.

[FL94]   P. Fraigniaud and E. Lazard. Methods and problems of communication in usual networks. *Discrete Appl. Math.*, 53:79–133, 1994.

[Fla97]   M. Flammini. Deadlock-free interval routing schemes. In *14th Annual Symposium on Theoretical Aspects of Computer Science (STACS)*, Rüdiger Reischuk and Michel Morvan, editors, LNCS Vol. 1200, Springer, New York, pages 351–362, 1997.

[FLS88]   A. Fekete, N. Lynch, and L. Shrira. A modular proof of correctness for a network synchronizer. In *Proc. 2nd Workshop on Distributed Algorithms*, LNCS Vol. 312, pages 219–256, Springer, Berlin, 1988.

[FPPP00]   P. Fraigniaud, A. Pelc, D. Peleg, and S. Perennes. Assigning labels in unknown networks. In *Proc. 19th ACM Symp. on Distributed Computing*, 2000.

[Fre83]   G.N. Frederickson. Trade-offs for selection in distributed networks. In *Proc. 2nd ACM Symp. on Principles of Distributed Computing*, pages 154–160, August 1983.

[Fre85]   G.N. Frederickson. A single source shortest path algorithm for a planar distributed network. In *Proc. 2nd Symp. on Theoretical Aspects of Computer Science*, LNCS Vol. 182, pages 143–150, Springer, Berlin, 1985.

[Fre93]   G.N. Frederickson. Searching among intervals and compact routing tables. In *Proc. 20th Int. Colloq. on Automata, Languages & Prog.*, LNCS Vol. 700, Andrzej Lingas, Rolf Karisson, and Svante Carlsson, editors, Springer, New York, pages 28–39, 1993.

[G81]   K.D. Günther. Prevention of deadlocks in packet-switched data transport systems. *IEEE Trans. on Communication*, 29:512–524, 1981.

[Gal76]   R.G. Gallager. A shortest path routing algorithm with automatic resynch. Technical report, Lab. for Information and Decision Systems, MIT, Cambridge, MA, March 1976.

[Gal82]   R.G. Gallager. Distributed minimum hop algorithms. Technical Report LIDS-P-1175, Lab. for Information and Decision Systems, MIT, Cambridge, MA, January 1982.

[Gav97]   C. Gavoille. A survey on interval routing scheme. Research Report RR-1182-97, LaBRI, University of Bordeaux, Talence, France, October 1997.

[GG97]   C. Gavoille and M. Gengler. Space-efficiency of routing schemes of stretch factor three. In *4th International Colloquium on Structural Information & Communication Complexity (SIROCCO)*, Danny Krizanc and Peter Widmayer, editors, Carleton University Press, Northfield, MN, pages 162–175, 1997.

[GG98]   C. Gavoille and E. Guévremont. Worst case bounds for shortest path interval routing. *J. Algorithms*, 27:1–25, 1998.

[GHS83]   R.G. Gallager, P.A. Humblet, and P.M. Spira. A distributed algorithm for minimum-weight spanning trees. *ACM Trans. on Programming Lang. and Syst.*, 5:66–77, 1983.

[GJ79]   M.R. Garey and D.S. Johnson. *Computers and Intractability: A Guide to the Theory of NP-Completeness*. W. H. Freeman and Co., San Francisco, CA, 1979.

[GKP98]   J.A. Garay, S. Kutten, and D. Peleg. A sublinear time distributed algorithm for minimum-weight spanning trees. *SIAM J. Comput.*, 27:302–316, 1998.

[GMS77]   B. Gavish, P. Merlin, and A. Segall. Minimal buffer requirements for avoiding store-and-forward deadlock. Research Report RC-6672, IBM, Yorktown Heights, NY, August 1977.

[Gol80]   M.C. Golumbic. *Algorithmic Graph Theory and Perfect Graphs*. Academic Press, New York, 1980.

[Gop85]   I.S. Gopal. Prevention of store-and-forward deadlock in computer networks. *IEEE Trans. on Communication*, Com-33:1258–1264, 1985.

[GP87]   A.V. Goldberg and S. Plotkin. Parallel $\delta + 1$ coloring of constant-degree graphs. *Inform. Process. Lett.*, 25:241–245, 1987.

[GP91]   K. Gilon and D. Peleg. Compact deterministic distributed dictionaries. In *Proc. 10th ACM Symp. on Principles of Distributed Computing*, pages 81–94, August 1991.

[GP95]   C. Gavoille and S. Pérennès. Memory requirement for universal routing schemes. In *Proc. 14th ACM Symp. on Principles of Distributed Computing*, pages 223–230, August 1995.

[GP96]   C. Gavoille and S. Pérennès. Memory requirement for routing in distributed networks. In *Proc. 15th ACM Symp. on Principles of Distributed Computing*, pages 125–133, May 1996.

[GP98]   C. Gavoille and D. Peleg. The compactness of interval routing for almost all graphs. Research Report RR-2002-98, LaBRI, University of Bordeaux, Talence, France, April 1998.

[GP99]   C. Gavoille and D. Peleg. The compactness of interval routing. *SIAM J. Discrete Math.*, 12:459–473, 1999.

[GPPR00] C. Gavoille, D. Peleg, S. Pérennes, and R. Raz. Distance labeling in graphs. Research Report RR-1239-00, LaBRI, University of Bordeaux, France, 2000.

[GPS88]   A.V. Goldberg, S. Plotkin, and G. Shannon. Parallel symmetry breaking in sparse graphs. *SIAM J. Discrete Math.*, 1:431–446, 1988.

[GRE84]   J.R. Gilbert, D.J. Rose, and A. Edenbrandt. A separator theorem for chordal graphs. *SIAM J. Algebraic Discrete Methods*, 5:306–313, 1984.

[GS86]   O. Goldreich and L. Shrira. The effects of link failures on computations in asynchronous rings. In *Proc. 5th ACM Symp. on Principles of Distributed Computing*, pages 174–186, August 1986.

[GZ94]   O. Gerstel and S. Zaks. The virtual path layout problem in fast networks. In *Proc. 13th ACM Symp. on Principles of Distributed Computing*, pages 235–243, August 1994.

[HA95]   J.S.M. Ho and I.F. Akyildiz. Mobile user location update and paging under delay constraints. *Wireless Networks Journal*, 1:413–426, 1995.

[Hal86]   M. Hall. *Combinatorial Theory*. John Wiley & Sons, New York, 1986.

[HHL88]   S. Hedetniemi, S. Hedetniemi, and A. Liestman. A survey of gossiping and broadcasting in communication networks. *Networks*, 18:319–349, 1988.

[Hil86]   R. Hill. *A First Course in Coding Theory*. Oxford Applied Mathematics and Computing Science Press, Oxford, 1986.

[HP97a]   R. Harbane and C. Padro. Spanners of de Bruijn and Kautz graphs, *Inform. Process. Lett.*, 62:231–236, 1997.

[HP97b]   R. Harbane and C. Padro. Spanners of underlying graphs of iterated line digraphs. *Inform. Process. Lett.*, 62:245–250, 1997.

[HP00]   Y. Hassin and D. Peleg. Sparse communication networks and efficient routing in the plane. In *Proc. 19th ACM Symp. on Principles of Distributed Computing*, July 2000.

[HR88]   A.R. Hevner and A. Rao. Distributed data allocation strategies. *Advances in Computers*, 27:121–155, 1988.

[HS84]   D.S. Hochbaum and D. Shmoys. Powers of graphs: A powerful technique for
            bottleneck problems. In *Proc. 16th ACM Symp. on Theory of Computing*, pages
            324–333, April 1984.

[HS86]   D.S. Hochbaum and D.B. Shmoys. A unified approach to approximation algo-
            rithms for bottleneck problems. *J. ACM*, 33:533–550, 1986.

[HS94]   M. Harrington and A.K. Somani. Synchronizing hypercube networks in the
            presence of faults. *IEEE Trans. Computers*, 43:1175–1183, 1994.

[Hu74]   T.C. Hu. Optimum communication spanning trees. *SIAM J. Comput.*, 3:188–
            195, 1974.

[HZ96]   S. Halperin and U. Zwick. Private communication, Tel-Aviv University, Tel-
            Aviv, Israel, 1996.

[IB94]   T. Imielinski and B.R. Badrinath. Mobile wireless computing. *Comm. of the
            ACM*, 37:18–28, 1994.

[Jaf80]   J. Jaffe. Using signalling messages instead of clocks. Unpublished manuscript,
            1980.

[Jaf85]   J.M. Jaffe. Distributed multi-destination routing: the constraints of local in-
            formation. *SIAM J. Comput.*, 14:875–888, 1985.

[JL95]   R. Jain and Y.B. Lin. An auxiliary user location strategy employing forwarding
            pointers to reduce network impacts of PCS. *Wireless Networks Journal*, 1:197–
            210, 1995.

[JLR78]   D.S. Johnson, J.K. Lenstra, and A.H.G. Rinnooy-Kan. The complexity of the
            network design problem. *Networks*, 8:275–285, 1978.

[KK77]   L. Kleinrock and F. Kamoun. Hierarchical routing for large networks; perfor-
            mance evaluation and optimization. *Computer Networks*, 1:155–174, 1977.

[KK80]   L. Kleinrock and F. Kamoun. Optimal clustering structures for hierarchical
            topological design of large computer networks. *Computer Networks*, 10:221–
            248, 1980.

[KK96]   E. Kranakis and D. Krizanc. Lower bounds for compact routing. In *Proc. 13th
            Symp. on Theoretical Aspects of Computer Science*, pages 529–540, Springer,
            Berlin, 1996.

[KKP00]   M. Katz, N.A. Katz, and D. Peleg. Distance labeling schemes for well-separated
            graph classes. In *Proc. 17th Symp. on Theoretical Aspects of Computer Science*,
            pages 516–528, Springer, Berlin, 2000.

[KKU95]   E. Kranakis, D. Krizanc, and J. Urrutia. Compact routing and shortest path
            information. In *Proc. 2nd International Colloq. on Structural Information &
            Communication Complexity (SIROCCO)*, Lefteris M. Kirousis and Evangelos
            Kranakis, editors, pages 101–112, Carleton University Press, Northfield, MN,
            1995.

[KL81]   B. Korte and L. Lovász. Mathematical structures underlying greedy algorithms.
            In *Fundamentals of Computation Theory*, LNCS Vol. 117, Springer, Berlin,
            pages 205–209, 1981.

[KL83]   B. Korte and L. Lovász. Structural properties of greedoids. *Combinatorica*, 3:359–374, 1983.

[KL84a]   B. Korte and L. Lovász. Greedoids - a structural framework for the greedy algorithms. In *Progress in Combinatorial Optimization*, W. Pulleyblank, editor, Harcourt Brace Jovanovich, Toronto, pages 221–243, 1984.

[KL84b]   B. Korte and L. Lovász. Greedoids and linear objective functions. *SIAM J. Algebraic Discrete Methods*, 5:229–238, 1984.

[KMZ84]   E. Korach, S. Moran, and S. Zaks. Tight lower and upper bounds for some distributed algorithms for complete network of processors. In *Proc. 3rd ACM Symp. on Principles of Distributed Computing*, pages 199–207, August 1984.

[KMZ85]   E. Korach, S. Moran, and S. Zaks. The optimality of distributed constructions of minimum weight and degree restricted spanning trees in a complete network of processors. In *Proc. 4th ACM Symp. on Principles of Distributed Computing*, pages 277–286, August 1985.

[KNR88]   S. Kannan, M. Naor, and S. Rudich. Implicit representation of graphs. In *Proc. 20th ACM Symp. on Theory of Computing*, pages 334–343, May 1988.

[Kor98]   G. Kortsarz. On the hardness of approximating spanners. In *Proc. 1st Int. Workshop on Approximation Algorithms for Combinatorial Optimization Problems*, LNCS Vol. 1444, Springer, Berlin, pages 135–146, 1998.

[KP98a]   G. Kortsarz and D. Peleg. Generating low-degree 2-spanners. *SIAM J. Comput.*, 27:1438–1456, 1998.

[KP94]   G. Kortsarz and D. Peleg. Generating sparse 2-spanners. *J. Algorithms*, 17:222–236, 1994.

[KP98b]   S. Kutten and D. Peleg. Fast distributed construction of k-dominating sets and applications. *J. Algorithms*, 28:40–66, 1998.

[KPR93]   P. Klein, S. Plotkin, and S. Rao. Excluded minors, network decomposition, and multicommodity flow. In *Proc. of the 25th Annual ACM Symposium on Theory of Computing*, pages 682–690, May 1993.

[KR90]   R.M. Karp and V. Ramachandran. A survey of parallel algorithms for shared memory machines. In *Handbook of Theoretical Computer Science*, J. van Leeuwen, editor, North–Holland, Amsterdam, 1990.

[KR93]   P.N. Klein and R. Ravi. A nearly best-possible approximation for node-weighted Steiner trees. In *Proc. 3rd MPS Conf. on Integer Programming and Combinatorial Optimization*, pages 323–332, 1993.

[Kru56]   J.B. Kruskal. On the shortest spanning subtree of a graph and the traveling salesman problem. *Proc. of the AMS*, 7:48–50, 1956.

[KS91]   G. Kalai and L. Stockmeyer. A lower bound on the complexity of regional matchings on the hypercube. Research Report RJ8461, IBM, Almaden, CA, November 1991.

[KS92]   P. Klein and S. Sairam. Parallel and dynamic approximation schemes for planar
           shortest paths. In *Proc. 24th ACM Symp. on Theory of Computing*, pages 750–
           758, May 1992.

[KV88]   E. Kranakis and P.M.B. Vitányi. A note on weighted distributed match-making.
           In *3rd Aegean Workshop on Theory of Computing*, LNCS Vol. 319, Springer,
           Berlin, pages 361–368, 1988.

[KW84]   R.M. Karp and A. Wigderson. A fast parallel algorithm for the maximal in-
           dependent set problem. In *Proc. 16th ACM Symp. on Theory of Computing*,
           pages 266–272, May 1984.

[LEH85]   K.A. Lantz, J.L. Edighoffer, and B.L. Histon. Towards a universal directory
           service. In *Proc. 4th ACM Symp. on Principles of Distributed Computing*, pages
           261–271, August 1985.

[LeL77]   G. LeLann. Distributed systems, towards a formal approach. In *IFIP Congress*,
           pages 155–160, 1977.

[Lin92]   N. Linial. Locality in distributed graph algorithms. *SIAM J. Comput.*, 21:193–
           201, 1992.

[Lin93]   N. Linial. Local - global phenomena in graphs. Technical Report 93-9, The
           Hebrew University, Jerusalem, Israel, 1993.

[LL90]   L. Lamport and N. Lynch. Distributed computing: Models and methods. In
           Handbook of Theoretical Computer Science, Vol. B, J. van Leeuwen, editor,
           Chapter 18, pages 1159–1199, Elsevier, Amsterdam, 1990.

[LL92]   C. Levcopoulos and A. Lingas. There are planar graphs almost as good as
           the complete graphs and as short as minimum spanning trees. *Algorithmica*,
           8:251–256, 1992.

[LLP+99]   C. Laforest, A.L. Liestman, D. Peleg, T.C. Shermer, and D. Sotteau. Edge
           disjoint spanners of complete graphs and complete digraphs. *Discrete Mathe-
           matics*, 203:133–159, 1999.

[LLR95]   N. Linial, E. London, and Y. Rabinovich. The geometry of graphs and some of
           its algorithmic applications. *Combinatorica*, 15:215–245, 1995.

[LMP+95]   G.L. Lyberopoulos, J.G. Markoulidakis, D.V. Polymeros, D.F. Tsirkas, and
           E.D. Sykas. Intelligent paging strategies for 3rd-generation mobile telecommu-
           nication systems. *IEEE Trans. on Vehicular Technology*, 44:543–554, 1995.

[LNS98]   C. Levcopoulos, G. Narasimhan, and M. Smid. Efficient algorithms for con-
           structing fault-tolerant geometric spanners. In *Proc. 30th ACM Symp. on The-
           ory of Computing*, pages 186–195, 1998.

[Lov75]   L. Lovász. On the ratio of optimal integral and fractional covers. *Discrete
           Math.*, 13:383–390, 1975.

[LS91a]   A.L. Liestman and T.C. Shermer. Additive spanners for hypercubes. *Parallel
           Process. Lett.*, 1:35–42, 1991.

[LS91b]   A.L. Liestman and T.C. Shermer. Grid and hypercube spanners. Technical
           Report TR 91-1, Simon Fraser University, Burnaby, B.C., Canada, 1991.

[LS91c]   N. Linial and M. Saks. Decomposing graphs into regions of small diameter. In *Proceedings of the Second ACM-SIAM Symp. on Discrete Algorithms*, ACM, New York, pages 320–330, 1991.

[LS93a]   A.L. Liestman and T.C. Shermer. Additive graph spanners. *Networks*, 23:343–364, 1993.

[LS93b]   A.L. Liestman and T.C. Shermer. Grid spanners. *Networks*, 23:123–133, 1993.

[LS96]   A.L. Liestman, T.C. Shermer, and C.K. Stolte. Degree-constrained spanners for multi-dimensional grids. *Discrete Appl. Math.*, 68:119–144, 1996.

[LS95]   A.L. Liestman and T.C. Shermer. Degree-constrained network spanners with nonconstant delay. *SIAM J. Discrete Math.*, 8:291–321, 1995.

[LT87]   K.B. Lakshmanan and K. Thulasiraman. On the use of synchronizers for asynchronous communication networks. In *Proc. 2nd Workshop on Distributed Algorithms*, LNCS Vol. 312, pages 257–277, Springer, Berlin, 1987.

[LTC89]   K.B. Lakshmanan, K. Thulasiraman, and M.A. Comeau. An efficient distributed protocol for finding shortest paths in networks with negative cycles. *IEEE Trans. on Software Eng.*, 15:639–644, 1989.

[Lub86]   M. Luby. A simple parallel algorithm for the maximal independent set problem. *SIAM J. Comput.*, 15:1036–1053, 1986.

[Lyn95]   N. Lynch. *Distributed Algorithms*. Morgan Kaufmann Publishers, Inc., San Mateo, CA, 1995.

[M89]   S. Mullender. *Distributed Systems*. ACM Press, New York, 1989.

[Man86]   U. Manber. On maintaining dynamic information in a concurrent environment. *SIAM J. Comput.*, 15:1130–1142, 1986.

[Med94]   E. Medova. Flow models for network design and routing. *BT Technology J.*, 12:57–62, 1994.

[MGS95]   P. Manzoni, D. Ghosal, and G. Serazzi. Impact of mobility on TCP/IP - an integrated performance study. *IEEE J. on Selected Areas in Communications*, 13:858–867, 1995.

[MHS94]   U. Madhow, M.L. Honig, and K.S. Steiglitz. Optimization of wireless resources for personal communications mobility tracking. In *Proc. IEEE INFOCOM*, 1994.

[MNS95]   A. Mayer, M. Naor, and L. Stockmeyer. Local computations on static and dynamic graphs. In *Proc. 3rd Israel Symp. on Theory of Computing and Systems*, IEEE, Piscataway, NJ, pages 268–278, 1995.

[MP94]   Y. Mansour and D. Peleg. An approximation algorithm for minimum-cost network design. Technical Report CS94-22, The Weizmann Institute of Science, Rehovot, Israel, 1994.

[MPS91]   Y. Mansour and B. Patt-Shamir. Greedy packet scheduling on shortest paths. *J. Algorithms*, 14:449–465, 1993.

[MR96] J.A. Makowsky and U. Rotics. Spanners in interval and chordal graphs. Technical Report, the Technion, Haifa, Israel, June 1996.

[MS80] P.M. Merlin and P.J. Schweitzer. Deadlock avoidance in store-and-forward networks–I: Store and forward deadlock. *IEEE Trans. on Communication*, COM-28:345–352, 1980.

[MS00] S. Moran and S. Snir. Simple and efficient network decomposition and synchronization. *Theoret. Comput. Sci.*, to appear.

[MV88] S.J. Mullender and P.M.B. Vitányi. Distributed match-making. *Algorithmica*, 3:367–391, 1988.

[MW86] S. Moran and M. Warmuth. Gap theorems in distributed computing. In *Proc. 5th ACM Symp. on Principles of Distributed Computing*, pages 131–140, August 1986.

[MZ86] Y. Mansour and S. Zaks. On the bit complexity of distributed computation in a ring with a leader. In *Proc. 5th ACM Symp. on Principles of Distributed Computing*, pages 151–160, August 1986.

[Nao91] M. Naor. A lower bound on probabilistic algorithms for distributive ring coloring. *SIAM J. Discrete Math.*, 4:409–412, 1991.

[NO99] L. Narayanan and J. Opatrny. Compact routing on chordal rings of degree 4. *Algorithmica*, 23:72–96, 1999.

[NS95] M. Naor and L. Stockmeyer. What can be computed locally? *SIAM J. Comput.*, 24:1259–1277, 1995.

[NS96] L. Narayanan and S. Shende. Characterizations of networks supporting shortest-path interval labeling schemes. In *Proc. 3rd International Colloquium on Structural Information & Communication Complexity (SIROCCO)*, Nicola Santoro and Paul Spirakis, editors, Carleton University Press, Northfield, MN, pages 73–87, 1996.

[NW61] C. Nash-Williams. Edge disjoint spanning trees of finite graphs. *J. London Math. Soc.*, 36:445–450, 1961.

[Pel89a] D. Peleg. Complexity considerations for distributed data structures. Technical Report CS89-31, The Weizmann Institute of Science, Rehovot, Israel, 1989.

[Pel89b] D. Peleg. Sparse graph partitions. Technical Report CS89-01, The Weizmann Institute of Science, Rehovot, Israel, 1989.

[Pel91] D. Peleg. Distributed data structures: A complexity oriented view. In *Proc. 4th Workshop on Distributed Algorithms*, LNCS, Vol. 486, pages 71–89, Springer, Berlin, 1991.

[Pel93] D. Peleg. Distance-dependent distributed directories. *Inform. and Comput.*, 103:270–298, 1993.

[Pel97] D. Peleg. Approximating minimum communication spanning trees. In *Proc. 4th Colloq. on Structural Information & Communication Complexity*, pages 1–11, 1997.

[Pel98]   D. Peleg. Distributed matroid basis completion via elimination upcast and distributed correction of minimum-weight spanning trees. In *Proc. 25th Int. Colloq. on Automata, Languages & Prog.*, pages 164–175, 1998.

[Pel99a]   D. Peleg. A lower bound on the time complexity of randomized distributed MST construction. Unpublished manuscript, 1999.

[Pel00a]   D. Peleg. Proximity-preserving labeling schemes, *J. Graph Theory*, 33:167–176, 2000.

[Pel00b]   D. Peleg. Informative labeling schemes for graphs. Technical Report MCS00-05, The Weizmann Institute, Israel, 2000.

[Per85]   R.J. Perlman. Hierarchical networks and the subnetwork partition problem. *Computer Networks*, 9:297–303, 1985.

[PKR82]   J. Pachl, E. Korach, and D. Rotem. A technique for proving lower bounds for distributed maximum-finding algorithms. In *Proc. 14th ACM Symp. on Theory of Computing*, pages 378–382, May 1982.

[Plo88]   S.A. Plotkin. *Graph-theoretic techniques for parallel, distributed and sequential computation.* Ph.D. thesis, MIT/LCS/TR-430, MIT, Cambridge, MA, 1988.

[PQ82]   J.-C. Picard and M. Queyranne. A network flow solution to some nonlinear 0-1 programming programs, with applications to graph theory. *Networks*, 12:141–159, 1982.

[PR98]   D. Peleg and E. Reshef. Deterministic polylog approximation for minimum communication spanning trees. In *Proc. 25th Int. Colloq. on Automata, Languages and Programming*, LNCS Vol. 1443, pages 670–681, Springer, Berlin, 1998.

[PR99a]   D. Peleg and E. Reshef. A variant of the arrow distributed directory with low average complexity. In *Proc. 26th Int. Colloq. on Automata, Languages and Programming*, LNCS Vol. 1644, pages 615–624, Springer, Berlin, 1999.

[PR99b]   D. Peleg and V. Rubinovich. A near-tight lower bound on the time complexity of distributed MST construction. In *Proc. 40th IEEE Symp. on Foundations of Computer Science*, pages 253–261, 1999.

[PRS94]   S. Plotkin, S. Rao, and W.D. Smith. Shallow excluded minors and improved graph decompositions. In *Proceedings of the 5th ACM-SIAM Symp. on Discrete Algorithms*, pages 462–470, ACM, New York, 1994.

[PRS97]   R. Prakash, M. Raynal, and M. Singhal. An adaptive causal ordering algorithm suited to mobile computing environments. *J. of Parallel and Distributed Computing*, 41:190–204, 1997.

[PS82]   C.H. Papadimitriou and K. Steiglitz. *Combinatorial Optimization: Algorithms and Complexity.* Prentice–Hall, Englewood, Cliffs NJ, 1982.

[PS85]   F.P. Preparata and M.I. Shamos. *Computational Geometry.* Springer-Verlag, New York, 1985.

[PS89]   D. Peleg and A.A. Schäffer. Graph spanners. *J. Graph Theory*, 13:99–116, 1989.

[PS92a]   A. Panconesi and A. Srinivasan. Fast randomized algorithms for distributed edge coloring. In *Proc. 11th ACM Symp. on Principles of Distributed Computing*, pages 251–262, 1992.

[PS92b]   A. Panconesi and A. Srinivasan. Improved distributed algorithms for coloring and network decomposition problems. In *Proc. 24th ACM Symp. on Theory of Computing*, pages 581–592, 1992.

[PS95]   A. Panconesi and A. Srinivasan. The local nature of Delta-coloring and its algorithmic applications. *Combinatorica*, 15:255–280, 1995.

[PS96]   R. Prakash and M. Singhal. A dynamic approach to location management in mobile computing systems. In *Proc. 8th Int. Conf. on Software Engineering and Knowledge Engineering*, 1996.

[PT95]   S. Plotkin and E. Tardos. Improved bounds on the max-flow min-cut ratio for multicommodity flows. *Combinatorica*, 15:425–434, 1995.

[PU87]   D. Peleg and E. Upfal. Efficient message passing using succinct routing tables. Research Report RJ5768, IBM, Almaden, CA, August 1987.

[PU89a]   D. Peleg and E. Upfal. A tradeoff between size and efficiency for routing tables. *J. ACM*, 36:510–530, 1989.

[PU89b]   D. Peleg and J.D. Ullman. An optimal synchronizer for the hypercube. *SIAM J. Comput.*, 18:740–747, 1989.

[Ray86]   M. Raynal. *Algorithms for Mutual Exclusion*. MIT Press, Cambridge, MA, 1986. Originally published in French in 1984. Translated by D. Beeson.

[RB97]   A. Rosen and Y. Bartal. The distributed k-server problem—a competitive distributed translator for k-server algorithms. In *J. Algorithms*, 23:241–264, 1997.

[RK87]   R. Reischuk and M. Koshors. Lower bound for synchronous networks and the advantage of local information. In *Proc. 2nd Workshop on Distributed Algorithms*, LNCS Vol. 312, Springer, Berlin, pages 374–387, 1987.

[RL95]   D. Richards and A. Liestman. Degree-constrained pyramid spanners. *J. of Parallel and Distributed Computing*, 25:1–6, 1995.

[RR95]   Y. Rabinovich and R. Raz. Lower bounds on the distortion of embedding finite metric spaces in graphs. *Discrete Comput. Geom.*, 19:79–94, 1995.

[RS94]   S. Rajsbaum and M. Sidi. On the performance of synchronized programs in distributed networks with random processing times and transmission delays. *IEEE Trans. on Parallel & Distr. Systems*, 5:939–950, 1994.

[RS98]   S.B. Rao and W.D. Smith. Approximating geometrical graphs via "spanners" and "banyans." In *Proc. 30th ACM Symp. on Theory of Computing*, pages 540–550, 1998.

[RSM+94]   R. Ravi, R. Sundaram, M.V. Marathe, D.J. Rosenkrantz, and S.S. Ravi. Spanning trees short or small. In *Proceedings of the Fifth ACM-SIAM Symp. on Discrete Algorithms*, pages 546–555, SIAM, Philadelphia, 1994.

[Rub99a]   V. Rubinovich. Private communication, Bar Ilan University, Ramat-Gan, Israel, 1999.

[Rub99b]   V. Rubinovich. Distributed minimum spanning tree construction. M.Sc. Thesis, Bar Ilan University, Ramat-Gan, Israel, 1999.

[RVVN90]   P. I. Rivera-Vega, R. Varadarajan, and S. B. Navathe. The file redistribution scheduling problem. In *Data Eng. Conf.*, pages 166–173, 1990.

[RY95]   C. Rose and R. Yates. Paging cost minimization under delay constraints. *Wireless Networks Journal*, 1:211–219, 1995.

[Sch91]   M.D. Schroeder, A.D. Birrell, M. Burrows, H. Murray, R.M. Needham, T. Rodeheffer, E. Satterthwaite, and C. Thacker. Autonet: A high-speed, self-configuring local area network using point-to-point links. *IEEE J. on Selected Areas in Communications*, 9, 1991.

[SCRS97]   F.S. Salman, J. Cheriyan, R. Ravi, and S. Subramanian. Buy-at-bulk network design: Approximating the single-sink edge installation problem. In *Proceedings of the Eighth ACM-SIAM Symp. on Discrete Algorithms*, pages 619–628, SIAM, Philadelphia, 1997.

[Sha86]   E. Shamir. Distributed network algorithms. Technical Report 86-8, The Hebrew University, Jerusalem, Israel, June 1986.

[SK85]   N. Santoro and R. Khatib. Labelling and implicit routing in networks. *The Computer Journal*, 28:5–8, 1985.

[SM86]   B. Schieber and S. Moran. Slowing sequential algorithms for obtaining fast distributed and parallel algorithms: Maximum matchings. In *Proc. 5th ACM Symp. on Principles of Distributed Computing*, pages 282–292, August 1986.

[Soa94]   J. Soares. Approximating Euclidean distances by small degree graphs. *Discrete Comput. Geom.*, 11:213–233, 1994.

[SS91]   L. Shabtay and A. Segall. Active and passive synchronizers. Technical Report 706, The Technion, Haifa, Israel, December 1991.

[SS93a]   L. Shabtay and A. Segall. On the memory overhead of synchronizers. Technical Report LPCR 9313, The Technion, Haifa, Israel, May 1993.

[SS93b]   L. Shabtay and A. Segall. A version of the γ synchronizer with low memory overhead. Technical Report LPCR Report #9313, The Technion, Haifa, Israel, January 1993.

[SS96]   M. Shneerson and S. Soloviev. Private communication, The Weizmann Institute, Israel, 1996.

[Sun82]   C.A. Sunshine. Addressing problems in multi-network systems. In *IEEE IN-FOCOM*, 1982.

[SV93]   M. Szegedy and S. Vishwanathan. Locality based graph coloring. In *Proc. 25th ACM Symp. on Theory of Computing*, pages 201–207, May 1993.

[T95]   D.M. Topkis. Repeated uncoordinated information dissemination by flooding. *Networks*, 26:13–23, 1995.

[Tan81]   A. Tannenbaum. *Computer Networks*. Prentice–Hall, Englewood Cliffs, NJ, 1981.

[Tar83]   R.E. Tarjan. *Data Structures and Network Algorithms*. CBMS-NSF Regional Conference Series in Applied Mathematics 44, SIAM, Philadelphia, 1983.

[Tel94]   G. Tel. *Introduction to Distributed Algorithms*. Cambridge University Press, England, 1994.

[TU81]   S. Toueg and J.D. Ullman. Deadlock-free packet switching networks. *SIAM J. Comput.*, 10:594–611, 1981.

[vLT86]   J. van Leeuwen and R.B. Tan. Routing with compact routing tables. In *The Book of L*, G. Rozenberg and A. Salomaa, editors, Springer, Berlin, pages 259–273, 1986.

[vLT87]   J. van Leeuwen and R.B. Tan. Interval routing. *The Computer Journal*, 30:298–307, 1987.

[vLT94]   J. van Leeuwen and R.B. Tan. Compact routing methods: A survey. In *Proc. 1st Colloq. on Structural Information & Communication Complexity*, Paola Flocchini, Bernard Mans, and Nicola Santoro, editors, Carleton University Press, Northfield, MN, pages 99–110, 1994.

[VRM+97]   G. Venkatesan, U. Rotics, M.S. Madanlal, J.A. Makowsky, and Pandu Rangan. Restrictions of Minimum Spanner Problems. *Inform. Comput.*, 136:143–164, 1997.

[Wir95]   P.E. Wirth. Teletraffic implications of database architectures in mobile and personal communications. *IEEE Communications Magazine*, 33:54–59, 1995.

[WLB+00]   B.Y. Wu, G. Lancia, V. Bafna, K.-M. Chao, R. Ravi, and C.Y. Tang. A polynomial-time approximation scheme for minimum routing cost spanning trees. *SIAM J. Comput.*, 29:761–778, 2000.

[Won80]   R.T. Wong. Worst-case analysis of network design problem heuristics. *SIAM J. Algebraic Discrete Methods*, 1:51–63, 1980.

[WWS98]   I.P. Weerakoon, A.L. Wijesinha, and D.P. Sidhu. On properties of read and write sets in Awerbuch-Peleg scheme for tracking mobile users. *Wireless Networks*, to appear.

[Yao77]   A. Yao. Probabilistic computations: Towards a unified measure of complexity. In *Proc. 17th IEEE Symp. on Foundations of Computer Science*, pages 222–227, April 1977.

Index